May Rihani's book is proof of the emptiness of three stereotypes: she challenges the idea that Arab women are submissive, that there are no democracies in the Middle East, and the notion of a "clash of civilizations." Her life demonstrates global leadership by a Lebanese Arab woman, and her memoir describes a golden age in Lebanon when democracy and freedom of expression were taken for granted. Perhaps most importantly, *Cultures Without Borders* finds the common ground among cultures despite apparent differences. This is an eyewitness account of the rich and profound goodness in humanity.

H.E. Amine Gemayel, former President of Lebanon

I have never met anyone who so adeptly mixes academics, philosophy, technical know-how, advocacy, and common sense like May Rihani. I have watched with awe as she has applied her unique set of skills and made a difference in the lives of women and girls around the world.

Stephanie Funk, USAID Mission Director, Zimbabwe

Cultures Without Borders contains important lessons for all those who aspire to live as productive global citizens in the twenty-first century. On the macro level, May Rihani's book demonstrates the falsity of the "clash of civilizations" theory that posits inevitable conflict between peoples of differing cultures. Instead, through personal anecdotes and authoritative evidence drawn from real-world experiences, she demonstrates the universality of the impulse to transcend frontiers of the mind and connect peacefully with "the other" through education and dialogue.

Suheil Bushrui, Professor Emeritus, University of Maryland

Weaving between poetry and politics; evoking the intimacy of family and the openness of public service; at once struggling for local girls' education/ poverty alleviation and negotiating with World Bank and UN officers; laboring every day for economic development for women and yet running high romance with Romeo lovers; conversing equally with illiterate village friends and global leaders – May Rihani invites us into a Lebanese and American garden throbbing with its unfolding mystery; enchanted by fragrances of East, West and South; and exhilarated by the empowering possibility of a life lived fully every moment and yet always with an eye to the possibilities ahead. She humbles, she empowers, she inspires.

Suad Joseph, Distinguished Research Professor,
University of California, Davis

Cultures without Borders is a historical and memoiristic account of several journeys, through time, place and the life of a remarkable woman. This beautiful and moving story starts with a young girl's childhood in the multi-confessional and multicultural Lebanon of the 1950s and 60s, and proceeds through the turmoil of the civil war that tore up the jewel of the Levant, and takes us up to the present in the United States where even as she succeeds richly in her new country she continues to keep a watchful and loving eye on her birthplace. With this book, May Rihani, who hails from one of Lebanon's great literary families, stakes her claim to her own unique vision, strong and triumphant.

Lee Smith, author "The Strong Horse: Power,
Politics, and the Clash of Arab Civilizations."

May Rihani makes beauty, love, and life shine through profoundly sad tragedies. Tracing her life through the enchantment of a child's eyes and later a woman's, we feel her wonderment, and champion her struggles in the blossoming of possibilities in Lebanon in the 60s and in African countries in the 80s, 90s and 2000. Written with economy of style and yet highly evocative, her interesting autobiographical approach pairs down to the essential, while drawing the reader in to her shared world: illumined by the quality of her writing, that doesn't draw attention to itself but offers a clear transparency into the place and event and their meaning.

Patricia Flederman, International Development Advisor

Cultures Without Borders is a deeply personal and profoundly political account of a lifetime of development action. May Rihani made a positive difference in the lives of women and girls throughout the world. The book is a fascinating exposé of development 'moments' and illustrations of good practice in girls' education across a wide range of cultures and countries, intertwined with personal reflections and experiences. *Cultures Without Borders* is also a rich record of efforts to advance girls' education by a wide range of actors from the Global North and Global South.

Nora Fyles, Head of the Secretariat of UNGEI,
the United Nations Girls' Education Initiative

May Rihani has worked tirelessly to improve the lives of girls and women, particularly through girls' education and gender equity. Her book *Cultures Without Borders* is required reading for policymakers, educators, university students and all those who share her important--and reachable--goals.

Elaine M. Murphy, Visiting Scholar, Population Reference Bureau

CULTURES
WITHOUT
BORDERS

FROM BEIRUT TO WASHINGTON, D.C.

A memoir

MAY A. RIHANI

authorHOUSE®

AuthorHouse™
1663 Liberty Drive
Bloomington, IN 47403
www.authorhouse.com
Phone: 1-800-839-8640

First Edition

Published by AuthorHouse   09/09/2014

ISBN: 978-1-4969-3646-2 (sc)
ISBN: 978-1-4969-3647-9 (hc)
ISBN: 978-1-4969-3645-5 (e)

Library of Congress Control Number: 2014915476

Printed in the United States of America

DEDICATION

To the girls of Africa, Asia, and the Middle East
who are fighting relentlessly for their right to learn, and
who are enriching the whole world by their efforts.

and

To my parents and mentors Albert and Loreen Rihani
who taught me that serving others is the
source of abiding happiness in life.

Acknowledgements

W RITING THIS BOOK HAS BEEN a joy, the main reason being the reflective process that a memoir requires one to go through. I had to reflect on the meaning of experiences, the impact of words and behaviors of the inspiring figures in my life, the events that marked me, and the elements that helped shape my character. Of course, I spent many hours asking myself the eternal question regarding the role of destiny versus the role of the individual in shaping one's own life.

Writing a memoir is a gateway to the path where memory and reflection intermingle. However, this joy would not have been as pleasurable if it were not for few individuals who accompanied me while writing this book. I am grateful to:

My husband Zuheir who was the first to read and encourage my initial efforts. We spent several evenings discussing events in my life and how I might describe them.

My brother Ramzi, who read the chapters in which he played a major role in my life and our family's, and whose acute mind and perceptive eyes made sure that details and nuances were captured.

My friend Professor Suad Joseph, who reminded me of the importance of participating, in the 1970s, in conferences on women, and how pioneering it was in those days to contribute to the discourse about the differences and common grounds between women in development and feminist theory.

My colleague and friend Carolyn Long, who reviewed our shared experiences at TransCentury and provided feedback that helped ensure the accurate portrayal of those glorious years.

My colleague and friend Patricia Flederman, who read chapters, shared insights, and discussed with me the unique literary approach of a person with a multicultural background.

I must also thank Professor Emeritus Suheil Bushrui for his encouragement when I mentioned to him that I plan to write my memoir and for his insistence that this book be written immediately and published as soon as possible due to the timeliness of the topics it addresses.

I extend my deep gratitude to those who accompanied me on this journey.

CONTENTS

CHAPTER ONE

DIVERSITY

WHAT AN AMAZINGLY DIVERSE WORLD we live in. In Freike, Lebanon, a villager works hard all day planting and harvesting, his wife bakes bread and prepares jams, his children work in the field after school and help their father pick figs and grapes, and there is a wonderful family gathering around a simple but delicious evening meal.

In Manhattan, a young woman wearing stiletto heels and a lavender three-piece suit hurries to arrive on time at her office where she presides over a fashion design meeting.

In Malawi, a campaign to increase awareness on the benefits of girls' education takes place in rural communities where villagers gather in a circle under trees to listen, ask questions, and propose solutions.

In Afghanistan, an eleven-year-old girl wants to go to school, but her parents are intent on marrying her off and her aspirations are crushed.

In Dakar, Senegal, the Minister of Education gives the opening speech at the United Nations Girls' Education Initiative (UNGEI) conference where 200 international education experts develop strategies to advance girls' education globally.

In Nepal, women spread dried red and yellow pepper on the mountain terraces in a colorful impressionistic painting of their lives.

In Paris at UNESCO, sixty-two education ministers and delegates meet to discuss the global status of basic education; analyses, commitments, and new strategies are discussed.

In Bangladesh, a villager beats cotton on a rooftop; his honest, hard work puts bread on the family table.

In rural areas around Kikwit in the Congo (DRC), women and girls carry water buckets on their heads; their tall slim bodies could have inspired Giacometti.

In Ghana, an American woman and a Lebanese-American woman drive north from Accra for two days; in Tamale, they meet with the district education officers to gather information and contribute to the design of a girls' education project for the region.

In Beirut, a poet signs a book that could not be published anywhere else in the Middle East due to its daring theme. Beirut's climate of free expression makes it the hub of Lebanese and Arab intellectuals.

In Jamaica, tanned bodies lie on gorgeous beaches; a little time for relaxation is acceptable.

In Thailand, visitors take riverboats to visit the many gorgeous temples; Buddha is everywhere.

In the Vatican, thousands visit La Pieta daily; standing in front of Michelangelo's sculpture is the purest prayer.

In Mali, children gather around two U.S. Congressmen who are interested in supporting international education; the natural joy of life on the children's faces inspires the visitors.

In Syria, demonstrations against a dictator are met with brutal violence; a cycle of destruction begins.

In Cape Canaveral, Florida, a rocket is sent to the moon; human beings dream big.

In Uganda, a young girl from a shantytown wants to become a brain surgeon; human beings dream big.

In Jordan, an education minister collaborates with the minister of Information Communication and Technology (ICT) to transform the Jordanian system of education; ministers dream big with their commitment to future generations.

In Morocco, women demonstrate in the streets for and against *Al-Modawwana*, the personal status code, or the family code, in Moroccan law; those who are for the changes in the code carry the day.

In Kivu in the Congo, soldiers rape women, declaring that rape is a weapon of war; humanity is deeply wounded.

In Liberia, the first woman president is elected; Africa is hopeful.

In Lebanon, with every dawn, a renewed commitment to diversity, pluralism, and freedoms take place. Writers do not give up, and hope in the future continues to exist in the Middle East.

These contrasts of diversity, these struggles and triumphs, hopes and fears, take me back to my childhood in Freike and in Beirut: what serenity, what bliss! A child embraced by love, surrounded by beauty, stimulated by different languages and cultures, always challenged to think and serve others. A teenager there begins to understand that some countries act superior and try, in direct and subtle ways, to undermine other cultures, often through the educational system. A young woman understands the transformational power of a university where freedom of thought as well as independent thinking is the norm.

As that young woman, I was privileged to have two role models who inspired me daily: a professional mother who worked on children's early education and made women's rights a central issue in her life, and a father who published the works of innovative thinkers, writers, and poets. My parents made our home a meeting place for

Lebanese and Arab writers, artists, professors, politicians, and thought leaders. I could not have had a stronger foundation for a journey on the highways of our global village. This foundation showed me how privileged I was and, as a result, stressed my duty and responsibility to give back and serve others who struggle for many things I could have easily taken for granted.

As I reflect on my life, it becomes clear to me that despite all the progress humanity has made in the past thirty-five years or so, there remains an urgent need to address basic issues. Poverty, economic development, equality, freedoms, and basic human rights must be dealt with in efficient and innovative ways in many corners of the world, if not in every country. Our global village needs the compassion of those with a vision and a commitment for a better future for every single human being regardless of race, religion, gender, or ethnicity.

The foundation laid all those years ago by my parents in Freike and in Beirut has been the basis for a lifetime of work toward that vision, and for a passionate devotion to that commitment. Those early years tell a tale whose ending has yet to be written.

CHAPTER TWO

THE FREIKE HOME

A S A LITTLE GIRL, I grew up in two homes that I loved: one was in Freike, a serene village in the Lebanese mountains; the other was on Hamra Street, one of the most cosmopolitan streets of Beirut, the Lebanese capital.

Our Freike home was enchanting. A magnificent balcony that oversaw everything encircled the home. Yes, everything. In the mind of a little girl, that balcony revealed the whole world. The balcony was a platform where everything paraded in front of me. During the day, depending on which side of the balcony I was on, I could see many proud peaks of mountains, villages with lipstick on their roofs, a beautiful valley that often draped its shoulders with the fog, the calm blue Mediterranean, and the tip of Beirut bathing in the sea. At night, my balcony offered me a different view; the mountains were transformed. Instead of lipstick on the rooftops, I would see strings of pearl necklaces adorning the many clusters of houses dispersed across the mountain. The villages that made the peak of the mountains their home, were adorned with diamonds borrowed from the starlit sky. The gentle moon helped the stars come down from on high to rest on the beautiful foreheads and necks of the villages. I could even hear the villages and the moon whisper to each other. I thought there was a very special relationship between the moon and one particular village that had its homes spread on top of a hill. The moon often rose from behind that village, bathing its homes in a gorgeous, transparent veil of evening light. At the age of six or seven, I wanted to watch the different scenes unfolding from the theater of my balcony every evening.

As much as I loved these scenes, my two favorite times on the balcony were dawn and sunset. My father Albert always woke up early. Sometimes I did, too, and I would run to the balcony to sit next to Daddy and watch the sunrise. From one side of the balcony, we could see seven mountaintops embracing each other. The tallest peak of the seven is called Sannine, and the sun always rose from behind its peak. Daddy would sit in his elegant silky *robe de chambre* facing Sannine, waiting for the dawn. I intuitively knew that this was a special time for my father, so I would tiptoe toward him without making noise, say good morning in a soft voice, and snuggle up next to him. It was important to be silent. The view was too precious to disturb and sound was not necessary at that moment. From the look on my father's face, I could tell we were in the temple of nature preparing to witness a magnificent ritual. Sannine would start changing color while I snuggled next to Daddy. At first, the color was gray, but it took only a couple of minutes for rays of pink to appear, then light blue, a stronger pink, then purple, and while the purple was spreading its wings over Sannine, hues of light gold would appear. What a palette! I do not think a watercolorist could have caught the subtle transformation. Finally, a powerful gold would shine and the forehead of the sun would appear from behind the peaks.

Sannine was dazzled by the sun, and became dazzling to those of us who shared the beautiful moment. The play of light on top of

Sannine was amazing, as if the sun were doing push-ups on top of the magnificent mountain. Within twenty minutes, that very special ritual would be over, and my father's meditation would be over, too. Pressed close to Daddy to watch God paint Sannine and the skies was so satisfying and beautiful that I never wanted it to end. But of course it did, and Daddy and I would return to the main sitting room of our home through the glass-arched doors of the balcony.

Before I describe our daily routine at home, I want to share my second favorite scene from the balcony: sunset.

At sunset, I would go to a different part of the balcony than where we sat in the morning and watch the huge ball of fire called sun dip itself in the Mediterranean. Depending on the summer months, sunset arrived between seven in the evening and eight-thirty. Often a breeze caressed the face of the magnificent balcony and whoever was there. I made it a point to be present at sunset to watch the Mediterranean change colors as the sun approached the horizon.

When I was six, I did not know where the sea ended and where the horizon started; they were both blue, they were both far away, they were both beautiful and mysterious, and they were always together; to me they were embracing—they were one. As I watched, the sun slowly slid down to touch the horizon. In anticipation, the horizon blushed and became a long line of red. Over several minutes, the horizon continued its display of powerful hues of crimson and gold. In the garden of our home next to the enchanted balcony stood a huge eucalyptus tree, which joined in the ritual of the sunset. Its branches and leaves slowly swayed while the huge ball of fire sank towards the horizon and the Mediterranean. The sound of the rustling leaves and the aroma of the eucalyptus added to the serene drama of the amazing evening scene. I loved the large eucalyptus tree that was taller than our two-story stone house; it provided an additional dimension of beauty.

If I moved to a particular spot on the balcony, I could see the Mediterranean, the horizon, and the descending sun through the veil of the swaying leaves of the eucalyptus all at once, and the tree's light green would be added to the powerful crimson and gold scene painted on the horizon. By the time the sun was close to dipping itself in the Mediterranean, it became a true ball of fire. The ball grew bigger and redder until it touched the water and the whole sea was blessed with the brush of God. In less than ten minutes, the Mediterranean tried on and discarded robes that were gold, crimson, purple, and pink. The last robe was usually pink, and somehow the pink became lighter and lighter as the blue regained its reign over the sea. The eucalyptus tree continued its chanting, the whispering of its evening love poem, and most probably the love poem ended with a line that expressed to the sun how the majestic tree would wait for its return.

Later in life, after enjoying the theater of plays, musicals, dance performances, and operas in many cities around the world, I still believe the Freike balcony, my first theater, remains the performance that taught me exquisite lessons about beauty, poetry, and serenity, and about the unity of the mountains, the sea, the sun, the moon, and humanity.

CHAPTER THREE

LEBANON IN THE FIFTIES

I GREW UP IN LEBANON in the early fifties, when my parents and many others were filled with hope for our small, newly independent country. Lebanon gained its independence from the French on November 22, 1943. The French mandate over Lebanon was established after World War I on September 1, 1920; in 1926, the Lebanese constitution was modeled after that of the French. The constitution provided a parliament, a president, and a cabinet. The president is elected by the parliament, which is popularly and democratically elected.

After the Allies won World War II, the Lebanese national leaders asked France to end the mandate. France proclaimed the independence of Lebanon in 1941, but continued to exercise authority. In 1943, the Lebanese leaders who were dissatisfied with the continued presence and authority of France decided to form the first independent democratic government. They also amended the constitution and voted to end the French mandate. The French authorities were not pleased and responded by arresting and imprisoning the president, the prime minister, and a number of ministers. Lebanese Christian and Muslim leaders united their forces to pressure the French government, and demonstrations led by Christian and Muslim political leaders filled the streets of Beirut. The French finally yielded by releasing the imprisoned political leaders on November 22, 1943, and recognizing Lebanon's complete independence.

The first independence president, Bechara El Khoury, and the first prime minister, Riad El Solh, were hailed as national heroes by the Lebanese population. The independent government of Lebanon, with some financial assistance from the international community, built the Lebanese infrastructure, economy, and social systems. The government developed a network of roads linking major cities, and enlarged the harbor of Beirut.

In 1952, a charismatic new president, Camille Chamoun, was elected. His government continued the building of Lebanon's infrastructure and main institutions. The Chamoun government strengthened the judicial system and improved the educational, agricultural, and public-health systems. Also, President Chamoun reorganized key governmental departments in an attempt to realize a more efficient administration. In some respects, his regime was thoroughly democratic; the press and rival political parties, for example, enjoyed full freedom. Towards the end of Chamoun's term, in 1958, the political opposition disagreed vehemently with him regarding Egypt's President Gamal Abdul Nassir's policies and politics, and as a result, Lebanon experienced a short period of conflict. In the early fifties, however, when I was a child, Lebanon seemed a country of tranquility, hope, and promise.

During my childhood, the Lebanese villages and towns of the mountains were serene and charming. Most of the villages were nestled in hills covered with a variety of trees such as pine, poplar, eucalyptus, oak, and numerous varieties of fruit trees. Homes were built from white marble or cream-colored stone, and a large number of the homes had red tile roofs. The use of arches was a major architectural feature in a number of Lebanese mountain homes. The main roads were asphalt and the side roads were of dirt. The pleasures of life were simple and innocent. The air was pure and unpolluted. Life in the village was closely linked to the generosity of the land. Most of the villagers were small farmers, and the land was the source of their daily lives. Scenes of farmers on their donkeys transporting agricultural produce and of women carrying jars of water were commonplace.

My village of Freike was a happy place in the summer—I only knew it in the summer. Men and women farmers worked hard six days a week planting and harvesting wheat, vegetables and fruits, baking their own bread, and attending to the needs of their children and their livestock. Children went to public schools and helped their parents in the planting and harvesting. On Sundays, families walked to church as soon as they heard the sound of the church bells. A common saying when I was a little girl was, "*Niyyal hilli 3indo markad anzi bi Libnan.*" The literal translation of this means "Lucky is the one who has a shed for a goat in Lebanon." What the villagers really meant was life in the mountains of Lebanon was good as long as the farmer owned a small piece of land and a few animals.

The city of Beirut on the other hand, where we spent the remainder of the year, was cosmopolitan and sophisticated. It was a bustling, busy city during the day and had a flourishing nightlife. Beirut was also an education center; it boasted two prestigious universities: the American University of Beirut founded in 1866, and Saint Joseph, a French Jesuit university established in 1875. Other higher education institutions included the Lebanese University, the Beirut College for Women, and a handful of other universities. Beirut hosted French, American, British, German, Italian, and Armenian schools in addition to its Lebanese primary and secondary schools.

The fifties saw the launch of a powerful publishing industry in Beirut. As the capital of Lebanon, the city rapidly became a serious competitor to Cairo as the publishing center of the Arab world, and a competitor to Baghdad in international trade and finance. Beirut also expanded its role as a hub of communication, shipping, and transportation. In addition, Beirut soon became the focus in the region for entertainment and fashion, an incubator of new visual and performing art trends, a center for luxurious hotels, and the home of a unique multinational community.

CHAPTER FOUR

OUR DAILY LIFE

WHEN I WAS A CHILD, the blaring horn of Daddy's 1953 Desoto would call my brother Ameen and me to immediately drop whatever we were doing and race out the main door of the house and up the garden stairs to the road, where we would literally jump with joy as we awaited his arrival. This was a daily ritual during the summer months when we lived in our Freike home. I remember reaching up to hug him, but would usually end up hugging his leg. When I was seven or eight, Daddy appeared magnificently big and tall.

Often, Daddy lifted one of us children for a kiss. When I was the one chosen, I was transported to a space where only joy existed—that space between his hands. Looking into his face, taking in his smiling eyes was more beautiful to me than looking at a rainbow, happier than receiving Christmas gifts, and more transporting than sweet dreams. I wanted it to last for hours.

On most days, Daddy left his office at the Rihani Printing House (*Dar Al-Rihani*, in Arabic) in downtown Beirut at around 2:00 p.m. The road to Freike was a wide coastal boulevard, or *autostrade*, on the edge of the Mediterranean Sea that linked Beirut to different main roads that were entry points into the hills and the mountains rising from the coastline. Daddy often stopped to buy from little shops and from street vendors who sold produce from large hand carts. Usually he bought Arabic bread that was still warm from a bakery; fish that carried within it the perfume of the Mediterranean; fruits and vegetables that we did not grow in our Freike gardens such as mango, papaya, avocado, and dates; and always sweets and nuts.

When Daddy arrived home, the very special part of my day began. It started with the joy of greeting him and helping him carry his bags of groceries. Even though I was the youngest and the littlest of those who ran up the stairs to greet him, I always tried to help. I wanted to carry whatever Daddy bought. After all, those were Daddy's grocery bags, and anything that had to do with my father enchanted me.

He would walk down the stairs from the car with at least five of us surrounding him: Ameen and me; our housekeepers, Jeanette and Leila; and our chauffeur, Edouard (in the fifties) or Mansour (in the sixties). In later years, my younger brothers Ramzi and Sarmad joined us as we ran up the garden stairs to meet Daddy.

Mommy waited for him at the foot of the steps on the terrace with a radiant smile. Their daily embrace was a reflection of tenderness, happiness, and love coming together in one moment. Very early on, while I was still quite young, I recognized their love and tenderness for each other. Somehow, subconsciously I knew that even though I loved the beauty of our home and gardens in Freike, and the centrality of the location of our home on Hamra street in Beirut, what made these two houses so special were the homes my parents created inside.

After they embraced, we would go inside the house for a late lunch. Mommy gave us children a snack at noon so that we could join her and Daddy for lunch when he arrived a few hours later. Our lunches were very special. On weekdays it was just the family, and we children would hear a detailed discussion of our parents' activities.

Mommy and Daddy offered us a living example of two lovers, two intellectuals, two individuals who were entirely engaged with their communities, and I'm sure as children, we took the beauty of their relationship for granted. They were deeply devoted to one another, and their love filled the air and lifted up all the members of the household. They talked to each other with kindness, interest, and warmth, at once tender and enthusiastic. They focused their attention on each other, no matter what the subject of the discussion. Mommy and Daddy were genuinely and unquestionably in love, and I delighted in watching them interact. They always looked each other in the eyes. He called her darling and sweetheart; she called him simply Albert; however, no one knew how to say his name with the beauty and love that Mommy did. Needless to say, our family lunches were a very special time and we usually—in contrast to dinners—enjoyed them as a family event. It was the children's quality time with just the two of them.

After lunch usually there was a short siesta. Daddy would go to his room and rest for fifteen or twenty minutes. Most days, but not always, Mommy did, too. During this period, our home was utterly quiet. If we children had to go from one room to another, we walked slowly, without making a sound. Then, after my parents came out of their room, the silence would lift, and the Freike home would put on a festive allure. Friends knew that my parents started receiving guests after 4:30 p.m. during the week, and on weekends, guests might arrive as early as 10:00 a.m. and would be received throughout the day. Our home was open to all, every day. The main door was never shut, but left wide open to welcome drop-by guests—a custom in Lebanon and the region at that time. Daddy only closed the main

entry door late at night before retiring and opened it again around
six in the morning.

Guests to our home were diverse: rustic villagers and sophisticated
Beirutis; Christians, Muslims, and Druze; poets and politicians;
secular and religious leaders; professors and businessmen; and of
course our extended family members and close friends.

Dinners in the Freike home were not to be missed since the
evenings and the weekends were about hosting friends. Mommy and
Daddy dressed up to honor their guests, and the dinner table was
not the same as our intimate lunch table. Friends who would have
dinner with us included, for example, the Maronite bishop from the
Mount Lebanon Governorate, Bishop Farah, dressed in black with
a large purple belt and a purple cap; a poet from Iraq, Ahmad Al-
Safi Al Najafi, who wore the Arab *abaya* and sat cross-legged on a
dining room chair; a woman diplomat from Syria, Alice Kandalaft,
who was a classmate of Daddy at Columbia University in New
York; and a Palestinian professor from the American University of
Beirut, Professor Ishak Moussa Al-Husseini. On another weekend,
guests at our dining table might include Professor Kamal Hage of
the Lebanese University, a professor of philosophy and an author of
many books; Daoud Salman, a political activist, and his wife Zahia,
one of the leaders of the women's movement in Lebanon; Youssef
Al-Khal, a poet, and Helen Al-Khal, his wife the painter; and Ramez
Schoucair and his wife, Mommy's cousins from Cairo. I cannot
forget the many dinners with marvelous people from Freike such as
our property caretaker Youssef Nakhle and his wife Leila, or Father
Youssef Al Mellah, the priest of the village.

When I was a little girl, I was fascinated by the attire of our
dinner guests, which ranged from a bishop's robes to the *abayas* of
some of the Arabs, from the village men's *shirwal* trousers, to the

haute couture dresses of the sophisticated women from Beirut and the sharply tailored suits of their men.

As a teenager, my attention shifted to the discussions. What a feast! Listening to Said Akl recite his poetry was the beginning of understanding how language can be used to stretch the world of symbols, how to create images that come from behind all horizons, and to master the Arabic language in a way that transforms it into a magical musical instrument. Those evenings were about the pleasure of learning to appreciate gorgeous poetry that hovers above where we think beauty lives. Such evenings also underlined for me the importance of how to recite poetry.

Other evenings might center on political debates. When Ahmad Mohammad Mahjoub, the Minister of Foreign Affairs of the Sudan, and Charles Malik the Minister of Foreign Affairs of Lebanon, discussed political issues, the Freike evening was a lesson in the complexities of the politics in the Arab world while recognizing that even though the Arab countries have a lot in common, each country has its special political conditions and expectations. The challenge was to acknowledge the importance of the common issues in the Arab world, but also to recognize and respect the particular aspirations of the peoples of each country.

Evenings with the marvelous people of our village were an immersion in the details of the daily lives of Lebanese village life. When Youssef Nakhle described how *arak,* a strong anise-based liqueur, was made, it was a lesson in the basic importance of making a drink that renders the special occasions of life real celebrations. It was about self-sufficiency, demonstrating how the Lebanese villager in the fifties and sixties was the lord of his land and the master of what it produced, and how families processed what the land yielded. Every year, Youssef would make the *arak* for his family and for ours from our vineyards. His discussions with Daddy about when he would start preparing for the yearly home production of *arak* were a scene of the most genuine part of village life. It would be hard to understand to understand the essence of the Lebanese village without listening to Youssef Nakhle talking about *arak*, or to Leila, his wife, discussing how, in September, the women prepared their jams, olives, olive oil, a dried yoghurt and bulgur wheat into a powder called *kishk*, tomato paste, cucumber pickles, eggplant pickles, wheat, carob molasses, the blend of spices called *zaatar*, dried figs, pomegranate juice, and other items they preserved, canned, dried, and set aside for the winter.

I still dream of making a movie about our visitors in the Freike home, and especially about those who stayed for dinner. It could be titled: *The Life of a Lebanese Publisher in the 60s*; or *Lebanon: The Meeting Point of the Rural and the Urban*; or even better, *Lebanon: Where Arab Intelligentsia Met*.

Whether with artists or teachers, politicians or religious leaders, rural farmers or urban merchants, the diversity and sharing of ideas during our dinners set my expectations high for such exchanges throughout life.

CHAPTER FIVE

THE PORTRAITS IN OUR HOME

DURING THE SUMMERS OF MY youth, and especially on Sundays, Daddy often dressed in white accented with a colorful tie. As a child, a teenager, and later as a young woman, I was fascinated by my father. I saw white as the permission-giver, the enabler for all other colors, as if Daddy was allowing colors, ideas, and different perspectives to co-exist and to enhance each other. I saw his life as the equilibrium between New York and Freike. He was a master in marrying the accelerated rhythm of the Big Apple with the serenity of the vineyards of our village. I think of my father as a lover of life who was capable of always enriching his life and ours. The life that my father lived was similar to both the daring skylines of the city that creates new horizons every day, and the calm traditions of the serene village where olive trees may date back to the days of Christ.

I saw my father as a refined alchemist who knew what to choose from New York, the city of his birth and his youth, and what to select from the village of his mature days in order to offer his selections on a silver platter to the wife he adored and to their four children. The climate of our home in Freike was an authentic creation of Daddy.

The home—with its books, paintings, music, garden, visitors, and discussions—created an ambiance where the urban and the rural met, where New York and Freike met, and where Lebanon, the Arab world, and the United States were engaged in a continuous, seemingly conventional, dialogue.

As a child and a teenager, I was influenced by the environment that Daddy and Mommy created in our two homes; however, I think the ongoing dialogue between Lebanon, the Arab world, and the United States that existed in those homes was the creation of my father.

In our main living room in Freike, there were five portraits drawn by different artists representing five authors whom my father liked and respected. On one side of the living room, likenesses of three Lebanese literary figures—Ameen Rihani (my uncle), May Ziade, and Gibran Kahlil Gibran—reminded us of the Arab literary renaissance. Ameen Rihani's was rendered by William Oberhardt, a prominent twentieth century American artist known for his portraits and for his special skills at delineating the human head. The portraits of May Ziade's and of Gibran's were drawn by Iskandar Haddad, a Lebanese artist and my father's friend. Rihani's portrait was elegant, attractive, and had presence; Gibran's was dreamy and ethereal; and Ziade's represented that elusive way a woman can combine being very feminine and totally brilliant.

On the wall facing these three Lebanese giants hung American paintings. In the middle was an imposing portrait of Walt Whitman with his long grey beard; to his right was a very handsome portrait of Max Eastman; and to Whitman's left were drawings by Troy Kenny. In addition to these portraits and the Kenny drawings, there were six or seven paintings by Moustafa Farroukh, a Lebanese artist who was a very close friend of my father, dispersed throughout the different living rooms of the house. I loved the Farroukhs; their pastel colors were soft, gentle, and serene. These paintings were an invitation to travel to a world so peaceful. The Farroukhs were like prayers; they took me along on a journey where nothing loud or aggressive could exist.

Starting quite young, and throughout my teenage years, my curiosity about these works of art led to many wonderful discussions with Daddy. Depending on my age, the discussions varied in depth and length. I remember for example Daddy telling me that I was named May in honor of the most important woman literary figure in the Arab world, May Ziade, and that her portrait was in our living room because she was an inspiring figure and because she was Uncle Ameen's and Daddy's friend. At other times, Daddy would tell me with pride that May Ziade held the most famous literary salon of the Arab world during the twenties and thirties in Cairo, and he would recount how all the leading literary figures of the Arab world such as Taha Hussein, Khalil Moutrane, Loutfi as-Sayed, Antoun Gemayel, Walieddine Yakan, Abbas Akkad, and Yacoub Sarrouf would gather at her salon to discuss the different literary trends and varying philosophical schools of thought of the early twentieth century.

Discussing Ameen Rihani's portrait would invariably lead to the vision Rihani had of bridging the Arab world and the West, and how he dedicated his life to creating a deeper understanding in the U.S. of the Arab culture and of Arab political issues. Gibran's portrait led us to talk about *The Prophet* and why this particular book of his became so popular.

When I asked about the portraits of the lesser-known (to me) writers in our living room, the Americans, Daddy tried to explain in terms that I could understand why Walt Whitman was important.

He would tell me how Whitman was the first poet in the world who wrote free verse, that Whitman was the poet who expressed bold ideas for the mid-nineteenth century such as the equality of all beings, and that Whitman's poetry created a new way of communication. My father always emphasized that Whitman opened doors for the new generations of writers. Of course, Daddy helped me understand that Uncle Ameen was influenced by Whitman, and that my uncle was the first Arab to write and publish free verse.

When I asked about the attractive portrait of the young Max Eastman, Daddy explained that Eastman was a New Yorker, a writer, and a political activist who supported many progressive causes. He had visited my Uncle Ameen in Freike and stayed in our home (Ameen Rihani's home at that time) for a week or so in the 1920s.

Farroukh's paintings would always elicit Daddy's lovely smile. I have no doubt he was my father's favorite painter, and I am sure that the seed of my love for art during my adult years was planted in my soul during those first lessons about color and light. Daddy described to me how paintings can recreate scenes through sensitive brush strokes and the subtle emphasis on light and its changing hues. He often concluded this wonderful dialogue about his friend Moustafa by telling me the name of the village or region depicted in one of the paintings which adorned our home. Then, when we visited that particular village, Daddy would remind me of the painting. In my young mind, the family visits to certain areas were also about how those villages were linked to Farroukh's paintings.

When I was growing up, the messages that brewed in my head were messages of that nature: writers and poets are individuals we like and honor, and we ask artists to draw their portraits to hang in prominent places in our homes. A woman writer is as important as men writers; May Ziade's portrait hung in the most prominent place of our living room and Daddy spoke about her with admiration. It did not matter from where the writers and poets came; if they inspired us, we honored them. In our second home, in Beirut, we had a lovely photograph of Tolstoy in our living room.

Painters whose works demonstrated the mastery of color and light were treasured. Our guests admired these portraits and paintings, and often the art of our home became part of the evening discussions. These portraits were linked to important books that influenced the thinking of many. Towards the end of my teen years and my early twenties, I decided to read the works of those who adorned our living room walls. Among the books I read during these years were: *Al Rihaniyat* by Ameen Rihani, *The Prophet* by Gibran, *Leaves of Grass* by Whitman, *Fleurs de Rêve* by May Ziade, and *War and Peace* by Tolstoy. I resolved to become familiar with as many artists as I could, and when we were at home in Beriut, I often found myself walking in Hamra Street in search of new exhibits at one of the many galleries in the neighborhood.

However, before I dwell on the teenage years of a Lebanese girl, let me continue sharing my years as a child, and what I believe influenced me then and in my mature years.

No doubt my father was a giant figure in my life. To me, he was an absolute role model. As a child, I thought of him as the ultimate source of knowledge, as the generous giver, as the lover of life, as the one with exquisite taste, and as the man who adored my mother. My father was not necessarily handsome, but he was incredibly elegant, and he could discuss any topic that one of his guests might be interested in. The discussions in his salon included debates about new literary trends, the importance of poetry, the difference between modernization and Westernization, the separation of church and state, the role of the government, Arab politics, and Lebanese politics.

They touched on the role of women in the Arab world, the role of youth in shaping the future, the relationship of Arabs with the U.S., how Arab and Lebanese music was or was not influenced by Western music, classical and modern art, paintings, and new painters. More local discussions centered on the planting and harvesting seasons, the scarcity of water and the respect for the environment, the magnificent bond between the individuals who worked the land and nature, the wisdom of villagers, how to honor certain traditions while embracing new ways of thinking and behaving, and of course, publishing and the new books Daddy decided to put into print. He was a publisher, and books were as important as the air we breathed.

I grew up feeling that I was privileged to be his daughter and to be part of his life. My favorite pastime in the summer when school was in recess, and when I spent most of my days in our Freike home up in the mountains, was to sit quietly in the living room with adults listening to their discussions. I never felt the need to be playing with friends or to have friends my age come over; it must have been odd for a little girl to feel that way. I was fascinated by Daddy and Mommy and their friends. Many of their guests were writers, and often friends would stay for dinner where the discussion would wander and touch on all kinds of subjects; however, the discussion invariably turned to books.

Sometime during the evening, a guest might say something like, "Albert, I brought with me the manuscript of my new essays, and I would be delighted if you would agree to read it and let me know if you might be interested in publishing it." Daddy would smile and most of the time his response would be, "I would love to read it. Give me a month or so, and then I will let you know what I think." For whatever reason that I cannot articulate clearly, as a child I was fascinated by the fact that Daddy was a publisher and that he was the one who decided if a handwritten manuscript would be turned into a book with thousands of copies published for readers to enjoy, instead of remaining a forgotten sheaf of papers gathering dust on a shelf.

Even as a child of ten or eleven, I intuitively knew how transformative the world of publishing could be; how the publisher, my father, could influence what the parents of my friends, and possibly many other Lebanese and Arabs would be reading. In the fifties, sixties, and seventies, my father's publishing house, *Dar Al-Rihani*, published poetry, novels, history books, philosophical books, political books, biographies, a children's magazine, and encyclopedias. Whenever Daddy came home after a long day at the office with a newly released book, the whole evening became a celebration. My parents and their friends would examine the design of the cover, the paper that was selected for the pages, the size and format, of course the contents. They would debate how the book might be received by readers and the media, who might write the book reviews, and the influence of the book on other writers, in particular on new generations of writers and on the youth. Daddy sometimes would even smell the book; Mommy and we, his children, would do the same. The perfume of newly published books is very distinct. To the publisher, his family, and his friends, a book is like wine: one must be able to enjoy its perfume. One must be a connoisseur and enjoy discussing how it came to life, and of course one must dwell on the content as part of the ritual of the birth of a new book.

I loved these rituals. Books, books, books, and all that is attached to them: writers, artists, historians, professors, politicians, editors, printers, distributors—all waiting for my daddy to make a decision about a manuscript, and if his decision was positive, after a certain number of months, the celebration of its publication would take place.

I grew up in this atmosphere, but to complete the picture, I should mention that Daddy transformed the east wing of our home in Freike into a museum dedicated to his brother, Ameen Rihani. So in addition to all the writers who would visit my father to discuss the possibility of publication, our home in Freike also saw a continuous parade of visitors who came to visit the Ameen Rihani Museum. Some of the visitors were journalists or university students writing their theses. All I could remember as a child growing up was that many of these visitors would ask if they could interview Daddy if he were home. They would discuss Ameen Rihani's life and *oeuvres* and include Daddy's words in the pieces they wrote. I grew up with writing and books at the absolute center of our lives. It felt like everything had to do with books, and life could not exist without the noble act of writing.

One summer day, an old man from our village came to visit with Daddy while a little observer watched the scene. They talked about a subject that I did not fully understand. All I could make out was that the villager wanted some papers signed. Towards the end of the visit, Daddy took a piece of paper, wrote something on it, and asked the man to dip his thumb in an inkwell and press his thumb on the paper. I was puzzled; I had no clue what was happening. When the villager left, I asked Daddy why the villager left the mark of his thumb on the page. He said the man needed to sign the paper. I asked why he did not sign his name like everyone else, and Daddy told me the man was illiterate. In reply to what must have been a blank expression, he patiently explained that many individuals, especially older people of the villages, did not have the opportunity to learn to read and write in school.

His words shocked me; I went to my room and cried. He came to my room, perplexed, and asked me why was I crying, and I explained that up till that moment, I had believed that every human being was born in order to write and publish a book. After seeing the old villager not able to sign his own name, I understood that was not the case; some of us will not be able to do that. To me it was as if I had seen the old villager without a hand or a leg, he was so terribly handicapped, and I cried. My dreams were shattered. I must have been eleven years old when that happened. Daddy comforted me by saying that even though books were very much a part of our lives, it did not mean they were the only source of happiness. He explained that his friend, the old villager, had a wonderful family and lots and lots of land, and that he was a very happy man. Daddy said I should not cry because the old man could not write and would never have the opportunity to publish a book.

In my continuing dismay, I must have dreamed of the old villager for many nights and years to come. Later on in life, and given what my life became, I wonder if this memory is what shaped and influenced my professional goals.

CHAPTER SIX

MOMMY, DUNIA AL AHDATH, AND WOMEN'S RIGHTS

SEVERAL LANGUAGES AND CULTURES WERE part of our daily lives. Mommy had a sister, Nasra, who married an Englishman; a brother, Fuad, who married an Austrian woman; and a brother, Wadi, who married a Lebanese woman. On my father's side of the family, there were also marriages with other cultures. Daddy's brothers Ameen and Joe were married to American women. His favorite cousin, who I called Uncle Roberto, was married to a Mexican woman. For these reasons, several languages were spoken at home. When we celebrated Christmas with our extended family, we sang carols in Arabic, French, English, and German. During the summer season when Uncle Roberto would visit, Spanish was added to the languages that floated around in our home.

Music also came from different parts of the world. Daddy liked a wide range of styles: classical, including Beethoven, Bach, and Tchaikovsky; opera, especially the great American tenor Caruso;

and Arabic, in particular the Egyptian composer Mohammad Abdul Wahab and the singer Asmahan. Mommy and Daddy were fond of the Lebanese diva Fayrouz. My brothers liked Bob Dylan and the Beatles, and I preferred French music.

Daddy was the meeting point of these different languages and cultures, while Mommy had the utmost respect for each. Mommy wanted us to know and respect, in an in-depth way, the different facets of each culture while Daddy wanted us to find the common ground among them.

In the midst of this very active cultural diversity, Mommy created a calm atmosphere in our home. She was the most serene in our family and at the same time, the most scientific. As a student, she excelled in math and physics but also loved literature and poetry. She wrote and published poems in English—one of them about trigonometry—while at the American University of Beirut (AUB) where she earned a BA in English Literature.

Mommy helped us with our homework and made sure we saw the value of each subject: literature, math, history, physics, art, and biology. She taught us discipline in a gentle manner, respect of others regardless of their station in a gracious way, and love of nature and all creation in a caring way. Mommy helped us realize how privileged we were and instilled in each of us a sense of duty to help others while being sensitive to their needs. The well-being of others was always uppermost in her mind. She was the chairwoman of the board of three non-governmental organizations and a member of the board of several social welfare organizations. Serving others was the driving force of her life and the primary expression of her selfless spirit.

Mommy's professional life resulted in the creation of the first Arabic weekly magazine for children in Lebanon. Ameen and I returned from our respective schools with French children's books and magazines, and Mommy was pleased that our schools were distributing these materials to encourage children to read. She asked us to request similar materials in Arabic, too. We did, but were told they were none to be had in Lebanon in those years. Mommy did her research and that fact was confirmed, so she set out to create the first children's magazine in Arabic in Lebanon.

In 1955, the premiere issue was published. *Dunia Al-Ahdath* (World of Youth)was a bi-weekly magazine for children between the ages of seven and fifteen. Mommy was the editor-in-chief. Many writers for the magazine became my parents' good friends, and some of them became very well-known writers in Lebanon. Emily Abi-Rashed, who became the novelist Emily Nasrallah, wrote children's stories for the magazine. Professor Mirhij, a science professor at AUB, wrote the science pages. Dr. Wadi Deeb, the poet and a professor at the Beirut University College, wrote poems and attractive short texts. Mommy often wrote a message for the children under a rubric entitled, "To My Son."

The magazine also had a number of artists who created imaginative illustrations and comic strips. I remember the celebration at our Hamra Street home when the first edition of *Dunia Al-Ahdath* was published. My parents invited all the contributing writers and artists for dinner. After we ate, and while bottles of champagne were popping, a huge cake was brought to the dining table. Mommy was surprised to see the icing was a replica of the cover of the magazine. Daddy was delighted that he had pulled off such a wonderful surprise for his beloved Loreen.

I was fascinated by the painted illustration on the cake and wondered how the artist had recreated every tiny detail of the cover of the magazine. Trust Daddy to find someone who could do this without ruining the cake! It was an unforgettable evening for everyone, and Mommy must have gone to bed feeling that all her efforts were recognized and deeply appreciated. Her dream produced the first children's Arabic bi-weekly magazine in Lebanon, one that had a profound influence on many children, as I learned in later years.

Beginning in 1955 and for many years after, my school and other schools in Lebanon distributed *Dunia Al-Ahdath*. Most of my class friends would buy it, read it, talk about it, participate in its competitions, and wait for it every fortnight. Mommy's magazine became the talk of the children of Lebanon in the fifties and the sixties, thanks to her vision. She made sure the children had access to an Arabic magazine dedicated to them in the same way they could access a French or an English magazine.

In addition to being the editor-in-chief of her magazine, Mommy was very active in the women's movement in Lebanon. In the fifties and sixties, my mother and other well-educated Lebanese women worked hard to improve the status of women and to advocate for equal rights. They considered women's advancement an integral part of the advancement of the newly independent and democratic Lebanese society. In those years, the number of girls enrolled in primary and secondary school rose rapidly, as did the number of women who entered universities.

On the other hand, most women in Lebanon were still not part of the paid workforce. Most rural women were very active in working the land with their husbands, and the majority of urban women did not even attempt to be employed or to start their own businesses. A small number of university graduate women decided either to join existing women's associations or to create organizations that focused on advancing women's social and economic roles. Women and men together debated ways to advance the role that women played and the

31

extent to which different roles, especially for mothers, might change social norms and possibly create societal problems.

Many of the progressive and better-educated women wanted to push forward and put women's changing roles on the national agenda. Mommy was a member of the Lebanese National Women's Council; the president of the Women's League; and chair of the boards for the Lebanese University Women, the YWCA, and the Organization of the Disabled Children. She was a member of a very active circle of women who made equity and equality between men and women a priority in their professional life. Among her circle of activist women friends, which included lawyers, doctors, and educators, were Laure Moghaizel, Najla Saab, Anissa Najjar, Edvick Shaiboub, Zahia Salman, Laure Tabet, Zahia Kaddoura, Ibtihaj Kaddoura, and many others.

During the fifties and the sixties, politics of all kinds played out against the background of a Lebanon moving forward in educating its human resources, building its infrastructure, promoting to the extent possible a democratic political system, and strengthening its economic base. The Palestinian-Israeli problem was always part of the headlines, political parties in Lebanon were mushrooming, and even the Communist Party had a strong voice. Political dissidents from the Arab world made Beirut their headquarters, and media in Lebanon gained stature because of the country's freedom— more than fifty daily and weekly journals representing far-flung causes were published in Beirut. Voices inside the Arab world that could not express themselves through their own communication channels used Lebanese publishing houses and media to get their messages out.

However, Mommy and her women friends felt that something was still missing. She and many of her colleagues felt that women needed to be more active in the political and economic life of Lebanon in order to gain fuller rights. They organized conferences, symposia, and forums where better health services, child care, women entering the labor force, women's political participation, and women's rights in general were discussed.

From my perspective as a child and later as a teenager, these were normal daily issues that became part of our dinner discussions. Possibly because my Daddy was so supportive of all these issues, in those days I did not see a divide between men and women. I did not think of these issues as women's issues; I understood them as societal issues that Mommy and Daddy agreed on, and on which Mommy took the lead. Only in later years did it become apparent to me that not all men agreed that educating girls, women entering the labor force, or women's political participation should be as natural as the air we breathe. What really marked me later on was that not all *women* were convinced these were fundamental rights that every girl and every women should have.

I still wonder about the power of seeds planted in the early years of childhood; about the power of words around the dinner table; about role models, and the deep, deep influence of parents' words, actions, attitudes, and daily lives; about the impact of what mothers and fathers value most; and about what they and their friends do and talk about.

Few things are more powerful when it comes to molding a child than what she/he has heard and observed parents say and do. I believe the words and deeds of mothers and fathers are inscribed on the pages of their children's unfolding future. With or without their being conscious of it, each word parents say, and every deed parents do will, in one way or another, have a major impact on the chapters of their children's future.

I have no doubt the design and architecture of my future professional life was being drawn by my mother without her ever knowing it, and without my ever being aware of it. She did it just by inspiring me through her value system and her actions, without ever saying: "This is what is important for you to do when you grow up."

CHAPTER SEVEN

MY FRENCH SCHOOL: COLLÈGE PROTESTANT

MOMMY AND DADDY MUST HAVE agreed that they wanted their children to learn three languages: Arabic, French, and English, and three cultures: those of Lebanon and the Arab world as well as the French and American cultures. To begin this journey, my brothers and I started our education in schools that had French as the language of instruction. For me, my parents decided that I would be enrolled in the *Collège Protestant Français des Jeunes Filles.*

The Collège, as the parents used to call it, was a French school with a French principal, Mlle. Louise Wegmann, and French teachers. It had kindergarten, primary, and secondary sections. The school campus was originally on George Picot Street in downtown Beirut. In 1956, the school moved to Mme. Curie Street in Ras Beirut, an upscale area adjacent to several mansions and the Beirut College for Women. French, mathematics, science, history, geography, social sciences, and sports were all taught in French. The Arabic language and the history of Lebanon were taught in Arabic. English was introduced at the secondary school level. The number of students in the early sixties was around 1,400. The Collège was a prestigious school, large and modern. It was very well established as the premier French-language school in Lebanon. Parents were proud to have their daughters in the Collège, and neighbors who were not able to enroll their daughters there envied those who could. Teachers had a haughty attitude. Mlle. Wegmann was more of a general than a principal, and the students were taught that they were privileged to attend.

I did not share the mainstream view regarding the Collège. I was miserable, very miserable. Everything that was valued in my parents' home was not valued at the Collège. The Arabic language, for example, which was praised in our home for its very rich expressions—often described by Daddy as an elegant vehicle of the Arab culture and rich with gorgeous poetry, a language that the Koran used to get its message across—was viewed by the Collège as a second-class language. Students were not allowed to speak it except when we were specifically instructed in the Arabic language and in the history of Lebanon. During all others hours, even during recess, we were not allowed to speak Arabic. If we uttered even few words in Arabic, we were punished by being given a "signal," a token we had to carry with us till the weekend. We had to try to get rid of it by passing it off to another student as quickly as possible. The girls who had a signal in their possession on Saturday were punished by being kept in detention Saturday afternoon. This practice encouraged the students to spy on each other, especially during recess, to catch a schoolmate who spoke in Arabic so the signal could be handed off, along with the requisite detention.

At home, Arabic was not just spoken, it was considered highly refined and expressive. At the Collège, Arabic was only permitted during Arabic class hours; otherwise, it was the cause of punishment. These contradictions disturbed my mind and made me uncomfortable at school. I became an introvert. I did not want to play with my classmates during recess and preferred to walk in the beautiful gardens of the Collège looking at the flowers and the different trees. One thing I have to acknowledge: the Collège had beautiful gardens and Samuel, the gardener, tended to the trees, shrubs, and flowers with great dedication. Despite my becoming more and more of an introvert, I enjoyed wonderful friends, among them Lily Rafeh, Fadia Riachi, Leila Solh, and Leila Osseiran.

Even though I did not appreciate how the Arabic language was treated at the Collège, I did well in certain subjects and the hours dedicated to learning Arabic were my favorite. I enjoyed them, felt at home, and did very well in these sessions. I also enjoyed mathematics and did well in it, too. I did not do as well in the sciences; biology and physics were a struggle. However, I enjoyed studying French. Even though I did not agree with the practices of the Collège regarding the Arabic language, this did not distort my appreciation for French. I knew, even when I was very young, that French was a beautiful and elegant language, and I wanted to learn it well despite the prejudicial atmosphere in the Collège.

And then the unthinkable happened.

Every morning at 8:00 a.m., all the students gathered in the main hall. The students of every grade knew exactly where to stand and the *surveillantes* checked our uniforms while observing every move we made. Mlle. Wegmann would say few words, we would all sing a *cantique*, and then we walked to the classes in a very orderly way. Discipline was the driving force.

One day, Mlle. Wegmann began by telling us she had reviewed our grades and that in general she was very pleased. The majority of the students were doing well, and we were getting good grades in French, mathematics, and sciences. However, she said, a small minority among the students did not get good grades in French. She explained that was not good because our parents must have made a conscious decision to send us to the Collège, and no doubt, she said, one of the major reasons, if not *the* major reason why was for us to learn French and to be able at one point to master it. She said if we did not focus and apply ourselves, we would not learn the French language the way we should, and we would not meet the expectations of our parents and the school. Up until that part of her speech, my young mind was telling me our principal was right and very logical, and that maybe I should spend more time with my French homework.

Then Mlle. Wegmann presented an argument that went something like this: "As you all know, you will need to use French when you become adults. French is the language of diplomacy. French is the language that your government often uses. French is the language of your living rooms, so students, do apply yourself, work hard, and spend more time learning French." She continued, "Of course we also teach Arabic at the Collège, but I am not worried about your Arabic because all of you will have the opportunity to speak Arabic with your maids and your nannies at home."

This made me quite upset and I was depressed for the remainder of the day at school. I could not wait for the end of classes to arrive. I wanted to go home. I wanted to find a place where Arabic continued to be respected and was not relegated to being the language of the maids and nannies only. I know the principal did not say that Arabic *is* the language of the maids, but somehow the message came across as, we need to speak and practice French with the teachers and the parents, but not to worry about Arabic because we can practice it with the maids.

I think this was the first conscious moment in my life when I understood what a rebellious spirit must be. I was silent, but troubled.

Most probably that day I did not listen carefully in class to what my teachers were saying. The mind of the little ten-year-old girl wondered, "Is the principal right? No way. What would Daddy and Mommy say? I want to speak Arabic with everybody—my teachers, my parents, my friends, *and* my maids. And I want to speak French with nearly everybody—my teachers, my parents, and my friends. Something was wrong with what the principal said this morning."

Daddy and Mommy were always available after dinner, and I could discuss anything with them. That evening, I asked Daddy if we could talk about what happened at school that day. I told Daddy what the principal had said and asked him if she was right. I remember extremely well the expression on his face that evening. He took his time after he heard my story and calmly said, "May *habibti* (darling), most of the time principals and teachers are right, but there are rare exceptions when they are wrong. This is one of those exceptions. It is true that your Mommy and I sent you to the Collège so you could learn French well, but we also want you to learn Arabic and the other subjects. Your mother and I do not want you to speak Arabic only with the maids; we want you to speak Arabic with us, with your brothers, with your friends, *and* with our helpers, and we want you to speak French whenever you wish to speak it. The Arabic language is very important to us. It is the language that your Uncle Ameen Rihani wrote and published most his books in. Arabic is a language that carries within it the history of the Arabs, and here in Lebanon when children are born, the first few words they learn are in Arabic. Arabic is the mother tongue of the Lebanese and of the Arabs. French is also important, and soon you will start learning English, also an important language. Please, *habibti*, do not let what the principal said disturb you. The Arabic language is part of who you are; however, who you are is also someone who wants to learn other languages, too. French and English are among the languages that we think will help you in your life."

I was so relieved. That whole day at school my mind was upset and angry, but Daddy knew how to dissipate my anger. He reassured me that the language I loved was important. Daddy knew how to avoid dichotomy. I went to bed that evening thinking that all languages were my friends, but my best friend's name was "Arabic."

The next day, I went back to school not angry at the principal, but with a thought lingering in my mind that she did not understand the beauty and richness of the Arabic language. Later on, I understood more.

During my teens, I began questioning many things that were happening at the Collège. Somehow, in the subtlest way, through the atmosphere and the ambiance at school, our French principal and teachers got messages across to us that I could not digest easily. In the most delicate way, the messages were saying we would be more important, more respected, or possibly more sophisticated, if we were like the French. We were influenced to believe that the French culture was superior, French literature more beautiful, and French history and geography more important.

As much as I loved reading Molière, Racine, Victor Hugo, and later Baudelaire and others, to me their plays, prose, and poetry were beautiful but not necessarily superior to the works of Al Mutanabi, Al Ma'arri, Ibn Al Arabi, and later on, Gibran and Rihani. I recognized that French culture was extremely rich, as was Arab culture. I had a problem with that notion of superiority. Between the ages of fifteen and sixteen, I began to decipher what colonialism was about. I became less and less happy at school, which affected my grades. After I completed my year of *troisième*, I must have had lengthy discussions with Mommy and Daddy, and they agreed to move me to Al Ahliah School for Girls.

Mary Kassab, a Lebanese writer, founded Al Ahliah in 1916. When I entered the school in the early sixties, the principal was Mrs. Wadad Cortas, a leading educator whom my parents knew well. The language of instruction was Arabic, and English was taught as a second language. The Arabic language was extremely respected and the teachers were friendlier than at the Collège. Discipline existed, but it was not imposed by creating fear or forcing students to tell on each other. Superiority was not in the air, and dichotomies were not part of our daily learning. The Ahliah school did not have the beautiful gardens of the Collège campus, nor its modern buildings or well-equipped science laboratories; however, I willingly accepted the loss of luxury for a better sense of acceptance and belonging.

I spent my last two years of high school at Ahliah and I did fairly well. In the evenings after completing my homework, I would read poetry, prose, and plays in Arabic and French. In those days I was not yet interested in English literature, so I read very little in English. I never gave up French. I continued to enjoy its beauty, but I did not have to endure constant intellectual battles about its superiority. Arabic was my intimate friend, and French became even more of a friend when no one imposed it on me.

Reflecting back on what happened at the Collège, I understand now why I was so uncomfortable in that academically excellent school. I believe Mlle. Wegmann and some of the teachers consciously or subconsciously were most of the time practicing cultural imperialism. In their lectures to students, the principal and some of the teachers conveyed that there is an unequal relationship between the French and other civilizations, in particular the Arab one, favoring of course the French. I now understand that the discourse and behavior of some teachers promoted the French culture over that of the Collège's host country and of the majority of the students; this made students eager to adopt the cultural values of France over their Lebanese and Arab values. It was only due to a solid and ethical value system at home that was built on respecting all cultures, and not minimizing the importance of any culture, that made me aware that the way the Collège taught, however unintentionally, was unacceptable to me.

CHAPTER EIGHT

MY AMERICAN UNIVERSITY: AUB

I ALWAYS KNEW THAT FOR my college education I would study at the American University of Beirut (AUB). In Lebanon, parents had a big say in what college or university their children would attend. For us, it was AUB. My parents had the utmost respect for it. Although Daddy earned his degree in economics from Columbia University in New York, Mommy was an AUB graduate. Moreover, her father Salim graduated in the 1890s from AUB, and her two brothers graduated from there in the 1930s. Her brother Wadi earned a degree in pharmacy, and her brother Fuad graduated in medicine at a very young age.

My brother Ameen was already a student at AUB when I was ready to enter. I think Daddy wanted us all to start at AUB. If we wanted to continue and get our higher degrees, we could consider universities in the U.S. He used to tell me if I did really well at AUB, and if I wanted to get a PhD, I could think about attending Columbia University in New York. Columbia had a very special place in his heart.

Reverend Daniel Bliss founded AUB in 1866. The university bases its educational philosophy, standards, and practices on the

American liberal arts model of higher education. AUB surpassed my expectations. It had excellent faculty members, a gorgeous campus right on the edge of the Mediterranean Sea, and terraced gardens covered with exotic trees and flowering bushes. The students were very active and deeply involved in numerous political, educational, and social associations. In Lebanon, political and cultural activities were as interesting to students as were the fields of study in which they were enrolled. AUB was a space for intellectual expression and discovery, where free thought, free speech, and open debates reigned.

When my family was not in Freike, we lived near AUB on Hamra Street. The university was a four or five minute walk along Jeanne d'Arc Street to the AUB main gate on Bliss Street. I woke up every morning thrilled about attending AUB. The atmosphere was invigorating, and its value system was closely aligned with the one in my parents' home.

AUB's faculty was drawn from many nationalities including American, Lebanese, Palestinian, Syrian, Iraqi, British, Italian, Greek, and Spanish. In the late sixties, the student body numbered about 3,500 and represented more than sixty-five nationalities. Many languages were spoken on campus. If there was a dream intellectual oasis in the world, a real melting pot, it was AUB.

I decided to major in political sciences. I also took courses in philosophy, literature, sociology, and cultural studies. As much as these classes stimulated me, I was equally stimulated by the activities on campus that were unrelated to my formal studies. Politically, AUB was a very active campus. I probably spent as many hours in the classrooms of Nicely Hall as I did in the Milk Bar café and the students' meeting building, West Hall, discussing politics. I also enjoyed participating in social and cultural activities. I was elected secretary of *Al-Rabita*, a student political organization, during my sophomore year, and as the representative of the AUB students on the Executive Committee of the Lebanese National University Students' Union the following year. The shy introverted student of the Collège became an engaged, politically active student in the liberating atmosphere of AUB.

Those special years at AUB coincided with what many Lebanese people consider the golden years of Beirut's intellectual life. In the late sixties and early seventies, Beirut was a city where the press was free, where publishing houses printed books that publishers in other Arab capitals did not dare release, where students had the right to demonstrate in the streets, and where freedom of opinion was respected. AUB reflected what Beirut represented, and most probably AUB influenced the intellectual identity of Beirut during these years. AUB was influenced by the freedom of expression in Beirut, and directly and indirectly helped expand and deepen those freedoms while strengthening the expectation that freedom was a right that needed to exist.

The year 1967 was a decisive one in the lives of the students of AUB. The Arabs lost the war against Israel. Gamal Abdul Nasser, the charismatic president of Egypt, had promised the Arabs that Israel would be defeated. It was not. The university students of the Arab world were disappointed, angered, and felt betrayed, and the AUB campus intensified its political activities. To start with, the students had their own weekly newspaper, *Outlook*, which became even more important after losing that war. AUB students also had their own political organizations, among them *Al-Rabita* for which I served as secretary. After 1967, these organizations increased their activities.

Also during this time, the students created their own Hyde Park. This campus tradition was inspired by the speaker's corner in

London's Hyde Park. At AUB, this space was between West Hall and Jessup Hall where, every Friday at 1:00 p.m., students gathered to discuss any topic they wanted to talk about. AUB's Hyde Park was a true, free intellectual space and an open physical place. We could speak for or against Gamal Abdul Nasser, President Lyndon Johnson, the Pope, the president of Lebanon, or any political figure. We could speak about politics, religion, culture, and student activism. We could debate the existence or non-existence of God, the reason for the Arab defeat in the 1967 war, and lay the blame at the feet of the U.S., Israel, or the Arab leaders. That space was sacred to students; it was a place where freedom of thought was exercised.

In 1966-67, the editor-in-chief of *Outlook* was Zuheir Al-Faqih. *Outlook* expressed the opinion of the majority of the students at that time. Arab nationalism was on the rise and Nasser was gaining in popularity. The Lebanese students on the AUB campus were a minority, and many of them felt that the wave of Nasserism did not respect Lebanese independence, or the aspirations of the Lebanese. This was reflected in the heated exchanges in Hyde Park. It also was reflected in the debates printed in *Outlook*, and the concerns and aspirations of the majority of the Lebanese students were expressed in the written statements of *Al-Rabita*.

Most probably the period between 1967 and 1972 was the most politically charged time of AUB's history. I remember when the executive committee of *Al-Rabita* would meet to decide on our political position and, as the secretary of the *Al-Rabita* who wrote well in Arabic, I would draft the statement. The executive committee would review the draft, and after it was finalized, we either mimeograph a couple of hundred copies—or if we had the funds, print a thousand—to disseminate on campus. Late in the evening, close to midnight, young men would hang copies of the statement on the walls of the university or pin them on the large, beautiful banyan trees. A couple of times these statements resulted in free-for-all fights between *Al-Rabita* and Nasserite students.

In the very early seventies when I was studying towards a master's degree and was no longer the secretary of *Al-Rabita*, one of these pro-Lebanon independence manifestos resulted in a huge fight among students. It was the Lebanese Independence Day. Lebanese students wanted to raise their national flag over West Hall and other students did not want to allow it. A statement from *Al-Rabita* was printed and distributed, a counter-statement was published, and the students fought each other in Nicely Hall using classroom chairs as weapons. My brother Ramzi, who was a very politically active student in those years, participated in many such confrontations. Major Lebanese dailies such as *An-Nahar* wrote about the political debates, activities, and the students' battles on the AUB campus. Needless to say, the AUB administration, headed by president Dr. Samuel Kirkwood, had its hands full.

During my AUB years, my mind was so incredibly engaged, my spirit was savoring the new dimensions of my life, and my heart was exploring new feelings. I studied political sciences with Professors Ralph Crow, Walid Al-Khalidi, Elie Salem, Hanna Batatu, and Yusef Ibish; philosophy with Professors Sadek Al-Azm and René Habashi; and literature with Professor Suheil Bushrui. The interaction with the professors was unlike anything I had experienced before AUB. Differences of opinions were respected, possibly encouraged, tolerance actively fostered, intellectual initiative seriously appreciated, and diversity recognized as an enriching factor. My political science professors taught us about schools of thought that ran the spectrum from capitalism to Marxism, while philosophy professors allowed us to question the existence of God. Professor Bushrui, an authority on William Butler Yates, James Joyce, Kahlil Gibran, and Ameen Rihani helped us understand that Lebanon's contributions to world literature were as significant as those of England or Ireland.

I enjoyed learning from my professors as much as I enjoyed my debates with fellow students. It seems we filled the air and space with discussions. I probably spent as many hours in the Milk Bar over a cup of coffee, talking and debating with my fellow students, as I did at Nicely Hall listening to, and engaging my professors in dialogue. During my AUB years, I made friends with students who were very different from each other—some were very studious and dedicated to academic achievement while others were focused on political activism.

My friends included Abdallah BouHabib, who lobbied for my election as *Al-Rabita* secretary, and who later became the ambassador of Lebanon to the United States. I believe I was the first woman student elected secretary of *Al-Rabita*. Amine Gemayel also became a close friend during these years. We worked together when he represented Saint Joseph, the French university in Beirut, on the Executive Committee of the Lebanese Universities Students' Union where I represented AUB. Both Amine and Abdallah were few years older than me and even more politically involved. Amine served as the president of Lebanon between 1982 and 1988.

It was during those years that I began teaching Arabic at the Collège, my old school. I also began my creative writing in Arabic, and I started publishing in the *An-Nahar* newspaper. My brothers Ameen and Ramzi were also writing during those years. Ameen published poetry, while Ramzi wrote about music for *An-Nahar*. In addition, he wrote plays including *Prova,* which was produced by AUB students in the West Hall Theater.

It was delightful to have a couple of overlapping years at AUB with two of my brothers: the eldest Ameen when I just entered, and Ramzi, the one immediately younger than me, when I was studying towards an MA and he was studying towards a BBA. Sarmad was much younger and still in high school. These were heady times. My horizons were expanding, learning was a joy, and political activism was the breath of every day. My brothers were interested in similar things: politics, activism, writing, and publishing; friends were special; my heart was actively exploring new territories. My days and evenings were so filled there was not enough time to sleep.

As I mentioned earlier, while a student at AUB I was asked to teach Arabic at the Collège. My first reaction was, no, thank you, I don't have time. However, Mlle. Rose Hawi, the Director of Arabic at that time, convinced me to accept. She invited me to teach part-time and to see if I liked it. She pointed out that I would be teaching Arabic, a subject I loved and excelled in, and that I would help improve the level of mastery of the Arabic language at the Collège. She also added that the new principal of the school, Mme. Bordreuille, was very different from Mlle. Wegmann and that she, Mlle. Hawi, wanted students to improve their Arabic.

This offer intrigued me, so after much thought, I accepted a part-time position—as if my daily life was not full enough. So there I was, a student and an activist at AUB, and a teacher at the Collège. AUB was a four- or five-minute walk south of my home, and the College, on Mme. Curie Street, was a fifteen-minute walk north of my home; so I walked to both. I arranged my schedule at the beginning of each semester so I could study and teach at the same time. Often, I would have class hours at AUB and at the Collège on the same day.

I was twenty when I began teaching, and my pupils ranged in age from thirteen to fifteen. I started with the *quatrième* grade, or what is considered ninth grade in the American system, and during the last year I taught at the College, I was teaching the *seconde,* or eleventh grade. I taught several hours of Arabic language and one hour of civic education each week.

When I was a student at the Collège, civic education was the least respected subject and the most boring, while Arabic classes were simply treated as unimportant. I wanted to change the paradigm and create a new attitude in my students towards these two key subjects. To that end, I decided to make the classes interactive. First, I wanted to minimize lectures and loading students with a lot of homework. Second, I wanted the classroom to be a place where they felt free to ask as many questions as they wanted, and to join me in providing answers, thereby engaging them intellectually and emotionally.

When I taught Arabic literature, I did not limit our study to classic poetry that reached as far back as the pre-Islamic poets of the fifth century. I added the poets of the twentieth century and included modern poets living in Beirut at the time, some of whom I knew from their connection with my family. I arranged for the students to interview them and then report to the entire class about their discussions. The well-known and influential Syrian poet Omar Abu Richi was one of many interviewed by my students, and they quickly found themselves in awe of him.

My students and I attended a Rahbani Brothers musical in the Piccadilly Theater in Ras Beirut one Saturday evening. They were amazed by the beauty and cleverness of the lyrics, and by the quality of the performances. I remember some of them telling me that it was the first time they had attended theater in Arabic and that they were entirely unprepared to discover its complexity and beauty. They did not expect to love the performances as much as they did.

For civic education, I engaged them even more. After I framed the importance of the subject to my class, the students and I selected the issues we wanted to study for the year. These included learning about the roles of government and the roles of citizens; understanding the three branches of our government; learning about what was centralized and what was decentralized in the Lebanese system; becoming aware of rights, responsibilities, and accountability; and being cognizant of the Lebanese heritage. I decided to add learning about other social classes. My students were completely invigorated by the range of topics and issues. We divided into small groups of about five students, and each group would research one topic and present it to the class. My responsibility was to provide guidance and, when needed, supplemental information. I reviewed the information they gathered for accuracy and helped them keep a clear and objective focus on the issues. In all instances, I took the role of learning facilitator. This proved to be very motivating; the more so as they had not experienced such an approach before.

Their learning emanated from personal discovery as we entered the interactive process where we learned from each other. Both the teacher and the student groups became sources of knowledge, and we all were learners. The students reacted in a most positive manner to this approach.

Even today, I cannot single out the most important factor that enabled the students to respond so positively to my way of teaching. The fact that I was close to them in age—perhaps the youngest teacher at the Collège at that time—and still a student must have been a factor. They could certainly identify with me more readily. My teaching approach was very different from other Collège teachers, and the students must have been thirsty for the respect they received as well as for the responsibility that I extended to them.

51

Most importantly, perhaps, was the absence of fear and intimidation. Learning took place in an open, win-win atmosphere where we all taught, learned, and benefited. But the underpinning element—the reason for their engagement—might be the fact that I was able to clearly demonstrate the relevance of the Arabic language and of civic education to their daily lives.

I loved teaching at the Collège. I saw excitement in my students' eyes; heard questions that emanated from a sincere desire to learn and not just to get a higher grade; and listened to presentations by fifteen- and sixteen-year-olds who were smart, inquisitive, analytic, and searching. I watched their minds blossom and witnessed their thirst for knowledge drive them to want to know more. I saw their attitudes towards Lebanon and the Arabic language change. A transformation was happening. The more I noticed it, the more excited I became about teaching.

AUB energized me as a student, and the Collège, to my surprise, energized me as a teacher. During those years my energy soared. In one of the civic education classes, we discussed the fact that the streets of our city were not clean. The debate was over who was responsible: the government, the municipality of Beirut, or the citizens? By the end of the class, we agreed that citizens had some responsibilities for the cleanliness of their streets and we organized a campaign for the cleanliness of Beirut. We wanted to put into practice what we learned.

We negotiated with the municipality of Beirut for Collège students, accompanied by a teacher, to clean Hamra Street in Ras Beirut on a certain Saturday afternoon. The municipality agreed to provide big brooms we could use and to ensure a truck followed along to collect the refuse. My students wanted to be action-oriented and I helped them organize the whole activity. We were ready to prove that we were responsible citizens.

That Saturday, shortly after noon, I received a phone call from the *surveillante générale,* an administrator at the Collège, telling me that the principal, Mme. Bordreuille, forbade me to allow the students to clean Hamra Street. I was completely stunned. I told the *surveillante* that it was too late to stop the event; we would be in Hamra in less than two hours, and the municipality had mobilized its work force to assist us. I reminded the *surveillante* that this activity was not taking place during school hours. Saturday afternoon was the weekend for the students, and I thought they were free to do what they felt was good for their city during personal time. The *surveillante* said the office would call the parents of my students to tell them the Collège forbade them to attend. I could not believe what I was hearing. I tried to convince the *surveillante* that the activity could not bring harm to anyone; that, on the contrary, it would teach elite adolescent girls a sense of responsibility. My pleading was to no avail.

It seems the Collège started calling the parents. What they had not anticipated was that many of the parents supported their daughters' participation in this activity. At two o'clock, my students and I were cleaning Hamra Street with big brooms provided by the municipality. Many of their parents, such as Dr. Salim Maksoud, came along to demonstrate their support. During the two-hour phone campaign to stop the project, somehow the media became aware of the confrontation brewing between the Collège on one hand and my students and me on the other. As a result, we had parents, photographers, reporters, and onlookers alongside us on the sidewalk as we cleaned Hamra for more than two hours.

The next day we were on the front pages of many Lebanese dailies and in the *Actualités,* a short video news clip that used to be shown in movie theaters before the feature film. We became the talk of the town. On the front page of *L'Orient-Le Jour*, the French daily of Lebanon, there was our photo sweeping the street, with a title: *"Les Boueurs du Collège Protestant."* My friends at AUB were delighted. They said that apparently what May is doing at AUB as a political activist is not enough, now she is also bringing activism to the Collège. They ignored my explanation that I was doing nothing more than teaching civic education in a relevant and practical way.

The principal of the Collège was frustrated. She was not used to the fact that the parents would not listen to her, and that the media in Lebanon made such a big deal of the small activity that my students and I decided to undertake. She decided not to renew my contract for the next year. When my students learned of her decision, they went on strike. The strike started on April 20 or 21, 1972. The Collège was then a forty-five-year-old institution (having been established in 1927), and there had not been a single strike up till then. The principal got even angrier and escalated the confrontation. She threatened to expel students who did not end the strike immediately. The students were not ready to give in. They wrote a statement, printed it, and distributed it to students, parents, and the media. They called their statement "Manifesto Number One."

The media had a ball. A majority—if not all—of the dailies and weekly magazines in Lebanon covered the conflict between the "elite students" of the Collège and the principal. I was frequently interviewed, the principal was interviewed, students were interviewed, and many articles were written. *An-Nahar, Al Anwar, Le Soir, L'Orient-Le Jour, Al Moharrer, Al Hawadeth, Al Hayat, Monday Morning* and many other dailies and magazines extensively covered this unprecedented strike by the daughters of the upper class of Lebanon. Mme. Bordreuille made statements that did not make a lot of sense; for example, she said that communist thinking influenced me. Nothing could have been further from the truth. During that same time, the leftist students at AUB were unhappy with me because I opposed Nasser's politics towards Lebanon, while at the Collège, the principal accuses me of being influenced by communist thought. The principal also said I was not fit to teach at a French high school but might be suited to teach at an American university. I considered that statement a compliment.

The situation triggered many events. The media covered the disagreement extensively. The *Actualités Libanaise* covered our campaign for over a week. Onsi Al Hajj, a luminary figure among poets, writers, and thinkers of the sixties and seventies in Lebanon, and editor-in-chief of the "Sunday Supplement" of *An-Nahar*, the most prominent newspaper in Lebanon, wrote two articles about what happened at the Collège and supported both my position and the students' action. The media saw the street cleaning as an act of patriotism and derided the notion it was inspired by communism. In short, there was a head-on collision between French elitist training on the one hand, and relevant education and service to the country on the other. The Collège maintained its philosophy; we remained true to ours.

Many other journalists and reporters provided extensive coverage of "the cleaning of Hamra Street" and the subsequent historic strike of the daughters of the elites. Some deeply engrained patterns began to change. The young women knew they were responsible for certain things in Lebanon, and the principals of their schools could not prevent them from being involved in the daily lives of their communities. The daughters of the elites wanted to close the distance between themselves and other members of Lebanese society, and they were not going to let a French principal of a French school stop them.

Many of my close friends today are students I taught at the Collège, some of whom participated in the cleaning of the Hamra Street and in the first students' strike at the school. Among those former students and friends are Mona Maksoud, a psychologist in London; Randa Azzam, an international lawyer in Washington, D.C.; Betty Abou Haidar, a public health specialist in Washington state; Leila Musfi, a professor of Fine Arts at AUB in Beirut; Nina Baydoon Idriss, a political activist in Washington, D.C.; and Najla Droobi, a scientist in Dubai.

That episode at the Collège, and the activism at AUB, helped me understand the power of teaching, and how teaching, if implemented in an interactive and dynamic way, can become a powerful force of transformation. I understood that teaching could be about a vision of a better future. I also understood that teaching is a noble profession that enables students to read and write, but can also result in empowerment, freedom of thought, and leadership.

CHAPTER NINE

TRAVELING INSIDE AND OUTSIDE LEBANON

I REMEMBER THAT THROUGHOUT THE sixties, Mommy and Daddy would take our family on day trips within Lebanon. Discovering the small beautiful country of ours was such a feast. We would drive and admire the scenery, have lunch somewhere and stop to visit and learn about historic cities on the coast of the Mediterranean or about special regions in the mountains.

My parents did not play teacher. They simply enjoyed an outing and assumed that their children would enjoy it, too. In those days, it was considered normal for children, including teenagers, to spend quality time with their parents. I think we enjoyed those outings and learned a whole lot just by osmosis. I recall the history we experienced while visiting Byblos, Tyre, Baalbeck, the Cedars, Sidon, and Beit Eddine, as well as the beauty of coastal regions such as Damour.

Byblos is a sunny coastal town inhabited by people who know they belong to a special place. School children live side-by-side with temples and amphitheaters that are over 2,000 years old. Priests pray in churches that could be a thousand years old, and fishermen sell their fresh catches while their blue fishing nets are stretched out in the sun to dry, waiting to be mended. It is a city where old and new exist together in harmony. Byblos' historic neighborhood is only a few meters away from the modern part of the city that is bustling with restaurants, cafés, and souvenir shops. We used to visit this town which lies just north of Beirut quite often, and spend a lot of our time absorbing its history and its sophisticated beauty.

Daddy explained that Byblos was founded around 5000 BC. For that reason, whenever we visited, I felt I needed to speak in a very low voice out of respect to the accumulation of stories, lives, events, cultures, weddings, births, deaths, celebrations, festivities, music, poetry, art, and the many other things this town had seen over the years. Byblos is said to be the first Phoenician city and the oldest continuously inhabited city in the world. Its Phoenician ruins are like writings on the earth; its Greek ruins echo with the voice of Homer; its Roman theater speaks of Virgil; and its Crusader castle inhabits the waters of the Mediterranean. It is a place that taught us, in a powerful way, the importance of history.

In contrast to Byblos' sophistication, Tyre is poetic in its beauty. It is the legendary birthplace of two beautiful women, Europa and Dido. The first had a continent named after her, and the second founded Carthage. Legend has it that Zeus fell in love with Europa, who was a Phoenician princess from Tyre. When her parents did not allow her to marry Zeus, he abducted her by assuming the form of a bull and took her to the island of Crete. So in love with Europa was Zeus that he named the continent after his beloved. I could not help but try to imagine how beautiful Europa must have been to have a legend of that nature created in her honor.

Dido, also known as Elissar, was the daughter of Belus, the king of Tyre, and she, too, was honored in legend. The story states she and her followers sailed the Mediterranean until they reached the shores of present-day Tunisia, where in about 800 BC she founded Carthage. To me, the southern city of Tyre was about Lebanon's ancient past and the thread that took us back to our Phoenician ancestry. But it was also about beautiful and powerful women. In addition, Tyre has a Roman hippodrome that made me dream of riding horses.

In the central Békaa Valley of Lebanon is the ancient city of Baalbeck. Baalbeck was about majesty, and about the link between Lebanon and ancient Rome. The ruins at Baalbeck are breathtaking. Its Zeus, Bacchus, and Venus temples take visitors on a journey where the windows of history offer a glimpse of Roman civilization so real one can imagine Julius Caesar riding along its streets. The remains of these temples are powerful, grand, and sacred. They defy time and evoke an air of mystery. It is as though these temples stopped time, threw it out of the window, and decided to enjoy the moment that was two thousand years ago. Every time we visited Baalbeck, I felt free. I felt like canceling the calendars and negating the hours and the days. Every time we visited, I wondered how those who built the monuments could move such immense stones and lift them into place to create the huge columns of the temples of Zeus and Bacchus. And every time we visited Baalbeck, I was drawn into a different world; sometimes I wanted to be a priestess burning incense in the temples, other times I wanted to be a ballerina dancing on the steps of the temple of Bacchus as Dame Margot Fonteyn and Rudolph Nureyev did. Baalbeck always carried me on its wings and stretched my imagination. Within its borders, there was no limit, not even the sky.

On the mountain range that separates the central valley and coast is the symbol of Lebanon: the Cedars. The Cedars seemed holy to me. We would drive north and go up and up the mountains until we reached the forest of Cedar trees. Often, we would stop for lunch in either Zgharta or Beshare before continuing upward for an afternoon walking among the stands of the Cedars. Daddy or Mommy always reminded us of the incredible age of these trees. It seems the forest was dense at certain times in history, but ancient demands for cedar wood were extensive. The dominant civilizations of more than two thousand years ago, Egypt and Mesopotamia, had very little wood. They became dependent on the Phoenicians for lumber and the Cedar forest was depleted to meet that demand. Unfortunately, the trees continued to be harvested until recent times. In the sixties, when I use to visit the Cedar forest with the family, only a small number of these majestic trees were left. May be that was one of the reasons I felt they are so precious and holy.

Another Mediterranean city we visited was Sidon. It also had a castle in the sea. These castles had a special relationship with the water, as if the sea continuously caressed the stones of their big walls, and as if the castles and the sea had a special language that was understood only when we listened very carefully and allowed our imagination to interpret what was said. I think it was soft poetry.

Away from the coast, in the Chouf mountain region, Beit Eddine Palace was about architecture. The prince, or emir, of Lebanon, Bashir Shehab, began building the palace in 1788. It took about thirty years to be completed. What I loved was the style that is a combination of traditional Arab and Italian baroque; the palace has so many arches. I think Beit Eddine instilled in me the love of anything that contained the beautiful shape of an arch.

In addition to these historic places, some of our outings with Mommy and Daddy were to lovely serene coastal towns such as Damour. Situated between Beirut and Sidon, Damour was the land of plenty. As we drove, we stopped at street vendors to buy all kinds of fresh vegetables and fruits: tomatoes, cucumbers, squash, radishes, lettuce, green beans, parsley, eggplant, cauliflower, mint, oranges, lemons, bananas, and many other seasonal produce. The smell of Damour was unique, a mix of ocean perfume, the freshness of young parsley, and orange peel. Someone from Grasse, in France, should study that enticing perfume and bottle it. With a name like Damour, especially if they add the apostrophe *d'Amour*, I am sure it would sell.

My first two trips to Arab countries were also in the mid sixties— one to Damascus, Syria, and one to Cairo, Egypt. The family went to Damascus for the weekend. What I remember about the city in particular is the old Souk Al Hamidiyyah. The market place, or *souk*, had shops for everything, some of which looked as if they might not have changed in centuries. Under the souk's covered arches were shops for clothes, tablecloths, sheesha water-pipes, toys, wooden engraved tables, shoes, sweets, carpets, and myriad other things. It was very crowded and perfect for people-watching. The drink sellers in their fezzes and bright garments were everywhere. I was fascinated by the ambiance of the souk, and all I could think of was how different Beirut and Damascus were. Beirut was forward-looking, always searching for new horizons, while Damascus was reclining in a space that enjoyed tradition—at least, that is how the two cities appeared to me.

Cairo was an entirely different story.

Mommy's cousins, the Schoucairs, invited my parents to spend a vacation in Cairo. I cannot remember why I was the lucky one chosen to accompany them, but once we arrived, I became Alice in Wonderland. There were no limits to my discoveries: the pyramids, the Cairo Museum, the Mohammad Ali Mosque, the Saladin Citadel, dinner on a boat in the Nile, belly dancing in one of the cabarets of the Nile Hilton, Groppy's tea room, and many more special and unique places. Mommy and Daddy were very close to Habib,

Shafiq, and Ramez Schoucair, who often spent short vacations in our mountain home in Freike.

The Schoucairs wanted us to see the historically rich Cairo as well as the modern city. A chapter could be written about each place we visited. The pyramids filled my head with centuries of history, and the Mohammad Ali Mosque opened a new chapter in my mind about the beauty of architecture. The presence of the pyramids in the middle of the desert was like the sun in the middle of the sky, so simple and so powerful. I knew I could not absorb all the importance of that presence during this first trip. It took several additional visits to Cairo for the pyramids to enter my consciousness. However, during that first trip, I took in an easier side of Cairo. I discovered and enjoyed places such as Groppy's, which was once a magnet for Egypt's high society when it was considered the world's ritziest tearoom. Groppy's is the creation of a Swiss pastry maker and has been featured in countless films and publications. That first visit to Cairo was only the beginning of a journey of discovery that continued over many decades.

In the spring of 1969, my world expanded beyond its previous confines. I received a grant or a scholarship—I cannot recall what it was called—to serve as a camp counselor in the U.S. for about eight weeks. My parents had encouraged me to apply. They promised if I were accepted, and if I had good grades at AUB, they would also let me visit Italy and France on my way to the U.S. It was a dream comes true. I could not contain myself; I felt I must have been born under a lucky star. My happiness must have been contagious because when my brothers learned about my good luck, Ameen and Ramzi lifted me onto their shoulders and, with Sarmad following behind, I was marched through every room of our Hamra home with the four of us chanting and fooling around. The fact that my brothers were as happy as I was made me even more excited about my upcoming great adventure.

The planning for the trip was a journey by itself. My parents' close friend Sheikh Maurice Gemayel, who was at that time the chair of the United Nations Food and Agriculture Organization (FAO), wanted me to be his guest in Rome for four days. I was delighted; I knew Sheikh Maurice very well. In addition to his friendship with my parents, he was also the leader of an informal organization called *Groupe Relève*, which he established and to which I belonged. Groupe Relève had student representatives from the different universities in Lebanon, all hand-picked by Sheikh Maurice. He made sure the religious diversity of Lebanon was represented and that active, engaged, promising student leaders were part of this group. We met on Sunday morning at his home where we studied and discussed with him the importance of human and economic development.

My parents also agreed that I could spend up to four days in Paris, on my own, before I went on to Le Havre to board a ship for New York. I had to pinch myself to believe that all of this would be happening in a few months' time. During June, July, and August of 1969, I discovered three cities that had inhabited my dreams: Rome, Paris, and New York.

By mid-June, I had finished my semester at AUB and was ready to start my trip. Several members of the family took me to the Beirut Airport to bid me farewell. The Middle East Airlines (MEA) flight took off, and in just three hours, the captain announced our descent into Leonardo Da Vinci Airport.

Sheikh Maurice was waiting to meet me. He always treated me as one of his daughters and often told my parents, "May is like my eighth daughter" (he had seven). He booked me into a room at the

Hilton close to the apartment he rented when he stayed in Rome. He picked me up each morning at around ten and took me on tours of the city. Sheikh Maurice was a dignified member of parliament, the minister of planning in Lebanon, and at the time of my visit, served as the chair of the FAO. Yet this man was willing to be my guide in Rome. I was humbled and delighted. He was very knowledgeable, well read, and appreciative of history, architecture and art, and how those things intersect. In four days, he provided me with a condensed tour of the most beautiful things in the Vatican and in Rome.

I kept wondering if I deserved such a renaissance, erudite man to be my guide. The only explanation I could find was that the behavior of Sheikh Maurice was a reflection of certain aspects of the Lebanese culture. Very close friends become family. Daddy and Sheikh Maurice were like brothers, and so he was paying homage to my father by treating me the way he did.

During my four days in Rome, I saw that enchanted city through the eyes of a connoisseur. We started by a tour of the city and drove around each one of the seven hills. We spent time visiting the Vatican City, the Holy See, St. Peter's Basilica, the Vatican Museum, and the Sistine Chapel. These incredible places came alive through Sheikh Maurice's explanation. He described the architecture, the history, the art, the colors, and the religious dimensions, and then waited to see where my real interest lay before elaborating on that specific angle. In the Sistine Chapel, for example, he explained that the famous ceiling is divided into nine sections in which nine stories of Genesis were painted. He noticed that I was particularly interested in knowing how Michelangelo was able to paint in such an intricate and precise way on a high, curved ceiling. Sheikh Maurice told me how Michelangelo conceived and constructed a unique scaffolding system, curved at its top, mimicking the curvature of the ceiling's vault. Michelangelo often had to bend backwards and paint over his head in order to capture the precisions of facial expression or muscle of each body he was illustrating.

While visiting St. Peter's Basilica in Vatican City, I was struck by the *Pieta* of Michelangelo (1498–1499). Sheikh Maurice explained that it is a masterpiece of the Renaissance period sculpted out of Carrera marble. The *Pieta* is a depiction of the body of Jesus on the lap of his mother Mary after the crucifixion. I was so overwhelmed by the purity of Mary that I studied her face to understand this absolute serenity. The face of the *Pieta* is a lesson in how sadness becomes beauty because of an inner understanding that her Son died for all of us. Her face, the face of the *Pieta*, transcends age, suffering, sadness, serenity, beauty, and even the pain a mother feels when her Son is crucified. Mary was holding the body of Jesus on her lap, but at the same time, she knew she was giving Him away to humanity. I did not know then that looking at Michelangelo's *Pieta* in June 1969 marked, for me, the beginning of my life-long love story with sculpture.

In addition to all the wonders of the Vatican City, we visited the Coliseum, Villa Borghese and its Gardens, Via Veneto, Piazza de La Republica, the Trevi Fountain, and the FAO headquarters. How we crammed so much into four days I do not know. Our energy was limitless, and we stopped only for lunches and dinners, which were interesting times in themselves. For one of the lunches, Sheikh Maurice invited Princess Lala Aisha, who was the Ambassador of Morocco to Rome. I was delighted to see an Arab woman ambassador as early as 1969. She was delightful, and the three of us had a wonderful conversation about Lebanon and Morocco. For another meal, he invited his sister, a nun who lived in Rome; and for a third, he invited an Italian couple who were so proud that the chair of the FAO knew their city well enough to be a better guide than they would be able to. At least that is what they said, and I believed them.

Every dream has an end, and my gorgeous dream in Rome had to end, too. On the plane from Rome to Paris, I wrote my parents a letter letting them know how lucky I was to have had their friend as my guide.

I landed at the airport in Paris, and went straight to a hotel I had booked in the Left Bank. This was my first trip to Paris. I had read so much about the "most beautiful city in the world," the city of light, the elegant and gorgeous city. My expectations had no limit. My boyfriend for the past few years had decided to meet me in Paris. I had not told my parents of his visit because they never approved of him, and I, too, was having my ups and downs with him. However, when he offered to come to Paris, I could not resist. All I could think was that was what Paris was for: lovers.

I knew I had only four days before my steamliner left Le Havre. In that time, I wanted to see the Louvre, the Tour Eiffel, Musée l'Orangerie, Notre Dame, Montmartre, Musée d'Orsay, Les Champs Elysées, and Saint Germain des Prés. I had done my homework; I was ready to take in all of Paris. I had waited so long to get to know the city that lived for many years in my imagination.

I wanted to start with Les Champs or the Tour Eiffel, but my boyfriend, wanted us to take the train to Deauville in the Normandy; he wanted to go to the Casino Barrière so he could gamble. I tried to convince him we should stay in Paris. He promised we would go to Deauville only for two days. As usual, he and his suave manner, he and his appearance of knowing it all, he and his argument that I would always have Paris but I would not go to the Casino Barrière except with him, won me over. We ended up in Deauville. He drank, and smoked, and gambled, and I watched a world I did not belong to. The two days in Deauville became four, and I left for Le Havre from Deauville, having missed Paris, and having quarreled with my boyfriend. Maybe I needed something as serious as four days at the Casino for me to break up with him for good.

On board the steamliner to New York, I had time to think and reflect. The time in Rome with the erudite older gentleman, my Daddy's best friend, playing the role of my guide represented the side of my life that is about knowledge, art, civilization, and the acceptance of a value system that has at its core respect of everything that exists. The time in Paris, or rather Deauville, with my boyfriend as my guide—a young, handsome gambler who spoke five languages impeccably, drank and smoked non-stop, and cared more about racing cars than art, history, literature, politics, or the rest of the world (and who was not an acceptable suitor to my parents) represented a style of life that was attractive but totally irresponsible. I had been entirely exposed to both in the past three or four years. My home life, my university life, and my work as a teacher were about the first lifestyle, while the escapades with my boyfriend were about that fast, attractive, exciting, crazy, and irresponsible life.

Somewhere in the middle of the Atlantic, between Le Havre and New York, and after some agony, I wrote to the handsome and attractive guy and ended our relationship.

They told us that the ship would arrive in New York very early in the morning, that we would see the shore before dawn, and that we would have a glimpse of the Statue of Liberty before 5:00 a.m. The night before I could not sleep; the anticipation was overwhelming. New York was the symbol of the new world, the new frontier, the edge of new ideas, the things that *would* happen, and the daring future. New York was also the city where my father was born, where he lived and studied at Columbia University, the city that shaped his liberal thinking, his love of music and dance, his openness to all kinds of new ideas, and his forward-looking approach to his life and the life of his family.

The steamliner slowly approached the New York skyline through the pre-dawn darkness and the morning mist. All the passengers were on deck watching silently. There was something surreal about the scene. It could be that the mist was a little heavier than usual, or it could be the early morning darkness cast a veil of mystery, or both. My heart beat faster than usual, my sense of acknowledgment of unique moments was heightened, a world of expectations filled my head, and my feelings regarding how I would react to New York started to flow with the mists towards the Big Apple.

There she was; I could make out her shape, her arm stretched upward holding a golden torch. The early light of the dawn unveiled her face. *Oh, my God! There she is: Liberty!* My Uncle Ameen saw her from the Brooklyn Bridge and wrote a famous article: "Why Not Turn Your Face Towards the East, Oh Liberty!"

When I saw her from the deck of the steamliner, I asked: Why are you not shining your torch on every home on this planet? Why is it taking you so long to free the poor from hunger wherever they are, to free the minds of people from the domination of despotic leaders everywhere? Here she was, the Statue of Liberty at the harbor entrance of New York, a gift from the French people to America. To my mind, it was a gift from every human being to every other human being. The steamliner approached slowly out of respect to the importance of what we were seeing, Liberty and the skyline of New York—a sight that would remain etched in my memory forever. Those huge buildings, as if they also had their arms stretched upward toward the sky, as if each one of them were a Statue of Liberty. There is something mysterious about first seeing the skyline of New York from the ocean, especially at dawn. The city was lifting itself up from the ocean and possibly stretching its arms upward to engage in a dialogue with whoever was up high.

The steamliner arrived at the shore; the passengers debarked slowly, as if in a haze. I felt I was sleepwalking. The smiling face of my wonderful friend Suad Joseph among the crowd brought me back to the reality of the moment. I had truly arrived in New York, and Suad was waiting to welcome me to her city.

We picked up my luggage and drove to the hotel where I was booked. Suad gave me a couple of hours to rest before she and her brother Alfred returned to take me on a tour of New York and, in the evening, to my first Broadway show.

Suad, Alfred, and I walked for possibly four hours: Time Square, Lincoln Center, Fifth Avenue, Central Park; we had an early dinner and then went to see *Man of La Mancha*. Suad's choice for my first Broadway musical could not have been better. Maybe everyone is completely taken by the first Broadway musical they see. The production, the choreography, the costumes, the stage set, the dances, the voices, the lights—everything about it was grandiose and bigger than my eyes could absorb all at once. But the lyrics of the feature song, "The Impossible Dream," were transporting. To me, *Man of La Mancha* was a symbol of what the U.S. aims to be.

After the show, Suad, Alfred, and I went to have coffee and discuss what we saw. I made them repeat the words of "The Impossible Dream" while I wrote it down on a piece of paper and tucked it in one of my pockets.

The lyrics (or some of them) were stuck in my mind throughout the summer that I spent as a camp counselor in upstate New York.

The words became a thread that linked me to a vision and continued
to inspire me:

> To dream the impossible dream,
> To fight the unbeatable foe,
> To bear with unbearable sorrow,
> To run where the brave dare not go.
>
> To right the unrightable wrong,
> To love, pure and chaste from afar,
> To try when your arms are too weary,
> To reach the unreachable star,
>
> This is my quest, to follow that star,
> No matter how hopeless, no matter how far,
> To fight for the right without question or pause,
> To be willing to march into hell for a heavenly cause.
>
> And I know if I'll only be true to this glorious quest,
> That my heart will lie peaceful and calm, when I'm
> laid to my rest,
>
> And the world will be better for this,
> That one man, scorned and covered with scars,
> Still strove with his last ounce of courage,
> To reach the unreachable stars. [1]

---

[1] Copyright © 1965, Words Joe Darion, Music Mitch Leigh. Andrew Scott
Music, Helena Music Company. ASCAP. Used with permission.

After a couple of days in New York with Suad as my guide, I had to join the camp I was assigned to on Lake Erie in Pennsylvania as an international camp counselor. A new experience totally different from my days in Rome, Deauville, and New York was to start. The Lake Erie camp was most probably typical of summer camps for teenagers in America. Camp Chicagami was on a forty-acre site on the shore of the lake. The grounds were beautiful, consisting of many acres of woodland and a half-mile of beachfront. Facilities were provided for all kinds of sports: basketball, volleyball, table tennis, and others.

The dining hall was under a huge tent and comprised of many wooden tables and benches. American teenagers entered in an orderly manner between 7:30 and 8:30 a.m. for breakfast. I was always amazed at the amount they ate. At noon, they would rush in for lunch, and between 5:30 and 6:30 p.m., they would line up for dinner. Even though the teens consumed huge amounts for each meal, they were always hungry.

The day was filled with sports activities, and I was utterly untrained in sports. I always worried that I would cause the team I joined to lose. In between the sports activities, we had drama programs, nature exploration, and social discussions. I was very interested in the social discussions in particular, finding the common ground and the point of differences between American and Lebanese teenagers based on the context of 1969.

My favorite time, however, was the campfire evenings. Many camp counselors played guitar and all of us—counselors and campers—spent the evening singing campfire songs and roasting marshmallows. My favorite songs were by Bob Dylan and Joan Baez. I learned so much about American music during my camp days, and I also learned about how competitive American sports can be.

In July, the camp director announced that we would all gather to watch the upcoming moon landing. The young campers were so proud that Americans would be the first human beings to walk on the Moon; excitement filled the camp. The countdown started a week before the scheduled landing. On the evening of July 20, we gathered in the great tent where a TV had been set up to watch Apollo 11 land on the Moon in the Sea of Tranquility. The minute Neil Armstrong's left foot touched the surface, the whole camp exploded in applause. Some were crying, some hugging each other, some continued clapping, some started dancing. Pride was in the air on July 20, 1969, as we shared an unforgettable day which represented the possibility of dreaming the impossible dream and making it a reality. The U.S. mission was considered the major accomplishment in the history of space exploration.

Launched from the Kennedy Space Center in Florida on July 16, Apollo 11 was the fifth manned mission, and the third lunar mission, of NASA's Apollo program. Neil Armstrong and Buzz Aldrin became the first humans to walk on the Moon. Their lunar module, *Eagle*, spent 21 hours 31 minutes on the lunar surface. The astronauts returned to Earth on July 24. Apollo 11 fulfilled U.S. President John Kennedy's goal of reaching the Moon before the Soviet Union and by the end of the 1960s, which he had expressed during a 1961 statement, saying, "I believe that this nation should commit itself to achieving the goal, before this decade is out, of landing a man on the Moon and returning him safely to the Earth." For me to be in the U.S. during this uniquely American time was to witness the fact that the sky is no longer the limit, and that impossible dreams can become a reality.

My camp ended after seven weeks. I went back to New York and spent another few days with Suad discovering additional dimensions of this great city. One thing I had not yet done was to visit Columbia University. Suad, who was a PhD student at Columbia, took me to the university. The minute I arrived on campus, I felt I got to know my Daddy even better. This was where he spent four years of his life studying economics. I saw the school's stunning architectural centerpiece, the Low Memorial Library, which is in the Roman classical style. A broad flight of steps descended from it to an expansive open area where students regularly gathered. I smiled as I imagined my father, as a student, going up and down the stairs of Low Memorial Library with books under his arm, several friends chatting happily around him.

I discovered where courses in economics were given during the late 1920s and visited those buildings as well as others. I imagined my father in certain classrooms, wondered who his girlfriends were, who his best friends were. I imagined him being curious, asking insightful questions in class, taking everything in, enjoying both classes and extracurricular activities. I was certain he had been popular because of his personality, and because his curiosity was endless. I also knew that these years in the halls of Columbia must have been among the most formative years of his life.

I wished the walls could talk so they could share with me special stories about Daddy. I was very happy to walk in his footsteps at this magnificent university. I learned that Columbia University was founded in 1754 as King's College by royal charter of King George II of Great Britain, that it is the oldest institution of higher education in the state of New York and the fifth oldest in the United States. I also learned that the famous philosopher and educator John Dewey, Irwin Edman the philosopher, Dean Harry Carman, and Mark Van Doren the well-known novelist and playwright were professors at Columbia in the twenties when my Daddy was a student.

I had only two days before flying back to Beirut via Paris, and I packed those days as fully as I could, walking from place to place in New York. So many things brewed in my head. This was the city that shaped Daddy; this was the city that pushed the edge of every idea and the contour of every concept; this was the city where the future might be more important than the past; this was the city that behaved as if it would be young forever. I enjoyed every moment, trying to feel, to understand, and to take in as much as I could.

Then it was time to leave. Suad organized a goodbye party for me. She invited several friends, Lebanese and Americans, and we ate and danced till three in the morning. I had just a few hours of sleep before going to the airport.

I did not know in 1969 how valuable that trip would prove to be. My exposure to Rome, Paris/Deauville, and New York was a turning point in my life; travel, journeys, different cultures, and constantly discovering new horizons became part of life's daily menu. To borrow a saying from Ameen Rihani, I did not know then that at one point I would become "a vagabond on the highway of life."

CHAPTER TEN

———◦◦◦———

WRITING AND PUBLISHING

A S IF STUDYING AT AUB, teaching at the Collège, being a political activist, serving as secretary of *Al-Rabita* and being elected to the Executive Committee of the Lebanese Universities Students' Union, weren't enough, I also felt the urge to jot down many of my thoughts and feelings. One evening during my first year at AUB, I came home and felt I had to express myself in writing rather than by discussing what I was feeling and thinking. When I finished writing the essay, I had to know what my father thought about it.

After dinner, with absolute trepidation I asked Daddy if he would read something I had written. He said he would be very interested in doing so. The emotions, feelings, and thoughts that invaded my brain and my heart were overwhelming as I retrieved the papers and joined Daddy in the living room.

What if Daddy did not like what I had written? Most probably it would mean that I would never write again.

What if he liked it? That might mean I would be propelled into a writing pathway.

There I was, in front of Daddy. He was reading my manuscript. What if the *publisher* did not like it? In those few minutes, I identified with the many, many, writers who had waited for his opinion to learn if he would publish their manuscripts.

I had always been able to read my father's facial expressions very quickly; however, that evening either I was completely overwhelmed or he did not show any expression until he finished reading my essay. Those ten minutes or so of waiting felt so long. Finally, he lifted his head, looked at me, and smiled. What a relief!

Daddy and I talked for over two hours that evening. He expressed his interest in what I had written, in my style, in the ideas I wrote about. We discussed my choice of certain words, the juxtaposition of words and phrases, the composition of sentences, the usage of certain metaphors. He commented on my deliberate decision to make symbolism a part of what I wrote, the fact that I was not yet writing poetry but that I would soon want to try my hand at it. We debated the legacy of classical Arabic poetry and the meaning of free verse as well as its freedom and its forward-looking nature.

Daddy said things like, writing is liberating, writing has no walls, no limits, and through it, individuals can reach ultimate freedom. I am not sure that I entirely understood the depth of what he said that evening, but I know that his words echoed through the rest of my life.

We discussed the internal, subtle music of free verse versus the obvious music of classical poetry. We discussed the power of writing; the fact that it is everlasting; the fact that it becomes part of history, culture, identity, and much more. We discussed how writing is a process, and how every writer continues to work on that process to improve what he or she is trying to communicate. We discussed the reader, the audience, whether a piece is targeted at a specific audience or not. I knew that if I had not had classes at AUB the next morning, Daddy and I could have spent another three or four hours discussing writing and publishing, but a little after eleven, Daddy reminded me that I had to go to AUB the next morning and that he had to go to his office.

That evening was a turning point in my life. If Daddy had not expressed any interest in my efforts, I do not think I would have continued creative writing. Around midnight, I went to bed transformed. I had been propelled into the world I used to observe around Daddy's dinner table when I was a little girl. I knew he gave me permission to enter the fabulous world of writers. I must have floated when returning to my room.

Every two or three weeks I wrote an essay. I made a conscious decision that I would send my first piece to Onsi Al Hajj, the editor-in-chief of *An-Nahar*. Another overwhelming period of waiting. That time it was not for ten or twelve minutes to see the reaction of my father. It was waiting for three or four days to see if Onsi Al Hajj would publish my first essay in the Sunday literary supplement of *An-Nahar*. The first time Onsi published me, I could not contain my joy. I must have floated on a white cloud for a full day. I was living in enchantment.

No doubt the fact that Onsi published my work strengthened my confidence in my ability to write and publish. I kept writing and Onsi kept publishing. My AUB friends started waiting for my articles to appear in *An-Nahar*; my students studied with me in class during the week, and read my essays on Sundays. I could not have dreamt of a better deal. In addition, a superb poet named Joseph Njeim became very interested in what I was writing. He became a close friend and wanted to be my first reader, reviewing any article I wrote before I sent it to Onsi in order to give me his feedback. I

sometimes took his advice and I would possibly revise a word or two
before I forwarded the article to Onsi. I could not believe that two
very well-known poets were interested in what I was writing and
were willingly engaged in my creative endeavors.

It is important to note that Onsi Al Hajj was a major poet in
the school of modern poetry and free verse while Joseph Njeim
represented the school that still valued classical poetry. At one
point they were friends, but by late 1967-68, when they were both
interested in my literary endeavors, they were not on speaking terms.
In addition to these two men, the one whose opinion meant a lot
to me was my father. Of course I wanted him to read anything I
wrote before I submitted it. I was privileged to have all three of them
reading my manuscripts before they were published. Onsi continued
to print everything I sent him, and I was thrilled. My dream of
writing and publishing was being realized.

In 1969, while I was still a student at AUB, I published my first
book of creative writing, *Hafrun Ala Al Ayam*, or *Carving on the Days*.
These were the essays that Onsi had published for me in *An-Nahar*.
Joseph Njeim wrote the foreword and the book was published by
the Rihani Publishing House. It was a collection of existentialist
articles and was well received by the press. The *Sénacle Libanais*, the
major cultural and literary institute in Beirut during the sixties and
seventies, held an evening about my book which was organized
by Michel Asmar, the known intellectual and *éminence grise* of the
late sixties. Whenever he organized a literary evening, it had to be
outstanding.

For the evening, Asmar summoned many literary figures and
asked them to comment on my book. The speakers included Said
Akl, perhaps the most famous Lebanese, and some say Arab, poet of
the twentieth century; Issam Mahfouz, a well-known playwright;

Nour Salman, a gifted woman writer; Joseph Sayegh, a poet and the editor-in-chief of the literary supplement of *Al Anwar*; and Jamil Jabre, a literary critic and scholar. They showered my book and my style of writing with *éloge*. Daddy, Onsi Al Hajj, and Joseph Njeim were proud of their protégée. That evening in the spring of 1969 propelled me into the wonderful and magical literary, artistic, and cultural world of the golden years of Beirut.

In 1969 I was baptized as a writer. My book was selling in all the major bookstores of Beirut. I continued to write and publish in *An-Nahar*. I was invited to many literary evenings, was asked to join several literary circles, and life seemed at its best. I had no idea that it was the calm before the storm, the rainbow before the hurricane. It was my golden year, my magical year: writing, publishing, traveling, and exploring wonderful new horizons. I never suspected that what came after 1969 would be filled with sadness, with unfairness, with questions, with doubt, and with challenges.

CHAPTER ELEVEN

MOMMY'S ILLNESS

ALL MY LIFE, MOMMY AND Daddy were clearly in love. I grew up thinking that all couples were in love the way my parents were. Somewhere, most probably in my mid-teen years, I learned that not all married couples remained in love.

Witnessing my parents' relationship was a privilege.

In the Freike home, Daddy would sometimes call me and ask me to pick little white jasmine blossoms from our garden, string them together on a white thread, and give them to him quietly without letting Mommy see. I loved being part of his little secret and enjoyed watching his eyes when I handed the string of fragrant jasmine to him. His eyes became so tender, so soft, and then he would go find Mommy. He would sneak up from behind and place the thread of flowers around her neck, tie it into a necklace, and kiss her. If the string was short, he would wrap it around her wrist as a bracelet and kiss her hand. I loved being his accomplice and enjoyed watching them be so tender with one another.

In the evenings, with guests in the living room, Daddy sometimes would ask about Mommy's work, the magazine, and her efforts on behalf of women's rights. He was so proud of her. She always spoke about the choice of the books that he decided to publish, about the latest painting he bought, or about the new water or electricity project that he was involved in for the village. She, too, was so proud of him. Listening to them was listening to the music of love mixed with the sounds of respect, and surrounded by the melody of admiration.

By early 1970, Mommy was at the top of her career. Her children's magazine was the premier Arabic magazine for children in Lebanon. Because of the increased demand for it, it became a weekly magazine and not a bi-weekly. She was at that time the chair of the board of the YWCA in Beirut, engaged in how to increase the employability of young women who did not make it to university. Before that, in the 1960s, she was the president of the Association of the Lebanese University Women, which published a newsletter about women's higher education and women's rights. Mommy often had articles in the association's newsletter. Also in the early 1960s, she was the president of the Women's League, an organization that had among its members Lebanese women activists as well as wives of ambassadors who were interested in learning more about the women's movement in Lebanon. Mommy was incredibly active leading a rich professional life, a full social life, an engaged activist's life, and being the wonderful mother of four and the beloved wife of Albert.

In early 1970, she began to have a problem with the vision in one eye. After several consultations with many doctors, it was discovered that there was a benign tumor behind the retina of her left eye that could be surgically removed. The doctors assured her and Daddy that the operation would be safe and that she would be back at home in a week. She remained working and fully engaged in her other activities till the day of the operation. I recall that just one week before the surgery she chaired a seminar that she had organized on social and economic development in Lebanon featuring Sheikh Maurice Gemayel, my wonderful guide to Rome in 1969. He was then a member of Lebanon's parliament and a former minister of planning.

My perspective of Mommy in the late sixties, and in particular in 1970, was that she was a soft-spoken woman; a beautiful feminine lady; a loving mother and wife; a selfless, ever-giving person who was intellectually and professionally strong, hardworking, dynamic, and engaged; and who was always chartering new territories.

She went to the American University Hospital for surgery in March 1970. Daddy, two of my brothers, and I went with her. Sarmad, the youngest, went to school.

Mommy was taken into the operating room very early in the morning at around six. The rest of us retired to the waiting room. We all expected that in two or two-and-a-half hours, the doctors would come to the waiting room to inform us of the success of the surgery and take us to see her in the recovery room. The hours went by...two, two-and-a-half, three. Daddy became anxious and started pacing the corridors, asking the nurses when the doctors would come out. He was not getting clear answers. He kept pacing, asking more questions. His anxiety increased, and the answers were never satisfactory.

After five hours, one of the surgeons came out. He told Daddy the operation was successful, but he recommended that we not go see Mommy because she was not awake yet. Another phase of waiting, another phase of pacing. I had never seen Daddy so disturbed.

After another two hours he went to the nurses' station and demanded to see a doctor. I heard him raise his voice—really raise his voice—insisting that he needed to see his wife. Finally, after another hour or two—we must have waited close to eight or nine hours from when Mommy was wheeled to the operating room—they allowed us to see her. Daddy went first and the three of us walked in after him, quiet and very concerned. Mommy was sleeping, her head was wrapped with white gauze. Many tubes were attached to her. Daddy spoke to her softly; he touched her hands, caressed her face. No response. Daddy tried again with all the tender and deep love within him, but she did not respond. The first fifteen to twenty minutes in her room were too long and too painful to describe.

Mommy was in a coma.

Daddy wept, broken-hearted. My eldest brother Ameen and I stayed by her bed for the night while Daddy took Ramzi home.

One drop of blood, one clot, changed her life and ours.

For forty days, Mommy remained in a coma. For forty days, Daddy was at her bedside, hoping that she would awaken. For forty days, he received their friends and their bouquets of flowers. For forty days, their best friends tried to console him. Sheikh Maurice came to the hospital every day. Albert and Claude Tohme, Jamil and Jacqueline Jabre, Fuad and Claire Sader, Gibran and Corrine Shamieh, Zahia Salman, Nadia Tabet, Mary Farha, Wadi Deeb, Youssef and Leila Nakhle, and many others stopped by to check on her nearly every day. Daddy was inconsolable. He spoke to the doctors and tried to understand what happened and what could be done. For forty days, the lion, Albert Rihani, was wounded, and his beautiful lady seemed to have slipped from his grasp.

At night, I watched by her bedside, sometimes accompanied by one of my brothers. I prayed, touching her hands, putting my fingers on her pulse to assure myself that she was still with us. I focused on her eyes to catch any movement that would tell me she was alert so I could call home and announce the happy news to Daddy and my brothers. For forty nights, she did not move or open her eyes. At night, by her bedside, questions swirled in my throbbing head. I forgot AUB and the upcoming graduate degree exams. I forgot that I loved writing. I forgot my wonderful summer in the U.S., France, and Italy. I forgot all the causes I was engaged in. I forgot my friends. My whole world centered on Mommy's bed and its still occupant.

For forty nights I prayed and meditated. I searched for meaning while I gazed at her sweet face. I asked God many questions but never received an answer. Mommy remained unconscious. I never knew she could be so vulnerable. In the hospital bed, Mommy was the ultimate vulnerable person. She could slip into the other world at any minute and we would lose her forever or she could remain, physically present, but with no clear end in sight. The doctors were not forthcoming. Their presence was not reassuring. They had few answers and seemed not to understand the place from where our questions were coming, a place called unconditional love. They were just another group that was irrelevant. In my anger, I perceived them as the cause of Mommy's unresolved condition.

Every night I waited, and every morning was a disappointment. I wanted to tell Daddy and my brothers, when they came to her room at seven or eight in the morning, that she was awake. I so much wanted to be the bearer of good tidings, but I was not given the opportunity. The four of them would come in the morning loaded with hope and expectations, and every morning their hope evaporated and sadness would gather around us like a fog.

For forty long days and nights we experienced a living nightmare. The doctors were useless. The nurses tried to help. The family was broken-hearted, tired, disillusioned, and despondent. We learned that during the operation, a small clot of blood had leaked and touched her brain, causing Mommy's unbearable situation and our pain, anger, and fathomless grief.

One drop of blood, one clot, changed our lives.

On the fortieth day, she opened her eyes, looked at Daddy, and smiled. He showered her with kisses. He kissed her hands, her face, and her forehead. He called the doctors. They explained that as a result of the clot, her right side would be paralyzed and that she would not be able to speak for a while. We later learned that she also would not be able to read or write—supposedly for a short time.

Finally, Mommy came home. Daddy arranged for a nurse to live with us to care for her, feed her through a tube, and take care of all her needs. He also hired a speech therapist to help her start learning to speak again, and a physiotherapist to train her to walk. Seeing these three medical assistants work with Mommy for the first six months was a mixed blessing. The nurse was helpful, but her presence was a constant reminder that Mommy could not do anything on her own. For the first two or three months, the nurse fed her through a tube. The speech therapist came every-other-day and worked with her. He tried to make her pronounce a few words, our names, but at first she could not.

Progress was incredibly slow and painful, and the sessions of speech therapy were hard to witness. The effort she had to make stressed all of us, and we argued as to whether Mommy was being helped at all by the efforts. After several months, Mommy was able to pronounce our names. I believe the first name she spoke was Albert.

The physiotherapist who was asked to come on alternate days so as not to overtax Mommy began by training her on a few exercises while she lay in bed. After an hour or so, he would put her in the wheelchair and take her to the living room where we all gathered around. It was great to see her in the living room; however, even physical therapy produced very slow progress. Her right side was completely paralyzed.

Through all the difficulties, Daddy was the eternal optimist. He deeply believed that one day she would be able to talk and walk again. He hoped, against all odds, that his beloved Loreen would completely regain her health and capacities. He was the soul of patience and steady optimism. He encouraged her and talked to her about the future, the days and years to come. He was not just still in love with her; he loved her more. He wanted her to believe she would be well, so he showered his beautiful, brilliant Loreen with love.

During the first couple of weeks at home, we learned that her mental abilities were intact and her awareness was as sharp as ever. We took turns reading poetry and the newspapers to her. She loved poetry. Daddy read to her the most. She always reacted in the most positive and happy way when he sat next to her wheelchair and read aloud.

At some point during those early months, Daddy slowly started selling off assets: two rental buildings and a valuable piece of land in Dbaye near the Antelias *autostrade*. In addition to the prolonged stay at the hospital, he had to pay the surgeon's fees, for medications, and the costs of in-home care: the nurse, the two therapists, and the regular parade of doctors. In those days, most Lebanese did not have health insurance.

I watched and silently asked God questions. I often wondered if he/she existed. Despite the fact that Daddy was selling what he owned to cope with this sudden, radical change in our family, he retained his strength, his optimistic outlook, and his strong will. He behaved as if he could will Mommy back to health. The tiny incremental progress she made energized him. Watching this only made me sadder and sadder; I was not as optimistic as he was. I reverted to my introverted self. At certain times, I was furious at God. He/she was either absent, did not care, did not listen to prayers and questions, or was too busy with things of no importance. None of these possibilities regarding God satisfied me. I remained despondent and deeply resentful.

Each of my brothers dealt with the situation in his own way. The atmosphere at the Hamra home had completely changed. It was no longer the happy home filled with writers, poets, artists, intellectuals, and scholars. It became a hospital where doctors, nurses, and therapists walked in and out all the time.

At last summer came, and we went to the Freike home. By that time, Mommy did not have tubes coming out of her body and she had started eating regular food. She spent a lot of time on the balcony in her wheelchair. Many of her friends came to visit regularly, and as they updated her about the women's organizations she was involved in, she would listen, nod her head, and smile. The villagers adored her. They came often with gifts—jams and cheeses they had made and those they knew she liked.

One short phrase that she recovered and dug out from the depth of her heart and brain, despite the clot, was "Thank you." She uttered these two words with such beauty. Ameen would bring her a glass of water, and he would hear her sweet voice smile as she said, "Thank you." I would bring her pills and receive in exchange a gorgeous "Thank you." Ramzi would tell her a joke, and she would shower him with "Thank you." Sarmad would put a plate of nuts on a small table next to her wheelchair and she would give him the gift of her "Thank you." And of course, Daddy would sit next to her and read whatever he thought might be of interest and she would say in her most loving voice, "Thank you, Albert."

That summer in Freike started healing us. The sight of Mommy and Daddy sitting next to each other late in the evening while he read to her and held her hand, as she looked at him with infinite sweetness and love, was real and precious.

For years and years, Daddy read to Mommy the headlines of the daily newspapers, political articles, book reviews, introductions to new books he was publishing, personal letters, news about their friends that would appear in some magazines, new poems by famous poets, old poems that she loved, and many other pieces. He read to her in Arabic and in English, he discussed with her what he was reading, and he was completely satisfied with her simple, "Thank you, Albert."

For years and years, he bought her clothing and accessories—dresses, necklaces, nightgowns, lipsticks, and perfume. Every now and then, he invited their closest friends for dinner to spend an evening. He would ask the helpers at home to prepare the kind of generous meal that Sitt Loreen would have arranged and made sure I helped Mommy dress for the evening. During those dinner parties, he treated the event and Mommy as though nothing had changed, engaging all his guests and his wife in the cheerful, intelligent, and dignified way that was the hallmark of his remarkable character and generous soul.

For years and years, he showered her with love, care, attention, patience, and an ever-ready smile. However, this did not alter the fact that his life had changed completely. He rarely accepted invitations after work because Mommy was reluctant to go out, even with a helper. Her condition made life's simple activities challenging. Beirut in the 1970s, like other major cities, was unprepared to accommodate the disabled. Rather than leave Mommy at home, Daddy stopped going out and instead spent quiet evenings at home with the family. Our home was no longer an open house where writers, artists, and intellectuals gathered.

Gradually, he curtailed his involvement with many of the associations in which he played an important part, such as the

Publishing Syndicate and the Cultural Council of the Northern Matn. He withdrew from these and other professional, social, and cultural associations to dedicate himself to his work and to Mommy. During the day he was at his office working, calling home several times to check on her. The evenings and weekends found him beside her.

Mommy continued to improve slowly and Daddy enjoyed watching her progress. He taught her how to play cards and backgammon. On the weekends, they played together. He helped her become interested in a new hobby, collecting stamps, and soon they were both avid stamp collectors. They developed a special language. A few words from her, a line of poetry she could say quite clearly from the depth of her heart, a gorgeous smile, the most beautiful thank you, were sufficient to make Daddy beam. On his part, he kept reading and discussing with her the political news of Lebanon, the Arab countries, and the rest of the world, as well as news about their friends and acquaintances to help her remain involved.

The helpers did the laundry, but Mommy insisted on folding the clothes with her left hand, the one that was not paralyzed. She also made sure that no one made noise when Daddy took a nap in the afternoon, as she had done all the years I can remember. She would ask a helper to prepare a drink for Daddy and put a plate of nuts next to his drink in the evening. And when he came in and sat in his favorite chair, she wheeled her chair beside him.

In 1976, Daddy decided to retire, sell his printing press, and spend the rest of his years with her. Those years they spent together continued a love story that I have rarely seen in other people's homes. Mommy and Daddy did not grow old together, they simply grew together, and the deep river of love continued to run beneath their feet.

CHAPTER TWELVE

EARLY '70S

I N THE EARLY SEVENTIES, MOMMY'S illness was the center of my life. During 1970-71, I was taking Master's courses at AUB, teaching at the Collège, and being the political activist that I was; however, in a silent way, all of these activities were colored by my mother's illness. Questions continued to swirl in my mind, and my disappointment with God did not diminish. He/she never answered my questions. The results of Mommy's paralysis were particularly ironic; she, the former president of the University Women of Lebanon, could not speak or write.

On the other hand, the silver lining in all of this was that the six of us developed a new way of communication. Mommy's facial expressions, accompanied by a limited number of sounds, were the new language within our home, and a most intimate one. Daddy and the four of us had to learn and understand this new language, and we all learned fast. It is hard to explain, but somehow, we were able to have interesting discussions with Mommy.

During the first year of my mother's illness, I developed my own way of communicating with her. I was determined that I was not going to give up having meaningful conversations with her.

Whatever the subject we were discussing, I would present several scenarios and she would nod her head after each scenario indicating if she agreed or not. If she agreed, we would move forward with our discussion; if she did not, I would come up with another scenario by giving her additional hypothetical possibilities so she could say yes or no. In many ways, I became her voice whenever we had a discussion, and I enjoyed that. It gave me the satisfaction of not allowing destiny to control my mother's voice. Those conversations between Mommy and me helped minimize my anger at God.

I continued to share with her the highlights of my life at AUB, the events surrounding my teaching at the Collège, and what I was publishing at *An-Nahar*. I learned to listen to her advice and wisdom in a new way. Most importantly, she was the one who tried hard to reconcile me with God. In her own way, she explained to me that I could not blame God for what happened to her. She also explained that every phase in one's life is a chapter to learn from, and the lessons come in different forms and ways. To please her, I tried to understand her logic. It was hard. The only time I got a glimpse of understanding was when I realized that her thinking emanated from faith and not necessarily from logic.

I had a problem with the non-alignment of rationality and faith; she did not. I had to stretch my mind to see her perspective and we had many conversations of that nature. I was the rebel; she was the wise woman. I was the one with frustration because of Mommy's situation; she was the one with serenity. I was the one with unending questions; she was the one with acceptance. Every now and then, she would ask me to bring the book of prayers of Saint Francis of Assisi and read to her his prayer:

Lord, make me an instrument of your peace.
Where there is hatred, let me sow love;

where there is injury, pardon;
where there is doubt, faith;
where there is despair, hope;
where there is darkness, light;
and where there is sadness, joy.

O Divine Master, grant that I may not so much seek
to be consoled as to console;
to be understood as to understand;
to be loved as to love.
For it is in giving that we receive;
it is in pardoning that we are pardoned.

After reading such a prayer, I began to understand Mommy better, and she encouraged me to go on with my life, to not allow her illness to become an obstacle in my pathway. I always wondered where she had acquired the strong faith that made her ever forgiving and hopeful.

Our friend Sheikh Maurice died suddenly of a heart attack while speaking at the Lebanese parliament on October 31, 1970. Losing Sheikh Maurice exactly eight months after Mommy's illness was a big blow to our family. To Lebanon, it was a terrible, unexpected loss of one of its most prominent figures, a man of reconciliation, vision and reflection. I was asked by Groupe Relève to speak on their behalf at his funeral.

In Bikfaya, on November 1, 1970, I joined the speaker of the Lebanese parliament, a representative of the lawyers of Lebanon, and Amine Gemayel who spoke on behalf of the Gemayel family, to bid farewell to one of the most enlightened and progressive politicians in Lebanon. It was an emotional day for me. There I was, speaking before thousands of mourners about an incredible man and mentor who brought students together from the diverse universities to discuss and debate the future of Lebanon from an international development perspective. These thousands and thousands of mourners did not know that I was not just representing Groupe Relève, but that I was also speaking about the closest friend of my parents, and about my mentor and erudite guide in Rome who loved me as a daughter.

Mommy's illness and Sheikh Maurice's sudden death pushed me to write more. Writing became my refuge. What I published in 1970 and early 1971 were essays filled with sadness and rebellion against destiny. I was not ready to accept that we can fall seriously ill or die at the whimsical wish of God. My struggle to try to understand destiny was growing deeper.

Writing as well as visits from poets, writers, and artists were becoming a greater part of my life. Writing was my therapy, and writers became the ones with whom I could continue asking those nagging questions about destiny and God. In the summer of 1971, I decided to create a literary salon similar to the one May Ziade had held in Cairo. I grew up admiring May Ziade and recognizing what a literary force she was. I decided to invite poets, writers, and artists to our Freike home every Wednesday evening to discuss literature and art. Daddy and Mommy were very supportive of my wish to have my own literary salon.

Every Wednesday afternoon, I filled our home with flowers and prepared some hors d'oeuvres. In the evening, I received the writers, poets, and artists on our vast balcony overlooking the valley with the mountains of Sannine and Kesrouwan as part of its panorama. Over drinks and hors d'oeuvres, we would spend the evening discussing newly published works of poetry, plays, or novels. Those Wednesdays became known among the circles of intellectuals in Lebanon and the media started writing about my salons.

I did not know at that time that those Wednesday gatherings would lead to strong and special friendships with many of those poets and writers. I had not realized that a young woman in her mid-twenties could create such a powerful literary platform where major poets, writers, and artists would discuss what were considered in those years to be major literary issues.

Among the regulars at my Wednesday salon were many well-known poets on the Lebanese scene. Said Akl, the giant in Lebanese and Arab poetry, taught us that among the major elements that define poetry are the condensation and intensity of beauty in each line, and the unexpected images and metaphors expressed in utmost brevity. When he read some of his poems, I was sure the villages of Kesrouwan facing the Freike balcony were rejoicing. Youssef Al Khal argued that modern verse frees us not just from old sets of meter and rhyme, but also from old ways of thinking. Joseph Sayegh insisted that when poetry is tied to political causes, it loses its freedom. He was a purist and strongly felt that politically committed poetry was bound to lose the essence of what poetry is all about.

Joseph Njeim was the Baudelaire or Abu Nawwas of the group, his two main topics being women and wine. Nour Salman often raised the importance of recognizing the contributions of women authors and poets. Jamil Jabre shared with us his latest readings and presented critiques of the newest published books. Issam Mahfouz brought us up to date on the latest in Lebanese and Arab playwrights.

Fadi Barrage and Farid Haddad, two artists whose paintings were highly abstract, added a different perspective that could only come from the world of color. Maurice Awad argued why writing in colloquial Lebanese dialect was important. Suheil Bushrui highlighted how the work of Lebanon's most influential thinkers, Gibran Kahlil Gibran and Ameen Rihani in particular, established the Arab Literary Renaissance. Hareth Tah Al-Rawi, who visited from Iraq, joined my salon and brought us up to date regarding the Iraqi literary scene. Mona Saba Rahhal added the dimension of English literature. And last but not least, my brother Ameen, who by then had published several books, brought to those evenings the unique beauty of having siblings as published authors be part of a salon together. He also helped me prepare and create the ambiance for every Wednesday of that very special summer.

At each of these gatherings, I felt privileged to be among those literary figures and my mood started shifting towards a space where rays of happiness were allowed to enter. By the end of 1971, I was ready to laugh again.

In the early summer of 1972, immediately after the strike of my students at the Collège, the YWCA asked me to serve as director of the annual summer camp in Dhour El Shoueir. I accepted. I had learned a lot from being an international camp counselor in the U.S., and I planned to adapt some of the lessons I had learned to a Lebanese setting. I also thought I might be able to create, as much as possible, an oasis of creativity for the Lebanese teenagers at the camp.

Our camp was on a beautiful hill at the top of Dhour El Shoueir that was covered with pine trees. We lived in tents under those aromatic and noble trees. I had seventy-five teenage campers and around ten camp counselors. Many of the campers were my former students from the Collège, and the counselors were carefully chosen by the YWCA and me.

I was perhaps the youngest camp director that the YWCA ever had, and I used that fact to my advantage. I asked them to allow me to change a few rules, regulations, and norms. They were quite flexible with me. The camp was not only about regimented chores, but it was also about creativity, responsibility, civic education, community service, and, of course, fun. During the months of June, July, and August, the camp became a workshop of creativity.

Poetry, theater, music, dance, and debates were central to the majority of the activities. We turned the movie *Billy Jack* into a play; we had discussions about young Lebanese women's aspirations for careers, and debates about the environment in Lebanon and the responsibility of both civil society and the government. We wrote poetry and held poetry recitals, and the campfires witnessed three or four teenagers with their guitars singing in English, French, and Arabic as the rest of us accompanied their beautiful voices till the late hours of the evening.

The campers, counselors, and I decided to offer our services to the municipality of Dhour El Shoueir by dedicating a few days to clean the Jafet Library and the old monastery. For whatever reason, these activities at the camp attracted the attention of the media, and again my students (now campers) and I became the talk of the town.

Different newspapers and magazines sent reporters and photographers to capture what was going on in our camp. *Al Hawadeth* magazine published a seven-page report about our camp on July 28, 1972. The *Al Mouharrer* daily published two articles, one in June and again in July. In both articles, the focus was on a new vision for society and an emphasis on strengthening the self-confidence of the girls during their teenage years. *An-Nahar* dedicated a full page for our camp and *Al Hasna'* magazine, two pages. Many other periodicals covered the news of the camp as well. Basically, the media in Lebanon thought our experiment was an innovative approach to stretch the ways of thinking of the daughters of the well-to-do class, and to train them in civic responsibility, equity, and community service.

In November 1972, the French-language daily *L'Orient-Le Jour* asked its readers to vote for the most provocative and forward-looking Lebanese women. On November 22, when *L'Orient-Le Jour* announced the thirty most audacious Lebanese women, I was ranked ninth behind women including the first to run for parliament and lawyers who were fighting for women's rights. I was pleasantly surprised, given that I never expected to be among such a stellar collection of Lebanese women, especially given my young age at that time.

Surprises continued to happen in my life. As a result of being seated next to Robert Kulka, the Swiss director of the Phoenicia Intercontinental Hotel, at a social dinner in Beirut, I was offered the position of Director of Public Relations at this internationally known, first-class hotel. He appreciated that I was fluent in three languages, that I had a degree from AUB, that I communicated well orally, and that I had published a book. I came home ecstatic.

The next morning, I happily told Daddy about the offer. He was surprised that it interested me so much because he thought I might prefer to continue my studies and complete a PhD. I argued that I wanted to work outside the education system for a while, to know the other side of life. As much as I loved books, teachers, and professors, I wanted to experience something else. Daddy's response was, "You might enjoy the glamour of such a job for a while, but I am not sure a job of that nature will engage your intellectual capacity to its fullest." I convinced him that I would like to try the position, and that we would continue discussing its impact on me. I promised him that after a year or two, if my intellect was not satisfied, I would resign.

And so, in January 1973, I became the Director of Public Relations at the Phoenicia Intercontinental Hotel. The media in Lebanon had a ball with my new role. The Lebanese English magazine *Monday Morning* printed in its January 22, 1973, issue:

> May Rihani is a young woman of many faces. She is a teacher, a writer, and poet, and holds a degree in Political Science. That is not all. May is the new and attractive PR manager of the Phoenicia Intercontinental. Very involved in youth activities, May is on the board of the YWCA, and she was the camp director last summer. Not bad for a young woman whose summers are barely over a quarter of a century. May's first book *Hafrun Ala Al Ayam* (*Carving on the Days*) was published in 1969, and her second, *Siwaya* (*The Other*) will be out in a few months.

Other dailies and magazines in Arabic and French also covered my new role, including *Al Moharrer*, *Al Ousbouh Al Arabi*, *Al Hasna'*, *Ash Shams*, *L'Orient-Le Jour*, *Al Hawadeth*, *Al Siyaha*, and *Al Rassed*, while *An-Nahar* continued to publish my prose and free verse.

The glamour of my new job was in sharp contrast with my mother's illness. The questions continued to swirl in my head. The nature of my employment was not in harmony with the other part of my life: my literary involvement. I was a participant or a speaker in many literary activities such as symposiums about literary schools, evenings and discussions regarding new poetry trends, and celebrations of literary and cultural milestones. One such evening was held at Dar Al Fann wa Al Adab, where Professor Suheil Bushrui, Dr. John Andrews of AUB, and I presented an evening on "Ezra Pound and the Revolution in Modern Poetry." In February 1973, I also participated in the celebration of the seventy-fifth anniversary of the first Lebanese Arabic-language newspaper published in the United States, *Al Hoda*.

Al Hoda was a landmark in the history of the U.S. Arab community. I spoke at many literary gatherings celebrating this milestone. Among the speakers in these *Al Hoda* events were Minister Albert Mokhaiber representing the President of the Republic; Riad Taha, the president of the Lebanese newspapers syndicate; Sheikh Khalil Takieddine, a very well-established author; Joseph Basila, the president of the Matn Cultural Club; Jamil Jabre, author and literary critic who was a member of my Wednesday salon, and me. On March 30, 1973, *Al Hasna'* published a four-page interview with me on the significant role of *Al Hoda* as the first Lebanese newspaper in the U.S.

My glamorous job at the Phoenicia became increasingly visible. I welcomed VIPs to the Intercontinental Hotel and organized press conferences about them. Among those I greeted and had dinners with in 1973 and 1974 were: Lebanon's President Suleiman Frangieh; Lebanon's former President Camille Chamoun; Lebanon's Prime Minister Saeb Salam; the heads of major Lebanese political parties such as Pierre Gemayel and Kamal Joumblat; many Lebanese ministers and members of parliament; several Arab ministers; the British media figure David Frost; the Belgian modern ballet choreographer Maurice Bejart; the designer and models from Jean Patou, the French *maison* of haute couture; the American boxing world champion Mohammad Ali (Cassius Clay); the Vice President of the Iranian senate Abbas Masoudi; the First Lady of Costa Rica Mrs. Figurs; the French/Belgian writer Dominique de Vespin; the Lebanese American comedian Danny Thomas; and many others.

In 1974, my literary activities escalated and one of my dreams came true. I had always wanted to present on the Lebanese national television a program about literary life in Lebanon. Joseph Sayegh, one of Lebanon's well-known poets and the former editor-in-chief of the daily *Al Anwar* literary supplement, decided to produce a television series titled *Lubnan al Adabi* (*The Literary Lebanon*), and asked me to be the presenter of the program.

On March 29, 1974, on Channel 7, we broadcasted our first episode. During the one-hour program, I presented literary life in Lebanon in three segments. The first was about significant literary and artistic events that were taking place, such as the London Opera premiere adapted from the Lebanese author George Shehade's play *Histoire de Vasko*. In the second segment, I presented a review of important, recently published books such as *Dulze*, the poetry book of Said Akl; *The First Death* by Issam Mahfouz; *The Caravans of Time* by Toufic Youssef Awwad; and *Water for the Family Horse* by Shawki Abi Shakra. The third segment was a discussion that involved either the authors and/or literary critics of three books: *The Entire Poetry Works of Yussef Al Khal*; the major poetry oeuvre of Joseph Sayegh, *Anne Coline*; and *The Book of Khalid* by Ameen Rihani.

The more I reflected on my life, the more I recognized that I was playing several roles. On the home front, I wanted to continue to be one of Mommy's caregivers; on the literary front, I was becoming more recognized; and on the professional front, I was the visible public relations manager of the Phoenicia Intercontinental.

The only way to handle this complex situation, the seemingly contradictory dimensions of my life, was to continue writing. I poured my feelings and thoughts onto the white pages and kept sending them to Onsi Al Hajj, and he continued publishing them. By 1974, I decided to collect what I had written since Mommy's illness and publish them in a book. Again, these were existential reflections on my mother's situation and possibly on human suffering in general.

The title of my new book was *Ismi Siwaya* or *My Name is the Other*. I had a serious and deep need to think about and empathize with those who were suffering, those who were less privileged, those who could not make ends meet, the poor of the world, and those who did not know and would never know the Intercontinental Hotels of the world. I also had a need to continue to try to make sense out of what happened to Mommy. My writing was my attempt to understand what happened to my mother; it also was my bridge to those less privileged, my connection with the rest of humanity. My writing allowed me to live not just with the rich and glamorous, but to remain connected with the Other.

The book was published in the spring of 1974, and *Librairie Antoine* invited me to hold a book signing ceremony. The hugely successful event took place on May 8, and was reported by the Lebanese media. The interviews about my book allowed me to talk about suffering, illnesses, poverty, destiny, and things that happen over which we have no control. I was delighted with the interviews and the book reviews that were being published.

I was especially pleased by women writers and journalists who wrote about my book, such as Etel Adnan, Hoda Naamani, Amal Nader, Noha Samara, and Evelyne Massoud. Also, I was delighted when some of the writers and poets who had come to my Wednesday salon, such as Joseph Sayegh, Jamil Jabre, and Issam Mahfouz, wrote about my book.

The period between 1970 and 1974 represented one of the richest segments of my life—and one of the saddest. It was as if God wanted me to experience extremes; as if destiny wanted me to stretch way beyond what I would have thought was possible.

Questions became more central in my life. Is it possible that we get to connect and understand others better if we suffer? Is it possible that God had given me the gift of living both the beautiful and the sad, the glamorous and the painful, the very visible and silent serenity, all at the same time so my sensitivity to the Other could be developed in an in-depth way? Was it a blessing from God to be baptized in a river of sadness and pain in order not to be allowed to live a self-centered life?

CHAPTER THIRTEEN

MY BEGINNINGS IN INTERNATIONAL DEVELOPMENT

I PROBABLY SHOULDN'T HAVE BEEN surprised, but Daddy was right. As much as I enjoyed my job at the Phoenicia Intercontinental, there was something missing. The job was exciting, glamorous, and fun, but it did not fully engage my intellectual capacity. Close to the beginning of summer of 1974, I resigned. My boss at the Phoenicia Intercontinental asked what prompted me to make such a foolish decision. I found it hard to explain without hurting his feelings, so I made some excuses and stuck to my decision.

By coincidence, I had just received an invitation to participate in the International Population Conference for Youth in Bucharest. For this conference, youth was defined as those students or university graduates who were between the ages of twenty and thirty, and who were active in youth movements around the world. The conference was a parallel event to the United Nations Population Conference that was taking place in Bucharest, Romania. The invitation I received included two parts: a two-week stay in Geneva, Switzerland, to attend seminars and workshops for nearly twenty selected youth leaders in preparation for the conference; and a week in Bucharest for the conference itself. I left for Geneva towards the end of July, a few days after my brother Ameen's wedding.

In Geneva, we had workshops that informed us about the importance of population growth and change in different parts of the world. In the seminars, we debated different governmental policies addressing population growth, the relationship of population growth to the social and economic systems of countries, as well as the role of youth regarding the future of population growth. The two weeks in Geneva helped me discover the importance of preparing well when one is expected to discuss a topic that can be addressed from many perspectives, and how to be able to present quantitative and qualitative arguments to defend a position. Even though I was aware that I was among the lucky ones to be in Geneva, I was anxious to move on to Bucharest and join young people from all around the world discussing the issue of world population growth.

The International Youth Population Conference took place from August 10-16, 1974, and was attended by two hundred participants from over eighty countries. The majority of the youth participating in the conference represented some type of leftist youth movements. There were many internationally known young activists at the conference; among them were: John Alexander, a British youth leader who was one of the organizers of the conference and who was given the role of conference facilitator and rapporteur; Jakaya Kikwete, who represented the Dar es Salam University students and who, in December 2005, became the President of the United Republic of Tanzania; and Nico Ceausescu, the obnoxious and arrogant son of the president and dictator of Romania, Nicolae Ceausescu.

The Youth Conference took place only a few days before the United Nations International Population Conference opened. One of the major objectives of the Youth Conference was to influence the debates and the final report of the UN Conference. During five days, we held intense debates. Possibly half of us took a strong anti-imperialist stand, insisting high fertility in underdeveloped countries was to be blamed on conditions created by imperialist countries. The other half of the participants related population growth to abject poverty, malnutrition, disease, massive unemployment, and serious inequalities and injustices.

A degree of polarization occurred along regional lines. Many delegates from the developing countries and Eastern Europe viewed the family as the only acceptable unit for reproduction and did not accept the distinction between population control and the right to birth control as an individual right. It was due to the mastery and amazing negotiating skills of some of our youth leaders at the conference, particularly John Alexander, that we were able to move towards a consensus. We had to produce our recommendations report in a timely fashion so that we could present it at the UN Conference.

After two all-night sessions where the energies were high, the debate intense, and the will powerful to produce an influential list of recommendations, we were able to reach consensus. During those two nights, John Alexander was the master of the nearly impossible job of helping us reach an agreement. Our recommendations included that youth and women be allowed more participation in their national development policies. We called for competent research and data interpretation, and for population education programs. We urged governments to intensify their efforts to reduce mortality rates, while recognizing the consequent impact of population patterns on education, employment, housing, and other welfare measures.

Women's education and decision-making were particularly emphasized. Our conference came down firmly in favor of a new economic order and of the rights of each country to control its own resources. We won the battle of influencing the UN report by presenting our recommendations to the plenary of the UN Conference and to several working committees.

The final report of the UN Conference reflected many of the recommendations of the Youth Conference report. Major common points were: 1) There is need for a more equitable distribution of wealth; 2) There is an interrelationship between population growth and other socioeconomic variables; 3) Every state should have the sole right to decide on the demographic policies most suitable for its people; 4) Family planning is not an engine of change to speed the development process; and 5) There is a need for serious attention to the role of women in development.

Something else happened during the conference. John Alexander and I had noticed each other during the intense debates. Even though the conference was all-consuming, we still found time to be together. The youth delegates had to go from their hotels to the conference hall by tramways; Bucharest still had the tramways in 1974, and John and I always found a way to ride together. During the two all-night sessions, when John was on stage for most of the night orchestrating how to move beyond the polarization so the two hundred youth could reach consensus, I was in total awe of his conflict resolution skills, his eloquence, and his charisma. I worked closely with him during the all-night sessions to draft and revise, paragraph by paragraph, the report and the recommendations. John, of course, was the one presenting the drafts to the plenary.

After presenting to the plenary of the UN Conference, a few of us including John and I decided to spend an evening listening to *Tzigane*

(Gypsy) music. Somebody found a superb outdoor club and garden, and six or seven of us spent a heavenly evening listening to this gorgeous music. Returning to our hotel at around two in the morning, both John and I thought it was too early to interrupt the enjoyment of the night.

After Bucharest, several delegates and I had to fly back to Geneva for a debriefing, and John's office was in Geneva. I never thought a city could be so enchanting. Our walks in the old town (*vieille ville*) and St. Gervais were unforgettable. The old town was picturesque and I was totally charmed by John. We walked everywhere. We would start somewhere near the tour boat dock on Lake Geneva, then go to the Bel-Air island and have lunch. In the evening, we walked uphill to the old town bridge crossing Mont Blanc to the English Garden with the famous flower clock, and then keep walking until we reached the long stairs passage and ended up at Saint Peter's cathedral where once we listened to a magnificent concert.

John knew the most charming places in Geneva, and we indulged ourselves. One evening we were walking and it started raining. I never liked walking in the rain, but somehow my likes and dislikes changed that evening. Walking in the rain became a delight. John pulled me tighter, closer to him; his arm around me while we were walking in the rain felt as if it was going to lift me up. And he did lift me up, look up, and laugh. The evening was magical.

My stay in Geneva was too short. In early September, I had to fly back to Beirut, and our goodbyes were painful. We promised each other we would write, and we discussed the possibility of John visiting Lebanon in the summer of 1975. In the plane, I reviewed all that had happened in Bucharest and Geneva and my tears became a veil to my smile.

Back in Freike, Lebanon, on our gorgeous balcony, I quietly shared with Mommy the story of a youth leader named John Alexander and the beautiful city he lives in.

CHAPTER FOURTEEN

THE BEAUTY BEFORE THE TORNADO

IT SEEMS THE BUCHAREST CONFERENCE marked out most of what was going to happen in my life after that time. In Bucharest, I learned the importance of international development, and I understood that individuals, organizations, and governments could work for the betterment of the world. As a result of the conference, I knew there would always be three main pillars in my life: love, writing, and international development.

Between September 1974 and September 1975, these three dimensions flourished for me. On the love front, the letters John and I shared colored my days with the most beautiful rainbow hues. On the writing front, I was publishing articles in *An-Nahar* on a regular basis, and I was asked by the editor-in-chief of the *Al Lubnaniya* to write the coveted last page of the magazine, where I would be given the freedom to publish my thoughts and reflections. On the international development front, I received invitations to participate in major international conferences.

My life in 1974 and during the beginning of 1975 was filled with achievements and enriched with hopeful expectations. I began to make peace with Mommy's illness, to learn to accept what I could not control, and to enjoy new horizons, unexpected vistas, and early successes.

During this blissful phase, many articles about my second book, *Ismi Siwaya*, and about my writing in general, continued to appear in the Lebanese press. One of the articles that affected me was by Edgar Davidian, published in the November 1974 *L'Orient-Le Jour*. The article, "*Quatre 'visages' des Lettres Libanaises, au feminin (très) singulier,*" was an essay about Nadia Tueni, Leila Baalbaki, Etel Adnan, and me. Basically, Edgar Davidian analyzed the literary works of four Lebanese women writers who represented four very different experiences; however, as Davidian put it, what linked us was an invisible thread called poetry. I was delighted to be in the company of these women.

A wonderful review of *Ismi Siwaya* by Dr. Assad Ali was broadcast on BBC and published in December 1974. Another interesting article about my activities was written by May Manassa and published in *An-Nahar* in June 1975. She wrote about my role in the Bucharest conference; how that role led to my representing Lebanon in a conference in Bombay, India, early in 1975; and that in July–August of 1975, I would be in Mexico City to participate in the first International Women's Conference organized by the United Nations. As a result of May Manassa's article, several other newspapers and magazines interviewed me about my role in those three international conferences.

The Bombay conference was a follow-up to the Bucharest conference. In Bombay, delegations of youth representing over twenty-five Asian countries met for four days to study and plan how to influence their governments and civil society organizations to ensure that the recommendations of Bucharest would be translated into action.

At the beginning of the event, I was elected chair of the conference. Amid some very serious discussions, when we were engaged in debates based on our deep belief that we as youth truly could improve the world, James Chui, the head of the Chinese delegation, instead of addressing me as Chairman May called me Chairman Mao. This gaffe broke the tense atmosphere as people throughout the hall laughed together. I believe James Chui's slip of the tongue helped all of us relax and made us—idealists who were determined to change the world—continue our debate with a little less intensity. A smile was added to the face of the participants every time they addressed me, their chairman.

The Mexico City conference was something else. It took place between June 19 and July 2. The conference was called for by the United Nations General Assembly to focus international attention on the need to develop future-oriented goals, effective strategies, and plans of action for the advancement of women. It was the first world conference on the status of women, and it coincided with the 1975 International Women's Year.

The purpose of the year's designation and of the conference were to remind the international community that discrimination against women was a persistent problem that affected much of the world, and that the world community needed to come together to address the issue. The conference, along with the United Nations Decade for Women (1976-1985) —proclaimed by the UN General Assembly five months later at the urging of the conference— launched a new era in global efforts to promote the advancement of women by opening a worldwide dialogue on gender equality. The conference set in motion a process of learning that involved discussion, debate, research, analysis, negotiation, setting objectives, identifying obstacles and solutions, and reviewing the progress made. To this end, the United Nations agreed on three objectives on behalf of women:

- Full gender equality and the elimination of gender discrimination;
- The integration and full participation of women in development; and
- An increased contribution by women in the strengthening of world peace.

In addition to the official conference, women also organized a parallel NGO forum, the International Women's Year Tribune, which attracted approximately four thousand participants. The Tribune represented civil society.

Sharp differences emerged among the women gathered at the Tribune, reflecting the political and economic realities of the times. It reminded me a little of the difficulties at the beginning of the Youth Conference in Bucharest. Women from the countries of the Eastern Block, for instance, were most interested in issues of peace, while women from the West emphasized equality and those from the developing world placed priority on development. Nevertheless, the Tribune played a pivotal role in bringing together women and men from different cultures to share information and opinions, and to set in motion a process that would help unite the women's movement. In addition, the Tribune's main objective was to influence the recommendations of the UN governmental conference. I believe we succeeded in doing so.

The conference adopted a World Plan of Action, a document that offered guidelines for governments and the international community to follow for the next ten years in pursuit of the three key objectives set by the UN. The Plan set minimum targets, to be met by 1980, that focused on securing equal access for women to resources such as education, employment opportunities, political participation, health services, housing, nutrition, and family planning.

This approach marked a change, which had started to take shape in the early 1970s, in the way that women were perceived. Whereas previously women had been seen as passive recipients of developmental support and assistance, they were now viewed as full and equal partners with men, with equal rights to resources and opportunities. A similar transformation was taking place in the approach to development, with a shift from an earlier belief that development served to advance women, to a new consensus that development was not possible without the full participation of women. The conference also called upon governments to formulate national strategies and to identify targets and priorities in their efforts to promote the equal participation of women.

As a result of my participation in the International Women's Year Tribune at Mexico City, I, too, was transformed. I knew that the three pillars of my life would remain the same: love, writing, and international development; however, I also knew that one of them, international development, would focus on women. I knew that one of the requirements for improvement of the world was based on action toward more equity and equality between women and men, girls and boys. I decided to dedicate my professional life towards that goal.

After the conference and before flying back to Lebanon, I made two stops. The first one was in Merida, Mexico, to see my father's cousin, Uncle Roberto Rihani, and his large family who were my wonderful second-generation cousins. I had a memorable time with my cousins as the Mexican Rihanis by far outnumbered the handful of us in Lebanon. Uncle Roberto and his family treated me like a princess. They organized visits to many Mayan ruins and to lovely places in the Yucatan including Chichen Itza, Cozumel, and Isla Mujeres. They organized endless lunches and dinners at their homes. The Rihanis of Mexico work hard and celebrate happiness just as hard. They are able to see life as a fiesta. Their *joie de vivre* wakes them up in the morning of every single day.

My second stop was in Geneva to see John Alexander. During my stay, John and I did not know where the day ended and the night began. Our year of waiting to be together made us fill every minute of our time with perfumed joy and enchanted happiness.

I returned to Lebanon before the end of July, just in time to attend my brother Sarmad's wedding.

CHAPTER FIFTEEN

EVERYTHING IS SHATTERED

A FEW WEEKS AFTER MY return home, and specifically during the summer months of August and September 1975, I began to understand that the April 13, 1975, incident that took place in Lebanon was not just an isolated and unfortunate political confrontation. The fact that unidentified Palestinian gunmen in a speeding car fired on a church in the Christian East Beirut district of Ain El Rummaneh killing four people, and the fact that the Christians retaliated and killed many Palestinians later that day, was still having serious ripple effects in the country. After this horrific and tragic event, additional unfortunate incidents took place every three or four weeks. The first couple of situations did not alarm the Lebanese population enough to consider what was happening as the beginning of a war. A ceasefire would be reached after every event and life seemed to return to normal. However, these incidents kept occurring and by the middle of summer 1975, I was one among many who began to understand that something very wrong was happening in my beloved Lebanon. I could no longer dismiss these incidents, nor could I consider them as isolated conflicts.

The political and security situation threatened what many of us thought was the beginning of the road for Lebanon's ascent towards a modern state—one that would recognize and respect individual freedoms, democracy, religious and ethnic diversities, innovative approaches to art and literature, new frontiers of thought, and the acceptance that new horizons were part and parcel of the culture. In my mind, the identity of Lebanon was tied to these qualities and concepts. For some of us at least, especially the new generation in Lebanon, these ideals had become an integral part of what we wanted Lebanon to be all about. This was our dream.

These values and practices had begun to bloom within the Lebanese context. They amplified the fact that Lebanon was not just a geographical space but was also a cultural space with a message about the importance of freedoms and the centrality of diversity. This did not mean that the geographically small, politically fragile, and militarily vulnerable Lebanon was always on solid ground. It was clear to some of us that, on the one hand, Lebanon was instituting new ways in the Middle East by taking an unchartered road and incubating new ideas and practices; and on the other hand, that Lebanon was a fragile, small nation. However, in the sixties and the early seventies, Lebanon had experienced a golden age where it provided opportunities for its people to grow in a daring and forward-looking way. That golden age, many of us thought, was a time that would propel Lebanon forward despite the political problems and security constraints. That golden age, we believed, would allow Lebanon to keep moving on the pathway that would consolidate the hard gains already made around the practices of freedom and respect of diversity.

I and many young women and men in Lebanon had hopes that, despite the need for reform in Lebanon's political system, the country was taking a bold position regarding the values mentioned above. For these reasons, many Lebanese and I were devastated when we realized that the security incidents might be an indication that Lebanon was on the verge of serious turbulent times that threatened those precious gains toward freedom and diversity.

I always knew that the government of my country, and its civil society, needed to implement certain basic reforms. At the top of the priority list was reforming the political system, improving the relevance of the education system, paying more attention to the development of the remote rural areas, and ensuring better enforcement of the laws. I also knew that my country was making progress on fronts that the geo-political region it lived in would not want, encourage, or support. The fact that Lebanon provided the space for freedom to be practiced, for religions to peacefully co-exist, and for diversity to be valued posed a serious threat to the neighboring countries, in particular Syria and Israel. I admired the fact that Lebanon, against all odds, was able to reaffirm freedom despite the fact that it existed in the middle of an ocean of regimes where freedom practically did not exist.

In Lebanon, freedom of thought, freedom of speech, freedom of gatherings, freedom of demonstrations, freedom of the press, freedom to practice one's faith, and many other freedoms were being practiced. In the neighboring countries, individuals were thrown in jail for such practices. Of course, the freedoms in Lebanon were not practiced in a perfect way, but compared to all of its neighboring countries, freedom in Lebanon was vastly advanced and people were in a much better place. Syrian opposition leaders, for example, fled their country in search of security and came to live in Beirut. Palestinians shared their political positions and thoughts in Lebanon when it was impossible for them to do so in the occupied territories. Arab writers and poets sought Lebanese publishers when other Arab publishers refused to print avant-garde manuscripts that questioned the existence of God or seriously criticized Arab leaders.

Beirut was the capital of free thought in the Arab world, the capital of free media, of students' demonstrations, of women's movements, of youth's demands, and of innovative thinkers. Beirut was bold; it knew how to take risks. The city enjoyed the avant garde in publishing, the experimentation in theater, the new schools in dance, the rebellion in poetry, the exploration in university activities, and the unexpected in visual arts. The sixties and the early seventies allowed many of us to dream of a Lebanon that was moving forward quickly, and that would soon be ready to address many of the inequities that continued to exist while the country was on the pathway of advancement and on the highway of innovation.

I was so devastated when I realized the violent political incidents of April 1975 could stop and even reverse the country's journey on this path of advancement. I did not want to believe that Lebanon was entering a dangerous phase that would erase our bold dream of a new future. It was hard to accept that the geographic neighborhood where Lebanon was situated—where oppression was the rule, subservience was the law of the land, and where freedom did not exist—might change Lebanon's trajectory.

My devastation was so profound because I firmly believed that what Lebanon experienced during those heady years of growth would be sustained and self-regenerate. I believed that the path envisioned by Lebanese free thinkers at the turn of the century, and by Lebanese activists at the beginning of the twentieth century, was reaffirmed and realized in the sixties and seventies, and that it would continue in the coming decades.

The two sets of avant-garde Lebanese free thinkers of the turn of the twentieth century were in the U.S. and in Egypt. They had traced the framework of freedom against all odds. In New York, in the early 1900s, free thinkers such as Gibran Kahlil Gibran, Ameen Rihani, Mikhail Naimy, Elia Abu Madi, and others published novels, poetry, essays, and plays that valued freedom and diversity, and wrote extensively against political and religious oppression. As a result of their powerful reformist voices, they became the founders of the Arab literary renaissance and they profoundly contributed to the transformation of Arab thought. In Cairo, it was the Lebanese who established the daring Egyptian media that questioned Ottoman oppression. Salim and Bechara Takla established *Al Ahram*; Jirgi Zaidan, *Al-Hilal*; Antoun Gemayel, *Az Zouhour*; and Yacoub Sarrouf and Fares Nimr, *Al Moukatam* and *Al Mouktataf.*

The Lebanese thinkers of New York and the Lebanese journalists of Cairo contributed to the foundations of freedom in the Arab world. In addition, we had been taught in our history classes in Lebanese schools and universities to be proud of our martyrs who were executed in Beirut on May 6, 1916, because they opposed the Ottoman oppression of Jamal Pasha, also known as *Al Jazzar* or "the Butcher," who was the Ottoman Wali of greater Syria. We were taught, and we always remembered, that the martyrs were both Christians and Muslims, and that their loyalty to a free Lebanon was what made them rise against the oppression of the Ottoman rule and of the Wali. Those martyrs had always inspired me and made me believe that, in addition to free thinkers, we always had in Lebanon free activists. The Burj Square in Beirut where they were executed later came to be known as Martyrs' Square, a reminder to all young Lebanese that our country had heroes. Those heroes died for our freedoms, and their martyrdom contributed to the Lebanese people's deep belief in the value and practice of freedoms. Those heroes were:

- Said Akl (not the famous poet, but the martyr)
- Father Joseph Hayek
- Abdul Karim al-Khalil
- Abdelwahab al-Inglizi
- Joseph Bshara Hani
- Mohammad Mahmassani
- Omar Hamad
- Philip el-Khazen
- Farid el-Khazen
- Sheikh Ahmad Tabbara

Like many other Lebanese, I believed that Lebanon's destiny was to carry the torch of freedom and to be the trailblazer of new ideas and practices in the middle of the difficult geo-political region that Lebanon inhabited.

As a result of my awareness in the summer of 1975, my overwhelming concern was that Lebanon was on the threshold of serious turbulence. I was afraid that the role of Lebanon as the carrier of the freedom torch might be seriously weakened and possibly annulled. This deep feeling of fear about the destiny of Lebanon made me want to do something. I wanted to become more of a political activist, to write more about the value of freedom and diversity, and to contribute to the empowerment of those who were not always heard such as women and minorities.

Two opportunities were presented to me that I thought would allow me to contribute to the strengthening of the premise that diversity and freedoms are at the core of Lebanon's identity.

The first was when I was asked to join Imam Moussa As-Sadr's Council of Cultural Advisors. Imam As-Sadr, the spiritual leader of the Shi'ah sect in Lebanon, was seen by a large number of people as a moderate. He worked tirelessly to improve the economic and social conditions of the less-privileged members of the Shi'ah community, and at the same time pursued ecumenism and peaceful relations with other sects and religions in Lebanon. He was an opponent of Israel, but also a critic of the Palestinian Liberation Organization (PLO) which repeatedly put Lebanese civilians at risk by crossing the border and attacking Israel. In 1969, Imam As-Sadr was appointed as the first head of the Supreme Islamic Shi'ite Council, and in 1974, he founded the Movement of the Disinherited (*Harakat Al Mahroumine*) in order to press for better conditions for the Shi'ah and other underserved communities.

By 1975, the Imam had established a number of schools and basic health clinics, many of which are still operational. As-Sadr wanted to reform inequities in Lebanon; however, based on my personal knowledge of him, he would have never accepted the use of violence to reach his goals. When I was asked by Michel Asmar, the director of the *Sénacle Libanais* who had organized the first literary panel about my first book *Hafrun Ala Al Ayyam*, to join the Imam As-Sadr Council of Cultural Advisors, I was surprised and honored. Imam As-Sadr had not met me, and I was surprised that he would invite a young Christian woman to serve as a cultural advisor. Michel Asmar explained that Imam As-Sadr intentionally sought diversity among his cultural advisors in order that all communities could be represented. He had specifically asked his inner circle to include young individuals among those who they would recommend. Asmar's explanation was convincing and I accepted his invitation.

During my first meeting with the Imam and the Council, I was impressed by many things, most notably that the Cultural Council was truly a diverse body. We were approximately thirty individuals who represented all the diversities of Lebanon: religious, ethnic, gender, and age. I believe I was the youngest member of the Council. The second thing that impressed me was that, despite the charisma of Imam As-Sadr and despite the influential role that the Imam already played in Lebanon, he seemed genuinely interested in listening to the diverse opinions offered by members of the Council, including myself as the youngest member who also happened to be a woman. In retrospect, I cannot measure in a precise way how much the Council of Cultural Advisors made a difference on Imam As-Sadr's thinking; all I can say is that this extremely important leader of the Shi'ah listened very attentively to all that was said, and he continued to be a voice for moderation and inclusivity despite the religious clashes in Lebanon. He worked diligently toward this end, even after the 1975 clashes, seeking to strengthen bridges of communications and understanding among the different sects in Lebanon.

The second opportunity which appeared at that time of my life was joining the Institute for Women's Studies in the Arab World (IWSAW). IWSAW was founded in 1973 by the Beirut College for Women (BCW). The history of the Institute is closely linked to BCW, which was the first women's college in Lebanon and in the Middle East. Established in 1924, BCW educated Lebanese and other Middle Eastern women for a half-century and became co-educational in 1973. In order to honor the college's unique heritage, IWSAW was established in 1973.

IWSAW was committed to pioneer academic research on women in the Arab world. This first such institute also sought to empower women through development programs and education, and to serve as a catalyst for policy change regarding women's rights in the region. When I joined IWSAW in 1975, it was still a fledgling organization trying to chart new territories in women's research and programs. The vision for IWSAW was that it would become a leading women's institute in the Arab world, and that it would facilitate networking and communication while cultivating ties with national, regional, and international organizations and universities concerned with women's and gender issues.

I joined IWSAW as an assistant researcher. After my participation in the conferences of Bucharest, Bombay, and Mexico City, I had become fully aware of the importance of gender equity and equality in societies, and I recognized that in Lebanon, in the Arab countries, and in the rest of the world, there was still a lot to be done to improve gender relationships so societies could benefit from all their human resources. I was delighted that I could contribute to this effort and that Lebanon, through IWSAW, was pioneering academic women studies in the Arab world.

I strongly felt that through Imam As-Sadr's Council of Cultural Advisors and IWSAW, I was given the opportunity to contribute to the improvement of the political as well as the social situation in Lebanon. Despite the political and security turbulence, the work of these two institutions gave us hope for the future.

During 1975 and 1976, I went to my office every day, not allowing the security risks to deter me. Often, Dr. Julinda Abu AnNasr, the director of the IWSAW, and I would be the only two at the Institute. Dr. Abu AnNasr lived on the BCW campus and I lived on Hamra Street, a ten-minute walk from BCW. Other staff members would often call in to let us know that they could not come to the office due to security problems on the roads.

Towards the end of 1975 and throughout 1976, the security situation continued to deteriorate in Lebanon. Car bombs exploded, kidnappings took place, electricity cut-offs increased, and the Lebanese spent some of their days and nearly all of their evenings at home and stopped going out. Even though after each major security incident a cease-fire would be negotiated, and often an agreement would be reached to end the cycle of clashes and allow life to have the semblance of returning to normal, somehow the short periods of quiet never lasted, as if an unseen hand was manipulating the situation to keep Lebanon on the brink of disaster.

The worse the situation got, the more I wanted to go to work. I felt if all the Lebanese would give up and stop going to work, to schools, and to universities, then those internal and external forces who wanted the violence to continue would have won. One way of fighting the violence, the security risks, and the clashes among the different factions was to continue to work and to proactively support moderation, freedom, tolerance, diversity, and productivity. I continued to go to my office at IWSAW and to attend the meetings of Imam As-Sadr's Council of Cultural Advisors.

At IWSAW, I was doing research on the role and contributions of women in Lebanon and the Arab world, and Dr. Abu AnNasr and I, with the approval of the Dean of BCW, Dr. Riyad Nassar, decided to produce a journal about women. Dr. Abu AnNasr asked me to propose titles for the newsletter. Daddy and Mommy enjoyed discussing with me the options I came up with. The next day I presented several possibilities to Dr. Abu AnNasr and Dean Nassar, and they chose *Al Raida* (*The Pioneer*). From the names I proposed, this was my favorite. The fact that the name of the journal would immediately validate and highlight that there were already many women pioneers in different fields, and that the journal would value the whole concept of pioneering was exactly what I hoped for. *Al Raida* became IWSAW's flagship interdisciplinary journal. It has addressed gender in historical and contemporary contexts since 1976. The publication strived to bridge the conventional divide between scholarship and activism, and *Al Raida* recently evolved into a biannual, peer-reviewed journal.

The first issue of *Al Raida* was put together by Dr. Abu AnNasr and me while the streets of Beirut were increasingly becoming a theater for violent clashes among different political factions. At that stage, it was becoming clear that what we were calling the *Lebanese* war was a war that also involved many regional players. Lebanon became the land where Syria, Libya, Iraq, Egypt and their Palestinian surrogates, as well as Israel, fought their battles. Money poured in from nearly every Middle Eastern country to back one side against the other, and the Lebanese political factions took sides and got entirely involved in this nightmare scenario.

I firmly believed that we needed Lebanese leaders who would put the interests of all the Lebanese first, and who would be courageous enough not to side with any of the outside players who were interfering in our country. I also believed that women had to make their voices heard and had to be equal players on the political and social scenes. IWSAW allowed me to highlight the importance of the role of women, and the Council of Cultural Advisors allowed me to be one of the voices that spoke to Imam As-Sadr about the value of diversity, peaceful coexistence among many religions, the need to respect all aspects of freedoms, and about the aspirations of the youth in Lebanon. These two powerful outlets gave me the opportunity to contribute, even though in a small way, to what might be a peaceful solution in Lebanon and allowed some hope to remain alive within me.

Towards the end of the spring of 1976, Dr. Abu AnNasr informed me about an upcoming conference at Wellesley College in the U.S. and asked if I would participate as a representative of IWSAW. Of course I accepted. The U.S. was where my father was born, and at the time of this conference, my two younger brothers were already in the U.S. Ramzi was employed in Washington, D.C., and Sarmad was studying engineering at Oregon State University. I thought I might be able to visit one if not both of them immediately after the conference before I returned to Lebanon.

I went to Wellesley. The conference which took place in the summer of 1976 was about women and development. It attracted one hundred seventeen women academicians and practitioners from thirty-two countries, scholars devoted to women's studies with the goal of evaluating the best practices of women in development studies, and strengthening the networks of scholars in this field. However, the conference did more than look at these narrow themes; it debated the definitions of women in development and feminism, and it brought together scholars from the North with scholars and practitioners from the South, many who did not have the same definitions for either feminism or development.

The Wellesley Conference raised complex issues about the politics of research and particularly the politics of international development research concerning the status of women. The seminal importance of the gathering was the opportunity for debate—heated debate—concerning the common ground and the differences between feminism and women in development. The perspectives of participants from the north and from the south often differed in essential ways.

The papers at the conference were first-rate, the analysis thorough and rigorous. Many internationally known academicians and practitioners participated. To my surprise and delight, my wonderful friend Dr. Suad Joseph was in attendance representing the University of California at Davis. Also at the conference, I was introduced to many impressive activists in the field of development, among them BJ Warren, a vice president of TransCentury. At the end of the Wellesley Conference, around twenty of us were invited to go to Racine, Wisconsin, to continue the debate on women in development and to produce a report. Suad Joseph and I were selected to attend this post-conference gathering.

While at the conference, I learned that the Beirut Airport was closed due to heavy shelling. I was worried. How would I return to my family in Lebanon? Dr. Abu AnNasr and I were in contact on a daily basis. She asked if I could delay my return by a few days, possibly a week or two, to see how the security situation in Lebanon would unfold. I told her that this was possible given that I have a brother in Washington, D.C., with whom I could visit.

I took the train to Washington, D.C., and was delighted to be with Ramzi, but I remained anxious about Lebanon, Mommy, Daddy, the escalating violence in the different regions, and my work. I followed the Lebanese news daily and spoke with the leadership at BCW on a regular basis. The airport remained closed.

After a week or so, Dr. Abu AnNasr informed me that given the airport shutdown and the security situation in Beirut in general and around BCW in particular, BCW preferred that I go to Paris for a few months, if possible, and work at UNESCO as a seconded staff. Dr. Abu AnNasr said IWSAW wanted to continue the research on Arab women in Francophone-Arab countries, and UNESCO had many of the French studies and documents concerning these countries. If I were willing to go to Paris, she and Dr. Nassar, the dean of BCW, would negotiate an agreement with UNESCO. Dr. Abu AnNasr also made it clear that BCW could not raise my salary despite the differences in the cost of living between Beirut and Paris. She asked me to think about their request and to give her an answer within a couple of days.

Ramzi and I had several long discussions weighing the pros and cons of such a move. I was worried about my parents in Beirut. Ramzi pointed out that they would be delighted to know that I would be living and working in Paris, but I was particularly concerned about Mommy. As I followed the news in Lebanon, I felt terribly guilty that I was safe in the U.S. while Mommy and Daddy were living in Beirut. The shelling in the city intensified, and no neighborhood was safe. Huge security risks were becoming part of the daily lives of its inhabitants.

I decided to accept the post in Paris; however, I remained deeply concerned about my parents who were living in the Hamra home (with Mommy's caregivers) in an extremely risky situation. My eldest brother Ameen and his family were also living in Beirut. My brothers and I discussed the situation and agreed to propose to my parents that they come to the U.S. on a long visit as soon as the airport opened. Ramzi and Sarmad wanted them to live with each one of them for a number of months hoping that after six, seven, or eight months' time, the security situation in Beirut would improve. We knew that it would not be easy for Mommy not to have the caregivers she has been used to for the past six years, but we thought our parents would be better off in the U.S. rather than Beirut during this time.

I called Daddy and Mommy from Washington, D.C., to discuss our proposal, and they agreed. We were delighted with their decision. In light of their acceptance, I decided that instead of flying directly from Washington to Paris, I would wait until the airport opened, fly to Beirut, help Mommy and Daddy in the preparation for their trip, fly with them on the same plane to Paris, and see them off to the U.S.

I called Dr. Abu AnNasr, told her I accepted the offer to work in Paris if I could return to Beirut for a week or so immediately after the airport opened and then fly to Paris from there. She accepted my condition; I was relieved. I needed to get my parents out of Beirut and on their way to Washington, D.C., where Ramzi would take care of them so I could begin my work in Paris with a clear conscious.

This was a totally unexpected development. I had gone to the U.S. to participate in a conference with the intention of returning to Lebanon to continue my professional and personal lives the way I had envisioned them. I was happy being involved with the two institutions—IWSAWand the Council of Cultural Advisors—that provided me with professional satisfaction and hope. While my days there included security risks, they were also filled with hard work, idealism, and dreams to improve the political and social inequities in Lebanon. In the evening, I would come home to a special atmosphere with a father who was as giving as ever, and a sick mother who radiated love, kindness, and bliss. In the evenings, I often wrote. At night, the three of us, with Mommy's caregivers, lived through the difficult hours of bombardments and shelling, but at least we were together.

All of that was going to change.

CHAPTER SIXTEEN

PARIS

EVENTUALLY, THE BEIRUT AIRPORT REOPENED and I
flew in to my beloved, bombarded city. With a heavy heart, I saw
the huge increase in number of buildings that were damaged during
the six or seven weeks that I was in the U.S. All I could think of were
the innocent lives that were lost. To me, most wars are not justifiable;
there must be a different way to deal with conflicts. There must be a
way to address conflicts without such horrific losses of innocent lives.
Gains as a result of most wars do not justify "collateral damage."

The once-gorgeous Beirut was scarred and disfigured by an
irrational war and by unacceptable violence. I was so incensed by the
destruction, so angered by the fact that so many buildings were burnt,
and so saddened by the increase in the number of innocent victims.

I could not, however, allow my concerns and sadness to overwhelm
me. I had a plan and I needed to work on it with focus and efficiency.
I wanted to help Mommy and Daddy get out of Beirut as soon as
possible. Despite the electricity cuts, the uncertainty of moving safely
on roads due to snipers, the shutdown of many offices including
several travel agencies, and the continuous bombardment day and
night, I was able to work with Daddy and Mommy in preparation

for this difficult trip. Mommy's doctors had to be consulted before she departed. Daddy was an American citizen; Mommy was not. Figuring out what visa to obtain for her in the quickest way possible was a constraint to be overcome. How to ensure Mommy's access to the plane was a problem that needed a solution. The easiest route between Beirut and Washington, D.C., had to be figured out, with Mommy's physical state taken into consideration. These and many more issues had to be dealt with. I was determined to find solutions to all of these problems, despite the continuous bombardments of the streets of Beirut, and I did.

The trip was scheduled for the end of October 1976. The three of us would fly to Amsterdam—the airport had a hotel within it and I figured Mommy and Daddy needed to rest for a night before flying to D.C.—and then I would see to it that they were on the plane to Washington.

Somehow, things worked out. We boarded the plane from Beirut to Amsterdam. Mommy was uncomfortable but never complained; that was who she was. I had booked two rooms at the Amsterdam airport hotel where we rested for the night. The next day, I wheeled Mommy to the plane while Daddy carried tickets, passports, and few other things. In those days, airlines allowed a family member to accompany a disabled person onto the plane to ensure that she was able to take her seat. With mixed emotions, and with tears running down my cheeks, I embraced Mommy and Daddy, wished them bon voyage, and walked out of the plane. They were on their way to Washington, D.C., and a few hours later, I boarded my plane to Paris.

I arrived at Charles De Gaulle Airport on October 30, 1976.

My head was spinning. All I could think of was my new reality: my parents would be in the U.S. within a few hours, the war continued in

Lebanon, and a new chapter was about to start for me in France. My emotions were so mixed; guilt intermingled with excitement, and my high expectations were dragged down by the reality of the war:

> Mommy and Beirut were ill, and I was landing in beautiful Paris.
>
> Mommy and Beirut were suffering, and I was supposed to lead a normal professional life.
>
> Beirut, my beloved city, was under siege, and Paris was as free as a flying bird.
>
> The sound of exploding bombs still rang in my ears while the sound of peace in Paris was the new reality.
>
> In Beirut, listening daily to the radio announcer informing us about which roads were seriously risky and which were less so was part of my routine, yet walking any street in Paris without concern would be my new mode of life.
>
> Beirut lost its lights in the evenings, and at night, Paris was, of course, *La Ville Lumière*, the city of light.
>
> When bombs fell like rain on Beirut, Lebanese children drew fear on the walls of the shelters; in Paris, children drew rainbows of dreams and hope.
>
> From the end of October 1976 till March 1977, Lebanon and its suffering lived in my heart, and I lived in the heart of Paris.

Ramzi called to inform me Mommy and Daddy had arrived safely. He said Daddy seemed happy to be in the U.S., and Mommy, as usual, was happy with whatever made Daddy happy. I was relieved and I knew that, with Ramzi, they were in excellent hands.

A week or so after my arrival in Paris, this most enchanting city was able to help me accept my new reality. After all, freedom and beauty are the essence of Paris, and I, like many other human beings, thrive on those two dimensions of life.

The first week while looking for a place to live, I stayed with Uncle Fuad and Auntie Claire Sader in their *16ème arrondissement* apartment close to the Arc de Triomphe. I was able to find a small apartment, an efficiency, which I shared with an older French lady named Denise. The apartment was on *Boulevard Malsherbes* in the *8ème arrondissement*.

Daily, I would take the bus to UNESCO. In Paris, I was not the known writer or political activist; I was one of millions going to work and trying their best to do a good job. This kind of incognito life presented a new way of being for me. In addition, I could barely make ends meet given my meager Lebanese salary, and I did not go out in the evenings. Despite all of this, I enjoyed discovering Paris.

During the weekdays, I did nothing but work. I was at UNESCO researching the role of women in the four Francophone-Arab countries: Lebanon, Tunisia, Algeria, and Morocco.

In the evenings, I wrote letters and read many books. Receiving Daddy's letters was a special joy. His words made my guilt of not being with him and Mommy go away. He detailed for me their daily lives and how wonderful it was for them to be with Ramzi. He always highlighted the small, incremental progress Mommy continued to make, and communicated the pleasure of living again in the U.S., the country of his youth. In addition, Daddy's letters represented that unconditional love towards me, his daughter, that he knew how to express in such a unique and beautiful way.

On Saturdays and Sundays, I spent most of the time with relatives and friends: the Saders, the Sayeghs, and French friends with whom

I developed new ties. Joseph Sayegh, one of the Lebanese poets who attended my Wednesday salon, by then was a friend living in Paris. The French friendships were developed with two lovely women: Bulle Vautier and Fabienne Mayeux. As these relationships grew, I also became a friend of their families, in particular with Benjamin Mayeux, Fabienne's brother; Ivan and Alexandre Chaumeille, Bulle's sons; and Michel Vautier, Bulle's brother. That circle of relatives and friends sustained me.

When I was not with relatives and friends, I walked in the streets of Paris, discovering the magical city. I was fascinated with the architecture, the large boulevards lined with magnificent trees. The great cathedrals and churches with their fascinating facades and the elegant opera house were stunning. Strolling along the majestic bridges over the Seine, through the charming Latin Quarter, and enjoying the special quality of light in the Jardin des Tuilleries and the lushness of the public parks offered momentary serenity. The romantic dimension of the *bouquinistes* by the Seine, the many languages to be heard in the Champs Elysées, and the *très chic* boutiques of the Faubourg Saint Honoré, displayed the *je ne sais quoi* that Paris is all about. I loved all these things, but what I loved most were the city's long, wide boulevards with their cafés. As if these cafés determined the Parisian scene. As if these cafés were the space that allowed French literature, poetry, philosophy, and art to flourish.

I imagined Guy de Maupassant and Emile Zola in the Café de la Paix enjoying the changing lights on the Opera. I could see in my mind's eye Henry Miller, Ernest Hemingway, Pablo Picasso, and F. Scott Fitzgerald taking their coffee and smoking at the Select as the sun draped over them on the terrace. I enjoyed thinking of Jean-Paul Sartre and Simone de Beauvoir debating their existentialist philosophy at Café de Flore, or sometimes across the street at Les

Deux Magots. I envisioned Pablo Picasso and Amedeo Modigliani in their very early journeys as starving artists, lingering in the Café de la Rotonde. Walking in front of La Closerie des Lilas, I had fun imagining where Oscar Wilde would be sitting, Emile Zola thinking, Paul Verlaine writing poetry, and Paul Cézanne dreaming of colors. Paris was magical.

On the weekends I walked and walked and walked discovering Paris, sometimes alone and sometimes with friends. I also wrote free verse and letters. The majority of my poems were about Lebanon and the majority of my letters were to my parents.

One evening in early December 1976, while in my apartment writing a letter to Daddy, I received a call from a woman named Carolyn Long from Washington, D.C. I was surprised, since I did not know anyone by such a name. She explained that she was a vice president from the TransCentury Corporation and that BJ Warren, another vice president of the organization, had met me while attending the conference at Wellesley College, and that TransCentury was interested in my experience. After a short discussion, Carolyn said that Warren Wiggins, the President of TransCentury, wanted to talk to me.

Mr. Wiggins came on the line and discussed the importance of the full engagement of women in international development. He said that TransCentury wanted to establish a Secretariat for Women in Development. They had a qualified candidate for the director's position, and after reviewing my resume and discussing my experience with BJ Warren and Carolyn Long, they wanted to talk to me about the possibility of joining TransCentury as deputy director.

I was dumfounded. I never expected a job offer from the U.S. while in Paris. My plan was to complete the research that IWSAW sent me to do at UNESCO and return to Lebanon. I intended to resume my duties on Imam As-Sadr's Council of Cultural Advisors and to work closer with the director and staff of IWSAW on pressing Lebanese women's issues. I wanted to continue writing and publishing in *An-Nahar*; and, when my parents returned from the U.S., I meant to offer all the love and care I knew how to my ill mother and to my aging but wise and fascinating father.

That evening in early December I told Mr. Wiggins that while I was honored by his offer, my plans were to complete the research assignment at UNESCO and return to Lebanon sometime in March 1977. Mr. Wiggins said he was not expecting an immediate answer, that he was calling to give me time to start thinking about his offer, and that he would mail a package of information about TransCentury so I could get to know the organization. In those days there were no computers, no Internet, no Google searches, no fast way to learn about an organization; information, annual reports, and other documents had to be sent by regular mail. Mr. Wiggins ended his phone call by saying I should take my time, learn about TransCentury, and that in two weeks or so after I received his package, he would call again to continue the discussion.

My letter to Daddy was interrupted. It had started out sharing my feelings about the first time I would celebrate Christmas without them, but hoping that it would be the last time we celebrated this wonderful occasion apart. I was going to remind them that towards the end of March, at the latest, I would be in Beirut, ready to receive them back in their home in Hamra as soon as they decide to leave the U.S. When Mr. Wiggins and I finished our discussion, it was close to 11:00 p.m. I was not sure if I would continue the original letter, or if I should introduce the new and unexpected offer. I decided to think about the letter and Mr. Wiggins' offer overnight.

Throughout December and January, I carried on a very interesting dialogue with Mr. Wiggins over the phone. He called every two weeks

135

or so to discuss TransCentury, women in development, international development, programs in Africa, programs in the Middle East, and his vision for the Secretariat of Women in Development. Warren Wiggins was eloquent and convincing. I could feel how genuine his commitment was to international development. I also could sense his absolute commitment to equality between women and men.

During those two months, I wrote to Daddy about the possibility of moving to the U.S. to accept the offer from TransCentury, and asked for his input. Daddy, as usual, was encouraging, and did not want Mommy's situation to interfere with plans for my future. He reminded me that when they decided to return to Beirut, Mommy would again have excellent help.

By the end of January, I accepted Mr. Wiggins offer. At the end of March, when I had completed the research for IWSAW, I would leave Paris and move to Washington, D.C.

Again, a new chapter lay ahead of me. A new culture, a new frontier, a new organization—all were waiting for me at the beginning of spring 1977. I began to wonder if part of my destiny was to live in different countries, to experience different ways of living, and perhaps allow myself to belong to different cultures. I remembered that before her illness, Mommy had said that it is a privilege and a responsibility to be an international citizen. That becoming an international citizen means becoming more tolerant and understanding of all cultures and not limiting ourselves to belonging to one culture only. I am not sure I fully understood what she meant at that time. Perhaps by 1977 I was beginning to decipher what that could mean.

As much as I loved Lebanon and France, I looked forward with anticipation to my big move to the U.S. Even though I had already visited the country twice, I wondered about the adjustment it would take to live and work there, and in particular, to understand in-depth a culture very different from the two I already knew. I wondered how much I could resonate with a new culture, how comfortable I would be in that new context, and most importantly, whether I would belong.

Onward to new horizons....

CHAPTER SEVENTEEN

MOVING TO THE U.S.

AND A NEW HORIZON IT was.

In the spring of 1977, Ramzi welcomed me into his home. Mommy and Daddy by then had left to be with Sarmad and his American wife Ina in Oregon. I spent approximately two weeks with Ramzi while I looked for a place to live. He recommended that I live in a group house. I am not sure I liked the idea at the beginning. My brother explained that this was exactly what he did when he first arrived in the U.S., and that those arrangements allowed him to get to know the Americans better. He also explained that there were some group houses shared by young professionals. *The Washington Post* had lots of ads for such houses.

When I found my new home, I knew Ramzi was right. I moved to a group house on Fulton Street in northwest Washington, D.C. It was a large and elegant home in a lovely neighborhood. Six professionals shared the residence: three American men, one Frenchman, one American woman, and me. Eileen and I had two rooms and a shared bathroom on the third floor; Philip, David, and Guy had three rooms and three bathrooms on the second floor; and Dan had his room and bathroom in the basement. Our living room, dining room, kitchen, library, and enclosed porch were on the first floor.

We all left the house at around eight each morning to go to work and all six of us would be back between 6:00 and 6:30 p.m. Dinners were fascinating to me, and I guess to Guy, too. I believe that is how I, the Lebanese woman, and Guy, the Frenchman, learned the most about how Americans think, interact, debate, cook, eat, drink, and go about their daily lives.

Of equal importance to learning about Americans through the prism of my housemates was learning about the U.S. through the prism of my colleagues at TransCentury. I started working at TransCentury in April 1977.

My first day at TransCentury included some initial shocks. I arrived at 8:30 a.m. dressed as usual for my work at UNESCO in Paris, where most of the women dressed in suits and high heels. TransCentury astonished me. The main door opened up to an area filled with people behind their desks—no separate closed offices, no privacy. My first impression was that such a place was not conducive to focus and concentration. I gave the receptionist behind the first desk my name and told her that I had an appointment with Mr. Wiggins. I expected to be asked to wait until someone could take me to his office. Instead, the young woman turned her head and called out to Warren, who was one of the people sitting behind a desk in the huge open area. I was sure she was mistakenly calling a different Warren, not the president of the company.

I was wrong; the president of TransCentury, like many others, was working in the open area. When the receptionist introduced me, a smile filled his face. He welcomed me warmly, escorted me the few steps to his desk, pulled up a chair for me, and asked me to sit and have a discussion.

Warren was as eloquent and as charming in person as he had been during his phone calls to me in Paris. He explained what my first few days might look like and said that Dr. Maryanne Riegleman, the Director of the Secretariat for Women in Development, was waiting for me on the third floor where our offices were located. He then called a young woman to show me upstairs.

A bigger surprise awaited me. As I followed my guide through the open office space, we encountered a large dog, a Saint Bernard, sleeping on the stairs. The woman smiled and said, "We will step over it." In a split second, all kinds of ideas rushed through my head: This cannot be true. I am dreaming.

First, I never expected to see a dog at work, let alone have to step over one. Second, I am afraid of dogs, especially huge dogs. Third, I was wearing high heels and a suit with a tight skirt. Fourth, this felt surreal! What did they expect me to do? The young woman nonchalantly stepped over "Robin" the dog, and kept going up the stairs. I had to muster all my courage, suppress my indignation, and cross silently over that huge monster while shocked, afraid, and a bit angry. Thank God I did not trip!

I arrived on the third floor where Maryanne was waiting for me and found we shared a large corner office with many windows. After all the other surprises at TransCentury, at least my office seemed normal. MaryAnne explained a little more about the expected role of the Secretariat for Women in Development, gave me many documents to read, and said that for the first day that was all that was needed from me. She assured me I could ask as many questions as I needed to, and then she went back to her desk.

My head was spinning. All kinds of questions floated through my shocked brain. Did I make the right decision to join TransCentury? Was this informality normal? Was Warren Wiggins as smart as I thought he was over the phone? Why was it that they called each other by their first names and not by the family name like we did at UNESCO? There, the Director General was referred to as M. M'Bow and not Amadou; here, Mr. Wiggins, the president, was called Warren. Why was it that many colleagues did not have enclosed offices? Why did the president sit in a huge hall with others? What about the dog—was it going to be there every day? Would I have to step over it often?

While I was reading the documents, a familiar face appeared in my office: BJ Warren. She welcomed me warmly and said she would come by at 12:30 p.m. to take me out to lunch. I was delighted. I knew I could ask BJ about all the strange things I had experienced that morning. I also decided that I would be subtle and very polite, and not show her how shocked I was.

BJ and I went to lunch in one of the Adams Morgan restaurants. If I recall correctly, it was Salvadoran. As we ate, BJ explained that Warren was a very innovative thinker, and that he, with the approval of his inner circle and senior staff, decided that an optional open space might increase active communication, new ways of thinking, genuine collaboration, and lasting cooperation. This was so new to me, in 1977.

She also said, that yes, professionals called each other by first names and that included Warren as president. He was a very approachable, brilliant, and humble professional, and the only way he felt comfortable was if we called him Warren and not Mr. Wiggins. When I asked about the dress code, BJ said only a small minority came to the office in suits, and then only on special occasions, while the majority dressed in a more casual manner.

Finally, I mustered my strength and asked why there was a dog at TransCentury.

BJ smiled broadly and said, "You mean Robin?"

I said, "Yes, the big dog!"

She smiled again and said, "Robin is my dog."

I had to hide my surprise. I did not expect such an answer.

BJ explained that she often worked late, and rather than walking home alone at night, she preferred the safety and company of her St. Bernard. Robin was a very docile dog. The TransCentury staff was used to him, and given that he was an old dog, he slept a good part of the day.

Some of her earlier explanations I was willing to reflect on and maybe understand and eventually accept, but not yet the dog story. BJ was a smart, gentle, professional woman who had a capacity to connect to others in a most genuine way. The fact that she was the one who explained many of the very different aspects of TransCentury on my first day in the office helped me look at things from a new perspective.

Things were very different from the UNESCO offices, even for 1977 Paris.

After my first day in the office, during the bus ride from 18th Street and Columbia to my stop near the National Cathedral and the final fifteen-minute walk home, I wondered if I could really adjust to such a work environment. Would I ever fit in? The gap between the style of work I was accustomed to in Beirut and Paris on the one hand, versus TransCentury on the other, was so huge. Would I always be uncomfortable? Maybe this organization was too far outside my comfort zone. Could I be as productive as I would like to be if I were in such a different atmosphere? And my coworkers: could I develop collegial friendships when our methods were so different, like passing ships at night?

Questions, questions, questions, and no answers.

I knew that in the coming weeks I would have to be a keen observer, a serious learner, in order to find out what made TransCentury work so well. My first few months became a study in discovery. I wanted to know the leadership of the company, Warren in particular, but also the other officers of TransCentury. I needed to better understand their vision and value system; their principles; their ways of thinking, interacting, and working. Surprises continued coming my way; however, many of them were actually pleasant, even inspiring.

Let me start with Warren. He was in his fifties when I joined TransCentury. I quickly understood he represented a different type of leadership than I had known before. I learned he was the major architect and organizer of the Peace Corps, an American civilian volunteer program established by President John F. Kennedy on March 1, 1961. The stated mission of the Peace Corps includes three goals: providing technical assistance; helping people outside the United States to understand American culture; and helping Americans to understand the cultures of other countries. The work is generally related to social and economic development. The first director of the Peace Corps was Sargent Shriver who, with Bill Moyers and Warren, formed the initial leadership of the organization. I also discovered that Warren wrote the foundational document of Peace Corps, "The Towering Task," that shaped its mission and its operations.

According to Patricia Sullivan of *The Washington Post*: "When 'The Towering Task' landed in the lap of Sargent Shriver just as he was trying to figure out how to turn President John Kennedy's campaign promise into a functional federal department, he was electrified by Warren's document."

Based on the accounts of many of my colleagues at TransCentury, Sargent Shriver's response after reading The Towering Task became legendary within Peace Corps. They referred to it as "the midnight ride of Warren Wiggins." It seems Shriver was taken by Warren's treatise urging that if the Peace Corps was going to be created, it needed to act boldly. In his foundational paper Warren wrote, "A small agency is more likely to fail because its projects would not be consequential enough."

Using specific examples, with a proposed staff size and budget, Warren suggested that Kennedy act through an Executive Order for the quickest start. Again, according to Patricia Sullivan, Shriver "fired off a telegram at 3 a.m., directing Mr. Wiggins to appear later that morning ... When Mr. Wiggins appeared, he was astonished to find that his exposition had been mimeographed and distributed to Shriver's task force."

According to my colleagues at TransCentury, Shriver ordered everyone to read the paper, which he described as closer to expressing his views than anything he had read before.

The *Washington Post* quoted former Senator Harris Wofford (D-Pa. 1991-95) as saying that Shriver "saw Wiggins as someone who had the spirit of moving big and fast."

In 1961, Warren was a 38-year-old deputy director of the Far East operations in the International Cooperation Administration. But he was not an ordinary bureaucrat. Even in those days, he was regarded as an innovative, creative, outside-the-box kind of a man.

Three weeks after the famous meeting between Sargent Shriver and Warren Wiggins, the Peace Corps was born by Executive Order from President Kennedy.

During my first couple of months at TransCentury, I learned that as associate director of program development for the Peace Corps, Warren was at a White House meeting when Kennedy's aides decided the fledgling agency should report through the established State Department bureaucracy. Alarmed at the prospect, Warren quickly sent a cable to Shriver, who was overseas. Warren then asked Bill Moyers, deputy director of the Peace Corps, to take a copy of the cable to Vice President Lyndon Johnson and argue the political benefits of an independent Peace Corps. Johnson agreed, addressed the matter with Kennedy, and the decision was reversed.

The information I gathered about Warren inspired me and made me want to know more. Whenever I would ask him about the Peace Corps, his eyes would shine. He would say things like: The Peace Corps was built on an absolute recognition that we can learn from all cultures, that America would be better off if our new generations better understood other cultures and if other countries got to know us better. The Peace Corps was built on the concept of recruiting appropriate volunteers—those who would want to live with local families even when the settings were remote and rural, who were curious to enjoy different traditions, who were deeply convinced of the value of respecting diversity, and who were interested in learning and understanding other cultures and new languages. He would say the volunteer's interest in learning new languages must include Thai and Bengali as well as French and Spanish. The idea that a Peace Corps staffer or volunteer should polish French, the language of diplomacy, rather than tackle a difficult Asian tonal tongue was an idea he did not agree with.

After serving as Deputy Director of the Peace Corps, Warren left the high-profile agency in 1967 to form TransCentury, not as a consulting firm, but as a social action organization dedicated to social and economic change both in the U.S. and in developing countries.

When I joined the organization in 1977, I understood that TransCentury was based on the same principles and ideals as the Peace Corps; instead of having volunteers, TransCentury did that same work through professionals. I was impressed and inspired. I also understood that Warren and the leadership of TransCentury believed that social and economic development was needed in the

U.S. and in other countries. That is why among the first programs that TransCentury implemented were job centers in Anacostia and in southeast Washington, D.C., and a remedial education program in New York. I also learned that given the stellar reputation of TransCentury, during the Washington, D.C., riots in 1968, the TransCentury building at 1520 Seventh Street NW was the only one on the block spared from arson and vandalism.

In the earlier-noted *Washington Post* article, Ms. Sullivan had written, "It's hard to say exactly why we weren't touched," Warren said. "It's partly luck, partly because we don't have any enemies, and partly because we think we do have some friends on the block. The people in the area know the kind of work we do."

After getting to know Warren and the circle of leaders at TransCentury that included at that time Dick Irish, BJ Warren, Carolyn Long, Ralph Bates, Brenda Eddy, and David North, I was glad I joined the organization. I also better understood that many of their different ways of leading and managing an innovative organization like TransCentury were based on new, forward-thinking ideas.

Warren truly embodied the spirit of international citizenship and globalization before such a term was even in vogue. He was ahead of his time in so many ways. His mind was always breaking frontiers; his heart drew in those who were not like him. His spirit was always optimistic and forward-looking, and his belief was that we can truly make a difference in this world by better understanding others and serving those who are less privileged.

Warren was an idealist, yes; a dreamer of a better world, yes; but he was also a serious pragmatist. After two months at TransCentury, I knew I was lucky to have been recruited by him to come to Washington, D.C., and join the ranks of this avant-garde organization.

CHAPTER EIGHTEEN

TRANSCENTURY

TRANSCENTURY AND WASHINGTON, D.C., THIS new chapter in my life, were far beyond my wildest dreams. My workdays required me to stretch my mind, constantly learn new things, contribute to a global service agenda, and immerse myself in a new life—at work and at home.

My first two months at TransCentury were about discovery. I was continuously bumping into new perspectives, new mindsets, and different ways of thinking. Work was about a vision that was fired by compassion and driven by a renewed sense of belonging to the whole planet. The American leaders of TransCentury were true global citizens. Warren had lived and worked in the Far East before founding TransCentury, and several other officers had been Peace Corps volunteers: Dick Irish in the Philippines, BJ Warren in Peru, Carolyn Long in Gabon, and Ralph Bates in Colombia.

My stereotypes about what defines an American were challenged on a daily basis. Nearly all the top leaders at TransCentury spoke a second language fluently. In comparison, my familiarity with English felt shaky. Many idioms used by my colleagues reminded me that

I still had a lot to learn before becoming comfortable with their dynamic language.

TransCentury was a hub of new ideas and an incubator of new programs, a space where professionals were able to contribute their best all the time. To me, TransCentury was the shining light on a hill, a light that sought to reach every corner of the world. I felt privileged to be part of this organization; however, I was not completely happy because Lebanon was constantly on my mind. In addition, I had never really reconciled myself with God. The war in Lebanon and Mommy's illness remained a deep wound that I suffered in silence.

The senseless war in Lebanon challenged my dream, and the dream of many others, of Lebanon as a country representing the peaceful existence of different religions where diversity and pluralism could be celebrated. Even though armed conflicts took place between political factions whose members were comprised of a majority of one faith, such as Christian or Muslim or Druze, the war in Lebanon was not about religions being unable to live together.

For some, the war was about the sovereignty of Lebanon; in particular, this perception was triggered by the role that Palestinians in general and their newly armed militias could or could not play in Lebanon, i.e., whether they could exist as a state within a state. Fatah was the Palestinian political and military organization entrenched in Lebanon. Those who objected to their presence believed Fatah's activities undermined Lebanese sovereignty and triggered strong Israeli reprisals that were extremely costly to Lebanon. What complicated the matter in the mind of those with such a position was the Lebanese government's inability to reach consensus for an appropriate response to Fatah, or to exercise what they saw as the country's legitimate right to protect its sovereignty over a Palestinian armed entity. Many Lebanese parties established their own armed militias to defend what they saw as a Lebanese sovereignty that was under attack by a non-Lebanese militia. Needless to say, in a scenario like this, regional outside support flowed into the country backing one militia against another. Most of the fighting factions, alas, were duped into becoming surrogates of conflicting regional forces.

For others, the economic disparities in Lebanon fueled the war. The fact that sufficient basic social services were not reaching the remote areas was a reason for disadvantaged populations to be angry and therefore to participate in violent action.

In reporting the war and its causes, most of the local, regional, and global media took a simplistic and irresponsible shortcut in describing the multi-faceted war as one based on conflicts between Christians and Muslims, on religious differences rather than a war about sovereignty and a lack of basic services to remote areas. In general, the media did not opt for the far more demanding task of tracking complex political beliefs, analyzing changing political alliances, understanding the covert meddling of external powers in the Lebanese scene, and tracing the flow of substantial non-Lebanese financial support for the different political positions.

Characterizing the war in this one-dimensional way was very troubling to me and to many Lebanese. Of course, it did not help that in Lebanon some members of the different political factions did, in fact, express narrow, bigoted religious views by committing atrocities in the name of one religion or another. However, to say the civil war in Lebanon was about religion is like saying the Revolutionary War in America was about the tax on tea.

This distortion was the main source of my inner pain and grief. Misrepresentation of a truly senseless war added insult to injury. As if it were not enough that a war raged in my beloved, small, fragile country, as if the death of innocents was not enough, the media, through hasty if not irresponsible coverage was damaging the precious concept of peaceful existence between Christians and Muslims in Lebanon. The media did not acknowledge that for decades many Lebanese Christians and Muslims lived peacefully together. They sent their children to the same schools, lived in the same neighborhoods, were partners in new businesses, and intermarried. They co-directed large progressive artistic, social, and economic enterprises such as the International Baalbeck Festivals and Middle East Airlines. They created model neighborhoods like Ras Beirut where I lived.

I was deeply hurt by the misrepresentation of what was taking place in Lebanon, and I decided to become an activist in Washington, D.C., on behalf of my troubled country. I spoke frequently at different gatherings and explained what was going on in my homeland. I joined the American Lebanese League (ALL), which presented hearings on Capitol Hill. We organized demonstrations against the Assad regime in Syria, a key meddler in Lebanon's affairs that played the most manipulative role of inciting different factions against one another.

Despite these efforts, I remained guilty about my own life, and especially about whether I had the right to be happy when both Lebanon and my mother were stricken. The war in Lebanon and Mommy's illness kept me up at night thinking, wondering what else I could do to help my mother and my country.

Mommy and Daddy were in Oregon during the spring of 1977 and had agreed to stay there till the end of June to attend Sarmad's graduation as an engineer from Oregon State University. After graduation, they planned to return to D.C. for a short visit with Ramzi and me before going home to Freike. I had not seen Mommy and Daddy since we parted in Amsterdam, and I hadn't seen Sarmad for possibly a couple of years. To say I missed them was an understatement. I decided to fly to Oregon to attend the graduation of my youngest brother and then accompany my parents to Washington, D.C.

Our week in Oregon was a total delight. Mommy and Daddy had a swell time with Sarmad and Ina. Sarmad had always dreamt of building bridges, and there he was—a qualified engineer with a bright future ahead of him. Mommy's face was radiant during his graduation ceremony, and Daddy's delight was clearly visible.

Afterwards, we flew back to D.C. where Ramzi met us. He happily wheeled Mommy through Dulles Airport. Ramzi and I had arranged for a large, beautifully elegant apartment in one of the D.C. suburbs where we could all stay together. For ten days, my brother and I did our best to ensure our parents enjoyed every minute of their stay. They had friends in D.C., among them Dr. Zakan Shakhashiri and his wife Adma who knew my mother when they were all students at AUB. We invited them for dinner and enjoyed a special evening.

The four of them talked about the good old days, remembered valued friends, highlighted special memories, and discussed at length the dreams of their generation of Lebanese and how the country moved forward from 1943 till 1975. They all wished the different governments had done more regarding social services to remote areas, but they were not convinced that this reason alone was sufficient explanation for all that was happening in Lebanon.

On another evening, I invited Warren Wiggins and Carolyn Long to dinner. BJ Warren was out of town for work and could not join us. During this visit, the topic of discussion was international development, and common ground among different cultures was the focus. A sense of optimism framed the discussions. Daddy, of course, invited Warren and Carolyn to be his guests in Freike.

During the day, Ramzi and I took our parents sightseeing. They had visited most of the monuments and museums of D.C. during their earlier stay in the city; however, it was fun to watch Daddy's pleasure in reliving the country of his youth. Mommy shared her excitement about the city she had enjoyed in 1953 when she participated in a conference in D.C.

That week was memorable thanks largely to Ramzi, who is deeply skilled at making other people relax and enjoy themselves. No one could make our parents laugh as much as he could! Daddy, Mommy, and the two of us had lengthy discussions about our life in the U.S., and about our work. Daddy, as usual, appreciated our individual efforts in his most positive way. He knew that wonderful opportunities lay ahead of us. Mommy was grace personified. I was sad when those ten days ended; I didn't know when I would see them again.

Ramzi and I had informed Ameen of our parent's date of return to Lebanon. Upon their arrival to Beirut's airport, Ameen was there to receive them. As in previous summers, he and his wife Samira planned to spend the summer with them in Freike. I bade my parents a loving farewell and immersed myself in my work at TransCentury.

TransCentury was a learning organization that valued new thinking and innovative approaches to challenging social and economic problems. The leadership also valued and respected all cultures and strived to ensure that our work reflected those values. I rose to this task and worked to meet their expectations. Warren, BJ, MaryAnne, and I held many meetings in an effort to come up with a strategic plan for the Secretariat for Women in Development. We agreed that the Secretariat would focus on three areas: research, policy, and implementation of programs. We agreed that in the coming three-to-four years, the Secretariat should add value in the research field about women, in the design and implementation of programs that could improve women's lives, and in influencing governments and civil society organizations regarding policies that impacted women. A tall order! But I was entirely motivated; I respected the team I was working with and knew that I would learn a great deal from them while hopefully contributing to the ambitious agenda.

On the research front, our priority was to learn about the status of women in the developing countries. I led the effort in mapping the research that already existed worldwide on women and development. I wanted us to read and learn about studies written by indigenous researchers, and in their own languages. I could use my English, French, and Arabic at the professional level, and my assistant researcher was fluent in Spanish. We set a deadline of early winter 1978 for an annotated bibliography about recent women studies in Africa, Asia, Latin America, and the Middle East. I titled the document: "Development as if Women Mattered: An Annotated Bibliography with a Third World Focus."

Warren was extremely pleased with the thoroughness and the quality of what we had produced in such a short time. He thought this annotated bibliography would contribute to and increase the knowledge base of the field of women in development, and decided to find a publisher. TransCentury submitted the manuscript to the Overseas Development Council (ODC), and they accepted it for publication. I could not believe this turn of events. I had never expected that a year after my arrival in the U.S. I would be publishing, in English, a technical book about the status of women in developing countries.

The abstract of my first book in English read as follows:

This new annotated bibliography on Third World women and development offers several special features. It gathers a large number of documents with an action/programming focus. A large proportion of the studies it lists was prepared by, and presented the perspectives of, Third World women. The bibliography makes accessible a large number of fugitive unpublished documents. The 287 studies annotated in the bibliography are grouped into subject categories that include: women in their culture and society; socioeconomic participation; migration; formal and non-formal education; rural development; health, nutrition, and family planning; and the impact of development and modernization on women. Within each of these subject categories, documents are subdivided by their geographic region of focus.

While working on the bibliography, I also became involved in two other major activities. I assisted MaryAnne in designing action-oriented programs, and I was asked by the United Nations Development Program (UNDP) to join a team that would assess the status of women in six Arab countries: Tunisia, Egypt, Sudan, Iraq, Kuwait, and the United Arab Emirates. The two-pronged objective of the assessment was to acknowledge the already-existing activities undertaken by the governments of these six countries, and to review with their major ministries—such as the ministries of women's affairs, social affairs, education, health, and planning—how they could better integrate women in national development efforts. I was thrilled to be part of all of these seminal programs and kept counting my blessings. I recall that I was working at least ten and sometimes eleven or twelve hours a day. I loved my work, and I wanted to learn and contribute in the best way I could.

The design MaryAnne and I contributed to was about how to train non-governmental agencies (NGOs) in integrating women in the planning and implementation of socio-economic programs in two countries in West Africa. The United States Agency of International Development (USAID) funded this activity. As a result of our work, and with input from Jane Watkins and David Brunell, lead trainers at TransCentury, we were asked to train the leaders of approximately twenty NGOs in Liberia and Sierra Leone in those methodologies.

I was delighted that both USAID and TransCentury trusted us with this task; however, I had misgivings about my ability to rise to the challenge. MaryAnne and I took what we were entrusted with very seriously. We suggested to USAID that we visit the NGOs in both Liberia and Sierra Leone to gain first-hand knowledge of their programs, priorities, capacities, and needs in terms of integrating women so that we could adjust the generic design we had prepared and better respond to their specific needs. MaryAnne and I recognized this would allow us to develop more responsive and specific designs. USAID concurred.

UNDP took me on an approximately seven-week trip to the six Arab countries that we would work in. I met many ministers and heads of women organizations during this period, and discovered Arab countries I was unfamiliar with, including Tunisia, Iraq, the United Arab Emirates, Kuwait, and Sudan. I also reconnected with Egypt.

The amount of information, statistics, and documents we collected was overwhelming. Our task was to assess and analyze the status of integrating women in the national development efforts of each country and to recommend strategies that might add value to the processes that already existed. All of this had to be done by a team of four, based on the result of the many interviews we conducted and all the documents we collected.

The UNDP team was composed of four women: two Europeans, a Swede and a British; and two Arabs-- an Egyptian and me. The Swede was our leader. She was very professional and very demanding, and the work was hard and fast-paced. During those seven weeks, I read documents and wrote reports every evening till the early hours of the morning. I again wondered if my work was at the top-quality level that was expected of me.

The year 1977 and the beginning of 1978 was a heady period for me. This phase was the beginning of the rich and powerful expansion of my career, a phase that made me think big, and consolidated the elements of optimism in me. It clarified my belief that my journey might lead to a sense of belonging not just to Lebanon, and possibly to France and the U.S., but also to our planet. My research was no longer about Lebanese and Arab women only, but about women in all the developing countries. I was so grateful for the opportunities I was given to contribute to women's national advancement in several countries in two continents.

If we succeeded in Liberia and Sierra Leone, USAID and TransCentury were ready to offer the program to NGOs in other African countries—so long as the NGOs expressed interest. And if the UNDP report was accepted by the several ministries of the six Arab countries, it might influence their policies and strategies on how to advance women's integration in their national development efforts.

In the summer and fall of 1977, MaryAnne and I made two trips to West Africa. The first one was to meet with the participating NGOs of Liberia and Sierra Leone to discuss their needs, and the second was to deliver a five-day workshop in Liberia for NGOs from both countries. The workshop focused on how to integrate women in the planning and implementation of educational, health, and economic productivity programs.

Visiting West Africa—specifically, Liberia and Sierra Leone for the first time—was breathtaking, to say the least. My mind had to be fully alert to see and understand everything, and my emotions took in every sight and every sigh.

Poverty and potential were totally intermingled.

Stubborn problems and soaring promises co-existed.

Vision and violence were always ready to surface.

Deterioration of systems and daring new dreams overlapped.

Yet corruption and creative solutions are part of nearly every government organization—a paradoxical situation to say the least. However, hope trumped all limiting factors. I felt that if only those two countries had honest leaders with a genuine commitment to serve their people, the horizons would shine and inspire the people to work harder and to believe in their future.

I had two reasons for my optimism: the new generation of Liberia and Sierra Leone, and their vibrant civil society organizations. I visited schools in both countries and was astounded by the children's thirst to learn. Working with the NGOs, I was very impressed by how active they were. What was missing was an honest and committed body of governance.

In addition to trying my best to understand the cultural and socio-economic context of each country, I could not help but notice the incredible natural beauty of both Liberia and Sierra Leone, especially when I went up-country.

My first trip to Africa made me understand the sun better. I began to perceive the sun not just as bright light, but as warmth that kisses the skin. I also understood forests better. Most of Liberia and Sierra Leone is plateau covered by dense tropical forests which thrive under annual rainfalls. The forests of these two countries must have at least thirty to thirty-five hues of green; green is king. In addition, I was enchanted by the calm of the ocean. Both capitals, Monrovia and Freetown, lie on the Atlantic Ocean. Often the business lunches I had took place at restaurants by the shore. I was always struck by how calm and beautiful the ocean was compared to the busy, crowded streets and neighborhoods of the capital cities.

Based on the evaluations of the participants of the workshop, the training MaryAnne and I delivered was successful, possibly very successful. The leaders of the NGOs asked for a continuing working relationship with the Secretariat for Women in Development, and I believe both TransCentury and USAID were pleased with these results.

The trip to the six Arab countries was a game-changer for me. I entirely understood that despite the common ground that tied these countries together, the Arab world is far from being monolithic. During this trip, both my analytic capacities and my emotions fluctuated at a depth and speed that I had rarely experienced before. There was so, so much to absorb in such a short time. The visit deepened my understanding of both the cultural dimensions as well as the socio-economic contexts in each of these countries.

Tunisia, for example, helped me understand how the fusion of an Arab culture with a French educational system and a Mediterranean ambiance could be different. Both Lebanon and Tunisia flirt with that fusion, but each of these countries mix those three dimensions in a mold that is particular to them.

Sudan, on the other hand, was in a constant battle with the environment. Northern Sudan where we worked has vast regions that are part of the Nubian Desert. These are dry areas plagued by sandstorms known as *houboob*, and during these sandstorms, the Sudanese stay inside their homes and offices and watch the wind, sand, and heat take over everything. The sand and the sun play a game of power, vying to block out the other. Thank God for the Blue Nile, which is truly a gift to this very parched land.

Egypt continued to fascinate me with its rich history and culture. The pyramids remind us that they are the oldest of the Seven Wonders of the ancient world and the only one to remain largely intact. The Egyptian culture is a wonderful mix of Arab context, Islamic architecture, Ottoman influence, and Coptic input. While in Egypt, I am reminded that Cairo continues to be a trendsetter within the Arab-speaking world with regards to music, film, and television.

Iraq intrigued me. It took more time to understand what appeared as a disconnect between Iraq's rich past and its suffocating present, in particular when I visited Karballa in southern Iraq. The area is marked by a history of self-flagellation, an act that many young men undertake to share the sufferings of Hassan and Hussein.

The United Arab Emirates was different from all the other Arab countries I visited. It was a country in the making, with a visionary leader who was determined to create a modern state in the shortest possible span of time.

Kuwait again was quite different from its neighbors. I was impressed with the fact that the Ministry of Planning had a woman as director in early 1978; Naima Al Shaiji was in charge of international cooperation.

While I was with the UNDP team visiting the six Arab countries, MaryAnne accepted an offer for a position within USAID. As soon as I returned from my whirlwind tour, Warren took me to lunch and offered me the job of the Director of the Secretariat. I accepted the challenge. He also asked me to commit to work with TransCentury with a long-term view. I told him that even though my father was an American, I had not yet applied for my green card. I had been accepted in the U.S. on the H1 visa that TransCentury obtained for me. Warren was of the opinion that given the fact that my father was an American citizen, and given that TransCentury needed me, the process of obtaining my green card would not be difficult.

He offered to write a letter, as the president of TransCentury, to expedite the process that would result in a green card and American citizenship. I accepted his proposal as I saw a future with a huge promise, and I was excited about my work that focused on integrating women in development in at least two continents.

Some paragraphs of Warren's letter of March 1, 1978, in support of my citizenship request read as follows:

> May Rihani is currently Director of the Secretariat for Women in Development, and her continued presence in the country and supervision of the work of this unit is imperative for its success. Her experience, professional background, and extraordinary array of skills makes her uniquely qualified for this responsibility, and, in fact she is the only one with the knowledge and experience necessary to carry out this vital program at TransCentury. ...Ms. Rihani's contacts around the world, her participation at numerous international conferences, her involvement as a member of the board with a wide spectrum of international organizations, and her recent participation as a consultant to the United Nations Development Program mission on the integration

of women into development has given her a unique
capacity to lead. ...Similarly her unique experience
and skills as a scholar and development practitioner
make her irreplaceable. ...As such, she makes a truly
unique contribution to TransCentury's work, both
as a provider of services, but more importantly as a
trainer of other professionals building similar skills. In
short, Ms. Rihani's considerable experience and skills
in the relatively new field of women in development
make her continued services to TransCentury and the
U.S. development community imperative.

When I read Warren's letter I felt very humbled, and I understood
how a leader empowers others.

Warren's confidence in me had a very positive impact. I was
determined to make the Secretariat for Women in Development
a department within TransCentury that made a real difference in
women's lives through as many programs as we could handle. Warren
deeply believed in women's empowerment, and I felt I had a superb
strategist, as well as a marvelous supporter, in the leader I reported to.

During the several working lunches that Warren and I had
during the first few months of my tenure as the Director of the
Secretariat, we discussed the necessity of expanding our donor base.
We were very thankful to USAID and its support, but strongly
felt that we would like to have expanded support from as many
organizations within the UN system as possible. We also discussed
the possibility of partnering with other international NGOs that
were designing and implementing international development
programs, as well as becoming further engaged with national
governments and local NGOS.

One of the principles we talked about was leveraging: how to make a bigger, more lasting impact by partnering with other agencies and organizations, and by building on what was already working and expanding it. Another principle we discussed in these serious, stimulating, and enjoyable lunches at La Fourchette, a French restaurant that was a three-minute walk from TransCentury, was the importance of building the capacity of the local agencies and organizations we worked with. Again, a very tall order.

With Warren the vision was always clear, the dreams were always big, the belief in the capacity of others was always profound, and hope trumped everything. Warren and I were on a journey. We were determined to make a difference in the lives of underprivileged and underserved women.

He gave me carte blanche, total support, and the benefit of being able to consult with him any time I needed to. I was motivated and determined. I knew that I needed to expand the base of our donors and the range of our partners.

My staff and I started planning for the rest of 1978, 1979, and 1980. I was in touch with UNICEF discussing a new research project, and was willing to bid on large USAID projects. I talked with Save the Children about possible programmatic partnerships in either African or the Middle Eastern countries, and explored with the Peace Corps how we could assist in their designs to ensure the integration of women into their programs. In addition, Warren wanted me to meet with Partnership for Productivity (PfP), an NGO that focused on economic productivity in Africa and the Caribbean. Excitement was in the air, and difficult, strategic work was the *plat du jour*.

Many of these plans started to come to fruition. UNICEF contracted with us for a small research project on girls' education. Save the Children asked me to attend a design workshop at their headquarters and to assist with the perspective of integrating women in designing holistic rural development programs. The workshop with the Liberian and Sierra Leonean NGOs had given me deeper insights on how to make such integration work in a successful way. The Peace Corps asked me to go to Fiji in June 1978 to assess how they could integrate women better into their activities, and Warren set up a meeting with PfP. During the spring of 1978, the Secretariat was like a beehive, busy planning and preparing for all these new programs.

Warren asked me to meet with him and the president and chairman of the board of PfP. I read several documents about the organization in preparation. The day of the meeting, towards the end of May, Warren and I took a short walk in Adams Morgan to PfP's offices, which were not far from TransCentury. We were greeted by the chairman, the president, and senior staff. The meeting went very well, the talk about collaboration was genuine, and their focus on increased economic productivity for entrepreneurs and small farmers was an area that interested us all. What Warren and I brought to the discussion was an additional dimension of how to better integrate women in their work. They proposed a second meeting in June to discuss specifics of how we could collaborate. I had to ask that we delay the meeting till the end of July given that I would be in Fiji for a time, and they agreed.

During the walk back to TransCentury, Warren and I agreed that the chairman, an older gentleman, might be a little old school; however, we agreed that the president, a younger gentleman named Andrew Oerke, appeared to be the innovative thinker and the one to continue our dialogue with. I tried not to show Warren how impressed I was by Andrew. I felt I might be making a too-quick judgment and that his handsome allure might be influencing me.

In May 1978, I was in constant dialogue with the programmatic director of the Peace Corps in preparation for my June trip to Fiji. One evening after a long day of work, while I was waiting at the intersection of Columbia and 18th Street for the bus that took me home, a car stopped and the driver asked if I would like a lift. To my surprise, it was Andrew Oerke. I accepted, and during the ride home, we talked about my trip to Fiji. We agreed to meet as soon as I returned to continue the discussion about the partnership between TransCentury and PfP. The drive took approximately twenty minutes, and I silently wished those minutes were longer.

June came and I flew to Fiji—a very different world. Fiji is an island nation in the South Pacific northeast of New Zealand. The country is comprised of more than 332 islands, of which 110 are inhabited. Most Fijians live in Suva, the capital, or in smaller urban centers. Most of the interior land is sparsely inhabited.

The first few days in Fiji gave me the impression that the country, possibly because it is an island, had something different about its style of life. I wondered if the inhabitants of islands have a mindset that created a lot of space for fun, relaxation, or happy hours. I also wondered if their mindset simply does not allow them to be overly worried and possibly does not permit a serious approach to life to dominate their daily activities. In the years to come, and after getting to know a number of islands and its populations, I became convinced that this was not the case, but understood how first impressions might leave a visitor with such ideas.

I worked very closely with the Peace Corps staff in Fiji to learn about their program so I could discuss effective ways of better integrating women in their efforts. The staff took me to different areas in the islands where their volunteers worked to implement their programs. In the first region, we were received by a marvelous group of indigenous performers. The singing, dancing, and welcoming speeches took an hour-and-a-half to two hours before we were able to start the meetings and the discussions. The same thing happened the next day, and the days after.

I loved the dances and the singing even though it took up a good chunk of my work day. I needed to understand the culture to do my work well, and how can anyone understand a culture without observing, living, and enjoying its values and traditions? Perhaps we could have said or done something to dedicate all the hours we had to just serious and analytic discussions, but I do not think this would have been respectful of the culture, and it would not have facilitated effective and insightful discussions. I understood and accepted that the welcoming rituals were as vital as the discussions. As a matter of fact, I ended up tremendously enjoying that aspect of the field visits.

It had become a part of my routine that whenever I traveled I included a few days in Beirut to see my parents. When I completed my work in Fiji, I stopped in Beirut to reconnect with the two marvelous and inspirational individuals in my life, refueled my emotional energy, refilled my reservoir of love, and kept going.

On the plane back to D.C., I made a list of what I needed to complete in the next couple of months: a report to the Peace Corps about their program in Fiji; a review of the research my staff was conducting for UNICEF; a series of meetings with Warren and other colleagues about the huge bid we planned regarding the USAID request for proposal (RFP) for a program in Morocco; follow-up with Save the Children about a possible programmatic partnership; and the promised meeting with the president of PfP.

The summer and fall of 1978 were so unbelievably condensed and rich, but more importantly, many new chapters in my life sprouted from the beautiful and transformative months of that period.

CHAPTER NINETEEN

MOROCCO, ANDREW, AND LOVE

D URING THE FIRST COUPLE OF months after my return
from Fiji, I completed many of the tasks on the to-do list made
on the plane flying back to D.C.

Two of these items—a proposal to improve young women's
literacy in Morocco, and following up with the president of PfP—led
to new developments in my life.

My team and I responded to the RFP issued by the USAID
Mission in Morocco, and when it was announced that we had won
the bid, I was overwhelmed. I knew we had designed an innovative
and creative program; however, I had not been confident that we
would win. I was new to the proposal writing business and leading
such an effort was entirely outside my experience. Perhaps I did
not yet have the self-assurance needed when working in such a
competitive environment. Despite all my uncertainty, we won with
our proposal to design a program of non-formal young women's
education in Morocco. This meant I needed to travel to Morocco to
negotiate and finalize the contract with the USAID Mission there
and with the lead ministry, the Ministry of Youth and Sports, which

represented the government of Morocco. It also meant I had to hire a full team of twenty or so professionals to implement the project. So many new territories to cover, so many new paths, and so many things to learn. I was quite nervous. I felt much better when Warren announced he would travel with me to Morocco. The two of us, as a team, could decide what needed to be done with our new partners.

Warren and I arrived in Rabat on a Sunday afternoon, and on Monday morning met with the USAID Mission. I knew I had to be a quick learner; I also knew that I had by my side the most strategic and subtle teacher and mentor. During the ten days we spent in Rabat, I underwent the most intense learning experience I'd experienced so far. Every evening over a long dinner, Warren and I discussed and planned for any possible scenarios of the next day. He stressed that even though our proposal was solidly designed, and even though we had won the bid, we should not be overprotective of the details of our approach. We could defend the philosophy and principles of our design, he said, but we needed to remain flexible and responsive to any specific needs USAID or the Ministry might express. If they needed to fine-tune certain aspects of the proposal in order to respond better to some subtleties in their priorities, Warren wanted us to find ways that would not compromise our approach and would represent a win/win implementation plan. I was learning from a wise man whose ego did not interfere with the path we needed to take to achieve results.

Our days were filled with meetings. Discussing and negotiating with USAID was done in English, with the Moroccan ministries in French. So many questions were asked, and Warren let me answer nearly all of them. Every now and then he would amplify some of my responses. When it came time to sign the contract, the Moroccan ministry wanted to have an official ceremony at their offices in the presence of the Minister and some of his directors, the USAID Mission Director and some of his senior officials, and Warren and me.

The Moroccans know how to plan such an event. On the day of the ceremony, we were ushered into an elegant conference room. Green leather folders were placed in front of every seat. Most likely the green leather folders were made in Fez. The Minister and his entourage entered; we, the Americans, were already in the conference room. Lemonade and mint tea were served in beautiful Moroccan hand-painted glasses and teacups.

After the introductory remarks about the spirit of cooperation, and the hope and expectations for improving the literacy and social and economic well-being of young Moroccan women, the Minister said the folders were ready for the three parties to sign: the Ministry, the USAID Mission, and TransCentury. The ministry staff placed the official folders in front of the Minister for his signature, and then the staff placed them in front of the USAID Mission Director for his. But when the staff placed the folders in front of Warren to sign on behalf of TransCentury, he very calmly, with a smile, looked at the Minister and at the Director of the USAID Mission and said, "For TransCentury, May Rihani will sign. She is the one who led the effort of the design of the proposal and she is the one who will be in charge of overseeing this program and ensuring the quality of its implementation. So, your Excellency and Mr. Director, if you do not mind, May will sign on our behalf."

I was completely surprised, as I think were the Minister and the USAID director. I signed. Every one applauded the agreement, and the Minister invited us to a celebratory lunch.

Warren never had to tell me how leaders empower their staff; he taught by example. From that day on, I always knew that one of the most motivating factors for staff who perform well is empowerment.

I also knew that empowerment, when it happens at the right time in the right way, propels professionals forward in a highly effective manner. I knew that only leaders who had self-confidence and who were sincerely committed to developing and supporting their key staff were able to develop promising new leadership. Warren was one of the very few I had the privilege of knowing who led in this way.

We flew back to D.C. with the excitement that new, long-term programs create. We had been given the opportunity to make a difference in the lives of thousands and thousands of young, illiterate women in Morocco. Through successfully designed and implemented functional, relevant literacy programs, we had the opportunity to transform lives. Of course, this would only happen if we listened and understood the cultural, social, and economic contexts of these young women, and if we recognized that only a powerful committed partnership with the relevant public and civil entities in Morocco would enable us to achieve the intended results. What a marvelous challenge! TransCentury and I were embarking on a journey to make a difference in Morocco.

A week or so after our return to D.C., Warren announced that I was appointed a vice president at TransCentury—barely two years after my joining them. I saw that the path ahead was filled with positive opportunities.

During this exciting time, the second new development in my life was Andrew Oerke. I kept my promise to meet with him, as the president of PfP, to see if there was an opportunity for his organization and TransCentury to collaborate. It soon became clear to both of us that the meeting was about not just our two organizations, but also about the two of us. At the end of the meeting Andrew asked if we could have dinner, and I accepted. Afterwards, I told Warren that if he wanted to pursue collaboration between TransCentury and PfP, he should appoint another vice president to oversee the matter. I told Warren that I would be seeing Andrew, but not in my capacity at TransCentury. Warren smiled and wished me the best.

The first few months of the courtship swept me off my feet. Andrew and I lived the love story that exists in many people's dreams. He was handsome; so bright, so engaging, so athletic, so intellectually stimulating, so multicultural and worldly, so articulate, so creative— and on top of it all, a published poet and the president of an international development organization. When we first met in 1978, he was forty-five and divorced. I was thirty-three and single. He made me feel both young and mature, beautiful and sophisticated, feminine and professional, creative and established, and much, much more.

During those first months, I learned that Andrew had been a Peace Corps director in Malawi and Jamaica, and president of PfP for two years. PfP focused on implementing microcredit programs for farmers and small entrepreneurs in the remote rural areas of developing countries. I also learned that he was a serious poet whose work had been published by *The New Yorker*, *The New Republic*, *Poetry*, and many other publications in the U.S. and England.

This man who blended America, Europe, and Africa fascinated me. He was born in the U.S., graduated from Baylor University, was poet-in-residence at St. Andrew's Presbyterian College in North Carolina, and was a part of the American literary and cultural scene. He was European due to his Norwegian roots, and because he had lived in Berlin as a Fulbright Scholar at the Freie Universität, he knew European philosophy and music like the back of his hand. He was African because of his deep knowledge of, and commitment to, the African people, and was deeply responsive to the continent's numerous cultures. Andrew's poetry focused on all three continents.

Our courtship was overwhelming. We discussed poetry, history, philosophy, culture, and economics. Andrew was passionate about new horizons and he always thought outside the box. He truly sought to understand "the other," whoever the other might be. He truly understood and acted as if our planet was indeed a global village, long before the term was coined. He and I could talk for hours and hours on end. Through his words, his concerned eyes, and his caring smile, I understood his passion for the underprivileged.

Andrew had done everything by the time I met him—well, almost everything. He had been a poet-in-residence, a Peace Corps country director, a sports fanatic (football and tennis), an avid traveler, and was now the president of a microfinance organization. In our discussions, Andrew often referred to Jesus, Buddha, Aristotle, Hume, Kant, Beethoven, T.S. Elliot, and Steven Wallace. I would bring in Lebanon, the Arab world, Mohammad, Kahlil Gibran, Ameen Rihani, Jean Paul Sartre, Simone de Beauvoir, and the Beatles.

Our late evenings together were magical. No one made me see the night with new eyes the way he did. When he entered my home on a Saturday evening, stars lit the room. When he read poetry to me, all languages became flutes he played. When he talked about our future, I became a bird with colored wings, flying in the most graceful way. When we wrote poems together, a new world was created.

After a time, Andrew and I decided to buy a home together on Irving Street in the Mount Pleasant neighborhood of Washington, D.C., not far from TransCentury and PfP. My only concern during all of this was the possibility of losing focus on my work. The Secretariat for Women in Development, the policy and research activities we were conducting, as well as our many programs and projects were naturally very important to me and I was committed to leading my staff in an effective way. I did not want this real-life love story to be all-consuming. I talked to Andrew about my concern, and he assured me we could have it all, our marvelous love story and our magnificent work and responsibilities. He helped me remain focused at work, but after work, it was heaven on earth.

Our home in Mount Pleasant became a nest where our love flourished. Our weekends were filled with music, especially Beethoven's Ninth; T.S. Elliot's poetry; and tennis. We shared stories about being the Peace Corps director in Malawi, and tales of Lebanon's history and heritage, including the country's role as a bridge between the East and the West. We discussed women's empowerment and the progress of my efforts at TransCentury, especially in Morocco. We translated my poetry from Arabic to English, and read his new poems aloud. We painted a room in the house, and enjoyed visits by Lebanese, American, and French friends. Among those who came and stayed with us in our love home were Gideon Waldrop, a music composer and dean of Juilliard in New York who was a very close friend of Andrew; Ramzi, my brother; Riyad Nassar, the by-then president of the Beirut College for Women where I had worked; two friends of mine from Paris, Bulle Vautier and Fabienne Mayeux; and many others. I loved Andrew's friends, and my friends fell in love with him.

As I mentioned earlier, Andrew was in love with Africa. He asked if I could accompany him on one of his trips, and while I was delighted he wanted me to travel with him, I needed to manage my own busy schedule. We made a deal that he would travel with me to one of the countries where my projects were being implemented, and I would do the same for him. He accompanied me to Morocco and I went with him to Senegal.

Both trips were about understanding a new culture through someone else's eyes. I was enchanted at being able to function as guide and interpreter for Andrew about the culture of one of the Arab countries. I wanted him to understand *al-Maghreb*, the rich history of Morocco, the fusion of Islam in North Africa, the difference between classical Arabic and the local dialect, and the fascinating faces of different Moroccan cities including Marrakesh, Fez, and Rabat.

When we went to Senegal, it was his turn to be the expert. He identified with Africa and was a superb listener. We went to villages in Senegal and Andrew became the facilitator *par excellence*. He asked questions and listened intensely to every word the villagers would utter; he could have listened to the villagers for weeks on end. He was interested in their well-being and the well-being of their children. He asked about the type of schools they had (if the villages had schools), whether they had health clinics, if there were wells in the village, who fetched the water and wood, and how long it took to complete those chores.

Of course he asked about farming, the agricultural products they were able to harvest, the difficulties they had in marketing their products, and the distances they needed to travel to sell their goods. He was also fascinated with the fishermen of Senegal, their lifestyle and their families. The list of his interests was endless, and I listened and learned.

Our time together in1979 and 1980 was unique. In addition to living a wonderful discovery process with each other, our trips to Morocco and Senegal added a special dimension to the beauty, and in-depth learning about facets of each other. Our travels created the possibility of discovering more about each other through another culture. We were delighted by the importance of multiculturalism and how it affected our lives, individually and together. Lebanon, America, France, Norway, Malawi, Morocco, Senegal—our exploration stretched our minds and hearts, and enriched us beyond measure. We understood that all cultures were incredibly rich and that each one could enrich the other. We understood that humanity would have a better future if individuals were capable of extending themselves to belong to more than just one culture, or were at least willing to recognize and respect the beauty, richness, and dignity of others. The world would be a better place if individuals could find and embrace the intersection of cultures.

Andrew and I were the East and the West coming together, international development and poetry intermingling. Fusion was happening.

CHAPTER TWENTY

A WEDDING IN FREIKE

As I said earlier, the years 1979 and 1980 were unique for Andrew and me.

Poetry was a major force in our lives. I was writing more than in previous years, and Andrew never stopped writing. I loved watching him on Saturday or Sunday morning at home in our sunroom, sipping coffee and writing. He often would lift his face to the sun and close his eyes while the muse inspired him.

I loved his poems, and he loved mine. At some point, he decided to translate my poems into English. I was a little surprised since Andrew did not read Arabic. When I asked how he would handle the translation, he suggested that we choose a poem of mine and then I would read it slowly, several times, while he listened to the sounds of the words and their music. After he had the feel of the poem through its language and sounds, he and I would go through the poem line by line and I would explain every word. Then he would render my poem into English. I was skeptical; however, I must admit his translations conveyed the meaning, spirit, images, rhythm, and mood of my poetry in a very transparent and sensitive way.

We gave bilingual poetry readings in many universities and public libraries in Washington, D.C., including Georgetown University, American University, and the Martin Luther King, Jr., Memorial Library. I would read my poems in Arabic and Andrew would read them in English. We deeply enjoyed preparing for these poetry readings, and in dressing up for them. Octive Stevenson, the founder of the "Poets in Person" poetry and literature series at the MLK Library, described our reading as "a special cultural event." He was anxious to present us both after learning that an American poet was translating the work of a Lebanese poet. "An exchange like this is a rare treat for poetry lovers," he said. Following the reading, Stevenson asked Andrew to explain his collaboration with me and to describe the translation process, and Andrew detailed it for him.

In addition to poetry, work, and international business-related travel, our life had many other pleasurable dimensions. Furnishing and decorating our home, entertaining American and international friends, reading by the fireplace, playing tennis—and I should not forget dancing—brought us joy. Andrew was a fabulous dancer, matched only by Ramzi. At that time, Ramzi was engaged to a lovely Australian woman named Karen who worked at the British Embassy. Ramzi, Karen, and their friends loved to go dancing and often invited us to join them at their favorite club, Piers 1, in Washington, D.C. Many Saturday nights saw the four of us staying up till the early hours of the morning having an utterly enjoyable time. Dancing with Andrew made me feel completely free as the rhythm and our bodies became one. It allowed creativity to overflow, and we relished living in the moment, forgetting the before and after.

In December 1979, I flew to Beirut to attend Ramzi and Karen's wedding. Andrew, alas, had responsibilities that prevented him from joining us, though he tried to. There, too, Ramzi, Karen, their close friends, and I danced till the early morning hours.

Since Andrew wanted to get to know my parents and Lebanon well, we spent two weeks in Freike during the summer of 1980. There are no words to describe the bliss I felt watching Andrew and Daddy sipping tea or coffee on the Freike balcony, discussing a wide range of topics from American, Lebanese, and Arab poetry to political and cultural changes in the U.S. and international development. They reviewed Lebanon's contributions to the West's heritage and shared memories of New York City; they compared the cosmopolitan side of Beirut and village life in the mountains of Lebanon. Andrew wrote many poems on our balcony, among them a much-cherished one about my beloved mountain Sannine, a majestic 8,622-feet that was usually covered with snow even into the early summer months. Lebanon and my family enamored Andrew. His discussions with Daddy were every bit as broad ranging, deep, and intellectual as he could have wanted; with Mommy, his communication was through silent interaction filled with love; and with my brothers, it was a celebration. They talked about local politics; Western and Lebanese music; European, American, and Lebanese art; and their professional lives.

With Freike as our home base, Andrew and I took the opportunity to spend several days visiting Lebanon's cities, ancient ruins, and mountain towns. Beirut and Byblos were at the top of the list. In Beirut, I showed him the apartment on Hamra Street where we had lived for many years, and took him to the lovely American University of Beirut's campus that sits on sixty acres right by the Mediterranean. Andrew and I discussed how AUB remained a positive force of good for the entire region.

In the northern coastal city of Byblos, we visited a site where, it is said, the world's first alphabet was invented, and the confluence of Phoenician, Greek, Roman, Crusader, and Ottoman civilizations exists.

Since we did not want the enchantment of those two weeks in Lebanon to end, rather than flying straight back to Washington, Andrew and I spent three or four days in our two favorite European cities: Venice and Paris. We arrived in Venice giddy with happiness. Andrew asked me to dress up before we went to San Marco. I wore a long white dress and a fuchsia shall. He dressed in white and wore a wide-brimmed white hat. As we walked from our hotel to Piazza San Marco, people must have thought we were celebrities because many stopped to stare and snap photos. What they were seeing were two people who were deeply in love and who found only beauty in the world. Sitting in a café trottoire in Piazza San Marco in Venice, Andrew proposed. Tears fell down my cheeks as I said yes.

Venice remains forever the most gorgeous poem I've heard. Andrew proposing in San Marco is a poem that was more beautiful to me than anything anyone ever wrote, and more beautiful than Beethoven's Ninth Symphony. Our days and nights in Venice and Paris were a crescendo of happiness.

In Paris, we agreed that the wedding would take place in Freike during the summer of 1981.

The fall of 1980 and the first eight months of 1981 were bursting at the seams. Both Andrew and I were totally dedicated to the quality and results of the programs and projects we were leading at PfP and TransCentury; we were committed to every community, region, and country we worked with in Africa, the Middle East, and the Caribbean; and we were involved in the planning of our wedding.

Our professional lives were hectic on their own, yet in addition; we had to manage wedding preparations at a site nearly halfway around the world. I do not know if we truly realized what it meant to be president and vice president of two different organizations, to assume all the responsibilities our jobs demanded, and to add to that the preparation of a long-distance wedding.

As if all of these responsibilities were not enough, in the fall of 1980, I was elected to the advisory board of the newly formed Women in International Development group at Harvard and MIT. Earlier in 1979, Natalie Hann, the study group leader at Harvard, had invited me to meet with the group to give a presentation about my work in Africa. As a result of that meeting, I was invited to join the WID advisory board. Further, Andrew and I were traveling extensively to launch or monitor sites where our respective programs were being implemented. Andrew went to Africa several times, and a couple of times to the Caribbean. I shuttled between the U.S. and Morocco, Tunisia, Mali, and Uganda, and managed to attend the second International Women's Conference in Copenhagen, Denmark.

Between business trips, our wedding plans were formulated. Andrew and I thoroughly enjoyed the preparations—selecting the music and readings, compiling guest lists, and making travel arrangements. We wanted our wedding invitations to appear in both English and in Arabic, and we found a skilled Arabic calligrapher who helped us design them and prepare the text. We were determined that planning a long-distance wedding would be delightful despite all the potential complications.

Summer 1981 arrived. At the end of August, Andrew and I flew to Lebanon. Ramzi and Karen, as well as Sarmad and his family, joined us there, and three close friends—Genie Holmes from Washington D.C., and Lisa and Ken Sullivan from New York—also flew in. The first few days of September were gorgeous. Daddy and every member of the Rihani family participated in decorating our Freike home and garden in preparation for the ceremony. The day of the wedding, September fifth, our home and its garden were covered in white: white flowers in the living rooms, in the dining room, on the balcony; and white butterflies made of organza at the entrance of the house and from the garden trees.

A little after four in the afternoon, Daddy entered the living room where I waited with my flower girls, Ameen's daughters Serene and Reem, and our ring boy, Cedar, Sarmad's son. Daddy put his arm around me and told me it was time to walk out to the garden where an altar was set and our friends were gathered. A rush of emotions and feelings overtook me as I realized that in an hour or so, I would be married to Andrew. I am not sure I know how to describe what I felt; floating with happiness is an understatement.

The Freike garden was transformed to an open-air church. Over two hundred guests were seated there, with Andrew waiting by the altar. The Maronite priests and Protestant ministers conducted the wedding in both English and Arabic. My maid of honor was Fadia Riachi Maalouf from my high school and AUB days, and Andrew's best man was my brother Ramzi. Our dancing nights in D.C. made them very close. The music during the wedding included selections from Beethoven's Ninth Symphony, Pachelbel's Canon in D, and music composed and performed by Ken Sullivan. Ameen and Sarmad read passages from Ameen Rihani's writings. Before exchanging vows, Andrew and I read a short poem. He began:

> Your eyes have become my home
> You are no more distinguished from light
> Than is the sunbeam from the beholder's sight

I replied:

> You are sitting at the right side of everything
> And I am your source and your mirror.

Then we said our vows, gave each other rings, were declared husband and wife, and kissed. Love was truly in the air. Happiness hovered around the guests. The pine trees at the entrance of the Freike home rejoiced, while the butterflies that decorated the house and the garden fluttered their wings. Andrew and I were transported to a magical world.

We mingled with our family members and friends during the cocktail reception, half aware of what was going on and half sailing on cloud nine. The celebration included politicians, writers, poets, university professors, artists, media representatives, the Freike community, friends from my AUB days, and many young professionals. Both Bashir Gemayel and Amine Gemayel, who later became presidents of Lebanon, were present. The Lebanese media covered our wedding extensively, and *Al Hasna'* and *Fayrouz* magazines each had a spread of several pages. On the cover of *Fayrouz*, one of the titles read, "The Rihanis marry from other civilizations."

Andrew and I had planned a honeymoon in seven Asian countries. We started in India, and continued on to Nepal, Bangladesh, Thailand, Indonesia, the Philippines, and Hong Kong. Except for India, those were new countries to me. Discovering new cultures is one of the ecstasies of life, more so when I was able to discover those countries with the man I loved and admired so much.

We visited a number of Buddhist temples and Hindu temples in India, Nepal, and Thailand. Small boats carried us on river trips in Thailand and Bangladesh. In India, Nepal, Bangladesh, and

Indonesia, we rode rickshaws. We enjoyed art in Indonesia, Thailand, and Hong Kong, and exotic foods in Nepal, Bangladesh, Indonesia, and the Philippines. Flower necklaces adorned us in Thailand and the Philippines, and we stayed in gorgeous hotels in Thailand and Hong Kong. The special, unique charm of every country we visited enchanted us; after all, we were so much in love, we saw everything through the lens of total happiness.

In Bombay, India (presently Mumbai), we stayed with a friend of Andrew's. The family was charming and hospitable. They took us around Bombay and explained that the architecture of the city is a mixture of Gothic, Indian, Art Deco, and other contemporary styles. Andrew's friend said that most of the buildings constructed during the British period, such as the Victoria Station and Bombay University, were built in the Gothic Revival style. Their architectural features include a variety of European influences and traditional Indian features. We ate lots of Indian cuisine, and I was not good at distinguishing the differences between the varieties of dishes offered. I felt curry dominated all other flavors. One thing though that I distinctly remember is that at the home of our Indian friends, I was introduced to chutney, which I really liked.

In Nepal, we stayed at a small boutique hotel. Nepal is wedged between the high walls of the Himalaya and the steamy jungles of the Indian plains. It is a land of snow peaks and old temples, serenity and mystery, yaks and yetis, monasteries and mantras. I immediately fell in love with the country. I felt that peace inhabited Nepal and I enjoyed its old traditions. Kathmandu is located in a very green valley surrounded by mountains. The valley is the home of the three ancient cities of Kathmandu, Patan, and Bhaktapur, and we visited many Buddhist temples there. The three cities housed seven UNESCO-designated World Heritage shrines as well as hundreds of other exquisite monuments, sculptures, artistic temples, and magnificent art.

Andrew and I took a rickshaw from Katmandu to Bhaktapur. Midway, Andrew decided that the skinny young man pulling the rickshaw might be tired, so he decided to walk. Then he convinced the young man that he would like to experience pulling the rickshaw. After several minutes of explanations in English, the young man allowed Andrew to pull the rickshaw and me for just a few minutes. It was a unique scene. Young Nepali men pulled all the rickshaws surrounding us, and mine was pulled by an American man with blond hair.

The natural beauty on the way to Bhaktapur was overwhelming, and once we arrived, we were stunned by its historic and artistic beauty. The square in the middle of Bhaktapur was by far the most elegant we had seen in Nepal. It has a large open space surrounded by a palace and several temples that date from the thirteenth to the eighteenth century. The extraordinary square with its breathtaking temples and palace reflected the glory days of the Malla Dynasty when art and architecture thrived in the three cities of the valley. The fifteenth-century Palace of 55 Carved Windows and its entrance, the Golden Gate, is a masterpiece which added splendor to the area. In front of the palace building are architectural showpieces and innumerable temples filled with intricate carvings and exotic statutes. Bhaktapur took us to a place where humans and gods live together, and where art, architecture, spirituality, peace, and incense are fused.

Andrew absolutely wanted to have Bangladesh be part of our honeymoon, so we went to Dhaka. It is another crowded, overpopulated city that suffers from many urban problems including pollution and chaotic city traffic. However, I loved Dhaka. The gentility of the people, the kindness of the rickshaw drivers, and the willingness of everyone we encountered during our few days in the city to remain optimistic despite the urban challenges, and regardless of poverty, all gave Dhaka a special flavor. The Buddhist and Hindu cultures co-mingle in Dhaka, and poverty made us, those coming from outside, reflective, thoughtful, and less self-centered.

In Bangkok, Thailand, we stayed at the Oriental Hotel. Warren's wedding gift to us was four nights in the Joseph Conrad Suite of this legendary hotel located on the banks of the Chao Ohraya River. It is known to have received literary legends such as Somerset Maugham, Joseph Conrad, James Michener, and Noel Coward, and there are suites named after each of them. Warren knew that staying in one of those rooms would add a special touch to our honeymoon, and it did; the poets in us loved being in the presence of Joseph Conrad.

Andrew and I often took riverboat trips on the Chao Ohraya River. We had learned that Thailand is ninety-five percent Buddhist and that there are hundreds of lovely Buddhist temples in Bangkok. Andrew and I decided to visit five or six of the most famous ones. Among those we visited were the Reclining Buddha Temple with its huge, lying-down Buddha; the War Arun Temple, or the Temple of Dawn, that is covered with Chinese ceramics and sits on the west bank of the river; and the Wat Phra Kaew, the temple of the Emerald Buddha that enshrines one of Thailand's most revered Buddha statues which is carved out of a single block of jade. My lessons in Buddhism came through the deep knowledge and admiration that Andrew had for this peaceful Oriental religion.

After Bangkok, we spent two days in Jakarta, Indonesia. At that time, in1981, Jakarta was extremely crowded and noisy, yet also cosmopolitan—a city of contrasts. The city is a mixture of languages and cultures, poverty and wealth. Andrew and I spent two evenings in Jakarta's famous nightclubs and we danced till dawn.

In the afternoons, after sleeping in the mornings, we visited the National Museum and the old section of the city.

From Jakarta we flew to Manila, where we spent just three days. We were interested in exploring the key sights in and around Intramuros, the city's only notable historical enclave. The stone houses and grassy courtyards of Intramuros remained as they were when the Spanish were in the Philippines. Manila prides itself on the quality of its nightlife, and Andrew and I went to a different club every night. Dancing with Andrew will always be one of the most enjoyable memories in my life, and I remember Manila as a city where people dance till the early hours of the morning and where Andrew bought me many flower necklaces.

In Hong Kong, Andrew and I splurged on the luxury of the super-chic Mandarin Hotel located in the heart of the city. After our first stroll in the city, we realized how densely populated and constructed Honk Kong is. The city is so incredibly vertical, I think I was looking up most of the time while we explored. It reminded me of New York. I felt these two cities had an important feature in common: they love reaching out to the sky. On the other hand, Hong Kong is very different from New York in that it has an old-world dimension. After all, Hong Kong is the place where China meets England, reflecting the culture's mix of its Chinese roots with influences from its time as a British colony. The modern and the traditional coexist on a daily basis as Hong Kong balances a contemporary way of life with traditional Chinese practices. Modern architecture lives side-by-side with superstitious traditions; buildings floors often skip the number four due to the similarity of the word "four" and the word for "die" in Cantonese. Both Andrew and I were fascinated by Hong Kong, and we bought a Chinese painting that in 1981 was over 150 years old.

What a honeymoon! Discovering new worlds; learning about a new religion; appreciating a totally different sense of beauty; embracing new forms of art; recognizing that diversity is what makes human beings more humane; and most of all, deeply learning to be appreciative within both very rich and luxurious surroundings as well as in very poor and dire surroundings. I have to admit that our honeymoon was not only about intellectual, artistic, and spiritual pleasures, but also about other vibrant pleasures that were a part of every day and every night of our honeymoon. I thought only Andrew could make all of this happen at the same time.

Andrew wrote many poems about our honeymoon. I did as well.

The titles of Andrew's poems were: "Honeymoon"; "Nepal, Mount Everest and Rice"; "The Emerald Buddha"; "The Temple of Dawn, Bangkok"; "Rickshaws and the Silent Racket"; "Champagne Room, Manila Hotel"; "New York/Hong Kong"; and "Making Love". The poems I wrote, inspired by our wedding and honeymoon, were in Arabic; the translations of the titles are: "A Poet, an Angel, and The Pine Tree"; "The Desert is a Woman in Love"; and "The Tenth Symphony."

Back to Washington, D.C., in the fall of 1981. Our lives resumed the hectic and rich pattern of two international development executives who were also avid poets. This meant enormous work responsibilities; more work travel—Andrew to Africa, Asia, and the Caribbean, and me to Africa and the Middle East; and more poetry writing and poetry evenings.

Something had happened that made Warren start writing poetry, and he decided that we would have evening poetry readings at TransCentury. Ten-to-fifteen poetry lovers would gather once a month, with the three regular readers: Andrew, Warren, and I. Often we invited others to read with us. I was delighted that Professor Abdul Aziz Said of American University often joined us to share the poetry of Rumi, Hafez, and other Sufi poets. During these gatherings, Lebanon and the U.S. merged, Buddhism and Sufism were fused, and international development and literature co-mingled. Warren was a master host and facilitator.

In 1982, I gave and participated in many poetry readings. One took place on March 7 on the occasion of International Women's Day. The Washington Women's Arts Center invited me to read with two other women poets, one from Cuba and the other from Panama.

Another poetry reading was held at Duke University. Professor Myriam Cook invited me to spend a day at the University to share my poetry with her Middle Eastern literature class and to discuss poetry with her students. As a result of these classes, Robert Statloff wrote on March 22 in Duke University's daily newspaper *The Chronicle*:

> Losing something in the translation is the stigma that Lebanese poet May Rihani and her husband, Andrew Oerke, have successfully overcome…Rihani, whose poetry often reflects her personal experiences in Beirut during the 1975-76 Lebanese war, and Oerke have devised a novel system for rendering the rhythm and tone of Arabic poetry into English. The couple read several of Rihani's unpublished poem—she in Arabic, he in English. "First, I absorb the sound and music of a poem," said Oerke, his wife's translator, the author of two books, and the former poet in residence at St. Andrew's College in North Carolina. He and Rihani then described a system of "free translation"

followed by a more liberal rendering. Once the couple has completed "the full circle," Oerke said, he listens to the poem once again to make sure he has captured the work's original rhythm. The task is formidable indeed to move freely from one language to another, Oerke said. Rihani read poetry written both before and after the war including one piece finished just one month ago. In recent years, Rihani said she has been able to deal more rationally with the war... "The deep pain is still there but now I can see why it is there." Rihani refused to classify her work within the bounds of a particular category, preferring to let it reflect her emotions and beliefs.

Below is one of the poems about the Lebanese war of the late 1970s that was translated by Andrew. I often read it in Arabic and Andrew read it in English in many of our poetry evenings:

A Certain Wednesday Night

Joy rides a winged white horse
I heard Joy calling:
I approached him slowly
He said: "Drink the water of the moon on the seventh
     day of each month
Light the olive tree standing straight as a temple in
     front of the castle
Without kindling a fire.
Draw a question mark on the face of the wind
And write his name on the breaking foam of the waves.

Sleep ten days and nights without closing an eyelid
Then wake up and follow me."
I did.

The white winged horse and Joy riding him grew
    even more spectacular.
While I was approaching
I heard him say
"To enter my kingdom
Wash your face with the ashes of the burnt houses,
Under the city bridge lies the corpse of a young man
Carry it to the sea.
On your way to the sea
Stop at the crossroad where women are repeating the
    names of those who left.
Repeat with them for seven months.
Then cross the river
And go to the other side
And search for a woman whose three sons died on a
    Wednesday night.
Tell her ..."

And the winged white horse rose into the sky
The voice disappeared
And Joy became a white dot on a white sketch in a
    gloomy sky.

In 1982, the Lebanese press continued covering my activities, especially my literary activities, and I was interviewed several times by major Lebanese media reporters. One interview that I particularly liked was with Akl Al Aweet. It was published in *An-Nahar* on October 17.

Akl started the lengthy article with this opening paragraph: "After five years of living in the United States, the Lebanese poet May Rihani came back to visit Freike, the playground of her nostalgia, youth, and memories. She came back to be in touch with the land and the people, and to be closer to her roots."

Akl asked perceptive and tough questions. During the interview, we discussed what it meant to not live in one's original country. We covered language, poetry, a writer/poet living in a land that does not speak her mother tongue, belonging and not belonging, the meaning of living in the U.S., the American culture and how a non-American interacts with it, engaging with a new culture, trying hard to understand human behavior within the context of a new culture, the act of multiplying our perspectives, poetry in the U.S., and how the U.S. impacted my way of writing.

I replied, in part:

> Even language cannot entirely express the feelings that one goes through when we live abroad. Despite language's richness, it becomes a limited tool when a poet wants to write about existential topics such as not living in one's original country. For a writer or a poet, the most difficult dimension of living abroad is language. I write in Arabic while I live in the U.S. When I write in Arabic, I do not have an immediate audience. I miss my audience; I miss my readers, and their reactions to my writings. While I am writing in Arabic in Washington D.C., I often feel like an actor who goes on stage to perform and discovers that the

theater is empty. My first reaction was not to perform, not to write; however, I could not live with such a solution, so I went back to writing. Writing was my solution. My passion is writing.

You asked me about if I always feel like a stranger in the U.S.; well, the answer is not at all. Even though I am often nostalgic, and Lebanon and Freike live within me, I enjoy living in the U.S. You might be surprised when I tell you it is extremely difficult to be neutral when you live within the American culture. You have to interact with this dynamic culture. I deeply feel that when you live within the American culture you have to become an active person within this culture. You can reject the culture, you can study it, you can fight it, you can accept it, you can add to it, but it is very hard to be indifferent or neutral towards the American culture. I found myself being enriched by this new culture. I felt like I am living in a place where many new windows get opened every day. I loved the fact that newness and new winds are so much part of the American culture and I embraced this fact. I loved it, I flourished within it. Sometimes, I found myself worried about not being faithful to my original culture, to my Lebanese culture. I felt as if I needed to protect my Lebanese culture from this new and powerful culture, the American one. Finally, I understood that I can embrace both of them, live and interact with both of them. I understood that I did not have to choose between the two and my loyalty can be for both; I understood that it is not an either/or. As if I experienced an epiphany the day I felt I can belong to both the Lebanese and the American cultures.

Towards the end of the interview, I mentioned to Akl that the fact that I feel I belong to both cultures was made easier because I married a poet who is extremely sensitive and who deeply appreciates different cultures and languages.

This wonderful interview, like many others, took place on the balcony of my parent's home in Freike. Being in Lebanon, in Freike itself, was going to the source of pure water, drinking and cleansing my soul at one time.

My life seemed perfect. Perhaps living in the U.S. with Andrew and working in international development, traveling to Africa and the Middle East for work, writing poetry, and visiting Freike and being with Mommy and Daddy once or even twice a year was too beautiful. Something had to interfere with this bliss.

It is hard to write about what disturbed this idyllic situation.

I wanted to have children, and Andrew, who shared so much of my soul and heart, was not able to warm up to my inner need. He believed our love was great and complete, and that we did not need anything more. Andrew felt that children would disturb our marvelous life together. I disagreed and explained in very clear terms why I needed to experience motherhood and how much that meant to me. Even today, nearly thirty years later, it is hard to write about this impasse. Suffice it to say, this became the issue that divided us. Andrew and I did not share the same vision. He was satisfied and I wanted more; I wanted my own children.

I thought I would be able to bring him around, so I did not press the issue at first. I did not want our happiness to be marred by anything, not even my dream of having children. I wanted to remain on cloud nine, and I did. During the day, I immersed myself in international development and in gaining a deeper understanding of the global village; in the evening, I stayed busy with poetry, stimulating intellectual discussions, and a rich social life; and at night, through the magic of physical love that is capable of allowing an experience of transcendentalism, I floated.

Even though 1980 to 1982 were years of bliss on the personal front—excluding my unfulfilled desire for motherhood—I continued to worry about what was happening in Lebanon. There were short periods of calm, like the period when Andrew and I got married, followed by continued violence. Different Lebanese factions, backed by different groups in the Middle East, fought over what they believed to be noble objectives.

Those who believed in the sovereignty of Lebanon were not going to give up until the Lebanese government regained full power over every inch of Lebanon's territory, but those who felt marginalized continued their struggle as well. Palestinian guerrillas and Israeli troops traded rocket fire across the Israeli–Lebanese border. In 1978, Israel had taken over a strip of southern Lebanon and continued to occupy it in defiance of UN Resolution 425, which called for an immediate and unconditional withdrawal.

By 1982, Israel became concerned that the PLO in Lebanon was gaining additional strength, and on June 3, a renegade anti-PLO Palestinian faction attempted to assassinate Israel's ambassador in London. The British police immediately identified Abu Nidal's forces as responsible, and revealed that PLO leaders themselves were among the names on the would-be assassins' hit list. The PLO had nothing to do with the London attack which left the ambassador unharmed, but Israel claimed the attempt was justification for war.

Three days later, on June 6, 1982, the Israeli army invaded Lebanon in operation "Peace for Galilee," crossing the Litani River and moving as far north as Beirut. They destroyed the feeble resistance from local villagers and the United Nations peacekeeping troops were swept aside during the assault. Israel remained in virtually uncontested control of the air and had overwhelming military superiority on land and sea. Beirut was besieged and subjected to merciless bombing for two months. Casualties were enormous, totaling more than 17,000 Lebanese and Palestinians, mostly civilians. Hospitals were hit, roads in southern Lebanon were destroyed, and the Palestinian refugee camps were leveled in massive bombardment.

Israel's invasion of southern Lebanon and the brutal violence they used to destroy the country's infrastructure while leveling the Palestinian camps became the nightmare of every Lebanese. For many days after the invasion, I woke up in the middle of the night worrying about an escalation of what was already an impossible situation.

CHAPTER TWENTY-ONE

LEBANON, NEW YORK, AND ZAIRE

G RADUALLY, THE CONTRADICTIONS IN MY life became more and more apparent. A good part of Lebanon was under occupation and the Lebanese population continued to suffer the atrocities of war, yet my personal and professional life continued to flourish.

My global travels deepened my commitment to working closer with the underprivileged and to sharpening my skills as a designer of programs aimed at improving the lives of women in the different countries and communities where my TransCentury team worked. I loved and cherished many things about international travel, including the fact that it permitted me to stop in Lebanon at least twice a year. During some years, I was able to see my parents even more often. During these visits, I had three priorities: seeing my parents and serving them, even if only for four or five days; staying in touch with the poets and writers of Lebanon; and catching up with the region's difficult and complex political developments, specifically how the geopolitical events of the area were impacting Lebanon. When I was not there in person, I followed the events daily.

On August 23, 1982, Bashir Gemayel, the leader of the Lebanese Forces which represented a segment of the Christians, was elected president of Lebanon. On September 1, 1982, one week after his election, he met with Israeli Prime Minister Menachem Begin. Israeli forces were occupying large portions of southern Lebanon. During their meeting, Begin demanded that Lebanon sign a peace treaty with Israel as soon as Gemayel took office. He also told Gemayel that Israel intended to stay in Lebanon until a peace treaty was signed.

Bashir Gemayel was furious and told Begin that the Lebanese hadn't fought for seven years and sacrificed thousands of soldiers and civilians to free Lebanon from the Syrian Army and the PLO in order for Israel to take their place. Gemayel also said that he would not sign the peace treaty without national consensus on the matter. He explained to Begin that he would seek the approval of Lebanon's parliament before agreeing to anything. The meeting was entirely dissatisfactory for both parties.

Even though President Gemayel was considered a leader of Lebanon's Christians when he was elected, he worked hard to represent all Lebanese and to unite the population. He met with Muslim, Druze, and Christian leaders and declared in the first week after his election that he would consistently work for a united, free, democratic, independent Lebanon that was pluralistic. He stated that Muslims and Christians could once again live together in peace, and that Lebanon needed to maintain good relations with the West as well as with the Arab world. He sought the withdrawal of Syrian forces that had occupied large parts of Lebanon since 1975, as well as the withdrawal of Israeli forces which had occupied the water-rich south since June 1982. He also wanted to disarm the Palestinian forces in Lebanon that had created a state within a state. He went beyond confessional conflicts to pursue the goal of uniting a sovereign, modern, and democratic Lebanon.

Exhausted by so many years of war and terror under foreign occupation, the Lebanese people welcomed such a discourse. They yearned for an end to violence and to the return of their independence and peace. Hope slowly reentered the minds and spirits of the people. Some Lebanese immigrants started thinking of returning to Lebanon; however, just three weeks after his election, President-elect Bashir Gemayel was assassinated by a pro-Syrian operative.

Andrew and I were in Lebanon when the assassination occurred. We witnessed first-hand the devastation and deep disappointment of many people who shared, with us, the broken dream of a united and free Lebanon. We saw how their dreams of a united Lebanon had grown larger and clearer when they watched on television as many Sunni, Shia, and Druze leaders such as Prime Minister Saeb Salam and Speaker of the Parliament Kamel El Assad meet with President-elect Bashir Gemayel to discuss the future of Lebanon. They had been praying for an end to war; they were hoping for an Israeli withdrawal, a Syrian withdrawal, and a sovereign Lebanon; but suddenly their dreams were shattered. Listening to many Lebanese during the week after Bashir's assassination, I heard the voices of disappointment, grief, sadness, broken dreams, and despair.

At the end of September 1982, Andrew and I flew back to the Washington, D.C. I was terribly concerned about the future of Lebanon, and fearful about the coming few years.

Back in DC, I again immersed myself in my work. International educational development energized me and lifted my spirits. In 1983, I was selected to the U.S. Global Advisory Board of the International Exposition of Rural Development. I was honored to be in the company of illustrious board members such as Robert McNamara, former president of the World Bank; Cyrus Vance, former Secretary of State; Andrew Young, Mayor of Atlanta and former Ambassador to the UN; and John Sewell, the president of the Overseas Development Council.

At home, life with Andrew was a continuous celebration. We were kindred spirits, truly global citizens with an abundance of love for all the cultures of the world. He and I wanted our efforts to be dedicated to those who were less privileged and those who did not have a voice; to the rural farmer in Senegal, the remote illiterate woman in Malawi, and the suffering people of countries in conflict such as Lebanon. The only difference was that I *became* a global citizen while he was probably born that way. Lebanon was my springboard. I used my love of Lebanon as a source to be able to love the rest of the world. He did not need a springboard or starting point. Andrew hit the global ground running. I understood that global ground from the perspective that I loved my Lebanon. I understood the local issues of Lebanon. I understood the diversity of Lebanon, and therefore I could translate that into programs for the world and become deeply committed to those issues while embracing the diversity of the world.

Two intellectuals, two executives, two professionals, two poets, two global citizens, two explorers, two travelers, two individuals committed to serving others, who happen to be in love and sharing their life—what could be better? I thought nothing...other than my abiding desire for becoming a mother.

In addition to our global travel, Andrew loved traveling within the U.S. Whenever we had a free weekend, we ended up in New York. Gideon Waldrop of Julliard often invited us to stay with him at his penthouse. When we were with Gideon, we read poetry, Gideon played the piano, and we watched the Hudson River and the bridges of New York from the penthouse balcony. Andrew and I saw Broadway shows together, visited the Metropolitan Museum of Art and the Museum of Modern Art over and over again, ate at fabulous restaurants like The Pierre and The Green, walked in Central Park, and had wonderful lengthy discussions. Through the eyes of Andrew, I began learning to appreciate American art. Among my favorites became Edward Hopper, Andrew Wyeth, Winslow Homer, John Singer Sargent, and others. During one of our visits with Gideon, we spent the weekend at his Woodstock home and took a long walk in the woods. We talked at length about Emerson, Thoreau, and Robert Frost. Back at Gideon's home, we read Andrew's poem "In the Village" that he had written in Malawi. I read "A Certain Wednesday Night," a poem I had just written a few months earlier about the events in Lebanon, and Gideon read "The Road Not Taken" by Robert Frost. In the early evening, I prepared kibbe, loubieh bi zeit, and hummos, a Lebanese meal that both Andrew and Gideon loved.

My professional career and international travel took new turns all the time. My previous work-related trips, until 1983, were either to deliver training like in Liberia, Sierra Leone, and Tunisia; to understand a context better so I could design a long-term program as I did for Morocco and Senegal; to assess and promote women's participation in different developmental sectors as in Tunisia, Egypt, Sudan, Iraq, Kuwait, and the United Arab Emirates; to participate in conferences like in Romania, Mexico, and India; or to negotiate contracts with governments and USAID like in Morocco. However, a particularly unique trip was my first visit to Zaire, now the Democratic Republic of Congo. I went there in 1983, shortly after the devaluation of its currency, the zaire.

The Zaire trip was different: my task was to research and analyze the relationship between poverty in rural agricultural areas and the access of children to schools, in particular girls—a fascinating topic. I was asked to spend a month in some of the rural areas around Kikwit in the province of Bandundu to analyze that particular dimension of poverty and its impact on girls' schooling. Of course I read many relevant documents before I embarked on this trip, which was absolutely necessary. It was essential to keep in mind that the real in-depth learning would happen after I arrived.

I started my assignment with a series of meetings at the USAID Mission in Kinshasa, the capital of Zaire. One of these meetings had to do with security. The embassy officer gave me a map of the country and pointed out boundaries outlined in red that he made clear I was not to cross. When I asked why, he rebuffed me and said, "Just don't cross them." I persisted, pointing out that I needed to know if I wanted to ensure that my driver didn't cross into those areas. He hedged, but I insisted on clarity. I was, of course, aware of political tensions among different tribes in Zaire, as well as problems Zaire had with neighboring countries. Finally, he stated that there had been several instances of kidnappings, disappearances, rape, and killings in the areas outlined in red. Such was Zaire in 1983. I obeyed the guidelines.

The next day, I returned to the embassy to exchange U.S. dollars for zaires, the local currency. The first difficulty I faced was that the exchange desk did not have sufficient zaires. I needed to stay at a hotel in Kikwit for a month and would have to pay in cash since many remote African establishments did not accept credit cards. The cashier explained that the zaire has been devalued to such an extent that he would need a huge amount of bills to make the exchange. He suggested that I exchange the equivalent of $100 or $200 for zaires that he had on hand, and that he would send the rest with an American NGO staff member who would be going to Kikwit a few days later. I accepted his offer.

I knew I had to pay for the hotel room and food for a month, for the driver's salary, as well as for incidental expenses including gas for the car; however, I did not anticipate how many notes I would be given in exchange for the U.S. dollars I presented. The Zaire currency had been devalued 3,500 percent very quickly, and the government had not had the time to print new notes for larger amounts. I understood the situation and empathized with the people whose lives must be in turmoil because of that situation, but I was at a loss what to do.

Finally, I realized that if I emptied my briefcase of all the documents I had, I could stuff most of the notes he piled in front of me inside the case and secret the rest in my purse and pockets. That seemed to work. My documents went into a cloth bag; the notes hidden away in my briefcase, purse, pockets, and wallet; and I left the embassy sort of ready for my assignment in Kikwit. I reminded myself repeatedly not to open my briefcase in public. I could only imagine the scene that might follow.

And so, armed with a small part of the zaire notes I would need to pay for my month, I started my trip to Kikwit and a new adventure in the African heartland, but I didn't doubt my ability to make it work.

The next day my driver picked me up and I left for Kikwit. It took nearly eight hours for our Land Rover to get there. The roads were rough and comprised of bumps and holes. When we finally arrived that evening, I was thoroughly exhausted. The manager of the small hotel who was expecting me explained that the hotel did not have electricity all the time. Some days, we might have electricity for few hours; on other days, we would not. He also said this situation applied to water as well. We could go for several days without water. I began to worry. I knew I could live on very little food, but doing without hot water and a shower was a far greater privation. I asked what the hotel did when the water was cut off, and he assured me they would send a bucket filled with water to each room so the guests could shower and take care of other needs.

I knew I was in for seriously new experiences. I had to learn how to cope with conditions I was not used to whatsoever. Again, this was 1983—way before laptops, smartphones, and other devices that link us to the outside world in seconds. My only way of communicating with Andrew, my colleagues and staff at TransCentury, and my parents and brothers, was through written letters. A letter from Kikwit to Washington would take two to three weeks, and letters to Lebanon might be a month or more. But there I was in Kikwit, by myself, having to live and work for a month under those trying conditions without being able to communicate with family, colleagues, and friends.

I realized I needed to dig deep into my reservoir of courage and strength to move ahead. I went up to my room, stuck my briefcase filled with zaires under my mattress, and had a good night's sleep.

Very early the next morning, I reviewed the plan my staff and I had set up for my fieldwork. The governor of Bandundu had invited me to meet him at 10:00 a.m. I needed to explain the objectives of my visit and get his approval to travel to the proposed villages. I also needed to ensure that he would dispatch a representative of the governorate to accompany me when I visited the chiefs, schools, and marketplaces in the villages. I wanted to fill him in on additional details such as community meetings with farmers, teachers, parents, and community and religious leaders to gather information for my research project.

The driver took me to the governor's office. I was able to navigate my way with French as most of the employees spoke it well enough for us to understand each other. I arrived a little before the appointed time and was well received by the governor, who was interested in my assignment and my proposed plans. He agreed to my proposals and reminded me that few people in those villages would be able to speak French. I asked about the teachers, and he acknowledged that they generally spoke French but that the rest—the parents, farmers, and community leaders—would not. I explained that I planned to ask a teacher in each village to be my interpreter, but the governor offered a better idea. Since I had asked him to provide a representative of the governorate to accompany me, he would choose someone who knew the local language and who could serve as a translator as well.

This was a good start. I asked if he could dispatch a representative as early as the next morning and he happily agreed. His positive attitude was encouraging; he did not allow bureaucratic procedures to become obstacles and delay the launch of my fieldwork.

In the afternoon, I spent nearly three hours studying maps of Bandundu learning the names of the villages I was going to visit. I worked with my driver to calculate the distances between one village and another in order to gauge how many villages I could visit in a week. I verified the names and locations of each community and prepared in detail the questions for the teachers, farmers, parents, and community leaders.

The background documents I brought with me were good references; they helped clarify the picture in terms of educational statistics and agricultural information of the region. I found the FAO and UNESCO information to be invaluable.

As I was reading more of these documents, the management of the hotel arrived to say that an American man was asking about me. I came down to the lobby to find the NGO representative the cashier of the U.S. embassy had promised. The young man asked that I step outside to the parking with him to get my money from his car. I was a little puzzled that he did not bring the money with him to the lobby; however, I went with the flow and walked with him to the parking lot. Again, I was puzzled when he did not open one of the car doors to retrieve a briefcase or something similar, but instead opened the trunk and pointed to a large wooden chest.

"This is your money," he said.

I did not immediately comprehend that the funds I had requested filled an entire chest. It was far too big for me to carry or even lift. I asked, "What do you mean 'this is your money'?" I had momentarily forgotten that the cashier at the U.S. embassy had explained the situation with the devaluation of the zaire.

The young man said the cashier had entrusted him to give me the necessary notes in Kikwit, so here he was, and here was the money in a wooden chest. He opened the chest and my jaw dropped. It was filled to the top with zaire bills. I felt I had been transported to a movie set. I do not know what the movie was about, but I know that one of the scenes was when the actress receives a wooden chest filled with money.

Back to reality. The young NGO man said very matter-of-factly, "I will carry the money chest for you to the lobby." He closed the chest, lifted it with strong arms, and carried it into the hotel. I walked behind him in a total daze. So many questions raced through my head.

Was it safe to have so much money in a hotel in Kikwit? I might be the only white woman in the hotel, and once this young man and I reached the lobby, anyone there would surely notice the wooden chest and wonder what was inside.

How would I get the chest to my room? Did I dare ask one of the porters to carry the chest upstairs?

What if the housekeepers suspected that the chest was filled with money? How great was this risk to my daily life in this hotel?

And so on and so forth—the questions swirled.

The young man was kind and pleasant. After depositing the chest in the lobby, he told me where he would be in Bandundu, and that if I needed any help I could reach him at the NGO office number or on his walkie-talkie. I thanked him and off he went.

There I stood, in the middle of the lobby—or in the middle of nowhere—with a chest filled with zaires. I sat down, tugged the chest nearer to me, and started thinking. What to do? This was really risky business. It was a highly perilous situation. I was more than a little frightened. I questioned how smart my decision was to ask for all of this money to be sent to me. On the other hand, there had been no other way. I had to have funds for a month, and I could not use my credit card in Kikwit or in any town or village I would visit during my month in this region of Bandundu.

After some reflection, I thought of a solution that would minimize my exposure to the risk that I was taking. I knew my idea might not eliminate the danger completely, but it was a start. I tapped my reservoir of courage again and went to the front desk. I told whoever was there that I needed to see the manager of the hotel. The person I spoke with said, "But Madame, tell us what you need and we will do our best to take care of your request." I insisted on speaking with the manager. After some back and forth, he told me to have a seat in the lobby while he asked the manager if he could meet with me.

I waited for a very long half-hour by my wooden chest, carefully observing the expressions of people in the lobby. A great lesson in Zairois facial expressions! However, I am not sure I was a keen observer during that time given how nervous I was. As time passed, I became even more nervous. Finally, the front desk man said the manager would see me. I thanked God that the office was right there and not on the second or third floor. I asked the porter to carry my wooden chest and follow me to the office of the manager.

I arrived in the office with my wooden chest in tow, a sight I am sure the manager had never seen before, and started by thanking him for receiving me. I reminded him that I would be staying at his hotel for one full month, and that I had decided to pay him in advance for my stay.

He politely said in his Zairois French, "But Madame, you do not have to. We received a telegram from an American NGO announcing your arrival two or three weeks ago, and we trust that you will be paying us."

I was relieved. Clearly, he was client-oriented and did not want to offend an American guest; American visitors must have been rare in this region and were likely good clients. He must also value repeat clients, I thought, so his instincts as a good salesman had kicked in. He wanted to assure me that no one in the hotel would ask me to pay in advance.

I explained that I understood, but that I wished to do so voluntarily. After some discussion, he agreed to receive advance payment for the thirty nights I planned to stay. He did his calculations and handed me the bill, stating that I would also be billed for any meals I took at the hotel. I took my time verifying the bill to be certain it was accurate. I did not want him to think that I did not care about the amount I had to pay. After a careful examination of the bill, I told the manager that I understood that the zaire had been devaluated a week or so earlier, and that any payment after the devaluation would require a larger number of bills than before.

He looked at me with an expression that basically communicated the idea: "I do not know why you are explaining to me all of that." I know I perplexed him, but I continued. Given the devaluation, I explained, the American Embassy where I exchanged my money gave me lots of zaire bills. I wanted to mention the American Embassy, believing wrongly or rightly that this could be a kind of protection. In a subtle way, I was conveying the message that I was not a white woman who nobody knew. In addition to my American organization that booked my room, the American Embassy knew where I was.

Then I said I wanted us to count the money together to ensure that I was paying the correct amount for my stay, and that I would need a signed receipt indicating he had been paid in full in advance for the room. As soon as I said this, I opened the wooden chest and the manager's facial expression totally changed. I truly think he was in shock. I honestly think he has never seen before a chest filled with money, and why should he? The zaire has just been devalued, plus, I could have been the first client to book a room for thirty days. This was uncharted territory for both of us.

I had to be smart and act quickly. I had to keep my calm, act as if I were in total control, and show him that what I was doing was normal. I spoke about the devaluation to introduce an element he was not used to and to take charge of the discussion. I did not want his being overwhelmed make him back away from the plan. I had to lead every action; I had to control every reaction; I had to fill the air in the room with a sense of trust and an air of normalcy.

I said I would count the zaires and create piles that equal the amount needed for each night. I asked him to verify each pile and make sure that I was counting correctly. I also said once the thirty piles had been counted and verified, we would have completed the transaction. He would be pleased that I offered to pay in advance, and I would be pleased to get my signed receipt.

I have no idea from where I got the strength and courage to do what I did. He did not know how frightened I was that my plan might not work. He did not know that under a façade of steel, there was a frightened young woman who was not sure how to get out of an immense problem she suddenly found herself in.

I started counting and creating the piles of zaires. He counted each pile to verify. I felt a little better when he agreed with my idea; it meant my plan was working. Still, I was afraid that in the middle of the process he might change his mind, stop counting, and decide to do something else. I think that while I was counting I was praying that nothing would interrupt us. No phone call, no visitor, no outside idea invading his mind. I wanted us to continue counting until we had thirty piles and he had signed a receipt stating I paid for my room in advance.

My goal was to get rid of as much money as I could as soon as possible, and then go up to my room to rest, and possibly cry. I wanted to have a small amount of zaires that I could hide in my briefcase, in my handbag, and possibly in the documents that I would carry with me. I did not want to leave any cash in my room to become a target of temptation for any of the hotel staff. *God please help me, let my plan be completed.* I counted and prayed, and he counted and verified, and the piles added up, from one to five to eight to fifteen to twenty. The sight of every added pile made me feel better. I was coming close to the end of this ordeal…. Pile number twenty-seven, twenty-eight, twenty-nine, and finally thirty.

With a big smile, I said, "Monsieur," —I cannot remember his name now—"I am pleased you verified my payment. I do not want to take more of your time. As soon as you give me the receipt, you will be able to go back to your other business."

He was not so busy, the hotel was not full, but I wanted to give him a sense of importance and let him feel that I understood his time was limited.

I looked at the wooden chest and saw with relief that the remaining amount of zaires was manageable. I asked the manager for a paper bag. He had my advance. He signed a receipt, gave it to me, and was gallant enough to give me a large paper bag. I put the money in the paper bag and gave him the wooden chest as a gift. He was delighted! As a matter of fact, he could not thank me enough. He repeated several times, *"Merci, Madame, pour votre gentillesse et générosité."* He also said several times, *"Madame, nous sommes tous à votre service."*

I thanked him and hurried to my room where I threw myself on my bed and cried with relief. After the tears were spent, I put the remaining zaires in things I could carry around with me. Thank God for my briefcase and a very large handbag. I could not believe that I solved my immense serious problem the same day it was thrown in my lap. *Oouf!* What an ordeal!

I wanted so badly to call Andrew and share with him what happened. I needed to talk about this shocking arrival of a wooden chest filled with money, how risky the situation had been, how frightened I was, and how I solved the problem. I needed Andrew's reassuring voice so I could regain my strength. I needed an intimate connection, but alas, I was in the middle of nowhere and was not able to connect with him.

Oh, what a good night's sleep can do! When I woke up the next day, I felt refreshed, energized, and ready to hit the ground running. I was excited that I was going to visit the first village on my list. By 7:00 a.m., my driver, the governor's representative, and I were once again off on dirt roads heading for our first destination. An hour later we were there. As soon as we drove in, twenty children or more popped out of their huts and started running alongside our vehicle. We stopped; the driver got out of the car and opened the door for me. The minute I got out, I was surrounded by children between the ages of four and perhaps twelve who jumped and talked together. I was delighted to be in the midst of so many happy children.

Some of the children wore torn shorts and T-shirts. Most only had shorts. Nearly all of their clothes were brownish or greyish, and had tears or holes in them. Nearly all of them were barefooted, and their lovely dark, agile bodies were covered with dust. Most important were their smiles—as if they were in the happiest place in the world. They were pleased to see me, a stranger who had landed in their village. I wondered how often they had seen a car in the village. How often did they see a white woman? How often did strangers visit them?

As I pondered these things, more children arrived and their faces and voices filled the space around me. I wanted to remain surrounded by them for a while studying their innocent, perplexed, intelligent, and excited faces; however, the governor's representative said something to them in one of the local Bandundu languages and they dispersed. He then led me a few steps towards where the Chief of the village was waiting for us.

It seemed this whole visit to Bandundu was going to be filled with unexpected events. The representative of the governor, my driver, a large number of children, and I arrived where the Chief with a full band was there to receive us. Several drummers, two players of Mangbetu guitars, and a few singers were dressed in their colorful African garbs standing next to the Chief. As soon as they saw me, the music started. As usual, the African beat was powerful and transporting. If I did not have work to do, I could easily have spent my days in Zaire listening to the magnificent music.

After the powerful drum beat ended, the Chief welcomed me and I explained why I was visiting. The representative of the governor translated. At the end of both speeches, I asked my interpreter to convey to the Chief that I wanted to start my work by visiting the market. Through the interpreter, I understood that the market took place only one day a week, and that it was not market day for the village. I asked if there was a shop that sold food that I might visit, no matter how small it might be. After some discussion, the Chief agreed that I could visit the small shop and that he would accompany me.

There I was, in the middle of a rural area in Bandundu, walking on a dirt road with the Chief of the village and the representative of the governor as my interpreter, to see a little shop. Over twenty children followed us. Curiosity was in the air, as was the sound of dozens of little voices.

Suddenly, the Chief turned around and, lifting his cane, he shouted at the children in one of the local languages, most probably in Lingala, and ordered them to disperse. The children hesitantly obeyed, but the walk was not short, so a couple of minutes later, they had gathered to follow us again. The Chief was upset, and again he turned around and shouted for them to leave.

Eventually, we reached the shop housed in a small hut with a low door. I was ushered in and had to stoop down to make my entry. I could not see at first because it was dark inside, but my eyes soon adjusted. The hut had no windows or electric bulb. The small door was the only way that light could enter. The Chief and my interpreter came in behind me, and when they did, it was dark for a few seconds until they cleared the door. The hut was so small there was barely any space for anyone else to come in.

A young, skinny man was the owner of the shop. Through the interpreter, I briefly explained the objectives of my visit and asked if he would mind answering some questions. He was very agreeable. I noticed his shop carried the essentials: cassava, peanuts, sugar, flower, oil, soap, manioc, yams, millet, corn, plantain, and few other small items. My questions were about the functions of buying the produce from the farmers, pricing it, and selling it; and the functions involved in the transfer of goods from the farmers or the household to other members in the immediate and not-so-immediate community.

As soon as I finished my explanations, and while I was asking my first question, the light in the hut dimmed. It took me a moment to realize that someone was at the door. I saw a group of children holding on to each other and peeping inside with curiosity. As soon as the Chief saw them, he lifted his cane, shouted at them, and told them to leave. I was frustrated that he had already shouted so many times at the children who were not disturbing us, but who were simply curious to see what the stranger was doing in their village. They tried so many times to come close to us, and each time they did, the Chief scolded them with a loud voice and a harsh tone and ordered them to leave. I felt chagrined that he responded harshly to the children's natural curiosity, but out of respect to him and to the norms of the village, I did not interfere.

After trying so hard to be part of our entourage, the children left for maybe the third or fourth time. I went back to my discussion with the shop owner and jotted his answers on my yellow pad. While I was trying to understand what the farmers kept from their agricultural produce for the subsistence of their household and what they sold to obtain a little cash, the light from the door dimmed again. I turned around and saw one boy, nearly ten years old, with a lovely face and bright eyes, lifting his hand up in the air and holding a small coin. I told the interpreter to ask the Chief to allow the boy in because it seemed he needed to buy something. The interpreter relayed my request, and thank God, the Chief allowed the boy in.

The hut was so small that I had to squeeze myself against the wall to make space for him to come closer. On a ledge, near the shop owner, there was a small pottery dish filled with hard candy bonbons. Unwrapped, the bonbons were catching dust. The boy uttered a few words, took one of the bonbons, and paid the owner with his small coin. I thought the transaction was over. Instead, the boy took the bonbon, lifted it up, looked at the Chief with a smile, and turned and offered the candy to me. It was a magical moment. The look of triumph and pride in the boy's eyes was clear. He had outwitted the Chief!

I took the candy with a "Merci," smiled, and put it straight into my mouth, dust and all. The boy walked out of the hut with a shining smile and eyes filled with a keen sense of accomplishment.

For several days I thought about this boy and the other children in the village. How smart, determined, and courageous he was. He and his friends had tried to get a closer look at me and be part of this unexpected event in their village. This smart boy figured out a way to attain his goal, and to outwit the Chief. Maybe the boy received a coin from his mother or his father once a month or so, or maybe he got the coin as a result of doing a chore. It did not matter to him; he had a coin, a rare coin, possibly the only one in his possession for several weeks if not more, as this was a very poor community. He figured out that if he could convince the Chief he needed to buy something, maybe he could get into the hut. His strategy worked.

In fact, he was able to preempt the role of the Chief by playing host to the visitor and favoring her with a rare gift: a dust-covered piece of hard candy from an old bowl. What he did was an incredible lesson in strategy, courage, and generosity. He basically told the Chief, "You cannot keep shouting at us and pushing us aside. I have the right to come inside the shop. I will use the only coin I have and I will come in. Not only will I come in, I will buy with my own coin whatever I want and I will offer it to the lady who is visiting my village." The boy was masterful. The act of offering me the bonbon was about dignity, generosity, pride, and basic rights. I do not think the Chief will ever forget the marvelous lesson that little boy delivered that day in a small crowded hut. I will always think of him as my African gentleman and his bonbon tastier than any Belgian chocolate I subsequently ate.

As I said earlier, my month in Bandundu was filled with unexpected events. Every day I learned about rural life in the region, about the farmers, the teachers, the parents, the community leaders, and of course, the children. As long as I put myself in that active listening mode that starts by respecting what I was hearing, the learning was rich and in-depth. I focused on the study I was conducting. I needed to understand the relationship between poverty in rural agricultural areas near Kikwit and the children's access to schools, in particular girls' access.

I worked very hard during that month. As long as I was awake, I worked. There was nothing else to do, no way to reach Andrew by phone, so I worked, and worked, and worked.

Before coming to Zaire, I had learned that Bandundu depends largely on its agriculture because, unlike some other provinces in the country, it does not have basic natural resources or industry. Most of Bandundu is rural, and most of its population lives on agricultural produce. There is subsistence agriculture and cash-crop agriculture, and I was interested in how each type affected children's access to school.

I spent a month interviewing rural individuals. I talked to subsistence farmers and cash-crop farmers, women farmers and men farmers, small plot farmers and fairly large plot farmers, parents who were farmers and parents who had other occupations, teachers and school principals, boy students and girl students, community leaders, religious leaders, and shop owners. My interviews were lengthy, and the conversations genuine, moving, and rich. The insights I gained were beyond my expectations.

My study looked into what rural farmers around Kikwit plant and produce. I had lengthy sessions with farmers (mainly women) who were living on subsistence agriculture, as well as with farmers (men and women) who were shifting from subsistence agriculture to cash-crop agriculture. I tried to understand the complexity of the marketing process that involved moving goods and services from the small farmer to the consumer. I spent time trying to figure out what was sold in the rural areas and in Kikwit, versus what was sent to Kinshasa and sold there. Understanding if there were enough returns from what was marketed to satisfy the needs of the rural families was a challenge.

A fascinating aspect that was of deep interest to me was the division of labor between men and women. It was not surprising that women worked more in the farms than men, but what was surprising was the number of hours women worked versus men: more than twofold. I gathered this information from the literature I was reviewing, in particular from FAO studies that I had brought with me as background materials. Of course, I verified all this during my long sessions with women and men farmers, checking to see if those findings applied to the rural region around Kikwit, and if so, to what extent.

To understand poverty and malnutrition, I addressed the issue of what small farmers produced, how much they produced, what they kept for the family, what they sold, and why. I dealt with the functions of pricing, selling, and buying in detail; I discussed the functions involved in the transfer of goods from one market to another. I discovered that transportation and other marketing services could constitute serious bottlenecks and constraints. I also discovered that many small farmers—women and men —no matter how small their plots were, needed to sell some of their produce to be able to pay for basic living necessities.

After a month of hard work I had these preliminary findings:

1. Even though the subsistence farmers (mainly women) lacked formal education, they were smart, astute, and cautious operators.

2. The small farmers in the surrounding villages of Kikwit did not have access to financing. Most of the banks financed only large farmers and large agribusinesses.

3. There was a total lack of government policies to assist the small farmers.

4. The cash agriculture, or the commercial farms, were concentrated largely on export crops (coffee, palm oil, lumber) and did not plant crops that provided families with subsistence products.

5. Poverty and malnutrition existed within the households of both the subsistence farmers and the cash farmers. There was a possibility that within the households of small cash farmers, malnutrition was more common. Due to the fact that the objective of the cash farmer was to plant and sell export crops like coffee, very little subsistence crops were planted and what was left for the family's nutrition was inadequate.

6. Foods in the region where I conducted my research were fairly diversified; however, not all the villages received all the ingredients or all kinds of produce. The diet in the villages where I worked tended to be very limited, consisting basically of the manioc root and the green leaves of the manioc. Most villagers ate only twice a day, in the morning and early evening. Manioc was the consistent staple.

7. When poverty was the condition in the context of a household, and when malnutrition was part of the daily life of a household, boys and girls were not encouraged to go to school. However, if an exception was made and the parents decided to send one or two of the many children they had to school, it would be the boys. Girls were the first educational casualties when poverty and malnutrition were the norm.

8. The development of a more effective subsistence agriculture and a more balanced commercial or cash agriculture could improve the livelihood of the rural population of the region and in particular the standard of living of the farmers. As a result of a more balanced approach to agriculture, the farmers might send not just their sons to school but their daughters, too. A balanced subsistence and cash economy agriculture might become one of the factors that would encourage the farmers to send their girls and boys to school, and keep them in school.

My month in Kikwit and the surrounding rural villages had a great impact on me. My soul was deeply touched. I saw poverty on a daily basis. I encountered so many situations where families were living on the edge of what is possible, where mothers worked extremely hard, but found at the end of the day that they did not have enough food to feed all of their children. I touched the noble foreheads of hungry children, the tired hands of exhausted women farmers, the extremely thin arms of sick elderly grandparents. I visited schools where children came to the classroom barefoot and without breakfast, and where students did not have books and notebooks. I visited hospitals where the sick children lay two to a cot. What transformed me, however, was a visit to a hospital run by Belgian nuns.

The small hospital that did not have electric power the evening I visited. One of the nuns showed me three or four rooms where sick children lay two to a bed. The mothers of the sick children were lying on the floor. I wanted to hold one of the children; I slowly approached one of the beds to lift a sick boy. I barely could see. The nun said, "You might not want to carry him; he is very, very ill. They brought him here too late. He might die of hunger." I lifted the boy and held him in my arms. I thought he was probably a year old or so; the nun said he was two-and-a-half. He had an inflated belly and orange hair.

I learned from the nun that this malnutrition was called *kwashiorkor*, a deficiency of energy-providing foods. It becomes a chronic condition of semi-starvation to which a child can adjust to some extent by reduced growth. The nun explained that in advanced stages, the children are robbed of any energy, and while *kwashiorkor* is found in all ages, it was more common in children between the ages of a few months and three or four years.

I asked why the mothers did not give enough food to their babies and children. With tenderness, the nun explained that the mothers often do not have enough milk to breastfeed, and whenever they are provided with baby formula, they dilute it to make it last longer. These incidences of extreme malnutrition for babies and children are associated with the food shortages that typically occur as a result of extreme poverty. I held the boy in my arms for maybe ten minutes. He looked as if he were sleeping. I caressed his orange hair, held his hands, looked at his half-closed eyes, and smiled. I tried my best to make him feel that a stranger cared, but I was heartbroken when I left the hospital that evening.

The next day around 6:00 p.m., after a long day of interviews with the farmers, I asked my driver to take me back to the hospital.

When we arrived, I looked for Sister Bernadette who had welcomed me on my first visit. I asked her about the little boy I had held in my arms. After some silence, and with a sad voice, she told me he had died. "They brought him to us too late. We could not save him."

I went back to my hotel in Kikwit in a state of total disillusionment. I cried for a long time. I could not understand why innocent children should die from hunger. Why innocent children should go through the pain and the suffering of losing every ounce of energy they have until they waste away. This was the reason why God and I were not on the same page. I had a very hard time understanding any argument that said God had plans that we do not understand and these plans are always for the greater good. What is the greater good that comes from innocent children dying from hunger?

I could not sleep that night. The face of the child I carried in my arms kept me awake. The more I thought about him, the more I thought about children dying from hunger, the more I became determined to dedicate my life to work for the children of poverty anywhere in the world, and in particular in Africa.

CHAPTER TWENTY-TWO

WORK, TRAVEL, AND POETRY

FTER MY VISIT TO ZAIRE, it was not easy to reconcile
my life of comfort with the life of poverty I had witnessed
and learned to respect while in Kikwit and its surrounding villages.

Andrew and I had several long discussions about this topic. Warren
and I also discussed poverty and malnutrition extensively. Neither of
these two wise men could console me. I was upset with this higher
power that we call God. This situation reminded me of Mommy
becoming paralyzed and losing her ability to speak, read, and write for
no rational reason. Now, I had learned first-hand that innocent children
also suffered, and sometimes died, from malnutrition and hunger for
no rational reason. I could not fathom a good reason for such situations.

I am convinced that an American child, an African child, and a
Lebanese child are all born equal and share those "inalienable rights,"
including the right to survive. The question that kept ringing in
my head was: Do children's most basic rights, including the right of
survival, depend on the haphazard circumstances of where and to
whom they are born? If that were the case, then injustice was flagrant

in this world, and I was convinced our duty—my duty—was to do something about it.

I could not set these nagging questions aside, nor could I avoid thinking about the young Zairian boy I held the day before he died of hunger. Perhaps that brief encounter with a dying child made me realize how important it is to dedicate our life to help others. Possibly this was the reason I became more determined than ever to work for poor children who are the most underprivileged.

The Zairian boy became the reason for many things that happened in my life after meeting him. For one, I stopped throwing away good food and became sensitive to overeating, wasteful habits, and our lifestyle in the U.S. and in many other countries. As a result, I became more respectful of poverty. In particular, I became less judgmental and I believe more reflective about the conditions people live in. I understood at a much deeper level than before my visit to Zaire that so many children are born into conditions over which they have no say, and that many adults, both women and men, find themselves in a cycle of poverty that is not easy to break.

The small farmers in and around Kikwit worked very hard; most of the women worked twelve-to- fourteen-hour days. However, that did not ensure they would ever lift themselves and their families out of poverty. Working hard in an enabling environment can help families and communities improve their lives and the lives of future generations. Working hard in a non-enabling environment rarely guarantees the same outcome. I understood at a deeper level that international development is in part about facilitating system reforms to create those enabling environments. I also understood that among the basic tenants of international development are concepts such as active listening, an ability to understand interlocking systems, a respect for local capacity, and a continuous genuine dialogue about relevant and sustainable solutions.

Oh, how much I learned from holding an innocent dying child! Thank you, Zairian boy. I wish I had been able to do something for you and not to just absorb the invaluable lesson your brief life taught me. Your silent suffering will always remind me how much I owe to poor hungry children. It will always motivate me to work harder. Your suffering expanded my heart so I can love more—especially to love those who were not born with the privileges that I was born with. You have marked my mind and my heart so I can never be indifferent to those who are less privileged. Thank you.

The Secretariat for Women in Development expanded its scope of work even further, and I continued to lead the design, management, implementation, and monitoring of its new projects. Many of these were implemented in Africa, and as I traveled to other remote rural regions of the continent, I learned to respect more and more the lives of others, and how to treasure each life.

Andrew and I led a life filled with love, work, and travel. We made an effort to find time to travel together as much as possible. From 1982-84, we went together to Senegal, Jamaica, Egypt, France, Italy, and Lebanon, and to other areas separately for work. During those three years, I also worked in Somalia, Ghana, Yemen, Jordan, and Morocco.

The Jordan trip was very special for me. Her Royal Highness Princess Basma bint Talal, King Hussein's sister, was the chairperson of the Jordanian Hashemite Fund for Human Development. She had asked TransCentury to assess the organizational capabilities of NGOs in Jordan in order to design a program to strengthen their effectiveness. Warren decided that he and I should travel to Jordan for about ten days, establish contact with the Princess to clarify the scope of work, become familiar with the context of their work, and ultimately to design the assessment. After our first round of discussions with the Princess, we were impressed by the clarity of her commitment to strengthening women's roles in each sector of human development in Jordan. We also discovered the extremely pro-active role she played in promoting the roles of women and youth in the development of Jordan. The Princess was particularly involved in supporting the implementation of sustainable development programs that addressed the social and economic needs of women, youth, rural communities, and marginalized groups.

Warren and I practiced active listening to understand in a clear and hopefully in-depth way what was expected from TransCentury. After a few days, we finalized the scope of our work with Princess Basma. To understand the NGO Jordanian context and its complexities, Warren and I met with NGOs in both urban and rural areas and held several community meetings. In addition, Princess Basma invited us to accompany her to one of the rural areas. She rode in a Range Rover with some of her aids and we followed in a second car leading a few other vehicles in a caravan. The Princess stopped in several towns where she stepped out of her car and greeted people as they welcomed her with flags and flowers.

When we arrived at our destination, a huge crowd was gathered to meet her. It was a stunning scene. Dozens of men on horseback with flags lifted up high called greetings to her while a group of male drummers danced and sang welcoming songs. A line of women in traditional dress ululated. Religious leaders, town and village elders, mayors, and community leaders from neighboring towns stood and cheered. I was very interested in the manner in which they welcomed her, not in a subservient way, but as family members greet an honored relative: "Sister of Hussein, we are pleased to have you among us."

After a few welcoming speeches, they ushered the Princess and her entourage to a huge tent, the floor of which was covered with Bedouin carpets scattered with large, soft cushions. The Princess sat on one of the cushions with her entourage gathered around. She gestured to me to sit close by her. The few hours that passed in the tent were fascinating. Mayors, community leaders, school principals, religious leaders and many others would address the "Sister of Hussein," and after some honorific terms, list several issues they wished to improve the lot of their lives. Many of them had very specific requests to make, all of which she took in, nodding her understanding, probing occasionally for details, asking about prior assistance and how effective it had been, and always listening carefully to their replies.

At this meeting, Warren and I learned a great deal about the seriousness with which this woman played her role; her clear recollection of what their needs were and her commitment to ensuring they got what they needed; her great dignity, yet the ease with which she could be approached; and her personal interest in their welfare. From the stories of my father, and especially from the books of my Uncle Ameen who had traveled extensively throughout the Arabian Peninsula in the early 1920s and met with the kings and emirs of the time, I realized we were witnessing Arab-Bedouin culture at its finest. I knew that Lawrence of Arabia, who had served Princess Basma's immediate ancestors, had witnessed just such scenes many times over.

After each speech, the Princess asked for a written list of requests and gave it to one of her assistants. Her responses were something like: "I have been listening carefully. I will check with the Ministry of Education and see why there is a delay in sending you the teacher you asked for. I will do what I can to speed the process." To another, she would say: "You said that your village needs an asphalted road. Did you petition the Ministry of Interior, and did you work with the mayors of neighboring villages to convince them to submit a collective petition for an asphalted road that serves all of your villages?" To a third requester she would say: "You asked for a mosque to be built, for a hospital to be constructed, and for the primary school to be expanded to include a secondary school. Did you have a meeting with the villagers and all the community members to prioritize your demands so that the government can prioritize the work?"

After possibly two hours of requests and answers, the Princess made some final remarks whereby she thanked everyone for their work for their people, promised each petitioner that she would follow up with the relevant ministries and agencies in the hope that many of their requests would be realized. She also asked them to check with her office after a month or so for information regarding the progress made with regards to their requests.

Just before ending this assembly, she held the written lists, raised her hand, and promised the crowd as a whole that she would work on their requests. The chanting, the ululates, the drumming, the flag waving, and the other demonstrative gestures of satisfaction intensified while the sister of the king shook hands and bade farewell to as many individuals as possible within the crowd. After nearly twenty minutes of farewell, the Princess got in her Range Rover and we returned to Amman.

That evening over dinner, Warren and I could not stop discussing the amazing experience we had just witnessed. Here was a royal princess who was nonetheless down-to-earth. She and about one hundred-fifty subjects sat on cushions or squatted on carpets in a tent to discuss their needs and priorities while two-to-three hundred more people gathered outside, listening and watching. Warren and I admired the closeness exhibited between the people and the Princess. We appreciated the lack of pomp and the absence of extreme formalities, and we were impressed by how knowledgeable she seemed and the manner in which she handled every request.

Warren wondered if this was unique to Jordan or whether it occurred in all the kingdoms, sheikhdoms, and republics of the Arab world. I shared with him my understanding of the traditional Arab practice of *Majlis Al-Shoura* where the king, prince, or leader would sit with a number of his advisers and subjects from his community to listen and debate with all of them before making any decision. I believed what Princess Basma was doing may have been inspired by this concept of *Majlis Al-Shoura*. Warren asked if this was still the practice in all the Arab countries, and I said I did not think so.

I told him that I knew from my Uncle Ameen's books that the founder of Saudi Arabia, King Abdul Aziz Al-Saud, used this approach. After some reflection, I told Warren that it was possible that this practice still occurred in some of the kingdoms of the Arab world, but that I doubted it was in the Republics. I could not imagine a president in Syria or Egypt or Iraq, for example, using the same approach that Princess Basma had. After a lengthy discussion, I promised Warren that I would research the issue and learn where the practice of a leader sitting and listening to his/her people was used in Arab countries.

When Warren and I traveled together, it was work, work, work, trying to absorb as much as possible about the new culture and the new context we were in. When Andrew and I traveled together for work, each of us focused on our individual tasks; however, in addition to duties, there was always poetry.

When Andrew and I traveled for pleasure, love was abundant and poetry was always in the air. Andrew was prolific and many poems were born on our journeys. Every country inspired him; every situation spoke to his most creative inner self. Poetry was the North Star guiding our journeys on the back roads and the highways of our planet.

In Dakar, Senegal, our hotel overlooked the Atlantic Ocean. In the late evenings after a long day of work, we would sit on the balcony of our room, sip a glass of wine, listen to the chant of the ocean, and silently watch the night fishermen. I loved this scene: the small canoe or carved shell looked like a horizontal black line in the ocean, and the fisherman in the middle of the canoe looked like a vertical black line. The geometry was abstract and beautiful—a red dot on the horizontal line next to the vertical line was the lantern of the fisherman. There were so many of these abstract black lines with red dots on a shimmering ocean of blue. The painting was superb. Some of the lines from Andrew's poem "Night Fishermen" say:

> The nightfishers are out,….
> ….. they glide
> gondola-like past the glittering darkness
> of light shedding electrical confetti….

In Cairo, Egypt, we stayed in the Mena House Hotel. In the morning, after a marvelous night, Andrew opened the curtains of our bedroom window and we were surprised by the closeness of the Pyramid, as if it wanted to come and visit us in our room. The Pyramid looked so close it felt as if we had slept at its feet. Andrew wrote:

> This is where they meet,
> The infinitesimal,

Too small to have been,
and the so-infinitely large
it can't be seen.
The upside-down descending pyramid of air
And rising pyramid of rock
Interlock
To square the circle
And cube the sphere of the sun.
There, balancing the opposites
Ice and fire dance.
This is where the stones
clap hands
and startle camels into clouds...
We flag a cab
whose driver knew the Sphinx
and bubble our wheels toward the sun
with a stop at Mena House, that swell hotel.

In Rome, I bought a glass horse made in Murano from a small shop. The horse looked like it was galloping with its feet in the air, and it inspired a few lines in Andrew's poem which read:

The clitter-clatter of horse's hooves,
One touching, three floating at any one time,
Freezes into a medallion of sound and light
in a narrow alley in Rome.
The hooves thresh cobblestone like a hovercraft
Harvesting seaweed and breakers
While wheels paddle the carriage into a flashbulb. Click.
When beauty happens it happens all at once:

The earth stops and its dust evaporates.
The secret of art is it pretends
It shelters motion and holds it still…..

In Paris, I took my American husband to all my Parisian favorite places. We spent a lot of time in the Louvre Museum. We sat in the sun in the Jardin de Tuilleries, and we promenaded along the banks of the Seine. We prayed at Notre Dame, and we spent a swell time on *La Rive Gauche*. We visited the museums of Auguste Rodin and Victor Hugo, and decided to treat ourselves with a visit to the cathedral at Chartres. Chartres is probably the finest example of French Gothic architecture and is perhaps the most beautiful cathedral in France. Andrew agreed and expanded, saying Chartres was probably the most beautiful cathedral in all of Europe. The perfume of the cathedral, the majesty of its pointed arches, and the ethereal beauty of the stained glass windows transported us to a spiritual space where peace reigned.

Before ending our French trip, we decided to indulge ourselves again, so we drove from Paris to Giverny and visited Claude Monet's home, garden, and museum. We sat by Monet's water lily pond and slipped into another world. Andrew wrote a poem about the stained glass in Chartres and one about the water lilies of Monet. The Monet poem starts with these lines:

Age softened his old eyes like chocolates
in the sun, and the fury of the lilies
exhausted the horizon.

Andrew's lines continued to say:

God is a girl who blow-dries Her hair
with the sun and lets there be sky,
at which Monet, intensified, stretches matter into a
    canvasing.

In Freike, Lebanon, Andrew wrote, and wrote, and wrote. He somehow fell in love with our Freike home; he spoke about the special light, the enchanting views, and the unique ambiance there. He and Daddy hit it off like friends from ancient times. Poets, artists, journalists, and other friends visited us every day. Love dominated the air, and joy joined us at our family table and shared our meals. Andrew, my poet friends, and I read English and Arabic poems on the balcony of my childhood. Poetry overflowed, became fused with daily activities, and the quotidian wore a new wardrobe. While in Freike, Andrew wrote at least a dozen poems, among them: "Freike Village," "Poetry Circle," "The Holy Mountains, Lassa," "Down Terraces of Centuries to Lebanon," "Time in a Chair in the Shade of a Grape Arbor, Lebanon," "To Ameen Rihani, on the 42nd Anniversary of His Death," "Byblos and the Alphabet," "In May be the Mountains, for Bashir," "Byblos through the Centuries," "Who He Was and Why, for May," "Fayrouz," and many others.

Many people write journals; Andrew wrote poetry. I felt so enchanted that our journey, our daily life, our moments of reflection and beauty, our magical moments were captured in his words. I would have loved to share with everyone all that Andrew wrote about Lebanon; however, I will choose only two poems and share them: the Freike Village poem, and the Ameen Rihani poem:

Freike Village

The missing bridge is only an idea
on the balcony of a young architect's mind,
as if contemplating the state of Tomorrow
by contemplating the yearning of Now
were the same as seeing today
through the eyes of several centuries ago.
The Mountain says, "I've been here for ever;
I am older than sky."
Sea sulks while Castle and House
Woo the Balcony whom they
love so desperately, they never budge.
The Balcony dances on their shoulders like light
when both Sun and Moon are showing in the sky,
and the Balcony hangs the badge of the Sun
on the chest of the Sea,
the medal of the Moon
on the mind of the Mountain
and elopes with Night.
Time is the Post Office that keeps everything
from happening at once.

We were in Freike in September 1982, the forty-second anniversary of my Uncle Ameen's death. My father's home, where we stayed, used to be Ameen Rihani's home. Andrew wrote:

Meeting you in your absence due to
a slight mistake because of birth and death—
which are, after all, inconsequential
in regard to their timing—is a real pleasure.
From your balcony where you watched, you saw

the female mountains and a male sky
make love every morning and evening so
the day would be full of infants of the sun,
and you were still, even as you ambled
all over the world, knowing if you were quiet
sooner or later the world would come to you.
So you drifted through the world as one of its
centers, one of its reference points, one
of its suitors like moon seducing
Saneen, mountain of Solomon and
Sheba. Being drunk with words and love
it was easy to ratchet a globe apart
and stick it back together in the shape
of the New Man and Woman in your mind,
though your bed sheets were empty as oceans
when they are glazed with a certain slant of light
till they look like a mirror of mirage
but are really the silver waste basket
for your thoughts from loneliness. Your horse
understood and steered you to words with the Wind,
who, like you, was never at a loss for gab
and was a consolation for a soloist
who arose so early the World was still in pajamas
and no one else yet though the Sun
was doing push-ups on top of the mountains.

During these three years, I, too, was writing. My poems were
still in Arabic, and Andrew continued to translate some of them.
Titles written between 1982 and 1984 included: "Palm Trees," "The
Night Flourishes," "Seven Years...and My Love," "On the Shore

of Your Eyes," "Alphabet," "On A Wednesday Night," "*Ghorba* or Living in a Foreign Land," and "Words, Words, Words."

A poem that Andrew really liked and asked me to share every time I had a poetry reading was "Alphabet." I believe he enjoyed translating it as much as I enjoyed writing it:

And the letters of the alphabet became the cave of
    Ali Baba
"Open Sesame!"
The letters emerge wearing new robes and jewelry
They dance in front of me
and embrace each other for the first time.
New words are born.
"Open Sesame!"
The alphabet announces in a strong voice
"I give you the freedom to use my letters however
you wish."
Magic falls on me.
My wand touches the edge of each letter.
I shuffle the deck
I change the rules of the game
The magic circles increase in front of me
Words enter each other
and languages not heard before grow out of the earth.
On the forehead of every 'A' blooms a red rose.

Our poems were a constant in our lives. Saturday and Sunday mornings we often sat in the sunroom in our home on Irving Street in Washington, D.C., reading poetry to each other while sipping coffee. Our sunroom was truly filled with light; it was Andrew's favorite room in the house, and he wrote most of his poems in that sun-filled space.

Our work and our poetry were equally important to us. We talked a lot about Africa, about education systems, subsistence farmers, and small financial loans to entrepreneurs. We discussed girls' education, rural life issues, civil societies, and economic productivity. We explored ways of expanding local capacity and the importance of listening to the realities, needs, and priorities of each community. We debated equity and equality and women's empowerment; local and international NGOs, the Peace Corps, and the role of governments in the development process.

Our private life was also central to us, and at the end of each day, our bedroom intimacy flourished.

During those years, my poetry was published both in Lebanon and in Washington, D.C. In Lebanon, *An-Nahar* continued to print the poems I mailed to Onsi Al Hajj. In Washington, D.C., Siham Wehbi, an editor of the *Lebanon News* that targeted the Lebanese diaspora, interviewed me several times and published many of my poems. In addition, Sobhi Ghandour, the editor of *Al-Hewar*, a magazine published in the DC area that targeted the Arab diaspora, published my work.

Between 1982 and 1984, Andrew convinced me that I needed to know the U.S. better. Only knowing the east and west coasts was not sufficient, he said. As much as I loved Washington, D.C., New York, Boston, and California, he insisted that I needed to know the South and the Midwest. So in addition to spending many of our weekends in New York, we took several trips within throughout the country.

One of the trips was a ten-day journey by car through the southern states. We drove from Washington, D.C. to New Orleans by way of Virginia, West Virginia, North Carolina, South Carolina,

Georgia, Alabama, Mississippi, and Louisiana. We stopped in each state to see something historical, artistic, or academic (a university).

We spent more days in New Orleans than in any other city, and there Andrew taught me about jazz and the blues. His love of New Orleans was contagious, and I fell in love with the city, too. We stayed at a hotel in the French Quarter and listened to music all day and all evening. Andrew taught me how the city brought together European instruments such as the horns with African instruments such as the drums. He said musicians in New Orleans were inspired by European melodies and African rhythms. He also felt it was New Orleans that put church music and barroom music together.

Andrew believed that New Orleans created the new American music that we call jazz which reflected the spirit and rhythm of the new energy in the U.S. He would say things like: "Listen to jazz and think of the energy in New York, and you will see the connection." He also believed the city and its music make people happy, which is why in New Orleans people dance in the streets even during the day. We were drunk with music. Every evening we went to a different jazz club. One night we visited Preservation Hall, a club in the French Quarter founded in 1961 to protect and honor New Orleans jazz. Our evening there was out of this world. The youngest jazz player in the Preservation Hall Band was about eighty years old, yet they played for at least three hours with just a ten-minute break every hour.

Suad Joseph, my friend from California, flew in to meet us in New Orleans for the last couple of days and we had a great time together. Discussions with Suad were always fabulous. We ate beignets in the morning at St. Louis Square, had Cajun food at noon, and listened to more jazz in the evening. The three of us took in the beauty of the city and enjoyed our special moments together. Suad captured our New Orleans getaway in wonderful photographs.

Another trip Andrew and I took was to Texas. We flew to Houston and stayed for a few of days with a family friend from Beirut, Said Wanna, a Lebanese engineer who was then with Bechtel. It was great to reconnect with a friend from AUB. When we attended a concert by the Symphony of Houston, Gideon Waldrop, the dean of Julliard, and few others within the symphony discussed with Andrew the possibility of putting his lengthy poem "Songs of the Southwest" to music. We had a lovely evening after the concert discussing Andrew's poetry.

The next day Andrew and I visited Rothko's chapel. The interior is not only a chapel, but also a major work of modern art. At first, I was dismayed on finding the walls of the chapel were decorated with fourteen black panels by Mark Rothko. Only after Andrew and I sat meditating for nearly a certain time did the beauty of Rothko's work appear, and I was overwhelmed by the gradual emergence of color. Instead of black, the paintings were in varying shades of dark green, dark blue, and greys. The artist's commentary on these provocative pieces states, "The familiar identity of things has to be pulverized in order to destroy the finite associations with which our society increasingly enshrouds every aspect of our environment." When we took the time to immerse ourselves in Rothko's work, his intent resonated with us and we left the chapel renewed.

Next we visited the Museum of Fine Arts; it rekindled our love for American paintings, and we saw some beautiful works by Georgia O'Keeffe and by John Singer Sargent that we had not seen before.

From Houston we went to San Antonio and the Alamo. Strolling through the Main Plaza we listened to live blues guitars, then wandered through the Spanish missions. We also spent time at the San Antonio Museum of Art. One of the most pleasurable moments during that visit was to stroll in the secluded parts of the River Walk. I found San Antonio to be a charming city where the old Spanish culture and the new American spirit merged to create a unique way of life.

From San Antonio we went to Corpus Christi and its incredibly beautiful beaches. We spent two days at the beach soaking in the sun and enjoying the scenery. I wrote my poem "Palm Trees" there. This became possibly my most popular poem for many years to come.

Another U.S. trip during those years was to Wisconsin, where Andrew's mother Agnes lived. We flew to Milwaukee and then drove to Agnes's home where we stayed. I thoroughly enjoyed being with Agnes. She taught me a lot about Wisconsin and Norway. She made sure that I knew that between 1850 and 1900, large numbers of European immigrants came to Wisconsin, and that among the Scandinavians who arrived, the largest group was Norwegian. She explained how Wisconsin was the leading state in cheese production, producing about a quarter of America's cheese, and that it was second in milk production, after California.

Agnes was a pharmacist, a smart and lovely lady who was full of energy in her late seventies. While in Wisconsin, Andrew, Agnes, and I drove to different cities including Racine and Eau Claire, and to different lakes. I had never seen such huge spaces of flat land before in my life. We would drive for hours and never climb the smallest hill. Andrew loved the flat lands. I attributed this to the fact that he grew up in such vistas, but he gently corrected me. He said that to him flat lands represented total openness. He appreciated the unobstructed view. To him, flat lands were about no borders, no barriers, no obstacles; horizons as far as the eye could see; imagination running loose; and always new possibilities. In many ways, that was Andrew.

He always saw the special and unique beauty of every place. Andrew also loved the farmhouses and the fields of corn. He felt farmers were the salt of the earth; they were noble human beings, and their connection to the earth was sacred. He admired them greatly and wrote about them in his poetry.

Traveling with Andrew was magical. When we traveled internationally, we basked in the rich cultural suns of all the countries we visited and worked hard to understand the many communities we had the privilege to work with. When we traveled in the U.S., I was in the presence of a teacher who not only knew inside and out the culture, art, and history of every city we visited, but who also was so insightful and sensitive to the uniqueness of every place and every situation that he made every chapter of our travels a chapter of discovery and love.

CHAPTER TWENTY-THREE

AN OCEAN OF PROBLEMS

LIFE WAS MARVELOUS, YET I was not fully satisfied. In the middle of what seemed to be an ocean of happiness, there were problems. I wanted to become a mother, and I was not happy to see Andrew did not care to have our own children. Maybe because he had three children from his first marriage, he was not eager for us to have our own. At first I was bothered by this, but then it became a point of serious contention between us. We started quarrelling. He would say our love was all we needed, that we did not need children to add to our happiness. I was very upset that he could not understand my need. He was totally satisfied; he did not need anything more, and I still needed to become a mother. He was happy with who we were and how we lived our life; he thought of our life as a great love story. But to me, our story was incomplete. I wanted a love story *and* motherhood. Our ocean of happiness experienced waves of deep sadness.

I wrote earlier that it is too hard to dwell on this subject.

As if what Andrew and I were living was too beautiful to last.

By the end of November 1984, we agreed to separate. I wanted to have children and I was worried that my biological clock was ticking, reminding me of the physical limitations that years bring to a woman. Andrew suggested that we spend a week in Bethany Beach before we separated so we could have a week of love and goodbyes. I wanted to go to Lebanon and spend ten days with my parents. He convinced me to have our week together before I left for Lebanon.

In December 1984, we went to Bethany Beach. The week there was surreal. Our goodbyes were suffused with love and tears. Andrew took many photos of me and asked passersby to take photos of us together. We strolled on the beach hand in hand; we walked the charming streets of Bethany Beach arm in arm; we sipped wine in lovely restaurants, and we hugged and kissed. Our goodbyes were washed with tears. Knowing that those were my last days with Andrew was so, so painful.

A few days before Christmas, I flew to Lebanon and spent the holiday season with Mommy and Daddy. It was the saddest Christmas ever. I do not think I ever cried as much as I did during that time. I was separated from my love and the war in Lebanon worsened by the day. My heart and the heart of Lebanon were bleeding. My years with Andrew had been too wonderful to last, and it seemed Lebanon's golden years of the sixties and early seventies were dissipating.

Andrew had offered to vacate our home while I was in Lebanon so we would not have to face a second week of goodbyes. I flew back in early January 1985 to Washington, D.C., to a home without Andrew. I could not stand it. I was miserable, and nothing could console me. I decided to sell the house.

Sadness equals a sign in the front yard that reads: "Home for Sale." I did not care if it was the right season to sell, or if I would get the right price. I did not want to live without Andrew in what used to be our love nest. Every nook and cranny reminded me of him: the sunroom where he wrote his poetry, the kitchen where we often made quiche together, the living room where we sat so many times next to the fireplace drinking wine and holding each other and, the family room where together we put up wallpaper to make one full wall become a forest. And of course, the bedroom, where we created our own world…it was very hard to sleep alone in our bed.

My decision to sell the house was final. I told the real estate agent I wanted to sell as soon as possible, and we found a buyer about a week after it was put on the market. The offer was less than encouraging, but I was willing to accept what was offered and not wait. I needed to minimize the daily pain I was experiencing.

I also decided to leave TransCentury. It seems the separation from Andrew made me need a total change. I have to admit that Warren had decided to begin reducing his time at TransCentury and to delegate some of his responsibilities to Lou Mitchell, the most senior vice president among our group. Warren had made that decision around the end of 1984, nearly at the same time Andrew and I agreed to separate. The decisions made between the end of November and the beginning of December of 1984 created an ocean of sadness in my heart. My decision to separate from Andrew as well as Warren's decision to no longer hold, on a full-time basis, the leadership of TransCentury eliminated the rainbow under which I was living.

In February 1985, I moved to an apartment on 4201 Cathedral Avenue in Washington, D.C. Even though we were separated, Andrew helped me find the apartment. It was in an elegant building and had a lovely balcony. In March 1985, I joined a new company, Creative Associates International. Andrew sent me red roses on my first day at Creative.

Creative was a women-owned, minority-owned company. In 1977, in a Washington, D.C., basement, four women with diverse cultural backgrounds founded the company: Charito Kruvant, a bilingual education specialist; Mimi Tse, who was interested in child psychology; Cheryl Jones, an accomplished education practitioner; and Diane Dodge, an early childhood specialist. When I joined, Diane had already left Creative and Cheryl was completing her work and preparing to leave; she left sometime during 1985.

When I joined my new organization, Charito and Mimi were leading the company, and two other solid professionals were moving up the leadership ladder: Brenda Bryant and Danuta Lockett. I have no doubt that the minority status and the fact that Creative was the first women-owned firm to be granted an 8(a) status helped propel the company forward. The 8(a) designation helped Creative win its first government contract, including its first contract with USAID in the early 1980s. In 1987, two years after I joined, Creative graduated from the 8(a) program. We were by then competing with all the big organizations and companies who specialized in international development.

When I joined Creative in March 1985, I was heartbroken but determined that the new professional chapter in my life would be as successful as the TransCentury chapter. At Creative, I was asked to contribute to several ongoing educational programs, including one in Yemen. I had already been to Yemen in 1984 as a member of the USAID-funded project Improving the Efficiency of Educational Systems (IEES). The team at Creative felt the knowledge I had of the unique and complex Yemeni context would be invaluable for the educational program they were implementing.

My trips to Yemen reaffirmed my conviction of the heterogeneity of the Arab world. Yemen is very different, for example, from

Lebanon, Egypt, Morocco, Tunisia, or any other Arab country. These other four Arab countries were modern nation states with progress clearly happening. On the other hand, although formally independent since the end of the Ottoman rule in 1918, Yemen under the government of the Hamid al Din dynasty placed little emphasis on formal social and economic development activities. The central government ruled largely on the basis of tradition, and the tribal authorities were semi-independent. This serious pattern of extreme decentralization had not been eradicated in 1984 and 1985 when I visited Yemen for my work.

During my visits, I wondered how a country could isolate itself from the rest of the world and move forward at such an extremely slow pace, or rather a pace that was totally unique to that country. How could a country so completely shield itself from global influences? This isolation was manifested in everyday instances in Yemen, small or large, significant and not so significant. For example, in the streets of Yemen, every man wore a dagger or a *jannabiya*. The jannabiya is a type of dagger with a short curved blade that is worn on a belt. I had not seen men wearing daggers in any other country I had visited in the past years. Other examples from the educational field, based on the statistics that I could find in 1985, attested to Yemen's isolation and a progress not in step with the pace of other nations:

- In 1982-83, there were only one hundred fifty-seven Yemeni teachers at the preparatory level and sixty-three at the secondary level.
- Three governorates had no Yemeni teachers in their post-primary schools, (only foreign teachers) and two other governorates had only one Yemeni teacher each.

- The 1975 census estimated that the adult literacy rate for men was 25.4 percent, and for adult women was less than two percent.

When I entered Bab el Yemen and went into the old city of Sana'a, I felt I was transported to a different era.

It was fascinating to visit Yemen several times in the course of a few years, to work with its Ministry of Education, and to learn about the historically rich, although isolated, country. While in Yemen, and specifically when meeting with ministers or directors in ministries, I was often asked if I were a relative of Ameen Rihani. They were all impressed when I told them I was his niece. It seemed that most of the educated Yemenis knew my uncle was one of the first outsiders to visit and write about their country in the early 1920s.

During my visits to Yemen, I stayed at the Sheraton Hotel at the edge of Sana'a. It was strange and disorienting. The minute I entered the hotel, it was like stepping into a modern Western country, and when I left and went to Sana'a, Taiz, or a rural area, it was like being transported in time. I felt as if the hotel had been dropped into Sana'a by a parachute. It did not belong there. Before the end of one of my visits at the Sheraton, I wrote a poem titled "A Borrowed Hotel, and the Waist of Zaid," in an attempt to understand the juxtaposition of a modern hotel and the daggers on the waists of men in the street.

My work at Creative occupied a great deal of my time and absorbed most of my energies; however, when I came home to my apartment after work, I could not help but think about how the abundance of love that carried my relationship and marriage with Andrew for nearly seven years could not last. Many evenings were filled with sadness and were spent reflecting and writing. I became less social and did not want to go out much.

The year 1985 was not just a miserable time for me; it was also one of the worst years of the war in Lebanon. I followed the news on a regular basis and tried to call Daddy and Mommy as much as possible. I would have called them on a daily basis if I could, but often I could not reach them by phone given the difficulty of the connections of international phone lines in a war-torn country. The news in the media was terrifying. It seemed the fighting, bombing, shelling, and kidnappings were escalating in many cities in Lebanon, but especially in Beirut. I read in the Western and Lebanese media things like:

- "At least 45 people died and 175 are injured in a car bomb explosion in Beirut, Lebanon." *BBC*, March 8, 1985
- "On this day a car bomb exploded in Beirut, with a final death toll of more than 80." *The Guardian,* March 9, 1985
- "It was hell in Beirut. Insane bombing continued in both sectors of the capital, crossing points had been closed illustrating the gravity of the situation." *An-Nahar,* April 30, 1985
- "Seven other Americans, in addition to the passengers and crew members of TWA hijacked last Friday, are being held hostage in Lebanon." *New York Times,* June 20, 1985
- "Death was moving around in West Beirut. Two car bombs exploded at Caracol-Druze [this is very close to our Hamra home] and Ghobeireh within half-an-hour, resulting in twenty-nine dead and a hundred injured. Several Christians were kidnapped at various crossing points right after the explosions." *An-Nahar,* August 19, 1985

I had many sleepless nights because of such horrifying news.

My brothers and I had several conference calls to discuss the situation and the safety of our parents. We agreed to propose to Mommy and Daddy that they leave the Hamra home in Beirut and live in the Freike home not just during the summer months, but yearlong. Freike in 1985-86 was a much safer place than Beirut. As a matter of fact, Freike throughout the years of war was a much safer place than Beirut; however, it had become utterly clear by that time that West Beirut was no longer safe and that Daddy and Mommy should not live there anymore.

We called Daddy to discuss the situation with him and were surprised that he did not argue. However, he suggested that Ameen and his family should go to Freike and live in our family home there, and he and Mommy would relocate to a smaller house not far away from them. The wise man struck again.

In 1985, three of my father's children were not living in Lebanon: Ramzi worked in Saudi Arabia; Sarmad was an engineer with the Zamel company, also in Saudi Arabia; and of course I was with Creative Associates International in Washington, D.C., and traveling extensively to Africa and the Middle East on assignments. The only one who was living in Beirut was Ameen. Daddy worried about the safety of Ameen and his family, and he had always intended for Ameen to inherit the Freike home while the rest of us would inherit land. In Daddy's loving and practical mind, it was reasonable for Ameen to take possession of the Freike home in 1986 rather than after Daddy left this planet. Also, Daddy wanted a smaller and more manageable house given Mommy's situation and the fact that he was aging.

We all agreed with Daddy's logic. The search for a new home started and Ramzi found a lovely four-bedroom apartment in Qornet Shahwan, a town in the mountains to the north of Beirut and five minutes from Freike. The apartment was new, its living room was spacious, and it had a large balcony. Balconies seemed to be a part of our lives.

Ramzi and I agreed that we would meet in Beirut and stay with Daddy and Mommy in the Hamra home to help them prepare for the move to Qornet Shahwan. Ramzi, like me, was separated by then. We were again the two single siblings with fewer family demands than Ameen and Sarmad.

The two weeks that Ramzi and I spent in the Hamra home with our parents were packed with all kinds of emotions. This was where we grew up and spent nine months of each year of our lives before we moved to other countries. This was the home where we spent our Christmases, Easters, most of the family's birthdays, and wonderful family dinners. This was where *Dunia Al Ahdath*, Mommy's children magazine, was created. This was where Ameen and I started writing poetry, and where Ramzi began writing and publishing his music critic articles. This was the home where our AUB friends spent so many hours, and where our parents and their Beiruti friends spent so many evenings. This was the home that weathered so many horrible days and nights when the fighting seemed never to end. Memories floated near the ceiling of every room of the Hamra home. We had to leave our loyal home, the home where every room held a thousand stories, every wall reflected intimate accounts, and every window could talk about special occasions. The beloved home and its special memories had to be left behind because of an insane war.

The four of us—Daddy, Mommy, Ramzi, and I—had to decide what could be transported to Qornet Shahwan without raising the serious attention of the many militias that occupied the roads. We agreed that we would take some risks and send a van, driven by someone we could trust, filled with things the family valued emotionally or preferred not to lose. Mommy, Daddy, Mommy's helper, Ramzi, and I would rent a second van with an experienced driver to take us from Hamra through the maze of potentially unsafe roads to Qornet Shahwan.

Ramzi and I, with Daddy's assistance, packed the many family photo albums; the movies Daddy had taken when we were children; the letters and personal correspondence that he and Mommy had kept. We boxed the collection of LP records of the fifties, sixties, and seventies; and the many paintings and Persian rugs which decorated the house. We gathered their medications and necessary health equipment, and of course books, books, and books. We decided not to transport heavy furniture such as armoires, buffets, the dining room table and chairs, beds, mattresses, televisions, desks, washer, dryer (in Lebanon washers and dryers do not come with the bought home), and many other pieces.

The evenings of packing were bittersweet; however, Ramzi was a master of making even the most difficult situation pleasant. He was capable of making Mommy laugh, helping Daddy look forward to living in a new home not far from his beloved Freike, and reminding me to cherish every moment we spent together packing memories and dreaming of a secure home for Mommy and Daddy.

The move was scheduled for the end of April or early May of 1986, depending on when we believed might be a fairly calm time without shelling. Our travel would be on roads filled with militias and dotted with checkpoints managed by armed men of different political persuasions.

On the day of the move, the first van arrived early in the morning. We loaded it with our emotionally valuable stuff, gave the driver a hefty sum of money, prayed for his safety and the safe arrival of our memories, and told him that as soon as he arrived at our new home in Qornet Shahwan, our brother Ameen would deliver the second half of his fee. We sent our things not knowing if any of them would arrive safely. We hoped that maybe the driver and the militia men who would stop him on the roads would not be interested in boxes of correspondence, family movies, records, or books. We feared they might, however, confiscate the Oriental rugs and possibly the paintings if they knew their value.

In the early afternoon, we received a call from Ameen informing us that the van arrived and he believed it to be intact. A big sigh of relief! The trip that should have taken an hour took nearly four given the many stops on the way by the different militias.

Now we were ready for the most important trip, in the van that would transport the five of us to Qornet Shahwan. Ramzi and I knew the move would not be without risk, so we had monitored the news extremely carefully for the days leading up to our departure, trying to determine what could be a safer route to take.

At around three in the afternoon, the second van and driver arrived at our home in Hamra, ready to take us to the new home in the mountains. We helped Mommy into the van; Daddy and Mommy's helper took their places; and Ramzi and I put our mother's wheelchair in the trunk. Then Ramzi and I had a difficult task to do: locking up the house. As we completed this painful step, tears ran down my cheeks. I did not know when I would see our home again, if it would soon be occupied by militias or the Syrian army, or if internally displaced Lebanese families would move into it. The usually buoyant Ramzi was silent and pensive; I was sobbing. Back to the van, Ramzi sat next to the driver and I sat in the back seat in the third row.

Off we went. The driver suggested a different route than the one that Ramzi and I had proposed, but we trusted that he knew better what roads were safe and which were not. We started our journey at nearly five in the afternoon, a bit later than expected. The driver took us through neighborhoods we did not know, where the streets were narrow and militiamen were at every corner. It seemed we were stopped nearly every ten minutes. Armed men brandished machine guns in Ramzi's and the driver's faces, asked a multitude of questions about our destination and the reason for our trip, and demanded our identity cards.

Ramzi stayed calm through the whole ordeal. He answered their questions, explained that Mommy was sick and paralyzed, and that the fresh mountain air was better for her health. They would look inside, take their time inspecting our faces, sometimes ask us to step outside while they examined the interior, and then let us go. The same questions, the same inspection, the same tension, every time we were stopped by a group of armed men. Mommy and Daddy remained stoic; our mother's helper was gentle and caring; Ramzi was the calmest possible; the driver sweated; and I tried my best not to show my concerns.

It started to get dark and we were still in Beirut. We had not yet reached the outskirts of the city when the driver turned into a narrow street and bullets started flying. My heart sank. He pulled the van to the side of the road and stopped. We were in a neighborhood where the photos of President Abdul Nasser, Imam Moussa Al Sadr, and many martyrs were all over the buildings.

We were approached by a large number of armed men, and the questions were tougher. As we had agreed before starting the journey, the questions were handled by Ramzi and the driver, and I would answer only if the armed men addressed me directly. We believed that is what the patrols preferred. A fleeting thought passed through my head: what if I told them I was a member of Imam Moussa Al

Sadr's Cultural Advisory Council? However, I immediately dropped the idea. Most probably they would not believe me. It was not at all the time to take such risks. Instead, I silently prayed for our safety.

After a series of tough questions and a very thorough inspection with flashlights brandished in our faces, we were allowed to continue. I reached for Mommy's hand as the driver moved ahead. Silence hung heavy in the van. Finally, we reached the outskirts of Beirut. It must have been after eight o'clock by then, and we breathed easier. Daddy looked back, caught my eye, and smiled. He, too, was holding Mommy's hand. Ramzi continued to be the courageous navigator and the calm representative of the family, ready to answer any question thrown at him by any group of armed men.

In normal times we should have arrived at Qornet Shahwan by six; instead, we arrived close to nine in the evening. Ameen was waiting for us anxiously. We went inside and collapsed, all by far more exhausted than we allowed each other to know during our difficult ordeal. All we wanted was a good night sleep. We took Mommy and Daddy to their new bedroom and helped them settle in for a good night's sleep. Ramzi and I went to the living room and shared with Ameen what we had been through.

The next morning, we woke up to a gorgeous spring sun, fresh air, and new lights. How could two parts of Lebanon be so different? Beirut was going through hell, and Qornet Shahwan was as peaceful as could be, at least during the beginning of May 1986. The mountains in Lebanon are magical in the spring. I prepared coffee, and Mommy, Daddy, Ramzi, and I enjoyed our delicious beverage on the new balcony, as if yesterday were a distant memory.

I cannot remember how many days—possibly five—we spent with our parents helping them settle into their new home. One thing

we were determined to do before we left Lebanon and flew back—
Ramzi to Saudi Arabia and I to the U.S.—was to hire a chauffeur to
help Daddy in whatever he needed: to take him to the bank, to the
doctors, to the dentist, and to do the shopping for him. When that
task was complete, we prepared to return to our busy lives.

Ramzi and I took a taxi to the Beirut International Airport.
While waiting for our flights, we reviewed with amazement how
much we accomplished in two weeks in the middle of a war, and
how flexible Mommy and Daddy were to accept this major change
in their lives. We also talked about how the trip between Hamra
and Qornet Shahwan could have been a disaster. We counted our
blessings, thanked destiny and God that Mommy and Daddy were
safe, and hugged each other warmly before going our separate ways.

Only when I arrived back in Washington, D.C., did I realize how
emotionally draining it had been to relocate Mommy and Daddy. I
rarely accept that the individual is not the master of his action and
destiny; however, that drive late in the evening on streets and dark
alleys filled with armed men was a journey filled with risks where
outcomes could not be controlled. Thank God destiny was kind to
us that evening.

After a month or two of being back in Washington, busy at Creative
with my international educational projects, I had my yearly check-up.

My doctor found a lump in my breast.

A biopsy was done, and to my shock, it was malignant. I had
always considered myself very healthy. I never smoked; I drank wine
in a very moderate way; I ate mostly vegetarian food; and I was never
overweight.

When my doctor told me I had breast cancer, many different
emotions surfaced all at once. I believe my heart skipped a beat. My

eyes swelled with tears, I gasped for air, and my stomach cramped. I was confused and felt like I was losing control. My mind wanted to be rational and start processing what it all meant, but my emotions took over—intense, overwhelming emotions. Sadness filled my chest, and uncertainty ruled.

I went home, called the office to tell them I was sick, and threw myself on my bed, sobbing. I cried for several hours straight until I became exhausted. I believe I slept for another couple of hours. When I woke up, I tried to understand what it really meant to have breast cancer; it still did not make sense and all I could do was cry.

I needed time to process my feelings. I was alone in Washington, D.C. I had separated from Andrew a year-and-a-half earlier. Ramzi and Sarmad were both living and working in Saudi Arabia by then, and of course my parents and Ameen were in Lebanon. I had my wonderful career, and my friends, but somehow during the first few days after the diagnosis, cancer seemed far more powerful than anything else.

Many questions surfaced: Why did I have cancer? What had I done to cause it? I wondered about treatment—chemotherapy, radiation, surgery. How invasive would treatment be? How painful, with what side effects? Could I recover, and if so, how long would it take? Would I even survive? Could I go through the ordeal alone, and if not, who could I turn to? Who should I tell that I had cancer? Questions, questions, questions—and no answers, instead tears.

In many ways, I was and still am a private person, and I was not sure I wanted all my communities to know what I would be going through. I knew I had to discuss with my oncologist what my next steps should be, and what would be the best course of action. It was hard to go back to the doctor in the first few days; I still needed time to process what I was going through.

A nagging question that dominated all other questions was why me? I tried hard to understand why I was chosen to get breast cancer and "Why me?" was the hardest question to deal with. I felt I was being forced into a journey that I did not choose to take. The first few days after the diagnosis were filled with sadness, fear, anxiety, confusion, and anger. I felt so alone and so miserable, with "Why me?" as my only companion. After three or four days, after I had cried my eyes out, after I had done some research about breast cancer, and while I was debating how to announce the bad news to my parents and brothers, a question entered my head unannounced: Why not me?

At that instant, I felt better. In the little research I had done, I learned that one out of every eleven women is diagnosed with cancer. Those statistics made me realize how wide-spread cancer is. I decided that if one out of every eleven women would be hit by cancer, then maybe it was better that I suffer rather than a poor African or Lebanese woman who did not have health insurance, who might be a widow with children, or who could not make ends meet. That thought comforted me. I may have been grasping at straws, desperate for consolation, but the idea that I may be shouldering another woman's burden made me feel better.

My reflections could have been irrational, but everything about cancer is irrational. Cancer has the power to make a person feel isolated. Maybe I could overcome that feeling, but an African widow who had lost her husband to HIV/AIDS, or a Lebanese widow who had lost her husband to the war, might have found the feeling of isolation impossible to bear.

After another day or two of reflection, I regained some of my strength and decided to tell a select group of my colleagues at Creative

Associates, as well as my brothers, about my diagnosis. I decided to spare Mommy and Daddy the horrible news.

Charito Kruvant and Mimi Tse at Creative had to know because I needed a month off and because the company's health insurance would cover the expenses of treatment. My three brothers had to know because we were so close; they were my support system. Mommy and Daddy had to be spared because the news would burden them with loads of sadness.

I was amazed that I was able to tell Charito and Mimi without crying; however, I sobbed when telling Ameen, Ramzi, and Sarmad. Even though the "Why not me?" question had helped me regain some of my strength and erase my anger, it did not erase my fears and my sadness.

Charito and Mimi were extremely caring and supportive, and they understood my desire not to spread the news beyond a certain inner circle.

Ameen, Ramzi, and Sarmad were unbelievably caring. Having brothers like them is a blessing. They called me often, did their best to console me, tried to understand my fears, helped me process what I was going through, talked to me at length about the importance of remaining optimistic, and wrote me loving letters.

The gynecologist who made the diagnosis, Dr. Constance Bohon, recommended Dr. Katherine Alley as my oncologist. They were both excellent physicians. After several consultations, we agreed that I needed to have a mastectomy. Ramzi decided to fly from Saudi Arabia to be with me during the operation and to stay at my apartment for the two weeks immediately following surgery. He was a gift from heaven. Seeing his face as I was wheeled out of the operation room was the most comforting thing.

Ramzi took me home and cared for me for two full weeks. The discussions I had with him during that time transported me back to a place of confidence and strength. He was the one who convinced me that I was still the same person after my mastectomy as before. He talked about my essence, my mind, and my heart, and challenged me to explain to him how these could possibly be changed by cancer. He insisted that cancer could not define me. Ramzi also took care of the daily chores, received the flowers that came from the few colleagues I had informed, answered Ameen and Sarmad's regular phone calls and informed them about my progress. He cooked for me or bought ready-made food, and made me laugh. Laughing with Ramzi was my therapy. I wish for every woman a brother like Ramzi.

When Ramzi returned to Saudi Arabia, I was doing much better. I was in a positive mood and had decided I would beat cancer, survive it, and make it just one more chapter in my rich journey of discovering our planet and our humanity, and a special page in experiencing suffering, sadness, and happiness.

My mother and father, Loreen and Albert Rihani, in Beirut, 1952.

My mother, brother Ameen, and I.

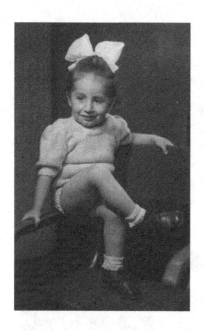

The hard life of being
the only daughter in the family!

With Daddy.

Friendship at a young age with
my brother Ameen.

View of our Freike home from the garden below.

A student at AUB, Beirut, 1969.

Another view of the home I grew up in.

The writers and poets who spoke at the Sénacle Libanais
about my first Arabic book, "Hafrun 'Ala Al-Ayyam,"
(left to right): myself, Said Akl, Jamil Jabre, Nour Salman,
Joseph Sayegh, and Issam Mahfouz, Beirut, 1969.

With former Lebanese President Camille Chamoun at
the Phoenicia Intercontinental, Beirut, 1973.

With Prime Minister Saeb Salam at the Phoenicia
Intercontinental, Beirut, 1973.

With the designer of Maison Jean Patou, the French Maison of haute couture, and the models of Patou, at the Phoenicia Intercontinental, Beirut, 1974. I am the first from the left.

With Mohammad Ali Clay at the Phoenicia
Intercontinental, Beirut, 1974.

In Geneva, preparing for the United Nations Youth Population
Conference that took place in Bucharest, Romania, summer 1974.

Christmas 1976 in the French Alps, with my friend
Bulle Vautier and her son Alexandre.

In Liberia, with women and children, 1978.

At a conference on Arab Women in Amman, Jordan, 1979.

Ameen, May, Ramzi, and Sarmad standing behind our parents
at our home in Freike during a visit to Lebanon in 1980.

With Edouard Saouma, the Director General of the Food and
Agriculture Organization (FAO) at an international conference in 1980.

Andrew and I at a poetry reading at the Martin Luther
King Library in Washington DC, 1980.

The Rihani family reunion in Freike, 1981: Back row (left to
right) Sarmad carrying his son Paul, Ina, Samira, Ameen, May,
Andrew, Karen, and Ramzi. Sitting in front of Mommy Loreen
and Daddy Albert (left to right) are: Reem, Serene, and Cedar.

September 5, 1981, on the balcony of the Freike home,
the day Andrew Oerke and I were married.

With Daddy, Andrew and I, the day of our
wedding in Freike, September 1981.

Andrew and I at our home in Washington, D.C., 1982.

A girls' school that I visited in Yemen in 1984.

Many of the schools that I visited in Africa were
outdoor schools with straw walls, 1985

Relaxing at home in Freike after a long work trip
visiting several African countries, 1985.

Platform International organized an exhibit in Washington
DC in 1987, for the internationally known artist Paul
Guiragossian. From left to right: Ramzi, Mrs. Guiragossian,
Paul Guiragossian, Mrs. Adma Shakhashiri, and myself.

An evening with friends during one of my visits to Lebanon in 1988 (left to right): author May Manassa, painter Souleima Zoud, Ramzi, and I.

Ramzi and I in 1989 at the opening of Platform International's exhibit for Lebanese women artists in Washington, D.C.

At a training session for the officials of the Ministry
of Planning in Mogadishu, Somalia, 1989.

CHAPTER TWENTY-FOUR

A NEW DAWN

FTER MY SURGERY, RAMZI CALLED me often from Saudi Arabia to discuss my progress. I shared with him that due to my fatigue after the mastectomy, I was considering asking Charito, the president of Creative, if at the end of the scheduled month off, I could return to work on a half-time basis until I was entirely recovered. He encouraged me to do just that. My meeting with Charito went extremely well. She wanted me to take as much time as I needed to recover and was comfortable with my working half-time.

One of Ramzi's phone calls brought a happy surprise. After some reflection, he had decided to move back to the U.S. in the fall. He had been working in the Arabian Gulf for several years, first as the CEO of the KDS Group of companies in Qatar, and then as assistant general manager of Technical Trading Company in Saudi Arabia. By 1986, he was a successful professional. I was impressed and delighted by his decision. Ramzi and I had always been very close, but after having experienced together the risky move from Beirut to Qornet Shahwan, and after the very special two weeks together immediately after my mastectomy, we had become even closer. By then, Ramzi was not just my brother; he was my best friend. When Ramzi told me of his decision to return to Washington, D.C., the rays of the sun that were beaming into my apartment's living room looked much brighter; they were shimmering with gold.

I went back to Creative half-time and continued working on educational projects. Ramzi moved back to Washington and rented an apartment in the same building I was living in, and I could not have been happier that we were neighbors. As I mentioned, both Ramzi and I were separated and going through a divorce process. Being single again allowed us to spend more time together. We often had dinner in one of our apartments or went out to concerts. Attending a concert with Ramzi was a special experience because he was a connoisseur of music. He introduced me to live performances of American music icons such as Bob Dylan and Bruce Springsteen.

During one of our evenings, we were, as usual, talking about the events in Lebanon. Our discussion centered on the poor image Lebanon received in the media. Ramzi and I were concerned that Westerners would never understand the positive side of Lebanon, the rich culture of our country, and its important contributions to the world's civilizations in the fields of literature, poetry, music, dance, and visual arts. As a result of this discussion, Ramzi thought that he and I could do something about the situation by informing the media in particular and the U.S. public in general about Lebanon's contributions. I asked how, and his answer was brilliant.

Ramzi suggested we form an organization that would have as its objective bringing top-quality Lebanese artists to the U.S. for performances in quality venues such as the Kennedy Center in D.C. and the Lincoln Center in New York. Media exposure for these concerts and performances would be the focus of our work. His excitement was contagious, and I agreed to be his partner in establishing this new organization. Ramzi was willing to invest his savings from his work in the Gulf for this noble cause. Our younger brother Sarmad also supported the idea and invested in it. I followed suit.

By the end of 1986, we had established Platform International. I decided that in addition to my half-time at Creative, I would work an additional half-time at Platform. Ramzi was a little concerned at the beginning; he thought I might be exhausting myself. I had to remind him several times that working with him at Platform was not stressful at all. On the contrary, it was delightful and extremely satisfying to have an opportunity to serve Lebanon.

From the end of 1986 till sometime in 1990, Ramzi and I worked passionately to improve Lebanon's image in the U.S. During these years, we brought to the U.S. many of the most important Lebanese singers, dancers, painters, and sculptors. We brought the superstar Fayrouz, who is considered the diva of Lebanon and is acclaimed by millions as magical. We booked a four-city tour for her, and she performed to adoring audiences in Washington D.C., New York, Boston, and Detroit. Venues like the Kennedy Center and the Lincoln Center had never before experienced an audience who believed an artist like Fayrouz could embody the sufferings and the hopes of a whole country. To the Lebanese and the American Lebanese, Fayrouz represented the dream and the hope of a peaceful Lebanon; she was proof that the war would end and Lebanon would return to its heyday. Fayrouz carried the soul of Lebanon in her voice.

The concerts in those four American cities were prayers for ending the war in Lebanon, and celebrations about the future of a suffering beloved country. Ramzi and I were delighted with the reaction of the audiences, and in particular with the positive coverage of the American media. *Newsweek, The Washington Post,* the *Herald Tribune,* and others wrote positively about Fayrouz, and about

Lebanon. Their articles underlined Lebanon's contributions in the cultural and artistic world. Ramzi and I were pleased that the strategy of Platform International seemed to make a difference at least in the minds of some of the influencers in the American media. Those small, early successes made us believe that improving the image of Lebanon might not be such an impossibility.

We expanded our efforts and brought in the Lebanese Caracalla Dance Theatre. As the premiere Arab dance company, Caracalla was Lebanon's innovative leader in the fusion of Lebanese, Arab, and Western music, where the creativity of its founder and choreographer, Abdul Halim Caracalla, captured the cultural richness of Lebanon through dance. Caracalla was highly acclaimed for its spectacular performances where dance, beat, color, choreography, and theater sets were breathtaking. Their choreographic style tended to be at the edge of new visions; the dance scenes were a fusion of the Lebanese *debke* and modern dance. The company presented a meeting point between a Lebanese village wedding dance, an uplifting Alvin Ailey dance scene, and a Maurice Béjart creative expressionist theatrical dance.

Abdul Halim Caracalla and his troupe captured the cutting-edge creativity in Lebanon and reproduced it on stage. The nine-city tour that Ramzi and I organized for them was a smashing success; audiences and media could not get enough. From Washington, D.C., to New York, Boston, Cleveland, Chicago, Detroit, Los Angeles, San Francisco, and Houston, they enchanted their audiences and impressed the media. With them, the image of Lebanon was that of a country where innovation in dance took place, where women and men experimented with the coming together of traditional Oriental dance styles and modern Western ballet-like dance approaches. No one could experience a Caracalla performance without thinking of Lebanon as an incubator of new trends in dance and as a country where daring art flourished. Caracalla was about leaps in the air and leaps of imagination. Like Lebanon—despite the war—Caracalla was about daring experimentation and a *joie de vivre* that had no boundaries.

Ramzi and I enjoyed sponsoring Lebanese artists in the U.S., and we wanted to do more. We wanted to introduce the U.S. to Lebanese visual art. We organized exhibits for single artists who were already known in Lebanon, the Arab world, and Europe, and sometimes we sponsored exhibits for a group of painters and sculptors to show the diversified and innovative work that Lebanon produced even through wartime. Among the visual artists we brought to the U.S. were the most well-known artists of Lebanon including Paul Guiragossian, Wajih Nahle, Hrair, the brothers Basbous, Mohammad Al Kaissi, Hassan Jouni, George Akl, Jacqueline Jabre, Souleima Zoud, Mona Sehnaoui, Nadim Karam, and Hoda Naamani. Their oil, watercolor, mixed media, and sculptor art exhibits were very successful. The shows attracted a larger number of viewers, and the media was, once again, interested in the rich artistic contributions of Lebanon. As before, both the audiences and the media were stunned by the diversity of art schools, the daringness of some of the topics, and the avant-garde nature of many of the oeuvres.

Next, we wanted to take this whole journey one step further and focus on women artists from Lebanon. We organized a special exhibit in a large Georgetown gallery for Lebanese women painters. Their work was stunning, diversified, and sometimes unexpected. For any viewer, it became clear that Lebanese women artists did not allow social boundaries or war conditions to limit their creativity. They were free to express their thoughts, identities, feelings, hopes, and dreams the way they wanted. Lebanon was showcased as a country where art flourished and where new frontiers were discovered.

During the Platform International years and my partnership with Ramzi to improve the image of Lebanon in the U.S. through Lebanese art, I continued to work half-time at Creative Associates on international development programs. My duties there took me back to Tunisia, a country I had connected with at a deep level, possibly because of Carthage and the Phoenician common ground between Lebanon and Tunisia. I was asked to participate in designing a women's leadership program for the *Union Nationale des Femmes Tunisiennes* (UNFT) or the National Union of Tunisian Women. Established in March 1956 at the dawn of the Tunisian independence, the UNFT was the first women's organization in Tunisia and was present in all regions of the country. It had twenty-seven regional delegations and three hundred fifty sections with presence in remote areas. In early 1981 when I visited Tunisia for the first time, I met with Mme. Fethia Mzali who was at that time the president of the UNFT. She was a strong leader with commitment and vision, but not necessarily a leader who made participation of others in decision-making a priority.

In 1983, Tunisian President Habib Bourguiba named the first two women ministers to his cabinet; one of them was Mme. Mzali, whom he appointed the Minister of Family Affairs and Women's Promotion. At that time, nominating two women ministers in an Arab or African country was considered a liberal move. I was delighted that Tunisia was setting an example in political power-sharing with women.

During my work in Tunisia in 1987-88, Mme. Mzali was no longer the president of UNFT, and the new leadership was looking for methodologies for greater involvement in decision-making by the leadership of UNFT at different levels. I knew that I needed an in-depth understanding of the strengths and the culture of UNFT in order to build on those strengths, and with the collaboration of the current leaders, gradually modify their organizational structure to increase participation in decision-making. Another consultant and I worked very closely with leaders of UNFT at both national and regional levels to design a workshop on leadership that would be responsive to the specific needs of the National Union. At the end of the workshop, I was humbled by the positive feedback and evaluations we received from the participants. No doubt I learned about leadership as much as anyone who participated in the session, if not more.

My work continued to require me to learn new skills, stretch my capabilities, and face new challenges. In 1988, Creative Associates and the Academy of Educational Development (AED) partnered in writing a proposal to bid on a project in Somalia, and I was asked to participate in the project design. I had worked in Somalia in 1984 as a member of the USAID-funded project Improving the Efficiency of Educational Systems (IEES). That experience in Somalia helped me understand the context of the country and enabled me to participate in the design in a meaningful way.

To my delight, USAID awarded the large project to AED and Creative. AED was the prime contractor and we at Creative were the subcontractor; I was in charge of the subcontract activities for this large program. We launched the project in 1989, and my visits to Somalia became essential to ensure the desired progress on Creative's activities there. One of our components was to assist in improving the management of a number of ministries. The learning curve was steep; I had to learn, as quickly as I could, efficient and result-oriented management. I needed to examine how ministries managed programs and implemented them, and how they handled challenging demands from bureaucracies while still moving forward.

I had to learn contemporary strategic concepts and strengthen my understanding of the elements of effective and efficient management.

A fascinating aspect of my work was that the learning process was continuous, and I could only succeed in designing and delivering technical assistance as long as my mind was fully aware that I was a constant learner. I needed to absorb as much as those who were receiving the technical assistance from me, my colleagues, or my staff.

In 1989 and 1990, I went to Somalia at least four times, worked with the Ministries of Planning and Labor on management issues, and designed training with two other consultants. We delivered the training to the top managers of the ministries and were hopeful that progress, however slow, would take place. While in Somalia, I could not help but reflect on the differences as well as the common ground among the different countries of our planet. The differences were clear: levels of poverty; spread of education; existence or lack of basic health services; the existence and nature of the infrastructure; and other basic rights and needs. The common ground was by far more subtle and less visible. It included things like the aspirations of parents for a secure, healthy, and happy future for their children; the suffering of a mother faced with the lack of sufficient food for her children; the intelligence and aspirations of children; the enchantment of discovering new things; and the spirituality that guided those elevated souls in cities and remote areas of our planet. Perhaps the most important common ground to be realized was the brotherhood or sisterhood of humanity that only a few deeply understand and live by, whether those few could be found in Somalia, the U.S., Lebanon, India, or France.

One day I took a long walk on the beach in Merka, not far away from Mogadishu, and tried hard to understand why we as humans differentiate among races and cultures. I failed.

On another day, I went to the main market in Mogadishu with two Somali colleagues. It was a beautiful, sunny day and the market was crowded. I became immersed in the sounds, noises, colors, and smells of the market, and intrigued by certain displayed items that I did not expect to see. Suddenly, I felt someone pull a hair from my head. I turned around and saw a little boy holding one of my long, straight, fairly light-colored strands of hair up to the sun and looking at it. To the boy, this was a novelty. A foreign woman in his market was different, and her hair was different. The hair he usually saw was black, curly, and not necessarily long. Because of his curiosity, he mustered his courage, stood behind me, and pulled out one strand to examine it. The fact that he lifted the hair to the sun and was gazing at it made me recognize how beautiful curiosity is. Who knew what he might have been dreaming? That blond hair could have been be a string on his imagined guitar, or maybe he was trying to understand when and how the sun decided that some hair would be golden blond and some would be jet black. The boy was on a discovery kick and I enjoyed watching him.

All children are curious. Their beautiful minds are not limited by their race or country of origin, and their expanding imagination is not dependent on their religion or color of skin. Children in Africa, the Middle East, and Asia were my best teachers about the common ground within humanity. Despite this common ground, the basic needs of all children are not always met, and I witnessed poverty in Somalia the way I witnessed it in Zaire.

One evening in my hotel in Mogadishu, in June 1989, I wrote a poem titled *"Kharej Al Shaba3"*; the translation would be "Outside the Circle of Plenty." This poem was published in several dailies in Lebanon, and was translated into English by Dr. Najwa Nasr, a professor of English literature at the Lebanese University in Beirut.

Another poem that I wrote during this same period is titled *"Woujouhi Al Arba'a,"* or "My Four Faces." Richard Harteis, an American poet, later translated the poem. *Delos,* a journal of translation and world literature published "My Four Faces" in 1994.

During the years between 1986 and 1989, like most of my other years since I left Lebanon, I visited my parents twice or three times a year. I would stay with them in Qornet Shahwan, reconnect with my friends from the AUB days and the writers, poets, and artists who were part of my life, and continue to learn more about the complex political scene in Lebanon. Often, I would be interviewed on Lebanese television channels or by some of the daily papers.

While visiting in September 1987, I gave a poetry reading at Beit Al-Moustakbal "The Home of the Future." The event was organized by Michel Maiki, a television anchor. Playwright Raymond Gebara wrote the introduction for the evening; Rifaat Tarabay, a well-known Lebanese actor, read some of my poems with me; and Oud player Charbel Rouhana accompanied me while I recited other of my pieces. It was a very special evening. Most of my poet friends attended it, and towards the end of the evening, the Lebanese President Amine Gemayel surprised me by arriving and joining the audience. He sat in the upper balcony and listened to my poetry. Michel Maiki created a unique ambiance for the evening: the stage was set with candles, flowers, and Oriental tent covers. Charbel Rouhana's Oud music was about nostalgia and travel, and Rifaat Tarabay's readings added a theatrical dimension to my poems. The opening remarks by Raymond Gebara captured who I was as a person; he talked about the bridge between Freike and Washington, D.C., and the connection between my Wednesday poetry evenings and my international work. Also that evening, Najwa Nasr presented an analysis of my poetry. The event was covered extensively in the Lebanese media.

A poem I read that evening is titled "*Ghurba*," "In an Alien Land":

Like spring those days ended too soon,
And now life is suspended until it returns.
Years of uncounted seasons pass
Yet the almond blossoms do not appear.
I saw her —
The East in her eyes
The West in her body —
Dreaming in a café,
Mixing the two in her cup.
There, roots extend to link her securely
To the incense of an old church,
To the mists of long summer nights
Among the columns of Baalbeck in the company of
    2000 years.
Here,
New York knows how to erase what preceded and
    start afresh
Here, the temperature of her body rises.
She raises her head, throws back her long hair
And overturns her cup to read her fortune
She leaves the café,
Without glancing at the cipher in her cup.

The taste of an alien land is like the taste of hesitation
In an alien land, long discussions with walls until
    twilight;
In an alien land, treading roads that have not echoed
    their footsteps.

283

Nights of dancing until daybreak,

In the morning, forgetfulness dawns.

I go to my office

I work earnestly

I work without stopping

And bury my nostalgia.

On the third day nostalgia rolls back the rock of work, and

Alienation becomes a sign that proclaims: House for
    Sale.

Even though I had to a certain extent decreased my involvement in Platform International due to the demands of my work at Creative, I continued to participate in planning certain cultural and artistic events with Ramzi. In 1988, Ramzi had thought of bringing to the U.S. some Lebanese classical concert players who were already known in Lebanon and Europe. One of them was Jad Azkoul, a Lebanese concert guitarist, who was Ramzi's friend from the AUB days. The plan was for Jad Azkoul to play at the Kennedy Center. Jihad flew from Geneva to Washington and met several times with Ramzi. They went together to the Kennedy Center to check on the hall, the acoustics, the stage setting, the lights, and rehearsal time.

Ramzi invited Jad for dinner at his apartment the evening before the concert so the three of us could have an enjoyable visit before the big event. Jad asked if he could bring a friend to dinner and Ramzi immediately agreed. I went to Ramzi's apartment a bit early to assist him in last minute preparations, and while I was arranging flowers in a vase, the doorbell rang. It was Jad and his friend.

As soon as they saw me, his friend said, "Do you remember me? We met before." I told him I did not remember, and added many men ask me that question. I do not know what got into me to answer in such a flippant way, but I did. The friend was Zuheir Al-Faqih. He and Jad were very close from their AUB days together. Later that evening I did remember I had met Zuheir once before at a dinner party at his father's home in Alley in Lebanon. I remembered the details of that time when we met seventeen years earlier, in 1971:

Daddy and Mommy were invited to dinner. Mommy was ill by then and could not go, so Daddy asked if I would like to accompany him. My original response was no, thank you. They were his friends and I would not know anyone there.

Then Daddy said, "But our host is an ambassador, and you like politics. I am sure you would be interested in the discussions that will take place."

I agreed to accompany my father for two reasons: one because of the argument that Daddy presented, but also because I felt Daddy really wanted me to be with him. Since Mommy's illness, he had minimized his going out in the evenings, and on the rare occasion when he accepted an invitation; he might not have wanted to go alone.

When we arrived at the large, lovely home of Ambassador As'ad Al-Faqih, there were already at least seventy guests in the gardens. I did not know anyone; the invitees were nearly all close to my father's and the ambassador's age. I sat on a bench in the garden and watched the elegant Lebanese guests enjoy the summer dinner party.

While lost in my own thoughts, I saw a young man, most probably my age, walking towards me from the other end of the garden. He introduced himself as Zuheir Al-Faqih, the son of the host. He sat next to me and we chatted for the whole evening. I learned that Zuheir did his BA at AUB during the same years when I was studying for my BA, and that he was the editor-in-chief of *Outlook* at that time. We had never met on campus. I also learned that after his BA, Zuheir went to the U.S. for his MA. He was in Lebanon to see his parents, and he would be leaving the next day to return to San Francisco where he was completing his studies. I mentioned that I was continuing my courses toward an MA at AUB and that I was writing and publishing. We had a wonderful conversation that spanned many topics: education, music, poetry, the U.S., Lebanon. He made me smile several times. Towards the end of the evening, he excused himself to go pack his suitcase because he was leaving in the very early hours of the morning.

So that was the friend of Jad's who came to dinner at Ramzi's apartment. Of course I remembered him during the evening, and kept wondering how he recognized me so quickly when I opened the door, given that seventeen years had passed.

Zuheir took my phone number and we started seeing each other. At our first get-together, he revealed that after his MA, he married an American. The marriage lasted several years, but at the time we became reacquainted, he was separated and in the process of finalizing his divorce. I shared with him my very similar story and that I, too, was in the process of divorcing.

Zuheir said it would be difficult to get on my schedule for a year or two. In many ways, he was right; I was very busy and I was traveling a lot in those years, but I was also trying to clear an emotional space within my heart. The American poet had left imprints that were not easy to erase.

CHAPTER TWENTY-FIVE

AMAZING ENERGIES

THE NEW ENERGY THAT SWEPT through my life starting in 1988 through the early 1990s was like the smell of ocean waves on a beautiful sunny day.

In 1988, Professor Leon Clark of the International Training and Education Department at American University (AU) asked me to teach a course at the school. My first reaction was perhaps Professor Clark thought I had a PhD in education because he knew of my work in international education. When we met to discuss his request, the first thing I clarified was that I did not hold a PhD.

Professor Clark believed that my international education experience would be sufficient to handle the course he wanted me to teach. The International Training and Education Program (ITEP) was a multidisciplinary master's program that focused on education both as an instrument of international development and as a means of promoting cross-cultural understanding. He felt my experience would make me eligible to teach at the master's level. He explained that the program would provide students with a strong theoretical background in the foundations and practice of education coupled with solid knowledge, skills, and experiences in policy formulation, program/project design and management, training in program design, and intercultural learning.

We discussed at length how in the current global environment, international education specialists played an increasingly important role as teachers, trainers, administrators, program managers, and change agents for improving social justice and welfare. Professor Clark underlined the importance for international education experts like me to find time to teach, so the lessons we were learning could be shared with the new generations of students who sought a career in international education. He also stressed that ITEP emphasized practical application as well as career development, and that ITEP students benefitted from faculty contacts and the alumni network for jobs, internships, and volunteer opportunities.

We reviewed how ITEP prepared students for professional careers in international development education, international exchange and study abroad, and how ITEP's location at AU in Washington, D.C., gave students an ideal proximity to a plethora of international organizations.

After our discussions, I told Professor Clark that I would be delighted and honored to teach a master's degree course in the ITEP program. My only concern was the demands on my time, given the amount of travel involved in my work. He said my course could be delivered in the evening after my hours at Creative. He pressed his argument as to why I should teach at AU despite my very busy schedule and concluded by telling me that his vision was to see the graduates of ITEP master's program be much better prepared and ready to be placed at organizations like Creative Associates International, CARE, NAFSA: Association of International Educators, National Institutes of Health, Peace Corps, Save the Children, U.S. Agency for International Development,

U.S. Department of State, World Bank, World Learning, and World Vision. Eventually, I was convinced; I agreed to teach a graduate course at AU.

I remembered my days at the Collège Protestant Français in Lebanon, and how much I loved teaching and respected the role of the teacher. Also, the prospect of working with Professor Clark was exciting. He was one of the earliest and most prominent professors in initiating and ensuring that international development, in its very best form—ethical, just, respectful, and people-focused—took hold and thrived at American University. He had carried out numerous assignments as an international development consultant in Africa and Asia and understood why it was vital to add seriously experienced practitioners to the mix of academicians, and why academia would benefit from practitioners teaching courses where learning was based on theoretical as well as experiential lessons.

Professor Clark and I agreed that I would teach a course about adult education. Planning, preparing, and delivering the course were invigorating activities. My students were from around the world and most of them were working and taking courses in the evening to complete their master's degree. I decided to base the course on two sets of knowledge: the theory of Paulo Freire and my experiences in Africa and the Middle East.

Some of the principles I used from Paolo Freire were:

- Conscientization is learning to perceive social, political, and economic contradictions, and to take action against the oppressive elements of reality.
- Conscientization is the ultimate aim of the educational process, and the starting point of the process of reconstitution.

- Conscientization describes the arousing of an individual's positive self-concept in relation to his/her environment and society through a "liberating education."
- Reading the world precedes reading the word.

The principles I used in the course from my experiences were:

- Learning can happen everywhere, and it happens best when it is relevant to the daily lives of the learner.
- Teachers, facilitators, trainers, and students learn from each other. They are all creators, givers, and receivers of knowledge.
- The global and the local contexts are equally important sources of knowledge; however, only if we understand the complexities of the local context can we then begin to understand the global context.
- Experiments cannot be transplanted; they have to be reinvented.
- Active listening is the beginning of the process of successful international educational development.
- Reforming the educational system needs the engagement and commitment of all the stakeholders; the Ministry of Education cannot reform the system by itself.

This graduate course at AU affirmed for me my love for teaching. My evening seminar was a platform for intellectual debates and learning. I think both my students and I deepened our knowledge of international education as a result of our exchanges. The frustrating side of teaching was that I had to travel during the semester which meant I had to find a lecturer to fill in. As much as I loved teaching, by the end of the year I told Professor Clark that I preferred not to continue teaching due to my travels. Given the excellent evaluations my course received from my students, he was surprised. It was my turn to do the convincing to make Professor Clark accept my decision.

In 1989, Creative Associates and the Academy for Educational Development decided to partner again and bid on a USAID-funded project. AED was the prime and Creative was a subcontractor; we won the project.

Advancing Basic Education and Literacy (ABEL) was a global project designed to address national and international concerns across the broad spectrum of basic education: formal education systems, girls' education, and informal education for out-of-school youth and adults. Broad consensus on the urgency of these issues was reached in 1990 when the nations of the world and the international donors met in Jomtien, Thailand, at the World Conference on Education for All. The leaders who gathered at the conference affirmed the importance of basic education as a tool to combat poverty and to stimulate the economy, as an approach to manage population growth and improve child health, and as a strategy to promote equality between women and men. Government representatives and donors committed themselves to making education a high priority.

During the Jomtien Conference, it was recognized that despite the significant gains that had been made in enrolling more children and in reaching the least-served populations such as girls and women, out-of-school youth, and minority ethnic groups, there was still a lot to be done. It was also recognized that a greater urgency was needed to bring girls and women into formal and non-formal education systems. In addition, it was acknowledged that the quality of education needed to be seriously improved.

The ABEL project was designed to address all of these issues. I was delighted that AED, Creative, and other partners won this five-year global project, and that I would lead the activities that Creative was charged with implementing. Contributing to the improvement of the quality and equity of education systems became my passion, and ensuring that girls would have the same educational opportunities as boys propelled my energies. Because I understood that improving the quality of any educational system needs concerted efforts in the areas of teacher education, curriculum development, efficient use of resources, empowerment of local school directors and teachers, and community engagement, I often worked twelve to fourteen hours a day.

Through ABEL, we ended up working in over twenty countries in Africa, Asia, Latin America, and the Middle East. The many teams of educational specialists that were hired by us, the consortium that led ABEL, assisted governments and USAID Missions in project design, policy reform support, pilot projects, evaluations, and applied research. ABEL also provided both short and long-term technical assistance. The most important work that ABEL delivered was the provision of short-term training to build capacity within ministries of education.

As a member of the leadership team of ABEL, I worked in several countries; however, the four countries that I focused on from 1990 till 1994 were Benin, Ghana, Mali, and Malawi. In Benin, I worked very closely with the Director of Planning at the Ministry of Education, Dr. Bienvenue Marcos. In Ghana, I worked in a very cooperative way with USAID's education representative, Dr. Sandy Ojikutu. In Mali, I worked hand-in-hand with Dr. Lalla Ben Barka, head of the Promotion of Women's Division of the National Directorate of Functional Literacy and Applied Linguistics (DNAFLA), and in Malawi, I worked with the minister and several directors. These education professionals—several Africans and one

American married to an African—were totally committed to the reform of the educational systems in their countries.

Dr. Marcos, for example, was leading the educational strategic plan for the reform of the system in Benin. His approach was inclusive; he engaged a large number of professionals from the ministry to lead the different components of the strategic plan. He had a vision for how to improve the quality and equity of education in his country and he was willing to address, in a serious and realistic way, all the constraints that faced the educational system. He was tireless, working long hours to change and improve the whole system in his country. What our project provided was technical assistance and expertise in areas that Dr. Marcos and his colleagues defined as areas that needed input from both the Beninois as well as from international consultants. Working with Dr. Marcos was a true pleasure. I learned from him the importance of believing that we can overcome obstacles and constraints, no matter how entrenched they are.

Dr. Lala Ben Barka was the consummate educational professional. A champion of education as a means of driving Mali's long-term economic development, Dr. Ben Barka's expertise focused on strengthening educational structures, increasing access of the underserved, and challenging traditional attitudes, in particular those regarding girls' and women's education. Working with someone like Dr. Ben Barka convinced me that many African countries would in fact reform their systems through the vision and the deep commitment of such professionals.

My trips to Benin, Ghana, Mali, and Malawi, reinforced my love of Africa, a continent with a rich and diversified history, and with populations who have dreams and hopes of a better tomorrow.

Benin was the former Abomey kingdom of the Dahomey, which was established in 1625. In Benin, a rich cultural life flourished; its wooden masks, bronze statues, tapestries, and pottery are world-renowned. Like Senegal, the country has a distinct connection with slaves who were transported across the Atlantic to the new world. I visited Ouidah, a city that is best known for its central role in the slave trade during the seventeenth, eighteenth, and nineteenth centuries, during which time nearly one million individuals were loaded onto ships from the beach at Ouidah and transported across the ocean. In Ouidah, there is a road that is called the *Route Des Esclaves*—the road of the slaves—that had numerous statues and monuments about slavery, including an arch named "The Door of No Return." It is through this door that the captured individuals were taken from their families, homes, and land to face the unknown in a life of physical and emotional pain. Benin today is a land with a promise of equity and equality among the Beninois, as well as a political system that aspires for a democratic approach.

Mali, although landlocked with large swaths of arid desert, is the home of some of Africa's most interesting cultural sites. Legendary Timbuktu is located in the northern region, and in the center of the country is the magnificently dramatic Bandiagara escarpment. Bamako, the capital, has its own charm, the charm of a city that still keeps a slow pace despite the tiny restaurants that pop up in the different quarters of the capital, and the numerous small businesses that try hard to stay viable.

The Malians, in the days when I used to visit and work in their country, dreamed of a future where rain would be generous and poverty would recede. I bought a gorgeous wooden statue called *Chiwara* from Mali. Chiwaras could be male or female; these statues represent and honor the mythological half-man/half-antelope hero who taught man how to cultivate the soil. The Chiwaras celebrate the union of male (sun), female (earth), and fiber costume (rain), signifying the cooperation needed for a successful harvest and for community survival. To me, Chiwaras are about hope and overcoming natural constraints. My Malian Chiwara sits with majesty in my living room as if he were the Mona Lisa.

Landlocked Malawi is among the world's least developed countries; however, it is nicknamed the Warm Heart of Africa, and indeed it is a warm heart. Malawi's economy is heavily based on agriculture, supported by a largely rural population. The Malawian government depends heavily on outside aid to meet development needs. In the early 1990s, the USAID Mission in Lilongwe and the Ministry of Education asked us, through ABLE, to design and implement a project on Girls' Attainment of Basic Literacy and Education (GABLE). GABLE took me to Malawi at least once a year throughout the first five years of the 1990s. I worked very closely with the ministry of education in Lilongwe, with the University of Malawi in Zomba, with a team that I hired to work long term in Malawi, and with many Malawian schools, communities, and NGOs. The Malawians are a hospitable population despite the poverty, a hopeful population despite HIV/AIDS, and a population that did not allow boundaries to limit its potential despite all the economic, social, educational, and health constraints. In Malawi, I learned that hope flowers like the jacaranda trees.

With all the new programs we were launching, and with the global responsibilities that I was taking on through the powerful ABLE project and many other programs, Charito, the president of Creative, decided to make me a senior vice president. There were only two senior vice presidents at Creative in the late 1980s–early 1990s; I became the third one. The three of us shared huge responsibilities. We had to grow the business, ensure the quality of the designs and implementation of the programs, and manage the programs and staff. I have never said no to a challenge, and a senior vice president I became.

While immersed in the demands of the various programs in the different countries, I got a call from Mansour, Daddy's chauffeur in Lebanon. Daddy had fallen and broken his hip, and the doctor was reluctant to operate given Daddy's age and the possibility of needing a blood transfusion. Mansour said the doctor refused to operate until one of us, Daddy's children, arrived to be with him.

By 1989-90, my three brothers and I were all living outside Lebanon. None of us were nearby to assist my father during his time of need. I immediately called Ramzi and informed him about Daddy's situation. The decision took no more than a couple of minutes. We would fly to Lebanon to be with Daddy during the operation and, in particular, to offer him blood in case he needed a transfusion.

Despite our decision to go to Lebanon as soon as we could, Ramzi and I faced many obstacles. The security situation in Lebanon was extremely precarious. The war had escalated in recent years. In March 1989, General Michel Aoun had declared a "war of liberation" against the Syrian occupation. This triggered a devastating set of battles that lasted throughout 1989 and into 1990. Daddy broke his hip during that period of time, and bombardments between General Aoun and the Syrian army made travel dangerous.

The Syrian army was shelling the Beirut airport, and often the airport would close for a day or two before reopening to accept incoming flights. The quickest way to travel to Lebanon was by flying to Cyprus and boarding a boat to Jounieh, a Lebanese town on the Mediterranean. From there we would need to find a way to reach Beirut. Ramzi and I were determined to reach Daddy's hospital as soon as we could, no matter what the difficulties were.

The day after I received the phone call about Daddy's situation, Ramzi and I boarded a plane to London, and from London to Larnaca, the port city in Cyprus that had boats to Jounieh. The flight from Washington to London seemed longer than usual. I could not sleep on the plane; I could not stop thinking about Daddy, how he was alone in the hospital waiting for us to arrive so that the surgeon could operate.

The flight from London to Larnaca seemed even longer. I was impatient; I wanted to arrive so Ramzi and I could arrange for our boat trip. We were not sure how often boats left for Jounieh, or even if there were daily trips. We were anxious and silent on the plane. Even though I was not sure if my prayers were heard by the power of goodness and compassion, I could not stop praying for my father's recovery. I wanted to pray; I needed to pray.

Daddy was the one who made Mommy's illness bearable. Daddy was the one who made Mommy happy despite the hand that was dealt to her by destiny. Daddy was the one who taught his four children, in the most subtle way, that no matter what destiny dealt, we ought to find a way to remain happy, compassionate, and loving. It was hard to think that the man who gave so much of his compassion to everyone around him was now suffering alone in a hospital bed.

Ramzi and I arrived in Larnaca and went straight to the port. We discovered there was a ferryboat leaving a little after midnight and arriving in Jounieh around 5:00 a.m. We booked two places and waited for the departure time.

At around midnight, we started boarding. Once on board, we were told by the Norwegian captain that they traveled by night because it was safer. He warned us that forty minutes before arriving in Jounieh, at around 4:20 a.m. until we debarked, he would put off all the lights on the boat and no one would be allowed to put

297

on any light, not even a cigarette. If the Syrian army spotted a boat approaching Jounieh, they might bombard it; the only safe way to approach Jounieh was under the cover of darkness.

The passengers on the boat were few; I think only those who had to enter Lebanon for whatever emergencies in their lives traveled in such a way. The service was, nonetheless, deeply appreciated by the passengers because that was the only way to enter the country when a serious need arose. On the whole, the passengers were very quiet and subdued, and the mood on the boat was ponderously heavy.

Nearly forty-five minutes before arriving in Jounieh, the boat captain addressed us. He reminded us of the importance to do exactly as he said, that he would be turning off the lights, and that no one had permission to even light a cigarette. He also told us that he would turn off the motor and guide us to the port with a much smaller engine that did not make any noise. No light, no noise.

We were told that when we arrived in port to forget about our luggage and to follow the path that the assistant captain would lead us to. We had to leave the boat as quickly as possible, but in total silence. The luggage would come later. I have never seen Lebanese obey instructions as well as they did that night. No one talked; no one questioned any of the instructions. We did exactly what we were told.

Traveling in total silence and in total darkness was an eerie experience. Couples held hands; a mother cried silently. Fear was on the faces of nearly everyone. The forty silent minutes in the ocean and in the dark seemed to last as long as a full day.

We finally arrived. We debarked quickly to follow the assistant captain on a narrow path that led to an underground hall in the port and began to enter the hall when hell broke loose. Bombardments fell on the port from all directions.

With the sound of the first bomb, someone screamed, "Everybody lie down!" Ramzi and I threw ourselves on the ground of this underground hall. It did not take more than a couple of seconds before the floor was covered with the bodies of the passengers from the Norwegian boat. The bombardments were so powerful, I thought the building would collapse on all of us. I did not know what would happen. All I wanted was for us to see Daddy and give him blood for his operation before we died.

I lifted my head a little and saw Ramzi next to me, lying down quietly. I looked the other way and saw a couple of young men bleeding. A few of us were lucky to have reached the underground hall before the bombardments started. Those who were still crossing the narrow path must have been hit by shrapnels. Still, I was not sure if we would survive. The bombing continued. The building shook.

I started praying. I, the not-so-sure of God, resorted to praying when everything else failed. My prayers were for the safety of all those lying on the ground. I had no doubt that most of them took that risky boat trip because someone in their family needed them inside Lebanon, and they were willing to risk their lives for that loved one. I tried to explain to God that it would not be fair if those who were lying on the ground died. I looked at Ramzi several times and his calmness reassured me. I continued praying.

The underground hall had tiny windows near the ceiling. Soon all the windows were broken and one person lying on the ground was injured by the glass. After maybe ten or twelve minutes, it appeared the shells and bombs stopped falling on the port. But we did not dare get up from the floor. What if we got up and the bombardments started all over again? What if we left the underground hall and found ourselves completely exposed and in danger?

We waited.

The calm continued.

We waited.

The silence continued.

Finally, one courageous soul got up and said it was time to leave and see what awaited us. Slowly but surely, one after the other started getting up. Several were bleeding, several were crying, and all of us were in a state of shock and disbelief. To me this was overwhelming. I saw Ramzi helping a woman up. She was crying. We crept out of the underground bunker, thankful that it had not collapsed on our heads. Outside, we saw burning cars. The air smelled of gasoline. Very eerie.

It took some time for us to regain a sense of reality. Jounieh is a gorgeous town on the Mediterranean; the contrast between the beauty surrounding us and what we had gone through was unbearable. What happened inside the bunker was so bizarre: innocent people being bombarded for no reason; innocent people bleeding; innocent people not knowing if they would live or die; innocent people expecting the roof of the bunker to collapse on them at any minute and kill them. Yet there we were, walking out as if nothing happened. The irrationality of war is only surpassed by its cruelty and injustice. There was no time to think or to process what had happened. Ramzi and I decided to walk to the main street in Jounieh to see if cabs were still running after such a nightmare. We needed to get to St. Georges' Hospital where Daddy was.

We found a cab and were willing to pay whatever he asked for; we just wanted to get out of the port area and to the hospital. In the cab, Ramzi and I sighed in relief and hugged each other. We replayed the horror in slow, halting sentences, still in shock. We shared our anger at the Syrians, and gratitude that destiny had allowed us to survive the ordeal.

We finally arrived at the hospital and ran to Daddy's room. Seeing his face was such a reward. Daddy was in a lot of pain, but the fact that both Ramzi and I were with him, standing next to his bed, holding his hands, made him feel much better. We discussed his situation and agreed that we would give the surgeon permission to operate. We also agreed to check our blood types and see which of us was a universal donor so we could be on stand-by if Daddy needed a transfusion during the operation.

We met with the surgeon, who agreed the operation could take place the next morning. The blood tests showed it was Ramzi who could give Daddy blood, and of course he was ready and pleased to do so. We were both exhausted and still suffering from shock, but we did not want to tell Daddy about our ordeal at that point. He was relieved to see us and was pleased to know we would be with him during and after the operation.

Daddy asked if Mommy knew we had arrived. We told him we had taken a cab straight to the hospital before going home. We tried calling her; however, during those war times, many phone lines were cut or disconnected. After finalizing our discussions with the different doctors, we went home to have dinner with Mommy and get some sleep, promising to return early in the morning to be with Daddy before he entered the operating room.

Mommy's surprise and relief when we arrived home were indescribable. She cried and laughed at the same time. Her gorgeous expressive face was our greatest reward. Ramzi and I spent the evening explaining the procedure that Daddy would be going through, and that we believed the operation would be successful. They were so much in love; he worried about her and she worried about him. Despite his pain, his mind and his heart were basically with her, and despite her disabilities, all her thoughts were about how

301

we could make him feel better. I truly believe their love continued to deepen through the years. They lived for each other—the other taking precedence over self. They were unique, and their love for each other was in the air they breathed.

Early the next day, Ramzi and I went back to the hospital. Even though Daddy's operation was successful, for the first few days, his pain was extreme. When someone is ninety years old, it is hard to expect the bones to recover in such a way that the person will be able to walk like before. Daddy stayed in the hospital close to ten days. When we took him home, Mommy's happiness lit up the house. They embraced, they held hands, and they were overwhelmed to be together again. You would think they have not seen each other for ten years! Being with them was always a joy, but seeing how much they cared for each other was a lesson in tenderness and love.

When Daddy started walking again, he had to use a walker. It became part of the quotidian in our home. Ramzi left nearly two weeks after our arrival in Jounieh, and I left a week later. By then Beirut's airport was open. Only when we were back in Washington, D.C., did we spend a whole evening remembering every second and every detail of our perilous journey from Larnaca, to Jounieh, to the hospital in Beirut. We had learned, while in Lebanon, that the Lebanese authorities had protected the bunker by putting dozens and dozens of sandbags on its roof. Many believed that if it had not been so well protected the bunker would have collapsed that night, and while Ramzi and I considered ourselves lucky not to have died or been injured during the bombing, Mommy and Daddy never knew what we went through. We thought that was how it should be.

CHAPTER TWENTY-SIX

WORK AND
POETRY REIGN

B ACK AT CREATIVE, OUR WORK was growing, our
programs expanding, our staff multiplying, and our
achievements rewarding. There was not one single day without
new horizons, new excitements, and new challenges. In 1991-92,
we launched educational programs in Egypt, Senegal, Lesotho,
and Uganda. I was traveling extensively to ensure the quality of
our work. To be able to contribute to their success, I believed in
remaining in touch with the field. I needed to listen to the priorities
of the ministries of education and of civil society, and to engage
in a constructive dialogue with the funders—in particular with
their representatives in the field. I spent time with our field staff to
better understand the pathways to progress and the challenges of
implementation. We visited schools and communities; talked with
students, teachers, parents, and community leaders; and remained
determined to understand the uniqueness and complexities of each
context. I found my continuous field visits to be an absolute must.
They were the source of my constant learning and the main source

for my insights into the multiple layers and the various dimensions of development.

Through these constant visits to the countries where our programs were being implemented, and through my engagement with the various stakeholders of each program, I developed a deeper understanding of the power of active listening. I consider active listening a must for the success of any development program. Active listening requires the ability to set aside any personal agenda and to open oneself to what is being communicated. Active listening is about immersing oneself in a new context, a new framework, and a new mindset, and then reconnecting the new information with a broader agenda.

- Listening to a young girl explain why her parents thought walking to school for thirty or forty minutes was a risk, and based on that reality, why the parents decided not to send her to school after a certain age;
- Listening to a Minister of Education explain why it was essential that donors not interfere with the national curriculum of the primary or secondary schools of his or her country;
- Listening to parents highlight the value of marrying their daughters off at a young age;
- Listening to teachers who insisted on the need for continuous teacher training and how that need was not always met;
- Listening to community leaders express their various views on the value of the different types of education; and
- Listening to the donors and their need for results based on their priorities.

The challenge was in *how* to actively listen, how to understand the reasons behind each argument even when you did not buy into the argument itself, how to reconcile priorities that often seemed non-aligned and still ensure a pathway to progress. My work and its challenges energized me. I would often wake up in the morning excited about what the day would bring in terms of new initiatives, new needs, and new challenges.

While I was immersed in the design and implementation of the new programs, Khadija Haq of UNICEF asked for a meeting at her office in New York. I spent a day with Khadija, during which she shared that she had spent the past years focusing on girls' education, and that she learned that I had been doing the same. She proposed that I join her in writing a book, a fairly short one, on policies and programs that were effective in girls' education.

I appreciated the idea, and we discussed how we could collect the lessons learned—and the best practices—around the policies and programs for girls' education in Africa, Asia, the Middle East, and Latin America. Khadija promised that if we succeeded in writing such a book, UNICEF would publish it.

In addition to my heavy workload at Creative, I joined Khadija and UNICEF in collecting information and evidence on policies and programs that worked well in girls' education. I always liked filling my days to the brim; 1991 and 1992 seemed like a whirlwind.

In addition to my work, I still had a personal life. Zuheir complained that it was hard to get on my agenda, but we found time to spend evenings together. Of course, I made sure not to be traveling on Ramzi's wedding day. Ramzi had decided to marry Ghada, a Lebanese woman who was visiting Washington and whom he had been dating. Also, I managed to take some vacations; I went to

Lebanon and spent time with Mommy and Daddy. And yes, I found time to continue writing poetry, mainly on airplanes, and sometimes late into the night in my different hotel rooms.

In 1992, UNICEF published the short book that Khadija Haq and I had written: *Policies and Programs that Work in Girls' Education.* I was pleased that UNICEF disseminated our book to all its offices around the world.

Maybe when we are totally driven by causes we are committed to, our energies multiply, our productivity grows, and our creativity flourishes. My travels were increasing, my work experiences were marking me even deeper than I ever thought they would, and my poetry was flowing. Poetry and my international development work intermingled. My understanding of poverty and inequalities transformed me, and I wrote about people who lived in a world that was so different than the world I had become a part of. My poems were about poverty, hunger, and inequalities, but also about the common ground among human beings: belonging, aspirations, hope, suffering, love, and giving.

Family members and friends often asked me when am I going to publish my next collection of poetry and of course Daddy continued to discuss with me my poetry and the importance of publishing it. The time eventually came when I was ready to collect the poems I had written in the past decade or so and publish them. I worked on my new collection on weekends. I talked to Daddy about my efforts and he was pleased I was finding time to prepare my work for publishing. I divided the poems into four categories: the first was about the different cultures and countries that I lived in or visited and had learned to love; the second, about love; the third, about the suffering of Lebanon; and the fourth, about the relationship humans have with language. After considering several titles, I was inspired one evening to name my third collection of free Arabic verse ...*Yalloufou Khasra Al Ard*. Translated, the title would read ...*Encircling the Waist of the Earth*. I purposefully wanted the three dots before the title to allow the reader to decide what encircles the waist of the earth: love, sadness, hope, or wars. My book of free verse was published in the spring of 1992, and I was thrilled with the reaction from fellow poets and writers, and from the literary critics in Lebanon, the Arab world, and the U.S.

Nizar Qabbani, the famous Arab poet, wrote me a lovely letter which said, "The most important thing about you is your huge capacity to love, to love everything in this world....the difference between us, oh May, is that my 'resurrection' is behind me and your 'resurrection' is still ahead of you..... Your poems are happiness, joy, and sunshine, ...may God keep your blue heaven over us."

Henri Zghaib, a well-known Lebanese poet and critic, wrote several articles about my new collection which were published in *An-Nahar* in Beirut and in the *Hayat* newspaper of London. These are some excerpts of what he wrote:

> May Rihani arrived in Washington bringing with her a sensitive poetic lens and the Rihani heritage. With this, she started her global journey.... [T]he human being in May's poetry is an international citizen..... Even though May's poetry is about world issues and human suffering, and about the connection among many parts of the world, her poems prove that despite her global outlook, Freike, her Lebanese village, remains at the center of everything...and despite her whirlwind travels, May carries Beirut with her wherever she goes.... May's poetry "encircles

307

the waist of the globe," and through her poems, she attempts to redesign the world based on a vision of compassion.

Joseph Sayegh, a Lebanese poet who participated in my Wednesday literary salon, wrote:

> Your book is part of Lebanon, part of all of us. It is not a book; it is the wind blowing through the pine trees of Freike. All the capitals of the world from where you wrote and about which you wrote were to my heart dimensions of Beirut. Your pen strummed the strings of my memory, and I am unable to determine which recollections were touched softly and which pierced my heart with pain. I do not know if I loved the book because it is your book, or if I loved it because it is you. Your poem about your child that never came is overwhelming.

Abdallah Beshara Al Khoury, a Lebanese poet, shared his thoughts:

> I will injure your modesty...I tried in every way, and with jealousy, to find just one line to criticize but did not succeed.... Our fields these years are barren except of chaff. Feed us "the bread of the poor." ...and as for "your child who never came," I believe he will come through poetry and will dream of writing like you.

Ghada Al-Samman, a Syrian novelist, wrote:

In her new poetry collection, May Rihani does not bend under the weight of the heritage of her family; instead, she carries that heritage with total capability on her strong poetic shoulders. Her creativity emanates from the authentic land of her Lebanese village Freike, and despite her continuous travel, she senses the pulse of her words from that authenticity, and that is why "her wound is the color of the rooftops in her village." ...Her entire collection of poetry is a love song to Lebanon that was written on five continents.... The publisher of the book sees May Rihani as a continuation to the Oriental prophets/writers who lived in New York such as Gibran Kahlil Gibran; however, she sees herself as the eternal lover of a country where "hope is still a seed of wheat in the ground."

May Manassa, a Lebanese author and critic, shared in *An-Nahar*:

May Rihani travels; a poem falls into her eyes and circumambulates the world. She lands in hungry countries, arid land, and empty deserts, and looks at the hollow gaze of hungry children. May travels, and in her luggage there is an olive branch.... Her collection of poems ...*Yalloufou Khasra Al Ard* is an inner journey across the continents of the globe. We listen to May Rihani turning the pages of the world with a whisper or with the flutter of a bird that does never tire of traveling because it is able to return to the source. The bird did not get tired of touching misery, regardless of the color, ethnicity, or religion of that misery. This traveling bird "understands languages when it listens, sees the globe becoming smaller when it prays, and marries populations in its entirety." ...May named the four directions of the world "My Four Faces." ...Her poetry is an autobiography of a Lebanese woman who carries her heart, and an American woman who carries her rationality, wherever she goes. Her poetry is the story of a woman who is at home everywhere and yet remains a stranger, who addresses any event with intelligence and engages with every event without removing the pain of nostalgia from her breast. Her poems are the result of that amalgam.

Jamil Jabre, a writer who also participated in my Wednesday literary salon, wrote in *La Revue du Liban*:

May Rihani's poems attempt to reconstruct the world.... Her life is a journey in search of elusive peace; however, hope appears on the horizon of her dreams: Beirut will be reborn from its ashes.... Her poetry imposes itself through the suppleness of rhyme, the grace of metaphor, and her pantheistic view of beauty. She travels in time and space with curiosity, sometimes amused, but never seduced. Her search is for the absolute.... I believe that May is persuaded that memory is the most durable thread of what is permanent.... Her poetry is inhabited by nostalgia.

Another Wednesday salon participant, playwright Issam Mahfouz, wrote in *An-Nahar*:

> May Rihani encircles the waist of the earth carrying with her her small village that sits on the waist of the Lebanese mountains. I wrote about May 20 years ago when her first book *Carving on the Days* was published, and I said, "May grows and the world will become smaller," and here she is today. She sees the world turning around her waist.... Even though May lives in Washington, she is a permanent traveler. I was imagining while reading her book that she and her carriage were passing by me, while on her way to Freike.

Raymond Gebara, a Lebanese playwright and critic, reported:

> May Rihani is movement in the form of a woman. She is poetry and a hidden rhythmic human pulse that embraces all faces, cities, stages, and dervish dances. The bridge between Freike and Washington allows faces, nostalgia, memories, capitals, and human beings to cross. May's poetry conveys her strong feeling about the universality of humanity.... From May's Wednesdays and her literary salon in Freike, to international development in the United States, to traveling in the cities of the developing world, she always returns like the migrant birds to Freike...that is how May is, her poetry travels in her luggage, on her shawl, in her reports, and on the wings of the plane.

Jacklyn Potter, an American poet, wrote:

> As you listen to May's poetry, you may notice a
> sense of largeness of universe, and of timelessness—
> or perhaps of all time bound together in her poem
> "Four Masks," her personal sense of her life and the
> act of describing her geography, her memories, and
> her knowledge come together. Rich in metaphor, the
> lines do not mention the first person "I" until the final
> stanza: "Returning to Beirut/I return to the womb./
> The years saturate my mind./Memory is sanctified,
> at repose on the throne of my kingdom." How the
> turbulent history as it is considered privately comes
> forward, reverberating—the poet May Rihani walks
> parallel to her history in a way many Western poets
> cannot or do not.

Myriam Cook, an American Professor of Arab literature at Duke
University, added these words:

> Your collection of poems truly embraces the world.
> Each poem that seems to stretch outside itself to touch
> other worlds speaks of so much love and tenderness,
> but also of terrible pain. Clearly you travel enormously
> geographically, yet it seems that you remain centered in
> yourself through the poetry that you create wherever
> you are. ...[H]ow powerful in 1980 to write of Beirut's
> sea having moved out and now longing for its return.

Elise Salem, a professor of literature at Fairleigh Dickinson University wrote:

> "I have been luxuriating through your poems and feel a kinship and an awe. The underlying notion of travel and fragmentation is one I understand only too well, and your ability to create independent wholes (i.e. individual poems) within the collective large epic poem is wonderful indeed."

Richard Harteis, an American poet who translated my poem "Four Faces," published in the magazine *Delos* the following:

> May Rihani assumes the voice of the earth, at one level lamenting the trials of her people, though the last stanza is an autobiographical account of the poet's return to her native land. The poet's voice and that of the spirit of the earth seem to merge and take on a ritualistic quality for me—the four sections become the incarnations of the earth, and they read almost like incantations. Using the word "masks" reinforces the religious or ritualistic tone of the poem…. I tried to capture the power of her images, choosing language that might resonate with an American reader…. I wanted to stress the four distinct incarnations I saw in the poem by using the first line in each stanza as a title for that stanza to emphasize the geometry of the poem, its neat architecture.

When Professor Abdul Aziz Said of American University read my new book, he decided to organize a poetry evening for me at the university chapel. Professor Suheil Bushrui from the University of Maryland suggested that I read my poems in Arabic and he would read the translated poems in English. Zuheir agreed, adding that Andrew Oerke and Richard Harteis should read their English translations of certain of my poems as well. Since Zuheir had also translated some of my work, I insisted those be included, too, and he finally accepted. The *Umsiya*, the poetry evening, was scheduled for March 1993. Zuheir became a major player in preparing the *Umsiya*, and he felt the evening should be produced with music and a stage setting. My friend Henri Zghaib, the well-known Lebanese poet, agreed to be in Washington to introduce the *Umsiya*.

When I arrived at the AU chapel dressed in a black kaftan adorned with golden Arabic, I was stunned at the beauty of the backdrop. Zuheir was a master at stage setting. He had a couch with an embroidered Oriental drape on it, an Oriental table with a charming lamp, and lots and lots of flowers. Zuheir had asked his friend Jad Azkoul, the concert guitarist, to softly accompany me. Professors Said and Bushrui were waiting with Henri Zghaib when I arrived. Jad was rehearsing, and there were around two hundred people in the chapel ready for the *Umsiya* to start.

While waiting in the antechamber until I was called to the stage, a huge basket of flowers arrived. The card was signed "Loreen May." Who was this? It took a few seconds, and then it dawned on me: it was from Ramzi. His wife Ghada had just delivered a baby girl and they named her Loreen May. My brother Ramzi named his daughter after Mommy and me. I could not have been ushered to this *Umsiya* in any other better way.

I stepped onto the stage. Professor Said welcomed the audience and then introduced Henri, who would introduce the *Umsiya*. Henri started by saying, "I would like to dedicate this *Umsiya* to the two Loreens, the mother in Lebanon, and the newly born daughter of Ramzi." It was good that I could hold my tears of joy.

After Professor Said's welcome and Henri's introduction, I read fifteen or so poems. Professor Bushrui read around nine translated poems, and Jad's guitar accompanied us in the most melodious way. Zuheir was the master of light; during the hour-and-a-half of reading and music, a play of light added to the beauty of the setting. An unforgettable evening, perhaps my best *Umsiya* until that time.

My audience was delighted. Among the poems that resonated the most were: "Alphabet"; "Palm Trees"; "The Wedding of My City"; "A Certain Wednesday Night"; "Oh Sea of Beirut"; "The Desert is a Woman in Love"; "Ghurba"; and "Words, Words, Words." After the *Umsiya*, I did not have enough words to thank Professors Said and Bushrui, Henri Zghaib, Jad Azkoul, and, of course, Zuheir.

Here are segments of poems from the translations that were read during the AU *Umsiya*:

From "Palm Trees" (written in 1983 and translated by Zuheir)

Do you think Palm trees dream?
What resides in their minds?
Do you think the Palms of Texas yearn for the Palms
    of Baghdad?
Which ones departed? Which migrated?
Are they twins, carrying between them a long mirror
Reflecting the character of the West, reflecting the
    face of the East;

Searching for a magical thread that links the far
corners with each other?

From "A Certain Wednesday Night" (written in 1982 and
translated by Andrew)

And the winged white horse rose into the sky
The voice disappeared
And Joy became a white dot on a white sketch in a
gloomy sky.

From "Four Masks" (written in 1988 and translated by Richard
Harteis)

Africa
Thirsty land
The sun's power radiates and overcomes.
Hunger's storm rages on.
The wind wracks the void.
Desert sands genuflect, rise, whirl
Into specters begging for mercy
From the light's intensity, the heat wave's harsh brilliance.
Its children drag their spent bodies
Toward the juncture of earth and sky, sparkling like
water.

From "Words, Words, Words" (written in 1982 and translated by me)

Language reaches a crossroad
It continues along its way,

Suddenly, it finds itself at a dead-end street.
It calls its troops
It dictates commands
And the show begins.

Words and sentences prance down the runway, pose,
and spin round,
Words come from the heart of the Great Book
And others from a vast kingdom ruled by a Mind as
bright as the Sun
And some from the beloved lady we call Yesterday.

At night
A mischievous, handsome Verb approaches the Letters,
The Subject kisses the lips of the Adjectives, and from
behind bliss comes the surreptitious
Words, words, words.

From "Alphabet" (written in 1982 and translated by Andrew)

Magic falls on me.
My wand touches the edge of each letter
I shuffle the deck
I change the rules of the game
The magic circles increase in front of me
Words enter each other
And languages not heard before grow out of the earth.
On the forehead of every "A" blooms a red rose.

From "The Wedding of My City" (written in 1985 and translated by Suheil Bushrui)

> Blazing fires are etched against the Beirut sky
> Ominous rumbling fills her head
> Fear lurks in her silent streets
> Children draw bomb shelters on the sky of their
>   notebooks
> And a tear trickles down the face of God.

The publication of ...*Encircling the Waist of the Earth* and the AU *Umsiya* came in the middle of a very full year. Zuheir had proposed just a week or so before the *Umsiya*, and the two of us were busy planning the wedding. We had agreed that in the summer we would travel to Lebanon so Zuheir could ask Daddy for my hand. We set the wedding for November in Washington, D.C.

CHAPTER TWENTY-SEVEN

AFGHANISTAN

A T CREATIVE ASSOCIATES WE CONTINUED to expand our work, and one of the new projects was about Afghanistan. Creative was the subcontractor to the University of Nebraska and its Center for Afghanistan Studies. The Center was headed by Tom Gouttiere and served as the only institutional base in the U.S. specifically and exclusively concerned with Afghan affairs, providing consultation and expert advice on matters related to the country. As such, it won a USAID-funded project about basic education in Afghanistan. Creative had to integrate a gender approach to this huge basic education project.

At the launch of the project in 1992, for many Americans, Afghanistan was a tribal country with a government that was anti-U.S., pro-Soviet, and where the law of the land was not respected by anyone. It was a kind of out-of-control country.

By 1993, the Mujahideen took over Kabul. Afghanistan at that time was a battleground, with rival factions fighting for power and pounding the capital with rockets. An estimated 10,000 people were killed in early 1993; 750,000 were displaced; and many neighborhoods in Kabul were devastated. Although the fighting decreased somewhat in the latter half of 1993, it was still unclear if Afghanistan ultimately would be governable.

Meanwhile, the pro-Soviet president of the country, Najibullah, had received a promise of safe passage from the UN when it negotiated his abdication, but he remained in the UN office in Kabul suffering from an ailment. The UN has been unable to secure his freedom. Continuing hostilities also delayed the homecoming of an estimated 3.8 million refugees—comprising the largest refugee population in the world—who were based in Pakistan and Iran. Given the unsettled situation in the country, the lawlessness, and the anti-U.S. mood, Americans in general did not care much about Afghanistan in those years; however, USAID and the Center for Afghanistan Studies at the University of Nebraska cared. As a result, a multi-year education project was funded. With the state of affairs in Afghanistan, this U.S.-funded effort had to be a cross-border project managed from Peshawar in Pakistan, a city situated in a large valley near the eastern end of the Khyber Pass close to the Afghan borders.

After the launch of the project and after nearly a year of implementation, the University of Nebraska, through Tom Gouttiere and the Chief of Party (COP) of the project, Dr. Jerry Boardman, who was based in Peshawar, asked if I could help them understand why the percentage of Afghan girls in school was so incredibly small—only at 2.7 percent—other than in Kabul. This was the lowest percentage anywhere of girls going to school at that time. I accepted the challenge and arranged to spend three to four weeks in Peshawar with the senior staff of the project, the large Afghan refugee community, and the Afghan shadow Ministry of Education in Peshawar to try to understand the status of girls within their communities and within the Afghan education system.

I arrived in Peshawar and was struck by the overwhelming number of Afghan refugees in the city. I visited the USAID office, discussed how I intended to conduct my work, and asked to meet with the Afghan senior officials of the shadow Ministry of Education. The answer was that most probably they would not meet with me because I was a woman. I explained that I did not believe I could do a good job if I did not understand the thinking of these senior officials, and my contacts said they would do their best to see if the Afghan officials would talk with me.

Next, I had a lengthy meeting with Jerry Boardman, the University of Nebraska COP in Peshawar, again explained my approach, and told him that in addition to the documents and statistics I had been provided regarding the educational system, I would need to meet with Afghan refugees in the camps; with the mothers, teachers, students, and administrators of the camps; but more importantly with the senior officials of the Afghan shadow Ministry of Education. I also asked to have an interpreter present during all of these meetings. The COP agreed that my proposal made a lot of sense, and that he would appoint one of his staff to begin setting up the meetings; however, he was doubtful they could arrange a meeting with the officials of the shadow Ministry of Education.

What was the problem? I asked.

He said the shadow Ministry was made of Mujahedeen who called themselves Taliban, and even though they were anti-Soviet, it did not mean they would meet with an American, especially an American woman.

I asked the COP for a favor. First, I asked if it were possible for him to make the appointment for me and not to delegate the task to one of his staff. And second, I asked him to tell the Afghan officials that even though I was an American woman, I was originally an

Arab, a Lebanese, and that my mother tongue was Arabic. I had read the whole Koran and I would be willing to conduct the meeting(s) with them in classical Arabic if they wished. Also, I agreed to wear the *chador* without covering my face, and to pray with them several times a day. The one thing I asked him not to offer information about was my religion; if they were to ask, though, he must tell them I was a Christian. I asked him to emphasize that as a Lebanese, I had the opportunity to study the Koran—which I did—and I was willing to discuss it with them.

A couple of days later, and to my surprise, the COP announced the seniors of the shadow Ministry of Education were willing to meet with me. He warned me they were all men, but that they would like to conduct the meetings in English. I was delighted with the news, and he offered to accompany me to the first meeting. In the meantime I had been reading the many educational documents that were given to me and reviewing the statistics provided to the project by the Ministry of Education in Kabul. Also, I had bought a long black *abaya* that was a kind of a chador, but without the veil that covers the face.

I arrived at the meeting dressed in the chador (but with my face uncovered), accompanied by the COP, and found myself in front of nine or ten arch-conservative, bearded men of the Afghan shadow Ministry of Education. The first meeting was very tense; I think they were testing me. They asked lots of questions about the project and about my company. They asked if I knew the Koran and when I read it. They asked why I was interested in the Afghan education system. However, they did not ask about my religion, and I did not offer that information. They asked where I studied, and when I responded AUB, one of them said he had a cousin who had attended there as well. This piece of information might have helped relax the atmosphere a bit.

The time for prayer was upon us and they said we needed to take a break. Each of them found a place to pray and I went to a corner, knelt, and prayed silently. I asked God to guide me in this difficult situation, and to make me extremely sensitive to cultural and religious nuances. I also asked God to make them understand that my only objective was to help the project help their children—boys and girls—go to school. When they came back to the meeting table, I stood from where I was praying and joined them.

Around the table, we were again one woman with nine or ten Afghan men. It was time to begin the substantive discussions. After I explained in detail the objective of my mission, the methodology I planned to use, the Afghan documents I relied on, and the series of meetings I had requested, I said that I would like to ask a few questions based on the statistics I had received from the Ministry of Education in Kabul. I thought it might be a safe approach to ask about the 2.7% of girls in school by suggesting maybe it was a typo and that the figure is in reality 27%.

After a few seconds of silence that seemed as long as ten minutes, one of the bearded men said no, it was not a typo. The figure was correct. The number of girls in school was 2.7%. He said that without any sign of regret or attempt to explain such an extremely low figure. The 2.7% was a matter of fact, and to them apparently not astonishing whatsoever.

I could write a full book about my meetings with the officials of the shadow Ministry of Education. I could write about their facial expressions, about the tone of their voices, about the differences between them, about the fact that several of them studied at universities in Iran, Pakistan, and Malaysia, and the rest of them studied at the university in Kabul.

Suffice it to say that I was pleased that after the first long meeting, they agreed to meet with me again the next day in their offices in

Peshawar. For four days, I met with them for two or three hours each day. I worked hard to get them to help me understand the situation concerning girls' education. I listened very carefully. I usually would start by asking some tame questions and slowly move to difficult or more daring issues. Many of their explanations were not convincing. For example, they said the reason why there were so few girls in schools was because the Soviets had declared war on Afghanistan and that bombs fall on schools and kill students, so they could not send their daughters to school. I asked if they valued the lives of their daughters more than the lives of their sons, and they quickly recanted that theory. They offered other straw dog explanations, but they were equally unconvincing. For four days, they tried hard to explain the 2.7% to no avail. I continued to gently, and sometimes not so gently, ask questions and listen carefully. Finally, one of them said, "We do not send our daughters to school because of our religion. The mullah tells us not to send them to school."

Now we were getting somewhere. This was my opportunity. Being versed in Arabic and knowledgeable about Islam, I asked them if they would allow me to write on the blackboard in our meeting room a sentence from the Hadith, the collected sayings of Prophet Mohammed. I made sure they understood that if I wrote on the board my hands would show, and asked their permission to do that; they agreed.

I wrote in Arabic, and then translated the sentence and wrote it in English. The quote from the Hadith says, "Education is the responsibility of every Muslim man and every Muslim woman." I explained that my understanding of this sentence indicated that Prophet Mohammad was intentional when he said, "...and every Muslim woman." I discussed with them my understanding, and said that the Prophet could have stopped at "every Muslim man," but he did not; he wanted all those who were listening to him to know that he wanted every Muslim woman to be educated. Then I asked them a question: Who is more important to you, the mullah or Prophet Mohammad? To make a long story short, we discussed this at length and, as a result, they allowed me to design with them, a new component of the USAID-funded project in order to increase the number of girls in primary schools, to be called "the home schools for girls."

I worked hard, very hard, during those three to four weeks. In the evening in my hotel room, I would design a strategy to increase the number of girls going to school, and during the day, I would take what I had written, discuss it with the representatives of the shadow Ministry of Education, the COP and his senior staff, USAID, and others, and then come back to my room and revise what I designed based on their feedback. After several back and forth attempts, I was able to come up with a design that was accepted by the different parties.

When I finished my design, Jerry Boardman invited me to dinner at his home with around twenty Afghans. While they were pleased that I was able to achieve as much as I had, I tried hard not to show how ecstatic I was.

Any gain that advanced the cause of girls' education elated me. I was so convinced that the power of education could transform a girls' life. I knew that without education, a girl would continue to be marginalized, not respected, not listened to, and without any rights. I also knew that with education, the potential of breaking all the barriers to girls' empowerment was real. With education, a girl can rise from a miserable reality to a different reality that is pulled forward by hope.

CHAPTER TWENTY-EIGHT

A WEDDING RECEPTION ON A BOAT

WHEN I RETURNED TO WASHINGTON, D.C., from Afghanistan, Zuheir and I finalized the dates of our visit to Lebanon and the exact date for the wedding. I told Zuheir I wanted to spend a few days with my parents before his arrival. Being at home in Lebanon with Daddy and Mommy was always extremely special for me. Their home was an oasis of peace, serenity, and tranquility, and when I was with them, I became free of worries and expectations; however, this time was different. I had concerns.

I wanted to tell my parents that I had accepted Zuheir's proposal of marriage, and I was eager to hear them agree with my choice and bless us. I was not sure, however, they would be as welcoming of Zuheir as they had been of Andrew. We are a Maronite family; the Al-Faqih family is Druze. Even though Lebanon's war did not start because of religious differences among the many Lebanese communities, those differences were exploited to expand and deepen the conflicts. Daddy and Mommy had been present in Lebanon throughout the war, and I feared those conflicts might have influenced their open-minded thinking. I decided to tell Daddy first and then, based on his reaction, inform Mommy.

One afternoon after he finished reading a magazine and while Mommy was resting in her room, I told Daddy that I had something important to discuss with him. He smiled and asked me to proceed. I told him that I was in love again, and the man I wanted to marry was Zuheir Al-Faqih. He had questions:

"Is he the son of Ambassador As'ad Al-Faqih?"

"Yes."

"So, if I remember correctly, his mother is Yacout Al-Faqih, who published her book at my publishing house, is that correct?"

"Yes, Daddy."

Then he asked about Zuheir's education, his work, his career, and his value system. After I answered all of his questions, he said, "You have my blessing and we need to tell Mommy."

Daddy did not ask me about Zuheir's religion, so I thought that, at the age of 93, Daddy must have forgotten the Al-Faqih family was not Christian. I asked, "But Daddy, are you aware that Zuheir and his family are Druze?"

Daddy answered, "So…?" And then he continued: "My dear daughter, what did I teach you? What did your Uncle Ameen teach all of us? There is no difference as long as the value system is based on the right principles. I know the parents of Zuheir and they are a noble family, and from what you told me, Zuheir, too, has high moral values." He also said, "You mentioned when you were talking about Zuheir that he follows the Sufi way. I believe that is an indication that he respects all religions, appreciates their common ground, and values the principles of love, tolerance, and sensitivity to the other."

I was stunned by my father's answer. Even at 93, he was ahead of me—and would always be ahead of us, his children. He was a true Renaissance man: forward looking, focused on the mind and the heart, respectful of differences and diversity but not bound by them, a man who honored elevated principles. I always felt deeply fortunate to have been born as my parent's daughter, and time only deepened that feeling.

Daddy helped me share my news with Mommy. She also had a lot of questions, and when I answered them all and explained that Zuheir's respect of Christianity's values was genuine and deep, she came to the same conclusion as Daddy.

Zuheir called me when he arrived in Lebanon a few days later. He was delighted with my parents' reaction. When he arrived at our Qornet Shahwan home, he carried two huge bouquets of flowers, one for Daddy and one for Mommy. The three of them hugged, kissed, and talked. Zuheir asked for my hand and Daddy blessed us again. He had already prepared a gift for Zuheir: the books of my Uncle Ameen. Even though Daddy's sight was weak by then, he wrote a lovely dedication to Zuheir in one of the books. Watching Daddy, Mommy, and Zuheir getting to know each other was pure joy. One of Zuheir's gifts to Daddy was a book about the Pierre DuPont Longwood Gardens in Pennsylvania. Of course, Zuheir knew that Daddy was a *fou de fleurs*, and they talked about Longwood and the garden in Freike. Daddy explained how over the years he had built up the gardens in the family home in Freike, and how he might one day plant some of the flowers that grew in Longwood.

Daddy was the eternal optimist, a planner who never allowed age to deter him or even slow him down, regardless of how much time might be needed to complete the tasks he determined to undertake. The book about Longwood took Daddy back to his years in the U.S. —New York and the East Coast—and he and Zuheir shared common ground, having spent their first years growing up in the U.S.

With Mommy, Zuheir discussed spiritual figures such as Saint Francis of Assisi and how he exemplified brotherly love at a dark period of Europe's history. Daddy, Mommy, and Zuheir truly hit it off. All I had to do was watch how three loving individuals who shared a deep enthusiasm for nature, cultures, and the values of love, tolerance, and service did not allow the difference of religion be an obstacle. They opened their hearts to one another. The days Zuheir and I spent with Mommy and Daddy were serene and charming. Our time with them was about two people who were starting their journey together watching the abundant love of two elderly parents whose journey continued to be filled with total tender care for each other. The river of love continued to flow under the feet of my parents.

Once we were back in Washington, we had a wedding to plan. I wanted to marry in a church and Zuheir agreed. We started looking into locations and discovered we had quite a challenge to overcome. Many of the lovely churches that caught our eye wanted us to be not just members, but long-standing members, before they would consider our request.

One day, driving through Chevy Chase Circle on our way from Ramzi's home in Kensington, we saw a beautiful church. I told Zuheir that I would like to stop and visit it. As we approached the entrance, I noticed a sign that indicated it was a Presbyterian church. I was delighted; Mommy was Presbyterian. No one was around, so we walked in and as we admired the beauty of the altar, a kindly, white-haired minister greeted us. He asked if he could help, so we told him our story: we wanted to get married and were having difficulties finding a church since I was Maronite/Catholic and Zuheir was Druze. The minister smiled and said we could get married there. We were ecstatic. His only condition was that we meet with him two or three times so we could discuss marriage and the importance of commitment, as well as our value systems. We heartily agreed, so we went to his office and booked our first appointment with the gracious Reverend Wesley Baker. We cherished those discussions with Rev. Baker and the warm welcome he extended to us.

During the wedding preparations, Zuheir was the creative one. He thought of holding our wedding dinner on a Potomac River cruise boat which could handily accommodate our two hundred guests. We checked several cruise companies and selected the Spirit of Washington, which had a pleasant layout; dining service, room for dancing, plus live entertainment.

On November 27, 1993, we had a dream wedding. Zuheir's sister Selma, who also made me a lovely orchid bridal bouquet and the boutonnieres for the men, decorated the church beautifully with white orchids. My uncle, Fuad Sader, walked me down the aisle. When in Lebanon a couple of months before the wedding, he had a swell time; he had Daddy sign a document he had prepared empowering him to serve as Daddy's proxy! Zuheir and I chose the wedding readings. Ramzi and Sarmad read from Ameen Rihani, and Khaled, Zuheir's brother, read from Meher Baba, the Sufi master. Our vows were loving and moving. Suad Joseph, Carolyn Long, and Sima Wali were bridesmaids, and Zuheir's best men were Khaled, Ramzi, and Sarmad. After the ceremony at the church, in the middle of a heavy downpour, our family and friends drove to the marina where we boarded the boat and cruised the Potomac till 11:00 p.m. The live entertainment, the toasts, and the dancing were unforgettable.

The next day, we left for Cancun for our honeymoon. I learned to appreciate the beauty of underwater sea life, including coral reefs. Zuheir was patient with me, teaching me to snorkel as I discovered the vibrant colors of fish and corals. Being the world's second-longest coral reef, Cancun had so much to offer. Our days were filled with the beautiful sun, a steady breeze, and margaritas served in fresh coconuts. Our days and nights were filled with tenderness.

During our first months as a married couple, I had to learn about a different world, the world of a disciplined Sufi. Zuheir and I had a lot in common; we were both Lebanese-Americans who had attended AUB, and our parents were friends. We both spoke English and Arabic, Zuheir knew some French, and we both valued a multicultural approach to our global village. Art and poetry were part of both our lives. We appreciated sensitive people who cared about others, and we shared a similar value system based on respecting others, recognizing the importance of diversity, and serving others.

However, I valued more than anything rational analysis, professionalism, intellectualism, passion, and freedom, and did not recognize the importance of disciplined and organized spirituality. Zuheir was a Sufi *par excellence*, and I was a free spirit *par excellence*; I never understood why spirituality or religion had to be organized or disciplined. He valued a school of Sufism where those who belong attended classes and meditations on a regular basis. I needed to adjust to this new way of life where one spouse spent many evenings in Sufi classes. I had to make room for disciplined spirituality and meditations, and the importance of Sufism in my married life.

Marriage is about love. In my book, it is also about how two people embark on a journey together and strive to become so close that there is only light between them. In Zuheir's book, it was about how two people embark on a journey together but remain independent, each one seeking his or her pathway. The journey started in November 1993, and Zuheir and I are still on a pathway of discovery.

CHAPTER TWENTY-NINE

MY THEATER IS THE WORLD AND PAIN INVADES MY LIFE

M Y LIFE CONTINUED TO BE filled to the brim. Throughout 1993 and 1994, my staff and I won additional new projects. We began large education projects in Malawi, Mali, and Egypt, and I had to visit these countries during each launch phase. My visits were to ensure that the Ministry of Education in each of these countries, the donors, and Creative as the implementing agency, were on the same page, agreed on the priorities, accepted the methodology of implementation, and had the same expectations for results. Getting to know each of these countries in a more in-depth way—Malawi, an Eastern Anglophone African country; Mali, a Western Francophone country; and Egypt, an Arab and African country—was a treat and a blessing. Getting to work in English, French, and Arabic was a privilege.

During these very busy two years, Nigel Fisher, the deputy director of the regional office of UNICEF for the Middle East and North Africa who was based in Amman, Jordan, asked if I could run a workshop for their approximately twenty educational officers who were based in the different countries of the Middle East and North Africa. He needed the session to focus on the importance of girls' education and, in particular, the needed strategies to ensure successful girls' education programs. Nigel and I had several meetings at UNICEF's New York headquarters to discuss the specific objectives and to agree on the framework of this workshop. Once Nigel and I agreed on the particulars, designing and delivering the workshop became my full responsibility. I decided to create a team from my staff to study and analyze carefully the strategies that we had been using in the past decade in different countries in the Middle East and Africa that were successful in increasing the access of girls to school, keeping them in school, and facilitating their completion of primary and then secondary education.

My staff and I found that our approach was holistic based on several complementary interventions, and that there was no silver bullet to advance girls' education. What proved effective was a combination of strategies that were context-appropriate, with the efficient implementation of those strategies to facilitate and contribute to the success of girls' education programs. Our reflections on what we had learned in the previous decade led us to conclude that among the key strategies that facilitate success were:

- Political will: Government representatives at both the national and local levels need to put girls' education on their agenda, and voice their commitment to advancing girls' education; political will is often a basic ingredient in the equation.
- Parental and community engagement: Families and communities are essential partners with schools. They should have a say in ensuring that the curriculum is relevant to the lives of their children including girls, as well as to the lives of

the parents, and parents and communities should have a say in how schools are managed.

- Low-cost education: Primary education should be free and where possible, there should be stipends and scholarships to compensate families for the loss of girls' labor within the household as well as girls' other chores and responsibilities outside the home.

- Schools close to home: Distance to school is an obstacle to girls' education since many parents worry about their daughters' safety and their walking or traveling long distances on their own.

- Importance of women teachers: In many contexts, parents are more comfortable having their daughters taught by qualified women teachers; therefore, increasing the number of well-trained women teachers plays a major role in keeping girls in school and in facilitating the completion of their of primary and secondary education.

- Girl-friendly schools: Schools need to be girl-friendly in their infrastructure (such as having separate latrines); in their human resources (for coeducational schools, it is important that the leadership include women and men); and in their curriculum and extracurricular activities (equity in the classroom and outside the classroom is key for keeping girls in school).

- Relevant curricula: Learning materials should be relevant to the girls' daily lives, and all educational materials should avoid reinforcing gender stereotypes, choosing instead to address girls' and boys' aspirations in an equitable way.

- Preparation for school: Girls and boys do best when they receive early childhood care which enhances their self-esteem and prepares them for school.

I designed the workshop based on these lessons learned, and in Amman, I delivered a three-day session to over twenty UNICEF education officers. Nigel and all the participating education officers contributed to the workshop and enriched our collective thinking.

I was delighted that UNICEF asked me to design and deliver such a workshop. It forced me to take time with some of my staff to reflect, analyze, and review lessons learned. At the end of the workshop, Nigel asked me to write a book about the strategies that make girls' education programs succeed in the Middle East and North Africa; he wanted UNICEF to publish such a book. I spent a good chunk of time during 1994 writing, and when I submitted my manuscript to Nigel, he was delighted with its content. He wrote a preface and asked UNICEF to publish it. My second book on girls' education was published in 1994: *Learning for the 21ˢᵗ Century—Strategies about Girls' and Women's Education in the Middle East and North Africa*. Nigel and UNICEF decided the book should be in the languages used in the Middle East and North Africa, so UNICEF translated and published *Learning for the 21ˢᵗ Century* into three additional languages: Arabic, Farsi, and French. In the second half of the 1990s, my book was used—in the four languages—as a reference for training educational officers in workshops and seminars in the approximately twenty Middle Eastern and North African UNICEF country offices.

Work never stopped me from doing things on the home front. Zuheir and I decided to buy a home together. We looked in many neighborhoods in the greater Washington, D.C., area and finally found a lovely home in Bethesda. We both fell in love with the house at first sight. We moved towards the end of 1994. Designing and decorating the interior of our home was so much fun. Zuheir was very artistic and had exquisite taste in choosing furniture and deciding where the sculptures and paintings go. The yard was Zuheir's domain; he added trees, bushes, plants, boulders, and a small pond. The area was transformed into a lovely garden with a variety of flowering bushes and plants including roses, irises, gerberas, and loostrifes.

In early 1995, the USAID Mission in Morocco asked me to assess the educational situation and submit a report about the areas and priorities within the Moroccan educational system that might benefit from USAID's support. I arrived in Morocco at the beginning of April for a planned stay of three weeks. During that time, I needed to collect all the information required to do such an analysis. I planned to meet with the Minister of Education and the directors of the ministry, USAID education officers, and officers of other donors. I scheduled visits to urban and rural schools where I met with principals, teachers, students, and parents. I also had many discussions with community leaders before I began writing the report.

I loved that aspect of my work, the field work. I felt energized when I was trying hard to understand a system within its own context and culture. I became a deep listener when parents told me that even though they wanted to send their daughters to secondary school, the socio-economic constraints they faced were too daunting. I engaged with teachers and principals when discussing their needs to improve the quality of teacher training. Rural schools were sometimes promised a full set of teachers, only to receive an insufficient number, and that concerned me.

When I was in the middle of fieldwork, I was aware that I needed to learn a huge amount of realities and complexities in a short time. I needed to absorb statistics and facts, and I needed to remind myself that all the information and analysis needed to fit within the context and culture of the country I was working in, both its urban and rural subcultures. My days were usually very full and rich with meetings, interviews, discussions, observations, and interactions, while my evenings were spent in my hotel room reading the documents I collected and the notes I took, and starting to analyze the situation. During my overseas work trips, I usually slept a maximum of six hours and devoted around sixteen hours of each day to work.

On April 11, about ten days after my arrival in Morocco, as I arrived back at the hotel after a full day of work, the receptionist told me that he had received several phone calls from my husband. It was urgent that I call him back in D.C. In 1995, we did not have cell phones the way we have them today. As I hurried to my room, I wondered what was so urgent for Zuheir to call me several times in the same late afternoon. I arrived in my room and immediately placed the call.

Zuheir, in his most gentle way, told me that Serene, my nineteen-year-old niece and goddaughter, after going for a swim, had been lost for the past twenty-four hours in the Mediterranean Sea. I could not believe what he was telling me. It was too shocking, too painful. I do not think I was able to hear his words of consolation. I was sobbing. I did not want to believe this news. I could not accept that destiny would do that to Serene, to Ameen my brother, and to the family.

Zuheir tried hard to calm me down by telling me that there might still be some hope to find her. He said she might have been carried away by strong waves to a far shore north of Lebanon and that Ameen had organized search teams in the hopes of finding her. Zuheir's attempts to calm me were to no avail. All I could do was cry. I was alone in a hotel room faced with this miserable, unexpected, and shocking news. We stayed on the phone for nearly an hour, and he heard nothing from me but crying. Deep down, I had a feeling we had already lost Serene.

Nearly half-an-hour after Zuheir and I hung up, Ramzi and Zuheir called. They both tried hard, but I was inconsolable. I told them I felt they knew that Serene was lost and were afraid to tell me except gradually, or that they really did not know anything further which indicated that it was going to be very hard to find her safe and sound.

I decided that in the morning I would explain to USAID what had happened and then go to Lebanon and be with the family. Ramzi, too, decided to fly to Lebanon from Washington. When I informed Zuheir of my plans, he said that if I wanted to return to Morocco to finish the assignment after the family crisis was over, he would join me while I worked. That night I could not sleep; all I could do was sit in bed and cry. I could not fathom the serious possibility of losing Serene in this way.

The next morning, I walked to the office of USAID and asked to meet with Monique Bidaoui, the education officer in charge of my assignment. As soon as she saw me, she asked why my eyes were so red. I explained my family situation and asked if she would approve that I interrupt my work for seven to ten days so I could fly to Lebanon and be with the family. I assured her I would then come back to complete my assignment.

Monique was extremely understanding. She immediately granted me permission to interrupt my work in Morocco, and insisted I not worry about the exact day of my return to Rabat. She said family emergencies like the one I was facing had to be attended to, and the completion of my assignment could be delayed by a week or two. I thanked her and went straight to a travel agency in Rabat, bought an airplane ticket for that afternoon, then went to my hotel to pack and go to the airport.

I was in a daze. I do not know how I arranged all of that in less than six or seven hours. I do not think I was able to eat that day. As

I flew to Lebanon, my only companion on the plane was my tears. Serene, the first grandchild in the family, was so sensitive, very gifted, pretty, and delicate. She had started writing poetry and had many of her oil paintings hanging in her room. Her studies at AUB held so much promise. I always thought she would become a great poet or a great artist, possibly both. I could not conceive that we would lose her to the sea. When I was growing up, looking at the sea helped me reflect and think, and usually it had a calming effect on me. It allowed me to dream of a world where peace reigns, where a breeze touches the face of every child, and where there are no thirsty or hungry children. If Serene were lost for good, and if the sea took her, all of those images would be erased. My friendship with the sea would be destroyed; more importantly, we would have lost our sensitive, loving, caring, gifted young Serene.

I arrived in Freike where the home was filled with relatives and friends. Ameen and Samira held out hope that Serene might be found. Ameen, with Ramzi and Sarmad, accompanied by a group of searchers and an army helicopter, were searching the coastline of Northern Lebanon to find Serene.

On the third day after Serene's disappearance in the sea, they found her body. I do not think there could be anything more painful for a parent than losing a child. I cannot imagine the pain that Ameen and Samira went through. Despite the hundreds and hundreds of friends who came to offer their condolences, Ameen and Samira's hearts were totally broken. They were in another world, a world that had questions and no answers. I spent close to ten days in Freike with the family. The silences in those days were more expressive and meaningful than words. All I could do was every now and then give a hug to little Khaled, Serene's younger brother; to Reem, her younger sister; and of course, to Ameen and Samira. My spirit was broken as well. I lost my first godchild, the nineteen-year-old poet, my sweet niece who was so close to me that often I felt she could have been my daughter.

When I flew back to Rabat to complete my assignment, Zuheir arrived from D.C. to join me. His presence was God-sent. If it were not for him, my evenings in the hotel would have been miserable. Zuheir let me work during the day, and in the evening after dinner, he would take me for a walk. It was spring and the weather was lovely. I do not remember if I had ever walked in Rabat as much as I did during those evenings. Zuheir's warm voice and the soft breeze of late April and early May caressed my broken heart and revived my low spirits. With his care, I was able to complete my assignment and submit my preliminary report to USAID Rabat. Monique was pleased that I met my commitment. Zuheir and I flew back to Washington and I returned to work in my office at Creative.

May, June, and July, as usual, were busy and filled to the brim, I rarely returned from a trip without feeling the need for a week or two of working extremely hard for very long hours to catch up with the development, progress, and issues of all the other projects and programs in the many other countries. My schedule was packed with meetings with my staff, my peers, and the different donors. Reports and proposals had to be written and finalized.

Towards the end of July, when I was beginning to feel that I had found a way to accept what destiny had dealt us, that life with deep pain and powerful sadness still has to go on, I got a phone call from Daddy's attendant in Qornet Shahwan.

My father had passed away early that morning. I think I lost my breath and collapsed.

Zuheir and I immediately decided to fly to Lebanon. Ramzi and Sarmad made the same decision. Ameen and his family were already there, having come from Bahrain to spend the summer in Freike.

The idea of losing Daddy was inconceivable to me. In that situation, rationality had no place. It was not part of my equation. From the minute I heard the awful news till the minute I landed at the airport in Beirut, my mind revolted and my heart wept. I could not accept the possibility. I did not care about his age or his health situation; Daddy was my anchor, my North Star, my first mentor, my intellectual guide. Daddy was the pillar in the family, the one who could face any challenge—including Mommy's devastating operation's results—and yet remain optimistic, finding solutions to the most complicated situations. Daddy, the man of principles, from whom we learned so, so much could not leave us. Daddy and Mommy taught us, by example, a value system that I built my whole life around; I could not fathom losing him. His death was as devastating as a tsunami. All my foundations collapsed. In the plane with Zuheir, I wondered why destiny had not allowed me to at least see him before he left this earth. Why didn't he fall ill so we would have time to be near him for his last days? I would have given anything to be by his bedside for a time before he passed in order to serve him, take care of him, and tell him how much I loved him.

We were greeted at Beirut airport by family members and friends who took us to Freike to see his body for the last time.

Zuheir knew that I needed support when I looked at the face of the person who influenced me the most in my life, my most profound teacher, the one who opened all the frontiers for me, my guide, my beloved Daddy. Zuheir held me as I knelt in front of Daddy's coffin and prayed for his soul. When I stood up to kiss his forehead and his hands, tears ran down my face and fell on his cheeks, forming a transparent thread between our two faces.

I slipped two letters in his coffin: one from me that I had written on the plane to Lebanon, and one from Suad Joseph, my closest friend, who knew Daddy very well and wanted to say goodbye. She wrote the letter in California as soon as she heard about his passing and faxed it to me just before I boarded the plane to Lebanon. I do not have a copy of my letter to Daddy; it went with him. I put it in the inner pocket of the jacket he was wearing, close to his heart. I do, however, have a copy of Suad's letter. She began by saying:

> You were a man of many centuries. Born on the precipice of one century, dying on the precipice of another century. You grasped the power of history.... I knew you as my closest friend's father, as my sister's father, as my Papa Albert. I saw you as the wings that protectively hovered over your family's experiments, risks, adventures, and challenges. The breadth of your wings knew no limits, widening to embrace whatever your family brought towards you. You soared with them, ahead of them, surrounding them, yet always letting them pass. I saw in you the endless stretch of space that permitted May the terrain from which to fly, to test, to become, yet to have always her ground.

The first week after Daddy's passing I felt lost. I had no compass. I was living in a foggy place. Nothing was clear. My heart entered a period of deep, deep sadness, and a sense of solitude invaded me. Mommy, Zuheir, and my three brothers could not dispel the sense of isolation.

My thoughts and emotions kept taking me back to when Daddy was with us. Whenever we were together, I belonged to the whole world. His expansive love of Lebanon, of the Arab world, and of the U.S. was contagious, and I got the bug from him. With him around, I felt I belonged to three cultures and to the whole wide world, but now I was no longer sure that my sense of belonging to those three rich cultures would remain intact.

His admiration for beauty and creativity, and how it expressed itself through poetry, literature, paintings, and music was stimulating. With him gone, I no longer knew whether art and literature would enchant me the way they used to in his presence.

His love for Mommy was pure, ideal, and inspiring. Now I wondered who would be my role model when it came to facing the challenges of love.

His respect for the intellect, for independent thinking, for freedom, productivity, and justice always guided me when it came to decisions related to these basic values. Without him, could I hold these values as guideposts in the journey of my life the way I did when he was with me?

And publishing and books—how would I view them now that the master publisher and the book connoisseur had left? But more importantly, how would I feel from now on without Daddy on this planet? Would I intrinsically change? The idea of not being able to call him whenever I wanted, not being able to hear his comforting and reassuring voice was disturbing. The idea that from that point on when I traveled to Lebanon to spend time in my parents' home he would not be there was inconceivable. What would happen to that oasis of serenity and love, their home—would I still find that oasis when I came back next time? How would I feel about everything and anything now that he had left us?

It took maybe a week before I stopped weeping, but it took possibly several months before I entirely accepted that I could not sit by his side anymore and talk with him, and learn and learn and learn. The brilliant man who was a river of love and wisdom had left me. I had to swim across a huge ocean of sadness before reaching shores where some new form of happiness could be found again.

CHAPTER THIRTY

LOSING THE KEYS TO THE HIGH GROUND

EVEN THOUGH I WAS IN the midst of a fog of sadness, we had to think about Mommy's situation. After some discussions, my brothers and I decided we needed to convince Mommy to move to the U.S. She could alternate her time at our homes so that we could each share in the joy of her presence among us. We knew she would need a live-in caregiver to attend to her needs. We anticipated that it would be difficult to convince her, but to our surprise, she readily agreed to the plan. Although she would be giving up her home, her reliable and competent caregiver of nearly ten years whom she liked very much, and undertaking two very long and uncomfortable flights, she nodded her agreement to the plan. That was Mommy. She always thought of what others needed and not about her needs. She gave up the familiarity of her home and visits by relatives and old friends. I think she wanted to look in on us and see how her U.S.-based children were doing. Ameen would deeply miss her presence, but like her, agreed to the plan as he felt she needed a change after Daddy's passing.

We arranged for Mommy's trip without too much difficulty, but when it was time to depart for the U.S., I found it extremely hard to lock up the Qornet Shahwan home. I experienced similar feelings to the ones I felt when Ramzi and I moved our parents from the Hamra home. On that day in 1986, after putting Mommy and Daddy in the van that took us on that very risky journey, Ramzi and I went back for a couple minutes to lock up. The sense of irreversible loss was overwhelming. The same sense of loss returned as we locked the door of the Qornet Shahwan home. We left the Hamra home because of the war, and now we were leaving the Qornet Shahwan home after Daddy had passed away. War and death seemed synonymous.

Due to Mommy's physical restrictions and the difficulty of helping her in the tiny flight cabins, she fasted for two full days and avoided water before we boarded the plane. Her sacrifice made the long plane trips from Beirut to Paris, and Paris to Washington much more manageable. We arrived to Dulles Airport, all of us tired and exhausted.

As soon as Mommy was in our home in Bethesda, and while showing her around the rambling house, she told us via her special way of communicating how beautiful our home was. She probably sensed that we had her in mind when we bought a house where all the living areas and bedrooms were on the same level. She found many things to like and admire. She would nod at a display case, for example, and make loving cooing sounds to express her delight. It was as if she wanted to lift our spirits.

Having Mommy with us was a total blessing. My only consolation after Daddy's passing was that I was able to come home after a day of work to her radiant presence. Our evenings were a source of intellectual stimulation for me. Mommy wanted to know everything about my work, and the more I described the girls' education programs and women's empowerment projects we had undertaken, the more she wanted details about how we approached the issues in each country, and how we worked with each government. I should not have been surprised by her interest and historical knowledge about these two fields; after all, she was one of the pioneers in Lebanon regarding women's rights and had helped launch several social welfare programs that enabled women to earn their livelihoods. As I mentioned earlier, Mommy had been the president or a board member of about seven NGOs in Lebanon, most of which addressed women's rights and women's issues.

Mommy also developed a wonderful relationship with Zuheir. Neither Zuheir nor I wanted to go out in the evenings without Mommy. We looked forward to spending our time at home with her. Despite her sense of loss, and the fact that she missed her Albert, Mommy never failed to radiate positive energy through her expression, the sound of her voice, and her small gestures. There was a palpable aura of peace on her face. She never asked for anything, despite her illness and physical limitations, and expressed to us that everything was always fine. I cannot remember Mommy asking for something even once, unless it was to buy a gift for someone. Whatever we prepared for dinner was wonderful; whatever television program we wanted to watch, she agreed to; whomever we invited over for dinner was someone whose company she enjoyed; whatever activities we planned for the weekends she agreed to. She was amazing, and nothing could upset her. The desire for material possessions held no sway over her. At the center of her life were an unlimited capacity of loving and giving, and an amazing calmness, serenity, sensitivity, and ability to reflect.

In August, I discussed with Mommy that Creative wanted me to go to Beijing to attend the Fourth International Women's Conference. I told her I was hesitant because I did not want to leave her for a week or more. She insisted that I participate in the conference and indicated that she would be upset if I did not go. She reminded me that she had Zuheir and her live-in caregiver, and that Ramzi, Sarmad, and their families often visited. I tried one more time to convince her I should stay home, but there was no way she would accept. Finally, I did what she advised me to do and started planning for my trip to China.

I left for Beijing on September first. I had attended the first conference in Mexico City in 1975, the second in Copenhagen in 1980, had missed the third in Nairobi in 1985, and now would participate in the fourth in Beijing in 1995.

The Fourth World Conference on Women met at the Beijing International Conference Center September 4-15, 1995. An estimated 17,000 individuals attended, from 189 countries. The participants were from UN agencies and from governmental and non-governmental organizations. As the host country, China held a welcoming ceremony at the Great Hall of People on September 4; Chinese President Jiang Zemin addressed the 10,000 of us who crowded the hall.

The conference had plenary sessions and a huge number of panel presentations. In addition, two committees were formed; their responsibility was the drafting of the Beijing Declaration and the Platform of Action.

Among the issues we discussed in the sessions were:

- Women and Poverty
- Education and Training of Women
- Women and Health
- Violence Against Women
- Women and the Economy
- Women in Power and Decision-making

- Institutional Mechanism for the Advancement of Women
- Human Rights of Women
- Women and the Media
- Women and the Environment
- The Girl-child

Nearly all of these issues were areas of work at Creative, and given Creative's focus on education, women and poverty, and on girls' education, these topics were extremely relevant to our projects and programs. I participated in at least five sessions each day. I found the debates and the different perspectives enriching and stimulating, and no doubt my learning expanded daily. To me, the highlight of the conference was when First Lady Hillary Clinton took the podium for her speech. I was one of the lucky ones who were able to enter the crowded hall to hear her. She spoke in a powerful and courageous manner, and I found her to be forward-looking and inspiring. Her speech was interrupted by applause many times. By the end, we all stood and clapped for a long time. It is noteworthy to mention that many ideas in Mrs. Clinton's speech became driving forces in the conference. She mentioned that it was "no longer acceptable to discuss women's rights as separate from human rights." These abuses "have continued because, for too long, the history of women has been a history of silence." She encouraged the participants of the conference to make their voices heard loudly and clearly. She spoke about the mistreatment of young girls as a violation of human rights, noting that some babies are often denied food, or drowned, simply because they are girls. What struck me clearly is the fact that she spoke eloquently and with clear knowledge and stunning courage about the different violations of women's rights and how these violations cannot be tolerated anymore. She ended her speech by communicating a powerful and simple message: "If there is one message that echoes forth from this conference, let it be that human rights are women's rights and women's rights are human rights once and for all." I remember everyone in the hall applauding loudly.

After Hillary's speech, many of us wondered if the Platform for Action that was being drafted would live up to the power of her ideas. As it turned out, the draft was not quite what we had hoped, and many participants expressed the desire for more direct and forceful language. Basically, the Platform for Action stated that it was an agenda for women's empowerment; it aimed at accelerating the implementation of the Nairobi Forward-Looking Strategies for the Advancement of Women; and it sought to remove all obstacles to women's active participation in all spheres of public and private life through a full and equal share in economic, social, cultural, and political decision-making. The Platform emphasized the importance of the principle of shared power and responsibility, and that it should be established between women and men at home, in the workplace, and in the wider national and international communities. The Platform stated that:

> Equality between women and men is a matter of human rights and a condition for social justice, and is also a necessary and fundamental prerequisite for equality, development, and peace. A transformed partnership based on equality between women and men is a condition for people-centered sustainable development. A sustained and long-term commitment is essential, so that women and men can work together for themselves, for their children, and for society, to meet the challenges of the twenty-first century.

On the long plane ride back to Washington, D.C., I reflected on the progress the world had made since 1975 when I attended the first international women's conference in Mexico City. I also reflected on the progress made since my mother started working on women's issues in Lebanon in the early 1950s. I saw that while much progress had been made, there was still a long way to go. I realized that until every girl and boy on this planet had the opportunity to be in school, to stay in school, and to receive quality, relevant education, we as a global community had a lot of work ahead of us. Until gender-based violence was mitigated and erased, we had a mountain of work ahead of us. Until women's integration into economic, political, social, legal, and all other fields was realized, we would need to continue the journey of transforming societies and communities. And, as Hillary Clinton said, until we all understood that "human rights are women's rights and women's rights are human rights once and for all," equity and equality between women and men, girls and boys, will be far from achieved.

When I arrived home in Bethesda, I could not wait to share with Mommy all that happened in Beijing. During work hours, I gave many presentations in Washington about the conference. In the evenings and on the weekends, Beijing was the topic of discussion with Mommy and Zuheir. During the few weeks after the conference, and as a result of these many discussions, I felt I was continuing the work she began in the fifties. That continuity between Mommy's work and my own became clearer than ever before. It gave me such satisfaction; I hope it did the same for her.

When Zuheir's birthday neared in October, Mommy did everything she could to help plan for it. Her presence and her loving smile were the best helpers to anything I did. The thank-yous she showered me with for the smallest things I did gave me energy and focus. I will never be able to describe in depth or in detail the blessing her presence was for us.

Toward the end of October, she indicated that it was time for her to go live for a time with Ramzi or Sarmad. They had been asking that she move to one of their homes, and she wanted to honor their requests. In her own way, she explained to me that she would like to live with each of us for three months. She basically said, "I have been with you and Zuheir since August; now it is the end of October, and it is time to accept either Ramzi's or Sarmad's invitation." I was so sad that she would be leaving our home.

Mommy spent November, December, and most of January with Sarmad and his family. For the first time in many years, we all celebrated Christmas with our mother. Sarmad and his family, Ramzi and his family, and Zuheir and I spent an unforgettable Christmas Eve and day with her. Mommy was so happy to be surrounded by her grandchildren Cedar, Paul, Michael, Loreen, and Jessie. Celebrating the holiday with Mommy allowed us to relive the spirit of Christmas in its true sense. With her, our Christmas was more about love and embracing others than about material gifts. It was amazing how her smiling, yet silent, presence could frame an evening in a far more eloquent way than all the talk or even the speeches that could be given by others.

Towards the end of January, Mommy moved again and spent the rest of January, February, and March with Ramzi and his family.

During January and February 1996, my team and I were busy writing many proposals at Creative. One of my senior staff, Patricia Flederman, was on maternity leave, and she had spent already nearly two months at home with her newborn. I felt our team needed Patricia's contributions on the many proposals we were designing and writing. I called her home and asked if she could come back to the office earlier than the agreed upon maternity leave period and resume her work. She agreed without hesitation, on the condition she be allowed to bring her baby Jamie with her. I answered, also without any hesitation, "Of course, bring baby Jamie and come back to work." I must have realized that a professional mother must have the right to a daycare center where she worked, and if such a place did not exist, then at least she should be able to bring her baby to the office.

Patricia came back to work with Jamie, a very calm baby. For six months, Patricia worked hard, contributed to all the proposals we were designing and writing, backstopped many overseas projects, and cared for Jamie in a small crib in a corner of her office. He spent his time sleeping or watching the office surroundings. When she needed to breastfeed him, she did that discreetly; it was a win/win situation. We at Creative benefitted from not having Patricia take a lengthy maternal leave, Patricia benefitted from coming back to work, and Jamie benefitted from continuing to be with his mother on a daily basis until he turned eight months old. We were pleased that our solution was mother-friendly and at the same time in support of the productivity of our team.

Soon spring was in the air, and during the first weekend of April, while I was visiting Mommy at Ramzi's, something unexpected happened. After lunch, when Ramzi and I were alone with her in the living room drinking coffee, she tried to tell us something that we did not understand; the word "Freike" kept coming up in her special way of communicating with us. Finally, Ramzi thought he understood and said, "I know what you are trying to tell us. You would like to visit Lebanon, and in particular, Freike." Mommy smiled and kind of encouraged Ramzi to continue, even though by the expression on her face, we knew that we did not yet capture what she was trying to communicate.

Ramzi and I continued the discussion with Mommy, and then she added the word "Albert." We said, "Now we understand, you would like to visit Lebanon, go up to Freike, and visit Daddy's tomb." Again, she seemed pleased that we understood a good part of what she was trying to communicate. Yet again, through her expressions, we knew we did not get it all. Something was still missing. To assure Mommy that we took her every word to heart, Ramzi and I promised that in June or in July we would travel to Lebanon together and go to Freike. We would spend time with Ameen and his family, visit Daddy's tomb, and then come back to the U.S. Mommy left it at that.

We enjoyed the rest of our afternoon until Zuheir arrived to pick me up. Mommy asked if she could come back with me to our home in Bethesda. Zuheir and I were delighted, but Ramzi said, "Mommy, the three months at my house are not over yet." She smiled, kissed him, and asked him to accept her request. I told Ramzi his three months were nearly up, and it was my turn to have Mommy. The coming week would be perfect for her to start her time with us. I noted the next Sunday would be April 14, Michael's birthday, and I wanted to celebrate it at my home. I was sure Sarmad and Ina would not say no, given that Michael was my godson.

Ramzi finally agreed, even though he would have liked to keep Mommy longer. While her caregiver and I packed her clothes, and while Ramzi was packing her medications, Mommy thanked Ghada for her stay with them. As she said goodbye to Ghada, Loreen, and baby Jessie, she kissed and hugged each one of them, and she gave Ramzi a warm and long embrace. Zuheir and Ramzi lifted her and her wheelchair across the few steps of Ramzi's front door, sat her in Zuheir's car, and the three of us, with Mommy's caregiver, returned to our home in Bethesda. Mommy cried in the car. I tried my best to cheer her up and barely succeeded; however, once we arrived at our home, she regained her composure. Zuheir and I prepared dinner, and the three of us had a lovely evening.

Everything seemed normal during that second week of April. During the day, Zuheir and I went to work, and as soon as I came home, Mommy's radiant face and smile welcomed me. The evenings were particularly lovely and Mommy and I planned Michael's birthday. We decided together the menu for dinner on Sunday, April 14, and discussed the gifts we wanted to buy him. During that week, both Ramzi and Sarmad stopped at our home after work just to visit Mommy. One of them bought her flowers and the other brought the mixed nuts that she liked. Zuheir, too, always knew how to make Mommy happy. He often asked lots of questions about Daddy, or would tell her stories that he knew regarding Daddy. Her face beamed with joy whenever any one of us talked about him.

On Sunday, April 14, the whole family came to our home in Bethesda to celebrate Michael's tenth birthday. Mommy enjoyed herself thoroughly. She had all the Rihanis of the greater Washington area around her: three of her children, three of her in-laws, and five of her grandchildren. During the late afternoon before dinner, Zuheir and I arranged to plant a maple tree in our front yard. The family gathered around and little Michael helped Zuheir plant the tree. Mommy was delighted. She asked us to name the tree "Michael's tree," and that is how we referred to it from then on.

At dinner, we were twelve at the table, with Michael and Mommy as the stars of our evening. After everyone left, I helped the caregiver prepare Mommy for bed. Once she was settled in, I kneeled next to her, like I always did when I said goodnight, kissed her hand, and tucked her into bed. She held my hand tightly and repeated her beautiful thank-yous several times. I also repeated several times that

I was the one who needed to tell her thank you for agreeing to come to the U.S., and for living with us in our homes. She shook her head and repeated, "Thank you, thank you, thank you."

I went to bed that evening with a happy heart.

Monday, April 15, I received a phone call at my office from Mommy's caregiver asking me to rush home. Mommy was not feeling well. I called Zuheir, asked him to call my brothers and tell them about Mommy's situation, and then meet me home. I left my office and drove as quickly as I could to Bethesda. When I arrived home, Mommy was not breathing well and indicated she was in extreme pain. I asked where she felt pain and she gestured from her head to her feet. Zuheir had arrived ahead of me and immediately made an appointment with her heart doctor, a wonderful man in Wheaton named Dr. Samuel Itscoitz. Sarmad arrived and we called Dr. Itscoitz to ensure he would see her. We got Mommy into the car and drove to the doctor's office. He saw her right away and said, "I can't detect a pulse." He advised we take her straightaway to the hospital; fortunately, Holy Cross Hospital was only a few blocks away. Dr. Itscoitz called ahead to prepare Holy Cross to receive her at the emergency entrance. We made a dash with Mommy to the hospital, where Ramzi met us.

We explained to the doctors the need for one of us to accompany her to help understand and to convey her gestures, and they agreed. Many doctors and many nurses were in and out. One explained they were having great difficulty finding a vein to insert a needle. Finally, they succeeded in finding one in her leg, and they discovered that she had a heart problem.

Every minute of that day was agony. Ramzi, Sarmad, and I took turns being with her in the emergency room. The doctors and nurses tried to run all kinds of tests and they needed to draw blood. Her veins had always been small and not readily visible; that day, they seemed to have faded away. The nurses poked her so many times looking for a way to insert an IV that she was covered with bruises. I held her hand and softly told her everything would be okay. I wished I could believe what I was telling her.

She was like an angel lying in a hospital bed, suffering but never complaining, not asking for anything. I knew she was in a great deal of pain, but she kept it to herself. After nearly two hours of poking her arms and hooking her to many tubes, one of the nurses came in and said she needed to draw blood. I have no idea what the nurse poked, but blood started gushing from Mommy's neck. I rushed out and called my brothers. Zuheir, Ramzi, and Sarmad went into her room to see what happened.

I sat on a chair at the entrance of the emergency room and cried. Why did Mommy have to suffer so much? Why did she have to go through twenty-six years of pain? Who was testing her faith and her patience? What was the meaning of all her suffering? Why was it that my mother had to carry a cross for twenty-six years and still the suffering continued?

Ramzi and Sarmad came out with frustrated looks on their faces. They could not understand why the nurse did not know how to handle such a delicate and sensitive medical procedure as drawing blood from Mommy's neck. They could not accept the fact that there was not another way to deal with the situation without poking her again and again, and especially in the neck. I was equally frustrated and distraught. Zuheir tried his best to comfort us.

Shortly before midnight, the nurses said it would be better to leave and come back the next day. We insisted that we wanted to see Mommy one more time before any of us left for the night. I also insisted that I needed to stay even if it meant sleeping on a chair next to her bed since Mommy could not speak except for a few words that only family members could understand. I would not be put off, and the nurses finally agreed.

We went in with sad hearts and tried to hide the tears in our eyes. Ramzi, Sarmad, Zuheir, and I stood by her bed looking at all of the tubes attached to her, and all of the bandages on her neck and her arms. I felt miserable and low, but I put on a fake smile. Mommy looked at all of us, smiled, and with a very weak voice said in Arabic, "Go and sleep." Typical Mommy; she was in a critical condition and in pain, yet she was thinking about others. To me she was always this amazing person, always concerned about the well-being of others and never herself. I do not know how she was able to muster those words in Arabic; as far as I know, she had not uttered them in twenty-six years. Her illness dictated that she should not be able to speak at all, yet somehow she drew those words up for our sakes, probably from an inner well of unconditional love that was so deep and rich that it never hesitated and always flowed out like a clear spring.

After my brothers and my husband kissed her forehead and hands to say goodnight, I wished them a restful night and stayed with Mommy.

I spent four days with an angel.

Mommy remained hooked to all of those tubes. Doctors would come during the morning hours to examine her. They told us that her heart condition was critical so it was hard to know how long it would take for her to recover. With all the pain, discomfort, and uncertainty that Mommy was going through, she continued to shower us with her beautiful smile and her faint thank-yous. Whenever, Ramzi, Sarmad, or any member of their families would come into her room, she would smile and indicate that she was fine. Whenever Zuheir came in, Mommy, in her own way, would ask him to take me home. I would go home only to shower and change my clothes, returning promptly to the hospital. Spending the days and nights with her, watching her beautiful calm face despite all the pain she was going through, was a lesson in patience and grace. No matter how critical her situation was, no matter how many times the nurses had to change her medication and tubes, she would find inner strength to utter her favorite words, "Thank you," in a soft, feeble voice.

One day, Sarmad brought Ina, Cedar, Paul, and Michael to visit. Then Ramzi brought Ghada and Loreen; little Jessie was very ill and they could not bring her to the hospital. Mommy was delighted to see them all.

Tuesday, Wednesday, and Thursday went by, and the doctors were not sure if Mommy's situation was improving; basically, they said she was stable. Zuheir's elder sister Selma visited, and after staying in Mommy's room for a while, came out with a wide smile and tears in her eyes, and said, "The room is *filled* with angels!"

Friday morning, April 19, Mommy was very uncomfortable and not breathing well. Zuheir and I called the nurses who rushed to her room, put an oxygen mask on her face, and added some new tubes. It was so painful to see them poking her again. Her arms were already black and blue. Zuheir and I came closer to her bed. Mommy became restless and shook her head back and forth, then suddenly she took the oxygen tubes off her face. We were alarmed. The bedside monitor alarm went off, and we ran out to call a nurse.

Holy Cross was an efficient hospital. Within seconds, we were ushered out as several nurses and doctors filled the room. I asked Zuheir to call my brothers and he hurried off to do so. I waited outside the door of her room until I could not wait anymore. I went in and held her hand. Zuheir returned and stood on the other side of the bed, also holding her hand. After a moment, he came around to my side and gently asked me to step back. I did not want to. Zuheir insisted. I stepped back. My Mommy passed.

Losing a mother is bad enough, but losing a mother who suffered for twenty-six years is unbearable. Losing the most loving person I knew on this earth, the least self-centered person, the most sensitive person, the person who never ever asked for anything, and the person who never said a word that could hurt someone, was so deeply painful.

After a short while, Ramzi and Sarmad arrived. They, too, were in disbelief. Like me, they were not prepared for this and could not believe that Mommy had in fact left us. The three of us knelt by the side of her bed and cried. I have never heard Ramzi sob out loud before, and I had never seen Sarmad in such a state of shock. Zuheir left the room out of delicacy for our need to grieve and be alone with Mommy, and he kept others out. We spent perhaps thirty minutes by her bedside, crying and praying.

During that time, Zuheir contacted Ameen in Lebanon and members of his family and close friends to inform them of our loss.

Mommy's passing felt like I had been disconnected from goodness in the world.

Her life before her illness was about others, how to love them and serve them. Her life after her illness was also about others, how to never judge them, how to forgive them, how to be thankful for whatever destiny dealt her even in illness and pain, and how to continue loving all those she knew and those she did not know. Losing Mommy was like losing the keys to the high ground, losing the source of pure water, losing not only our home but the pathway to it, to where love abides.

We accepted condolences. Family members, relatives, and friends were generous with their sympathies and support.

A few days after Mommy's passing, Ramzi and I realized what Mommy was telling us on that Sunday afternoon in his home. We believe she was asking for something, and that would have been the first time she asked for anything. We believe she was trying to tell us, "When I pass away, please take my body back to Lebanon and bury me near Albert in Freike." In all those years, she never asked for anything, not material things, not vacations, not anything for her. Finally, when she did ask, it was to take her back and lay her to rest near Daddy. She wanted the river of love to continue running under their feet.

Of course, we honored her wish.

We all flew to Lebanon, walked behind the coffin of an angel, and laid her to rest in Freike next to her Albert. Ten-year-old Michael walked silently behind her. I hoped that someday he would realize how lucky he had been to witness how an angel had made a decision to come to the U.S., bless three homes, live in each one of these homes for three months, and then return to Freike and rest next to the love of her life.

In the twelve months between April 1995 and April 1996, I lost my niece who had been my goddaughter, my father, and my mother. Sadness continued to accumulate. But with the loss of Mommy, I was overwhelmed. I am not sure whether many individuals in midlife experience feeling orphaned, but I did. I am not sure independent, successful professionals can feel so bereft, so lost, so uprooted and disoriented by the loss of parents, but I did.

The loss of Mommy and Daddy changed me. There was a time in my life when I felt totally anchored. Now, and for the rest of my life, I would be searching for a way to re-anchor myself. There was time when I consciously relied on an oasis of peace, serenity, and unqualified love. Now I was adrift, not knowing whether I could ever recreate such a place or find a similar one under a rainbow.

CHAPTER THIRTY-ONE

A WINNING STREAK

BACK AT CREATIVE, I IMMERSED myself in our programs. The Morocco Mission put out an ambitious RFP for girls' education in Morocco. We bid on it. The competition was very tough; all the reputable international education organizations submitted bids. I was concerned that we might lose out to the Academy for Educational Development (AED) or to Research Triangle International (RTI), but we did not. We won the large five-year project, which the USAID Mission called Morocco Education for Girls (MEG). My team and I got busy recruiting the Chief of Party and a team to assist her in implementing this very important project. I traveled to Morocco to ensure a smooth launch. The Moroccan Ministry of Education was pleased that I came and I was delighted to work with a very knowledgeable, strategic, and thoughtful Minister, Dr. Rachid Benmoukhtar. The minister thought my analysis in the 1995 report to USAID, "Promoting Girls' Education in Rural Morocco," was accurate. He had a copy of my report and reminded me of what I had written in five key areas:

- Access: Very large disparities existed between urban and rural enrollments—"two worlds," in the words of the education minister. The absence of girls in the rural area schools was particularly acute.

- Retention: In rural areas, the dropout rates for boys and girls were 50.4 percent and 54.0 percent, respectively.
- Attainment: High rates of efficiency in urban areas were observed, but fewer than half of rural students—boys and girls—were completing grade six.
- Achievement: Once girls entered school and were retained, their chances of succeeding were equal to those for boys.
- Quality: Improvements were needed, including curriculum, teacher preparation, and instructional materials.

After he reviewed what I wrote in the report, he said he expected the MEG team to work very closely with the Ministry to address all five educational issues highlighted in the report. During the planning of my several future trips to Morocco while Dr. Benmoukhtar was minister, I made it a point to inform him of my time in Rabat so we could resume our lengthy meetings. I needed to gauge the ongoing satisfaction of not only Dr. Benmoukhtar, but of the directors of the ministry regarding the progress and accomplishments of the MEG program.

It seemed Creative was on a winning streak. Between 1994 and 1997, we won a large number of basic education projects, and our implementation teams were hard at work in Benin, Malawi, Morocco, Egypt, Uganda, and South Africa.

In Benin, we had supported the national primary education reform since 1995 through the USAID-sponsored project. Our long-term advisors worked together with Benin educators and ministry officials to enhance local capacity to both plan and implement educational reform. We assisted in defining standards of educational quality for Benin's primary schools. Our team worked with ministry professionals on curriculum development, teacher and inspector training, revision of students' assessment instruments, and on refining methods for tracking educational data and results.

In South Africa through project ABEL, we assisted NGOs and the government in the design and execution of basic education programming. Our Creative Associates team provided technical assistance to the National Department of Education (NDE) and to local NGOs identified by NDE as partners in South Africa's education reform efforts. A major activity was to support South Africa's Curriculum 2005, an initiative that sought to improve classroom pedagogy in the direction of student-centered and continuous assessment approaches.

In Malawi, through the USAID-funded Girls' Attainment in Basic Literacy and Education (GABLE), and through the support of both USAID Washington and the USAID Mission—in particular Program Officer Stephanie Funk—we had two large funded educational projects: a Social Mobilization Campaign (SMC) project and a Policy Planning and Curriculum (PPC) project. The SMC team implemented a campaign designed to change the attitudes of the Malawian communities—particularly local leaders, teachers, and parents—about girls' education.

Our approach to the social mobilization campaign was built on a process in which government ministries, local government organizations, businesses, parents, and grass-roots communities and organizations assessed the barriers to girls' education, identified culturally appropriate solutions, and implemented those solutions. Our campaign included four key elements: 1) interactive folk theater; 2) training of trainers, community leaders, and grassroots organizations to develop advocacy skills in support of girls' education;

3) village-based initiatives that identified and implemented action plans and solutions to overcome the barriers to girls' education; and 4) dissemination activities, including a weekly radio broadcast and a variety of print materials. All of these activities were designed to stimulate dialogue and encourage sustained changes in behavior.

The PPC team of long-term advisors supported the Ministry of Education in its efforts to upgrade the quality of primary education. Reform efforts emphasized those planning, policy, and curriculum issues that related most specifically to the retention and achievement of girls in school. By providing on-the-job, individualized technical support, our local and ex patriot staff strengthened the capacity of the Ministry staff to plan their reform efforts. In addition, we had a special long-term advisor work with the Malawi Institute of Education to reform the social studies curriculum to ensure that it focused on both young girls and young boys as citizens and active members of their communities.

In Uganda, we worked through the Support for Ugandan Primary Education Reform (SUPER) project. The Creative Associates team promoted parent/community involvement in the country's primary education reform effort. We identified parent and community needs, developed a community mobilization manual, and trained local mobilizers to work with community leaders. Our team also assisted the Ministry of Education staff in planning and implementing an incentive program to further motivate parents to send their children, particularly their daughters, to school.

In Egypt, the USAID funded-project we directed planned to assist in increasing the participation of girls in quality basic education. The goal of Project ISIS (Institutionalizing Success in Innovative Schools) was to create a minimum of 1,000 girl- friendly classrooms that would provide quality education to boys and girls in the underserved rural communities of Beni Suef, Beheira, Minya, and in poor urban districts of Cairo.

Finally, in Morocco—possibly our largest project—our team of long-term advisors based in Rabat was to assist the national Ministry of Education, through project MEG, to increase the access, participation, and retention of Moroccan girls in selected rural primary schools. Our MEG model focused on providing higher quality, more gender-relevant primary education; ensuring girl-friendly school environments; and engaging communities in the support of primary education for girls.

In addition to these multi-year, multi-million-dollar projects, Creative designed smaller innovative projects that contributed to advancing the field of international education in general, and to the cause of girls' education in particular.

Towards the end of 1997, the Creative Associates Division of Education and Training that I led was growing quickly and expanding its programs in many countries. I therefore wrote to our colleagues, collaborators, partners, and donors to reintroduce the division, emphasizing our educational vision and highlighting our approaches. I felt it was helpful to clarify the role our division was playing around the world and why.

My letter read:

Dear Colleagues,

Perhaps the single most determining factor impacting the quality of life for future generations is what happens in the schools and classrooms of the 21st century. The Education and Training Division at Creative Associates International is driven by one central purpose: to enhance the lives of children and adults by ensuring quality basic education.

We focus on assessing, designing, and implementing programs and activities that improve educational systems. For example, we created the concept of home schools for illiterate girls in Afghanistan. In Benin, through collaboration with a variety of stakeholders, we are assisting in the reform of the educational system. In Malawi, our social mobilization campaign is working in the heart of the country's social norms to reinforce elements of its culture that will gradually build an equitable educational system. In Uganda, we are developing an alternative basic education program for out-of-school youth. In Guatemala, we are assessing literacy programs and special educational needs for adults. And in Morocco, an innovative model is being implemented in rural areas to increase girls' access, retention, and achievement. In addition, we conduct research that enables us to continue refining strategies that are being implemented as part of our work in the global village—in Africa, Asia, Latin America, and the Middle East.

Our work, by definition, is shared. Our partners are government ministries, NGOs, community organizations, local leaders, private sector institutions, and donor agencies. We value these collaborative efforts which benefit the people we serve, and which in turn inspire us.

The Education and Training Division has developed
innovative solutions to educational problems that
enrich the quality of life.

I welcome your collaboration as we confront the new
challenges of the 21st century.

I loved my work: it energized me and inspired me. I was capable
of regularly working twelve to fourteen hours a day without feeling
tired. My work helped me through the deep, silent sadness that
engulfed me after the loss of my parents and my goddaughter. It
was as if working hard and serving the underprivileged honored my
parents' value system and allowed me to feel that I was walking on
their path.

In the summer of 1997, USAID invited bids to support Lebanon.
It was one of the first large RFPs in perhaps two decades. I hired a
Lebanese consultant who resided there to help collect the necessary
data and information, and I assigned some of my best staff to join
me in designing and writing the proposal. I was motivated to work
hard in the hope of winning this project to benefit Lebanon. The
RFP called for supporting small agro-business enterprises in different
parts of the country in order to boost the economy of remote rural
regions. I loved the spirit of the program, and my team and I worked
very hard.

Again, the competition was tough. My concern this time was
that Creative Associates could lose this project to an NGO that was
well established in Lebanon such as World Vision, or to another
non-governmental agency that had been working in Lebanon for
years or even decades, and there were many. The results were to
be announced around the end of 1997; however, there were delays.

Finally, on March 25, 1998, Creative Associates received a letter from James Jeckell, an agreement officer at USAID, informing us we had won the Lebanon proposal.

I was jubilant, and my team and I celebrated the win. When I arrived home, I cried. It meant so much to me that we would be able to assist small farmers in Lebanon increase their productivity. A dream came true. I had always wanted to add Lebanon to the list of countries my team and I were able to serve and finally we did. Tears of joy and gratitude accompanied my dinner at home that evening.

While my team and I were designing and writing several other proposals in 1997 and early 1998, I was involved in planning an International Girls' Education conference for the spring of 1998. Susie Clay, a senior officer at the USAID Women in Development office, had created a committee of ten professionals from ten different organizations to work with her on planning this international conference, and when she asked me to join the committee, I accepted. The conference was called "Educating Girls: A Development Imperative."

Our planning committee wrote several documents explaining why we were putting this conference together:

> Common sense and thirty years of research show that by not educating girls, society is shortchanging them, their children, and itself. Educating girls, particularly at the primary and lower secondary levels, is one of the most productive investments that society can make in terms of its social and economic development... Educating girls initiates a process of intergenerational poverty reduction that contributes to both family welfare and household income. Educated women are more likely to find employment, earn higher wages,

and be more economically productive, have fewer children, increase the chances of both maternal and child survival; have healthier families through better nutrition and health practices; and ensure that their own children—daughters and sons—are educated, initiating a virtuous cycle that contributes to the well-being of future generations.

Working with Susie was always invigorating as her commitment to girls' education was deep and genuine.

The conference, which took place May 6-8, 1998, aimed to strengthen partnerships between the public and private sectors in countries around the world in support of girls' education. Specifically, the conference goals were to:

1. Build linkages, partnerships, and means of collaboration between public and private sectors.
2. Examine the roles, responsibilities, relationships, and activities of the public sector, private sector, religious leaders, NGOs, communities, and media to support girls' education.
3. Learn from leaders in all sectors who were promoting education improvement efforts.
4. Present new knowledge on cost-effective and sustainable approaches for increasing girls' educational opportunities.
5. Encourage countries to design innovative ways to increase the number of girls in school, and focus media attention on efforts to expand girls' education.

The participants were four hundred senior representatives of the public and private sectors from forty-two countries in Africa, Asia, the Middle East, and Latin America. Conference presentations were informative and thought provoking. Among the highlights were contributions made by delegates from Afghanistan, Benin, Egypt, Ghana, Guatemala, Guinea, Haiti, India, Malawi, Mali, Morocco, Peru, and Zambia.

However, from my perspective, the main highlight was the speech of the First Lady of the United States, Hillary Clinton. She spoke as if she were a specialist in girls' education, recognizing the progress made to date, but also urging us all to multiply our efforts and to be more creative and innovative in thinking about how to overcome the obstacles to providing girls' education. Mrs. Clinton ended her speech by saying:

> "Certainly USAID and the United States government want to stand with you in helping to bring to reality our dreams that we will see opportunities for every girl and every boy everywhere in the world to receive a quality education that will enable them to take responsibility for their futures."

During May and June of 1998, I received offers for senior positions from several organizations around Washington, D.C. I was intrigued by the offers, and one in particular piqued my interest. In my thirteen years at Creative, I had never been unhappy or unsatisfied. I was excited about our work, passionate about the transformation that took place in the field, and delighted to work with the excellent professionals in the office; however, when I got the new offers, I was thoughtful of the resources that some of the larger firms would provide.

After much thought, reflection, and deliberation—and long discussions with Zuheir and Ramzi—I submitted a letter of resignation to Charito at Creative and accepted the job of Senior Vice President at the Academy for Educational Development. At that time, AED was larger than Creative and worked not only in education, but in health, nutrition, HIV/AIDS, social marketing, civil society, and the environment. That diversity of expertise appealed to me, and a larger, well-known and respected organization was also attractive. When I accepted the position in August 1998, I told Steve Moseley I would need a month or so off before beginning work. Steve agreed, and I was pleased to have time to reflect on my years with Creative.

My conclusion as a result of that month of reflection was that anyone who worked in the field of international development, and in particular international education, must recognize the importance of the role that is bestowed on her or him, and must be totally aware of the need to continue to listen and to learn. On one hand, anyone working in international development is privileged; on the other hand, the responsibilities can be daunting. Working to alleviate poverty, to ensure that girls and boys have access to quality education, to ensure that gender perspectives are integrated in all international development programs, to channel the contributions that give voice to those who do not have a say, and to serve remote marginalized populations is a responsibility given to a select few, and those few who are within that circle need to tread carefully with compassion, knowledge, humility, respect, and an open attitude that allows them to continue to learn.

CHAPTER THIRTY-TWO

GIRLS' EDUCATION AND WOMEN'S EMPOWERMENT

OCTOBER 1998 MARKED A NEW beginning for me. AED was a very large NGO that worked in different sectors of international development. After joining the organization, it took me approximately two months to learn the culture of AED and its way of functioning. Unlike TransCentury— a smaller organization that was totally driven by a visionary, innovative leader and a creative senior management—and unlike Creative—a smaller (at that time) for-profit organization driven by the fact that it was women- and minority-owned, which were among the elements for its success— AED was a large NGO driven to be totally responsive to its clients so it could deliver results. These three very different U.S.-based organizations working in international development had different cultures and different motivations. What they had in common was a philosophy of respect to all cultures. I knew I was lucky to have the opportunity to work in all three of them.

Early in 1999, I decided that I needed to focus on building a portfolio of programs and projects that I could lead and could oversee the implementation of within AED. I discovered that internal competition within AED was much greater than I had experienced in my two previous organizations. This was neither good nor bad; it was simply a new feature that I needed to adjust to. After some thought and discussions with some of the leaders of AED, I decided that the portfolio that I wanted to build had to have girls' education at its center, and needed to include women's programs focused on leadership, empowerment, and participation in economic productivity, as well as activities and projects to combat gender-based violence and human trafficking. A tall order. It seems I still enjoyed challenging myself.

I started the year by flying to Pakistan to oversee a project AED was already implementing and to discuss with our Dutch funders the possibility of expanding and extending the project. I came back hopeful that the possibility of expansion was good given the results we were producing and the fact that the Dutch were so committed to girls' education.

Back in Washington, the need to add new programs to my portfolio became a total priority. To be able to do that, I recognized that I had to scan the world of the other donors and see where their priorities were. I was delighted to discover that Susie Clay at USAID was interested in funding a new girls' education project based on facilitating and promoting partnerships among the public sector, the business sector, the religious leaders, and the media within the host countries. After several meetings with Susie, and with Margarette Lycette, the director of the Women in Development Office at USAID, we agreed that if I wrote a proposal for Guinea whereby I could show that there were enough entities from within those four sectors who were willing to work together to advance girls' education within their country, the USAID Women in Development Office might fund such a program. I flew to Conakry, Guinea, met the former Deputy Minister of Education Dr. Aly Badara Doukoure, and worked with him for nearly ten days to identify leaders within those sectors who would be willing to work together toward this goal. Once back in Washington, I wrote a proposal and submitted it to USAID.

While waiting for USAID's response, Judy Mann from *The Washington Post*, who had attended the 1998 "Educating Girls: A Development Imperative" conference, contacted me because she wanted to write about girls' education. On October 27, 1999, Judy published an article in *The Washington Post* titled "Educated Girls Can Help Heal Broken Nations." I am going to quote several sections of this article because it captured some of our major approaches regarding girls' education in the late 1990s. She started her article by stating:

> May Rihani, director of girls' education at the Academy of Educational Development, went to the remote Baloshistan province several months ago to see how girls' schools she had helped start were doing. She found a success story not only for girls, but also for their mothers.... Rihani, who has worked for 22 years to improve girls' education in developing countries, was not sure the formidable obstacles this project faced could be overcome. Baloshistan is Pakistan's biggest and least-developed province. It is a conservative region. In its rural areas, only two percent of the females are literate. Girls and boys cannot attend school together, and only women teachers can instruct girls. The AED Dutch-backed project goes in and builds schools for girls and trains teachers, who then are paid by the government. The

operation of the school stays with a local women's committee.

One of the first steps in setting up a school is to form those women's education committees. The most important principle is to involve them at all levels—whether they are literate or illiterate, Rihani said. She spent two hours talking with committee members during her most recent visit. "I challenged them to tell me why girls' education is important. I heard: 'Until we sent our girls to school, we did not see changes in our lives. Once we sent them, we started seeing changes in our lives.'"

One mother told her that by creating the education committee, the women in the community got their first taste of power. "Our voices have been heard by the school and by the teachers, [as well] as by the representatives of the government, so we women are gaining power," the mother told Rihani. Another woman said, "Now they hear our voices on the schooling of our daughters, they will have to hear our voices on other things."

Rihani said, "I always heard women say, 'We want to send our daughters to school because we want them to have a better life than us,' but what was said by these mothers in these remote areas was very revealing and quite new. Schools for girls are not a priority in these communities. We learned we have to work through

local NGOs, we strengthen the local institutions and
we create leadership, and they in turn work with their
communities and convince them to build schools for
girls. Once this happens, we come back and train
women teachers. The communities did not want their
rural women traveling to teacher training centers. We
said, fine we will bring the training to you. We did
mobile training," Rihani said.

The *Post* article went on to explain how we tackled many of
the obstacles we faced when we designed and implemented girls'
education projects, especially in remote conservative rural areas.

I was extremely grateful that Judy Mann wrote and published
this article. It affirmed the key importance of girls' education and
its centrality within the process of comprehensive international
development schemes. My phone did not stop ringing for nearly a
week from the date of its publication. Some callers just wanted me to
know they were pleased with the article; some were being educated
about the obstacles of girls' education and wanted to express their
concerns; some wanted to know more about how we overcame those
obstacles; and some wanted to conduct further interviews with me. I
must have given another five or six interviews about girl's education
that year.

As soon as the year 2000 arrived, two exciting things happened:
USAID announced we had won the Guinea project, and Steve
Moseley, the CEO of AED, asked me to co-chair the company's
Strategic Planning Task Force.

Winning the Guinea girls' education project was a big deal. Susie
Clay and Margarette Lycette of USAID had told me if they agreed to
the design of AED's proposal, and if they saw during the first year of

implementation that key players of the four sectors were partnering in support of girls' education, they would be willing to fund projects that followed the same approach in other countries. I was excited about the possibility of implementing similar projects elsewhere, and about the opportunity of comparing whether the framework, the methodologies, and the basic principles, remained the same or changed slightly depending on the context of each country. My staff and I discussed names for this promising and forward-looking project and offered SAGE: Strategies for Advancing Girls' Education. When I suggested this to Susie, she happily endorsed the name.

In Guinea, I hired Dr. Doukoure to head the local effort. Aly and his team of Guinean education experts did an excellent job in mobilizing major actors from the four sectors in support of girls' education. In Guinea, under Aly Badara's leadership, the staff of SAGE created local alliances in support of girls' schooling in many rural towns and large villages. They were also able to facilitate meetings whereby the religious leaders, the business leaders, the representatives of the local media (radio in particular), and the representatives of the Ministry of Education agreed on many strategies, among them the following:

1. Every week during the Friday sermon, the mullahs would speak about the importance of sending girls to school and the benefits of girls' education. Our local team provided them with details on the benefits of girls' education and included quotations from the Koran and the Hadith about why it is important to educate girls and women.

2. Every month or so, local radio stations would air a program in support of girls' education whereby the reporter would interview local representatives of the Ministry of Education,

a principal of a school, a teacher, or a parent to discuss the importance of girls' education.

3. Business and community leaders agreed to fund the construction of latrines for the schools which did not have appropriate facilities.

4. Business leaders agreed to offer scholarships for the girls who obtained high grades by the end of the year, and whose parents did not have the means to support their continuing education.

5. Reporters of the main newspapers in Guinea agreed to cover news of the schools that SAGE was supporting in the rural towns and large villages in order to raise awareness about the local partnership formed among the four sectors in support of girls' education.

6. Aly convinced the Ministry to declare an annual Day of the Girl Student. They chose a day in June. Most of the schools in Guinea celebrated that day, and many successful girl students were key speakers at the event. Parents, community leaders, business representatives, and local ministry officials gathered to participate in the celebrations and to hear passionate reports from the young speakers.

7. Local alliances reached a level of engagement in education whereby every year they would develop a plan of action for the school(s) they supported. These plans became major sources of support for the girl students, the teachers, the principals, the infrastructure of the school(s), and the local Ministry of Education representatives. In addition to building latrines, these local alliances committed to dig wells for the schools that did not have running water; fix the buildings—roof, windows—where the need existed; buy textbooks for the impoverished communities where parents could not afford

378

them; and find housing for teachers in remote villages when the government did not provide it. The local alliances became the empowered proactive agents, and a voice representing what were formerly underserved remote communities.

The local SAGE team in Guinea, with support from the international consultants from our headquarters, empowered local communities and helped build local capacity within the four sectors to support girls' education.

As a result of the approach we adopted in Guinea, Susie Clay asked me to submit proposals for other African countries. My senior staff and I, in consultation with USAID Washington and several of the USAID Missions in Africa, decided to submit proposals for Mali, Ghana, and the Democratic Republic of Congo. Senior staff were sent to each of these countries to identify local educational experts so they could work together to design a SAGE project for each of the three countries.

During that same year, 2000, I began my duties as co-chair of the Strategic Planning Task Force at AED. Working ten-to-twelve hours a day became the norm. To understand better strategic planning and prepare for my task, I read many books, among them *The Fifth Discipline* by Peter Senge and *Innovation and Entrepreneurship* by Peter Drucker, and reread Steven Covey's *The 7 Habits of Highly Effective People*. These books anchored me in the theory of change and how organizations can address change strategically. They reminded me that organizations and effective leaders cannot thrive without learning to adapt their approaches and practices to continuously changing environments and priorities. These books deepened my understanding of how organizations—leaders and employees—need to work together to anticipate the challenges that change brings.

These books also reminded me that the success of an organization is based on a vision and a mission that cannot be adopted by the leader and senior management only, but one that needs to be embraced by the rest of the staff. Every employee needs to believe in the vision and mission and to advocate for them. A key point emphasized by all the authors I read regarding strategic planning and healthy organizations was that successful organizations had to embrace and reward work habits and practices that valued innovation, initiative, excellence, effectiveness, win/win approaches, leadership at all levels, and fulfillment. I tried my best to distill from these books all that was relevant to co-leading AED's Strategic Planning Process.

The year 2000 felt like a crash course in topics that I enjoyed. It was demanding, enjoyable, and rich beyond any imagination. As a result of our strategic planning, AED decided to flatten its organizational structure, decentralize decision-making to a certain extent, create centers of excellence, and enable more leaders to head major technical areas. In the restructuring, twenty-six Centers of Excellence were created. These Centers were grouped in three programmatic groups, headed by senior vice presidents, and either senior vice presidents or vice presidents headed each of the centers.

As a result of my work with the strategic planning, I was asked to co-direct the Global Learning Group and to lead the Center for Gender Equity. During the year 2000, I also got to know some colleagues who I would not have had the chance to know well if not for the strategic planning appointment. Among those colleagues who became work collaborators and friends were: Bill Smith, Frank Beadle De Palomo, Mary Maguire, and Greg Niblett.

Given AED's international education work and history, the Global Learning Group was the largest AED group, and the Center of Gender Equity was one of the newest centers within AED. Challenge always energized me, and these two leadership positions required two different sets of skills. Co-directing the Global Learning Group (GLG) meant overseeing and ensuring the quality of large educational and/or information and analysis programs; establishing the Center for Gender Equity (CGE) meant being creative and innovative in designing gender programs, convincing donors to fund them, and overseeing the quality of implementation of these new programs. For CGE, I thought it would be wise to build on SAGE, expand it, and add to it a research agenda. Our funder, Susie Clay of the Office of Women in Development at USAID, agreed to this new vision of SAGE. As I mentioned earlier, my staff and I were in the process of designing new SAGE approaches for three new countries.

Three new SAGE proposals were submitted and all were funded; my staff and I were ecstatic. However, launching three new programs at the same time and continuing to manage the Dutch program in Pakistan, the SAGE program in Guinea, and overseeing some large programs of GLG was not a small responsibility—but when in my life had I ever said that I expected to be given small responsibilities? CGE was on its way to building a strong practice within AED, ensuring that gender perspectives were integrated into the designs, implementation plans, and monitoring approaches that were put in place. The research agenda of SAGE was ambitious: my staff, our donors, and I focused on studies and analyses of the obstacles which prevented a large percentage of girls from completing primary school and transitioning to secondary. We also wanted to rigorously analyze the strengths and the weaknesses of facilitating national and local partnerships in support of girls' education. In addition, we needed to understand better the relationship between HIV/AIDS in Africa and girls' education. I hired excellent researchers to undertake this ambitious agenda, including: Dr. Andrea Rugh, Dr. Howard

Williams, and Karen Titjen. My staff and I also worked closely with Frank Beadle de Palomo and his HIV/AIDS Center on reviewing all the research to date that focused on this health issue in Africa.

My staff and I organized a conference on the new and crucial topic of HIV/AIDS and girls' education. We invited lead researchers from Africa and from the United States to discuss the issues related to this topic and to present their findings. Over one hundred individuals participated in the conference we organized, including representatives from the donors, the UN system, researchers, and practitioners. Our objective was to present the most up-to-date information about the link between HIV/AIDS and girls' education, and to influence the donors to fund further research and projects designed to decrease the spread of these infections among youth, women, and men through changes in social behavior.

Lead researchers Andrea, Howard, and Karen focused on a deeper, more analytic understanding of the existing partnership among the public sector, the business sector, the religious leaders, and the media, and how to make these partnerships more effective and efficient. As a result of their work, CGE, through AED, produced three books presenting the findings of our researchers.

In addition to designing and implementing the SAGE programs in four African countries (Guinea, Mali, Ghana, and the Democratic Republic of the Congo), the USAID Mission in El Salvador asked us to design a program for them. By 2001, SAGE was being implemented in five countries, and its research arm was busy organizing seminars, symposia, colloquiums, and conferences to continue presenting findings and to widen the circle of dialogue and debate around all the issues related to girls' education.

During 2000 and 2001, the media continued to be interested in our work in girls' education. Judy Mann had struck a chord when she published her interview with me. Barbara Crossette published in the *New York Times* under the rubric "Week in Review" an article titled "Making Room for the Poor in a Global Economy" where she mentioned our work at CGE. From my perspective, the fact that local media in the countries where we were working were also interested in our programs and wanted stories about them was as significant and helpful to this task as the articles published in *The Washington Post* and the *New York Times*. When a Guinean or a Malian newspaper published an interview with me or with our local staff about our girls' education projects, part of what the newspapers were doing was raising awareness about the fact that girls' education is an imperative for the advancement of their countries. *La Nation* in Guinea, and *Le Republicain* in Mali, two daily newspapers, covered SAGE activities and accomplishments on a fairly regular basis. In addition, our local staff in El Salvador convinced one of their major dailies to have a full page on SAGE, girls' education, and women role models every single Thursday for a full year.

Some of the interviews, specifically those conducted by Lebanese or Arab journalists, wanted to understand the link between my work and my poetry. One of the interviews that I really appreciated was by Nada Al Awar, published in Beirut, in *The Daily Star* in November 2000. Nada described in a precise way how my travels and my poetry intermingled. She said in her article:

> On those many trips overseas, where after a long working day the only place to go is an empty hotel room, Rihani turns to writing. She uses a computer to type the technical reports. Beside it, she places a yellow note pad and a pen, her escape route into an hour of poetry writing, this time exclusively in

Arabic, before she finally goes to sleep. The location where each poem was conceived and created is clearly marked on every page of Rihani's poems, testimony to the importance of place in the development of the "international identity."

Nada quotes me saying: "Because I travel so much, poetry is my link to my identity. It is an identity that sees Lebanon as the essence of what home is—as a mixture of childhood and the future that I keep dreaming about."

She continues:

> Yet despite all the words and all the countries and all the longings in her heart, Rihani says she has still not written the book she has always wanted to. It is a future work that is still growing and developing within her, and one which will help her articulate her own ideas about being a citizen of the world. Rihani says, in that future book, "I hope to communicate to my readers a deeper understanding of how similar we all are." Rihani explains: "After all, we are nothing but brothers and sisters with the same joys and the same sorrows."

Sometime in the fall of 2000, I testified on Capitol Hill about the importance of girls' education. Among those present at the hearing was Congressman Earl Pomeroy (D-ND, 1993-2011). He became very interested in my testimony and asked if he could visit one of our USAID programs. I was delighted, and said of course we wanted him to see our work first-hand. I pointed out that visits by Congressional representatives would help them see the positive differences that the U.S. was making in the lives of impoverished communities through the funds that Congress allocated to international development through USAID and other donor agencies.

Upon returning to my office, I mentioned Congressman Pomeroy's request to Steve Moseley, AED's CEO. Steve was very interested in the idea, and through the Basic Education Coalition, he helped organize a visit for two Congressmen—a Democrat and a Republican—to visit Mali and Ghana.

In January 2001, Congressman Pomeroy, Congressman Mark Green (R-WI, 1999-2007), AED Senior Vice President for Communication Mary Maguire, Steve, and I visited Mali and toured communities and schools outside Bamako where project SAGE was being implemented. The leaders and community members of several rural towns and villages welcomed us. The communities were delighted that two U.S. Congressmen had come to visit them. The rituals of drums and dance were even more spectacular than usual, and the welcoming speeches included a sincere request for further assistance. The Congressmen asked permission to visit a sample of schools, and the community leaders responded positively. The delegation visited four or five schools, and the time spent there was one of two significant highlights of our stay. After Mali, the others continued on to Ghana where they visited schools and communities.

Perhaps nothing sheds light on an education system better than classroom observations. Sitting in the back of a classroom allows observers to notice physical things such as how crowded the classroom may be or the presence—or lack—of educational materials on the classroom walls. They can easily see the ratio of teacher to students, and how teachers interact with boys and with girls. The quality of information and instruction is readily visible, as is whether or not all students have textbooks. Differences become clear among the students, such as who asks questions and who does not, and how often girls ask questions versus the boys. Observers can see how instruction is delivered: if the teacher uses a lecture form only, or if he/she introduces other methods. The more rural the school the better; the observer can understand if all the services offered by the system of education are reaching those remote areas and if quality teachers are deployed to the rural communities.

The Congressmen were fascinated by what they saw, and after each classroom visit, they asked many questions. They wanted to understand the difference that project SAGE was making. Congressman Pomeroy asked about the supplemental educational materials he had seen used by both teachers and students in all the classrooms they visited. The teacher explained they were the Life Skills materials produced by the SAGE staff after consulting with the communities about relevant topics. She explained that SAGE conducted many teacher-training workshops during which the supplemental materials were distributed: one for the teacher and many sets for the students.

Congressman Green asked why the SAGE materials were used in addition to the textbooks. Another teacher said that during the community meetings with the SAGE staff, it was noted that the more relevant the topic of the teaching, the longer parents would keep their children in school. The SAGE materials covered topics that were relevant to the students, their families, and their communities, including issues of hygiene, nutrition, health, water, reproductive health, diseases, with specific lessons on the necessity of washing hands before touching food, how to treat an infant with diarrhea, how to avoid malaria, the facts about HIV/AIDS, how to avoid "sugar daddies," and so on.

In their initial discussions, the Congressmen had also asked for a few meetings with parents and community leaders. These gatherings led to lively discussions about the new approach in the school; while much of the talk was in English, some French and Bambara crept in and, of course, translation was key. At one point, Congressman Pomeroy asked if the new Life Skills materials made a difference in the education of their daughters and sons, and if so, how. After some hesitation, a mother responded timidly:

> My daughter has been going to school for five years. This is the first year she comes back from school and says, "Mother, I learned something at school that I want to teach you because it would be useful for our family." She taught me that when her baby brother and sister get diarrhea, we can do something to stop it. She said, "The teacher taught us that it is easy. First, we need to boil water and then mix in one-quarter of a small spoon of salt and one small spoon of sugar, and give it to the infant with diarrhea. This will help them not be dehydrated and will help stop the diarrhea."

The mother continued, "I am so pleased that my daughter comes home and teaches me useful, practical things that I can do to help the family."

It was so rewarding to hear this smart, brave, intelligent rural Malian mother explain in such a practical way why relevant education was critical. On the way back to Bamako after that meeting,

Congressmen Pomeroy and Green and I discussed in detail the importance of relevance and how through the proper materials, we could increase the retention of students in school and improve the quality of the teaching/learning process.

Another highlight of our visit to Mali was meeting with President Alpha Oumar Konare, at his request. President Konare had been elected in 1992 at the end of the democratic transition instituted by Amadou Toure, and he was re-elected for a second term in 1997. His time in office was noted for the restoration of democracy in spite of the 1997 difficulties, his management of the Tuareg Rebellion in the north, and his decentralization of the government. However, corruption remained a significant problem under Konare's administration.

Before becoming president, Konare began his professional career as a tutor in Kayes, then as a teacher at Markala and Bamako, and later became a professor of history and geography at the *Ecole Normale Supérieure* of Bamako. In the course of his career, he headed several professional organizations, including the Association of Historians and Geographers of Mali, the West African Association of Archaeologists, and the Union of West African Researchers. Between 1981 and 1992, Konare served as a consultant for UNESCO and UNDP. Due to his scholastic background as a teacher and a professor, President Konare was very interested in the educational system of his country and he wanted to discuss with us how this system could be improved.

The two-hour meeting with President Konare was refreshing. I had not expected a political president to discuss in such detail the possible improvements that could take place within the educational system of his country; usually that was the expertise of the Minister of Education. In this case, we had a president who was knowledgeable about the Malian system of education and genuinely interested in its success. He discussed with Congressmen Pomeroy and Green, and the rest of our delegation, the collaboration with USAID, the innovative approach of SAGE, the lack of resources that prevented the Ministry of Education from doing all it needed to do such as build more schools, train and deploy more teachers, ensure science and mathematics laboratories for all the secondary schools, provide running water for all the rural schools, and renew the curriculum to reflect the current needs, information and relevance. President Konare even addressed the gender gap between boys and girls in the Malian schools, and how poverty, social norms, and traditions could delay the necessary closing of such a gap.

At dinner that evening, our group discussed how satisfying it was to have a president who was genuinely committed to education and who was willing to search for ways to reduce the gap between boys and girls in Mali.

On March 12, 2001, *Le Republicain* had a full page about our visit: "The Visit of an American Congressional Delegation to Mali," with a photo of Congressman Pomeroy, the local director of SAGE Kadiatou Coulibaly, and me. The article offered details on our innovative approach to reforming the system of education, and how SAGE was implementing this approach and working to narrow the gap between the girls and boys of Mali.

Back in Washington, I immersed myself again in the demands of the Global Learning Group, the Center for Gender Equity, and the needs of the other AED groups to integrate gender in their work. In addition, the Social Change Group had a large multi-year environmental project, WEPIA, that addressed the issues of water in Jordan, and WEPIA asked for my assistance in integrating gender perspectives in their project.

WEPIA was a strategic social marketing program that focused on immediate and long-term water issues in Jordan. The management of scarce water resources was among the most significant challenges faced by Jordan. Like many other countries in the Middle East, Jordan grappled with rapid population growth, an aging water infrastructure, and a lack of public awareness regarding the severity of the problem and of measures required to ameliorate it. Because there were few opportunities to develop new supplies of fresh water, most experts agreed that the key to a sustainable future lay in managing demand.

To address the growing demand for water, USAID and the government of Jordan agreed upon a course of action to affect concrete changes in water consumption; AED was to handle implementation of the project. Over the life of the program, WEPIA worked cooperatively with the government of Jordan to build popular commitment for conservation of water, promote the use of water-saving technologies, and institutionalize strategic communication methods.

I was asked to review with the leadership of WEPIA ways to integrate gender perspectives regarding water conservation and consumption, and in particular how to ensure that the curriculum of the secondary schools sufficiently addressed the strategic issues of water. I also worked with the WEPIA Chief of Party, Dr. Mona Grieser, and the Jordanian partners to ensure that the approaches adopted were gender sensitive and acknowledged the roles of women and men in water conservation. The goals of the program included NGO capacity building, partnering with the Ministry of Education to produce environmental curriculum emphasizing strategic water issues, community grants for local water projects, water audits, media campaigns, and training workshops.

The work in Jordan was an opportunity to stretch my mind and learn *with* others and *from* others. The challenge of integrating environmental processes, educational work, and gender perspectives helped me trace new pathways. This project reaffirmed and deepened my understanding of how gender social norms affect every aspect of the daily life of communities, and how designing and implementing strategies to improve human and natural resources issues could not be successful without the integration of gender perspectives.

CHAPTER THIRTY-THREE

THE UNTHINKABLE HAPPENED

WHILE IN THE MIDDLE OF this extremely busy and productive period of 2001, the unthinkable happened: a tragic, horrific act that would change our lives forever.

On the morning of September 11, 2001, I was working in my office when several of my staff rushed in, alarmed. Their voices carried anxiety and fear as they told me something horrible was happening. We gathered in the big conference room to watch the television reports together. A plane had hit the World Trade Center in New York and the first tower fell in flames. The images were repeated over and over. Suddenly, the reporter stopped in the middle of his sentence and said, "The second tower was just hit by a second plane and is now burning."

The number of staff in the conference room had grown by then, and we all screamed, *Oh God, no!* as the images became more horrific. Watching the Twin Towers of the World Trade Center burn and collapse was impossible to comprehend. It felt like the whole world was going mad. Those horrible images will be imprinted in my memory until I leave this earth.

The worst part of it all was knowing that so many innocent people were going through hell while this was happening, and that most of the people in the Towers were killed. It was heart wrenching. I hurt everywhere and felt sick to my stomach. My colleagues in the conference room cried. Even though I felt horribly disoriented, as a senior vice president, I had responsibilities. I left the conference room, went back to my office, and called Bill Smith, the executive vice president who was in charge of AED during the month of September while the CEO was on vacation; his line was busy. I called his assistant and left a message asking him to call me immediately. A few minutes later, Bill called, as distraught as I was. He was considering closing AED and asking all our employees to go home, but he was consulting with D.C. security officers to make sure it would be safe for them to leave.

Bill hung up. I put my head in my hands and I gave in to tears. I could not believe what was happening. Deep down, I was convinced it was an act of terrorism. It could not be a freak accident; it had to have been planned. My inner pain deepened. My head ached. My throat was dry. My eyes were getting irritated, and my stomach churned. Every fiber in my body wanted to deny what was happening, but the reality—the television screen and the images we had seen in the conference room—screamed that it was true. Bill called back and said very sadly, "I am going to ask each senior vice president to inform staff that we would like them to go home, and that their security is the most important thing for us." He told me to remind them to drive calmly while going home. After staff was gone, the senior management would meet for a short while before leaving.

It was like a funeral. Staff members hugged each other as they left, sharing sentiments of concern such as stay safe, hope to see you tomorrow, call me when you arrive home, do you need a ride, if you need anything call me, and we are all in it together. After they were gone, I went to Bill's office where a few senior vice presidents were gathering. The mood was grim. We had a short meeting. By then most of the television channels had confirmed that it was a terrorist act. Bill recommended we all go home but stay in touch with him and with each other. He asked that we check the AED phone message before coming to work the next day to know if our offices would be open or closed.

While driving home on that clear, sunny, late summer day in September, I was unable to understand how human beings could kill so many innocent people, no matter what cause they may have had. The mind and heart of a terrorist will always be an enigma to me. There is no cause, no religion, no belief, and no objective worth killing thousands of totally innocent people. I was so upset, so hurt, and the images of the Twin Towers burning and collapsing while thousands of people tried to flee would not exit my mind. The drive home was not easy. I was distracted. I was overwhelmed. I was in pain.

Once home I was glued to the television. I stopped watching only to talk to Zuheir, to phone Ramzi and Sarmad, or to respond to the many calls from Lebanon and France asking about our safety. Everyone heard that the Pentagon in Washington, D.C., was also attacked, and they were worried about us given our proximity. They were also worried about Americans in general.

September 11, 2001, became a wound in America's spirit, a wound that hurts the heart even more than the brain; 9/11 is an unwanted tattoo that no one can erase. A fall morning that started serenely and with such beauty was interrupted with the horror of hate that transformed us all. That day became a storm of ashes that assaulted the eyes, eerie sites that disturbed the memory; horrific visions of bodies falling from on high became the most sensitive poetry ever written; whispers of last goodbyes were prayers of love. September 11 became everyone's fourteen stations of the Golgotha. Perhaps shared suffering and pain transforms the collective soul of a nation; hopefully such a devastating experience can propel humanity's soul into the realm of light where hate has no place.

In the days that followed, all of us at AED were transformed. The outpouring of concern for each other, and specifically for those of Middle Eastern backgrounds, was overwhelming. Phone calls, emails, cards, and letters kept coming in asking if we needed anything, hoping that no one was profiling us. From day one, when I came to the U.S. and joined TransCentury, I knew that Americans were extremely caring about their co-workers and neighbors. I never knew, however, that the caring could be so deep. During that phase, I was grateful for this avalanche of genuine concern.

A few weeks after we all returned to work, Bill called an executive meeting and proposed that we implement a program in Afghanistan for the Afghan children. He felt we should start the program as soon as possible, before securing funds from donors. He suggested that AED could fund the launch phase and, while it was being implemented, seek funds for continuation. Given that our government planned to bomb Al-Qaeda in Afghanistan because of 9/11, which would result in Afghan civil casualties, Bill believed it was important to demonstrate that the American people cared about the Afghan people. Implementing a program that would benefit Afghan children might prove that point. The executive team agreed, and we proposed an educational program.

The program was a simple one. We wanted children in Afghanistan to receive the basic materials required for them to enter school. When we started the project, we targeted young children between the ages of five and eight. Project BluePack, as we called it, was to provide specially made blue backpacks filled with basic school and hygiene supplies to individual Afghan children. Each BluePack contained pens, pencils, colored pencils, eraser, sharpener, chalkboard, chalk, the traditional Afghan small wooden board, special plumes for writing, six paper notebooks, a coloring book, and a ruler. The pack also contained soap and a thermos so children could bring clean water to school from home.

We at AED wanted to let the children of Afghanistan know that the American people cared about them. We raised funds from our own staff to begin the program, and I was asked to be the officer in charge. I hired a superb Afghan professional woman, Sara Amiryar, who was working at Georgetown University at that time. In one of our meetings, Sara and I agreed that she would be the project director in Afghanistan. She moved from Washington, D.C., to Kabul to ensure that over the first year of the project, 200,000 Afghan children would receive the BluePack. While she was in Afghanistan, Sara and I communicated by phone nearly every week; I was so impressed by her leadership and dedication. She took all kind of risks to ensure the BluePacks were distributed to first and second graders in the poorest and most remote areas of Afghanistan. I have pictures of Sara with one or two young Afghan men riding donkeys, with additional donkeys next to them loaded with BluePacks, traveling to a remote village school to distribute the supplies. Sara always told me that seeing the joy, the hope, the aspiration on the faces of the Afghan children when she gave them BluePacks was worth all the risks she took. I am sure that without Sara—without a trusted, professional Afghan leader—the BluePack project would not have been as successful.

In 2002, Sara became a delegate to the 2002 Afghan Loya Jirga. Besides becoming one of the Afghan women leaders and activists, she also became known for a statement she kept repeating: she said that even if the new Afghan constitution sought to guarantee the rights of women and ethnic or religious minorities, true equal protection under that constitution would only come about through education. In one of her interviews, she said, "The war of twenty-five years has deeply scarred Afghanistan, but we have made progress in the last two years, except for women's rights." She expressed concern that Articles 44 and 45 of the draft constitution might exclude women from free education in Afghanistan. "Women need the right to education; it will mean freedom for Afghan women."

Whenever I read about Sara, I am delighted that I had the insight to hire such a capable, courageous, proactive leader to head our project in Afghanistan.

The year 2002 brought with it new chapters. We started a new Dutch-government-funded project for girls' education in the province of Baluchistan in Pakistan. The Baluchistan Girls' Education Program was to provide access to quality basic education to a large number of girls and boys over the next three years. Overall, the state of education in Pakistan was far from satisfactory. It was even less so in Baluchistan, where the total adult literacy rate in 2002 was a little over thirty percent, with the female literacy at seventeen percent.

My staff and I designed the program in consultation with the government and local stakeholders, and it was implemented through partner organizations in Baluchistan. Our intent was to address issues of access to, and quality of, education with a particular focus on girls. I hired a team of Pakistani educational experts to implement the project and appointed one of my American senior staff to oversee it. Over three years, the Baluchistan project improved the existing infrastructure of close to 250 schools, benefiting nearly 30,000 girl and boy students. Teacher training, with a focus on child-friendly, participatory teaching methodologies, was a major component of our project. We worked in close collaboration with the provincial government of Baluchistan and hired local organizations to help us implement the project. As detailed in the evaluation, the basic objectives of the program included: increasing access of the children to schools, especially girls; improving the quality of education; enhancing teacher training in order to make the teaching/learning process more student centered and more interactive; increasing parents and community engagement in school affairs; improving the educational planning and budgeting; and, together with local organizations and communities, working on a better understanding of gender roles and equitable approaches to these roles.

The Baluchistan project was challenging, but it was a project that made me wake up every morning even more excited to go to work, knowing my team of international and local professionals could make a difference in the lives of girls and boys.

Also in 2002, CGE created and maintained a website providing information on human trafficking. Supported by the U.S. Department of State, the site provided thousands of pages of up-to-date information on human trafficking and exemplified the best use of the Internet as an advocacy tool. Accessed by policymakers, activists, service providers and academics in 160 countries, the information on the site has been used by individuals to assist the removal of victims of trafficking, as well as by the U.S. Department of Justice to facilitate the safe and voluntary repatriation of victims of trafficking from the United States. In addition, it is used to prevent trafficking as it raises awareness about how to identify victims. My staff and I were conscious that through the information on this website, we were contributing to empowering local NGOs who assisted in the reintegration of women who were victims of trafficking.

As if those projects weren't enough, in 2002 I joined the Global Advisory Board on the United Nations Girls' Education Initiative (UNGEI). UNGEI is a partnership of organizations committed to narrowing the gender gap in primary and secondary education. It seeks to ensure that, by 2015, all children complete primary schooling, with girls and boys having equal access to free, quality education. UNGEI was launched in April 2000 at the World Education Forum in Dakar, Senegal, by then-United Nations Secretary-General Kofi Annan in response to a troubling reality: Of the millions of children worldwide who were not in school, more than half were girls—a reality that continues today.

I was delighted to join the advisory board of UNGEI to see how I could contribute to reducing this sad reality. By that time, I had been working on that issue for twenty-five years, and no doubt serious progress had been made, country by country; by joining UNGEI, I had an opportunity to influence and hopefully accelerate change at the global level.

Despite my increased work, the longer trips I had to take, and the longer hours I put in to the national and global programs I was involved in, I continued my engagement on two other fronts: I wrote poetry, and I was fully engaged in family life.

In the spring of 2002, the Center for Global Peace at American University of Washington, D.C., in conjunction with The Ameen Rihani Institute (ARI), organized a two-day international symposium titled "Ameen Rihani: Bridging East and West." The event was held on AU's campus in the Washington College of Law building, and addressed many of the themes to which Rihani dedicated his life. I worked closely with Professor Abdul Aziz Said and the staff of the Center for Global Peace on this symposium. The generous support of his Royal Highness Prince Talal Bin Abdul Aziz of Saudi Arabia made this event possible. Professors and researchers from the U.S., Lebanon, the United Kingdom, Russia, and Australia participated.

In his opening remarks, Professor Said said:

> Ameen Rihani was an original bridge builder. He never lived on the bridge. He kept it open for others to travel.... Rihani pursued knowledge through total existential surrender. He blended passion with reason to achieve critical thinking. The Eastern mystic and the American industrialist are two poles of the same realities. Rihani blended the materialism of the West with the spirituality of the East, by causing both elements to "meet and fuse." The most highly developed being is neither Western nor Eastern, but rather a person who combines the finer qualities of Western genius and Eastern prophet. Otherwise the materialism of the West and the spirituality of the East become narrow.

Professor Said continued:

> Ameen Rihani was ahead of his time. He was a remarkable futurist. Rihani introduced us to an all-inclusive epistemology. He recognized that the deeper we go in the core of sciences, the closer we come to the fundamentals of perennial wisdom. He was an original post-modernist, post-structuralist and deconstructuralist. Rihani developed the view that

human consciousness comprises both analytic and intuitive modes. He saw the individual parts of reality as well as the whole. For him the complimentary functioning of the rational and intuitive was a measure of human creativity. Rihani opened the universe of our imagination to a broader understanding. We often think of creative power as a possession or attainment of certain special individuals. Rihani taught us that creativity has a great deal to do with how we relate to each other. When we cultivate creative powers, we gain the confidence to realize what we uniquely have to contribute.

In conclusion, Professor Said added:

Rihani the social critic, the political analyst, and the reformer stretches our sympathy and moral imagination to include the wider human community. Like every Sufi before and after him, through his spiritual development, Rihani worked his way up the ladder of consciousness from limitation to abundance, from human opportunity to divine proximity.

Listening to Professor Said and other professors such as Suheil Bushrui, Geoffrey Nash, Terri DeYoung, Hisham Sharabi, Nathan Funk, Nijmeh Hajjar, Mikhail Rodionov, and Henry Melki, made me even more aware how much I had been influenced by the writings of Ameen Rihani, and how much more I still need to learn from him.

In the summer of 2002 while visiting Lebanon, I was surprised by a call that informed me that Said Akl, Lebanon's foremost poet, had selected me for his award. Even more surprising, the award was not only for my poetry, but for what he saw as my professional accomplishments and my political action on behalf of Lebanon. On September 19, at the Lebanese Press Syndicate in Beirut, writers, poets, journalists, university professors, and friends gathered for the presentation. Mohammad Baalbaki, the president of the Lebanese Press Syndicate, gave the opening remarks and welcomed the great poet and the "lady coming from overseas." Said Akl spoke and I felt he was describing someone other than me. He said:

> I am honored to receive our poet May Rihani, who represents our Lebanon in the U.S. through her work and her writings. May is part of the old foundation of Lebanon, the Phoenician foundation. The Phoenician woman was so successful that she became the ambassador of her culture abroad. May is like her predecessors the Phoenician women, a successful poet, and an activist with a big impact. She works tirelessly to advance education worldwide and she advocates with different global organizations to ensure equality for girls and boys. Lebanon should be proud to have May Rihani for her professionalism and leadership. My award gains prestige when it is given to May Rihani.

I was so moved by what this giant poet said about me. In my response, I talked about how my generation was influenced by his ideas and his writings, and that through his poetry we learned about the glory of our Lebanon, and we ended up believing that it was our duty to continue expanding on the powerful foundation built by authors like him:

You challenge many of the politicians of my country; they do not understand that the central point of leadership is vision and calculated optimism, and you water our land with hope.... The comparison saddens me; however, this moment is a moment of celebration, so allow me to count the reasons why I am celebrating today. A giant from my country crowns poetry as queen, and knowledge expands. A thought leader from my country keeps reminding us of the contributions of Lebanon, and the new generations learn. A poet from my country crowns the heads of the creative writers and artists, and the horizon dances on blue light. A touchstone from my country tracks the history of creativity, and the history of Lebanon becomes richer. The giant writer and poet of Lebanon celebrates today the achievement of a Lebanese woman who carries Lebanon with her wherever she goes; she draws at the center of the American capital a profile of the nobility of the Lebanese mountains. Thank you, my mentor, for honoring me.

Back in Washington, my work front remained as active as usual. Our CGE won a new contract from UNICEF. They were interested in mapping the field of girls' education and gathering together in an annotated bibliography all the research and project documents written on girls' education in Africa, Asia, Latin America, and the Middle East. A team from my staff spent most of 2003 putting together this document.

The year 2004 brought three huge and significant programs. Two of the programs represented a leap in the field of girls' education, and the third one represented an innovative way of collaborating and putting together lessons learned from the U.S. domestic educational scene and from the Middle Eastern scene to respond to a request from a gulf country. Each of the programs was to be implemented over several years, with a total value of approximately $90 million.

Two of the new programs were milestones in the journey of girls' education. My staff and I had bid on two USAID RFPs: one for fifteen African countries, and one for Morocco. We won them both.

The first, the Ambassadors Girls' Scholarship Program (AGSP), was designed to provide comprehensive support for girls' education in fifteen countries spread across east, central, and west Africa: Kenya, Uganda, Tanzania, Rwanda, Democratic Republic of Congo, Ethiopia, Burundi, Cameroon, Niger, Chad, Somalia, Sudan, Djibouti, Eritrea, and Guinea Bissau. This was a key component of the U.S. President's Africa Education Initiative (AEI), which was to serve forty-five African countries. AGSP addressed the constraints to girls' participation, retention, and achievement at school. These obstacles included financial and opportunity costs, socio-cultural factors such as early marriage, as well as the devastating impact of HIV/AIDS on girls and their families. AGSP provided comprehensive support for girls' education in the form of scholarships at the primary and secondary levels; mentoring; parent and community awareness programs; and HIV/AIDS awareness activities to prevent and mitigate the spread of the diseases. Scholarships were intended to ensure access to educational opportunities, and were geared to needs within each country.

AGSP was funded by USAID for four years; it was extended for another three years, continuing from 2004 till 2011 as one of the most important girls' education projects that my staff and I implemented. I will come back to the reasons why I believe this program had a serious impact on the lives of more than 188,000 girls and boys in Africa.

The second girls' education project was Advancing Learning and Employability for a Better Future (ALEF) to be implemented in Morocco. I have to admit that when I named this project ALEF, I had a feeling that the Moroccan partners would really like the name—*alef* means new beginning in Arabic, and it is the first letter of the Arabic alphabet—and that was exactly what happened. We launched the project with the Ministry of Education in Morocco by the end of 2004/beginning of 2005. During the launch, I spent nearly a month in Morocco, ensuring that all the partners agreed on the vision of the project and the first year plan of action.

The third project was part of Education for a New Era in Qatar. The leadership of the country had declared that education was one of their top priorities, stating it was the key to Qatar's economic and social progress. Long concerned that the country's education system was not producing high-quality outcomes, and was rigid, outdated, and resistant to reform, the highly committed Qatari leadership interviewed a number of international education organizations before selecting a few of them to work with the Supreme Education Council on improving the K-12 education system.

Dr. Denise Borders, Senior Vice President and Group Director of Domestic Education at AED, and I presented to the representatives of the Qatari Supreme Education Council the educational expertise of AED. We stressed how by merging together the lessons learned from our experience in U.S. education as well as our experience in international education, we could offer Qatar innovative, relevant, and effective approaches to improve the quality of education for their K-12 students. Denise and I were ambitious; we recommended options for building a world-class system consistent with other Qatari initiatives for social and political change. A couple of months after our presentation, the Supreme Education Council contacted AED and stated they were ready to negotiate a contract allowing us to be part of the Education for a New Era in Qatar.

The end of 2004 presented a situation loaded with opportunities to serve in ways that were more effective than ever before. The launching of these highly effective projects opened new venues of service for AED. For AGSP, we subcontracted with over forty local NGOs as our partners in order to implement the programs in the noted fifteen African countries. From day one, sustainability was an important concept for us; both USAID and AED agreed that the best approach would be to contract with African NGOs, build on their existing capacities, train them for additional capabilities, and make sure all the components of AGSP were being implemented in the most efficient and effective way.

For ALEF, I hired an excellent Chief of Party, Dr. Josh Muskin. He moved with his family to Morocco, and he completed the local hiring that I had started. We hired close to thirty Moroccans to work with him and the Ministry of Education on implementing this very promising program.

For our participation in Education for a New Era, Denise and I hired Dr. Ibrahim Sharqieh and Meghan Jordan to lead AED's efforts. They hired around fifty staff to implement the project.

The year 2004 was the opening of the floodgate of new energies, strategies, activities, projects, programs, innovations, lessons learned, insights, partnerships, co-operations, collaborations, and—thank God—results. It felt like my staff and I were at the foot of the Himalayas, and we were determined to go to the top of the mountain.

As usual when I am terribly busy, I find time to make myself even busier. In the middle of this avalanche of new projects, Zuheir and I decided to buy a new home in Potomac, Maryland. We moved during the Thanksgiving weekend of November 2004. Adding a few features to the house, decorating the rooms, and furnishing it was a source of enjoyment for both of us. The house became a place of beauty that we both love.

Also, during 2004, as in many previous years, my brothers and I were invited to attend events honoring Ameen Rihani, these events were happening in Lebanon, some of the countries of the Arab World, Australia, and in the US. One of those invitations was to attend the unveiling ceremony of Rihani's bust at Tufts University in Boston. The ceremony took place on December 1st 2004, and the bust was placed at the Fares Center for Eastern Mediterranean Studies. The Rihani ceremony was conducted at the Hall of Flags at Cabot Intercultural Center on the Tufts Campus. Ramzi, Khaled my nephew, and I represented the Rihani family.

With the Minister of Education of Togo and
colleagues in Lome, Togo, 1991.

With the Minister of Social Affairs and Women's
Promotion in Conakry, Guinea, 1992.

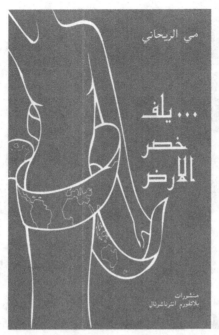

The front cover of my third Arabic book, a poetry
collection ". . . *Yalloufou Khasra Al-Ard*," 1992.

During an interview about my third Arabic book:
"....Yalloufou Khasra Al-Ard," 1992.

With the teacher trainers of the Ministry of Education in
Malawi, 1992. I am in the middle of the second row.

"An evening of poetry with May," at the American
University in Washington, DC, 1993.

During the same poetry evening at the American University, 1993.

Zuheir and I in Lebanon, after we received my parents
blessing for our upcoming wedding, June 1993.

Mommy, Daddy, and Zuheir on the balcony of the
Qornet Shahwan home in Lebanon, summer 1993.

Zuheir's and my first dance at our wedding day,
Washington, D.C., November 27th 1993.

With professor Abdul Aziz Said at the American University,
Washington, D.C., during one of my poetry readings, 1996.

At the poetry reading at the American University, 1996.

413

At another poetry reading in 1996.

With Zuheir and my stepdaughters Selma and Ivy in California, 1997.

An outdoor classroom in Africa, visiting such classrooms made me more determined to work to advance education in Africa, 1997.

Another classroom in Africa, 1997.

With my brothers Ameen, Ramzi, and Sarmad,
at my home in Bethesda, 2000.

Reminiscing about the glorious days of TransCentury
(left to right): Warren Wiggins, myself, Ralph Bates, and
Carolyn Long. At my home in Bethesda, 2002.

Surrounded by children at a school in Mali, 2002.

With Said Akl the Lebanese "Poet Laureate" the day I
received his award in Beirut, Lebanon, summer of 2002.

At the Said Akl Award Ceremony in Beirut, from left to right: Zuheir, Uncle Fuad Sader, myself, and Ameen.

With Mrs. Churchill, the Minister of Education in Ghana, and other ministry officials, 2002.

At the Mosaic Foundation ceremony in 2004, where I accepted an award for AED's girls' education project in Egypt, Yemen, and Djibouti. Left to right Harriet Fulbright AED board member, Steve Moseley AED's CEO, Peter Russell AED's Chairman of the Board, myself, and Mrs. Nermin Fahmi wife of the Egyptian Ambassador, and Chair of the Mosaic Foundation.

During the interview conducted by AUB's *MainGate* Coeditor Lynn Mahoney, Fall 2004.

At the unveiling ceremony of the Ameen Rihani bust at Tufts
University in Boston, December, 2004. From left to right:
Ghada Rihani, Ramzi, myself, Khaled Rihani, and Zuheir

Through our USAID funded program: Ambassadors Girls' Scholarship
Program (AGSP) my staff and I administered the distribution
of over 188,000 scholarships and delivered educational support
services to African girls at the primary and secondary level in 15
African countries. Among the girls who received the scholarships
and the educational support services were Ugandan girls.

The cover of my book: "Keeping the Promise—The Five Benefits
of Girls' Secondary Education" Washington, D.C., 2006.

My staff and I produced a series of Mentoring Guides that were originally used in 15 African countries. The first guide got translated into French for Francophone African countries, Portuguese for Guinea Bissau, Arabic for Yemen, and into Lao for some Asian countries. Above is the cover of volume one in the series, *Girl' Success: Mentoring Guide for Life Skills.*

As the co-chair of UNGEI, welcoming African Ministers of Education and Mr. Anthony Lake, the Executive Director of UNICEF, during the Girls' Education Conference of 2010 that took place in Dakar, Senegal.

During one of my visits to project ALEF, in a
classroom with Moroccan students.

Professor Emeritus Suheil Bushrui and I, after I
received the Juliet Hollister Award of the Temple of
Understanding in New York City, October 2012.

At the Juliet Hollister Award of the Temple of Understanding (left
to right): Zuheir, Souad Assaf, Ramzi, myself, Jacqueline Jabre
and Marwan Charrouf. My friends Jacqueline and Souad flew
from Lebanon to New York to attend the award ceremony.

CHAPTER THIRTY-FOUR

CLIMBING MOUNT EVEREST

A T THE END OF 2004, my staff and I expanded our work even further. We continued to reflect on the lessons learned from past experiences in order to deepen our knowledge of best practices, and to analyze those practices against different contexts. We were determined to work as strategically as possible, making sure innovations were an integral part of our designs, and ensuring that for each context, we customized our programs for each local partner to encourage local capacity building. We expanded our pool of donors. We monitored our results and refined our means of measurement. It was important to be part of the discourse that was advancing girls' education and women's empowerment in order to ensure that the programs of AED integrated a gender lens in their design and implementation work, and contributed to local, national, and global agendas regarding girls' education and women's empowerment. In other words, we wanted to challenge ourselves, stretch our capabilities, and do it all. In my mind I called this "climbing Mount Everest." The amazing thing is my staff and I were united in wanting this challenge. We knew it would take several years to reach the top of the mountain, but we were up to the task.

Before I describe the climb, let me say few things about my staff.

In the years between 2000 and 2010/2011, some of my staff was housed at the AED headquarters in Washington, D.C., and the rest were scattered in many African, Middle Eastern, and Asian countries. At the headquarters we were like a mini United Nations. During those ten years, my excellent and eminently capable headquarters staff hailed from so many different countries: Michele Akpo from Benin, Dr. Ibrahim Sharkieh from Palestine, Hala Al Hoshan from Saudi Arabia, Renu Jain from India, Dr. Uzma Anzar from Pakistan, Ahlam Kays from Lebanon, Boubacar Cisse from Mali, Aissatou Balde from Guinea, Helen Albert from Romania, and Adam Maiga from the Ivory Coast. Of course many Americans were also among my staff, such as: Dr. Cory Heyman, Dr. Howard Williams, Dr. Andrea Bertone, Stephanie Psaki, Eugene Katzin, Greta Stults, Jill Hartsig, Lisa Kays, Julia Kirby, and Charles Hess. The headquarters staff combined the qualities of idealism and pragmatism. Many of them brought with them the rigorous analytic discipline of their doctoral work, but they also brought a work ethic that was as solid as Mount Rushmore and as productive as a rich harvest. They were committed to improving the world, and they were creative in finding solutions to stubborn entrenched problems. In their determination that partnerships with local institutions and leaders had to produce results, they were aware that local capacity-building was at the core of all that we wanted to do. They were innovative in their approaches, and above all, they were learning and evaluating every step of the way. My staff and I were guided by the conviction that we needed to serve the communities we worked in with the best we had to offer: a sharp, ever-learning mind, and a compassionate, ever-encompassing heart.

I learned so much from my headquarters staff, and I owe them loads of gratitude for being my partners in climbing Mount Everest.

In the field, of course, international staff from the countries we were working in outnumbered Americans. Extensive programs such as Qatar, Yemen, and Morocco had large teams, with fifty-, forty-, and thirty-plus staff respectively. Other projects such as Guinea, Kenya, Tanzania, Ethiopia, Nigeria, Mali, the Democratic Republic of Congo, Ghana, Djibouti, South Africa, Afghanistan, Pakistan, and Saudi Arabia had between five and ten staff members each. In some countries such as Cameroun, Burundi, Niger, Chad, and Equatorial Guinea, we worked through our partners and subcontractors, the local NGOs. Among the leaders of the teams in the field were: Dr. Josh Muskin, Sara Amiryar, Dr. Kadiatou Coulibaly, Dr. Aly Badara Doukoure, Dr. Bienvenu Marcos, Lilian Tarimo, and Percilla Obunga.

We started our climb to the summit in 2004. Many existing projects such as the Human Trafficking project, the Afghan Teacher Training project, and the research for UNICEF continued while my staff and I were busy launching the three very large projects that we just won, and still designing and winning other new projects. Those next few years were heady indeed.

In Morocco, ALEF provided AED and my team with the unique and exciting opportunity to not only implement a major educational undertaking from the ground level up, but also to participate in national educational reform.

In October 2003, Morocco's king launched a nationwide campaign against illiteracy under the theme *Massirat Nour* (a march toward the light). The campaign was part of a larger program to fight poverty, exclusion, and marginalization by reducing the illiteracy rate of people older than ten years of age to less than twenty percent by 2010, and to eradicate it by the year 2015. In 2004, The Ministry of Education in Morocco decided that ALEF would contribute to *Massirat Nour*. Information, communication, and technology (ICT) were central components of this national effort, as well as a major component within ALEF. For that reason, the Ministry decided that the ICT aspect of *Massirat Nour* would be aided by ALEF. When we launched ALEF, we targeted four main regions in Morocco: Casablanca, Meknès, Chaouia, and Oriental.

Another major component of ALEF was focused on women's literacy. My staff worked with twenty-eight different Moroccan NGOs and associations to implement this element. ALEF used relevant, learner-friendly materials based on the newly agreed upon *Moudawana*—which was the new Family Code the Moroccan government approved—in the adult literacy curriculum that was implemented. The adult women's literacy classes were conducted in Moroccan Arabic and in Berber dialects.

ALEF focused on a number of aspects of the Moroccan education system including relevance, teacher training, parental and community engagement, extra-curricular activities, girls' dormitories, the use of technology, the linkage between education and entrepreneurship, and literacy training for women. My staff and I were able to increase the funding for the program by convincing the Middle East Partnership Initiative at State Department (MEPI), UNIFEM, and Cisco to add to the original USAID funding. By the end of the second year of implementation, and as a result of the success of the first phase, the Ministry of Education asked AED to expand its work to additional regions.

At a press conference on June 26, 2006, Secretary of State for School Education Latifa Abdida said she had visited schools involved in the ALEF project and had seen for herself a new state of mind and a new approach among the pupils and project stakeholders. Mrs.

Abdida noted that ALEF had given valuable and concrete support to the national education system. She added that her department intended to explore all possible ways of ensuring that ALEF was rolled out across the country and made permanent.

Many others spoke during that press conference as well.

"The implementation of the ALEF project," said USAID Mission Director Monica Stein-Olson, "demonstrated that the use of a package of flexible but rigorous strategies, with adequate support and scope for innovation, can enable Moroccan schools to help young people in their care to thrive, even in isolated and deprived areas, despite the lack of material resources available to them." USAID noted that work on the front lines involved over 3,300 teachers and 260,000 pupils since the beginning of 2005, as well as inspectors and headmasters at more than four hundred schools.

The Chief of Party that I had appointed, Dr. Joshua Muskin, talked about the importance of improving the quality and relevance of education, and the necessity of encouraging the active and strategic participation of parents, civil society, and various sectors of the economy in the process of improving education.

Fatima, a fifty-two year old woman said, "As well as learning to read and write, I was also able to find out what my rights and responsibilities in society are."

Atili Lhoucine, a technology teacher, said that the creation of a multimedia room in the school where he taught had a positive effect on both the pupils and the teachers, who were able to participate in on-site training.

The groundbreaking ALEF ended up working with four Moroccan ministries to support the adoption of its key education strategies in more than 475 primary and junior secondary schools and four agricultural training centers, reaching over 300,000 students in several of Morocco's regions. The project generated tremendous enthusiasm in all areas of educational activity. Teachers, trainers, directors, and officials across ALEF's partners had taken seriously their central role in improving education and training in Morocco. ALEF produced several concrete results, among them was the fact that girls from the most isolated areas in the Moroccan Kingdom had increased their access to schools; pupil and teacher absenteeism and dropout rates fell in the schools and in the institutions where ALEF worked; and students' exam performance improved. Equally important, multiple public and private institutions chose to adopt the ALEF methods piloted and refined by our staff to their programs nationwide. During its fifth year, ALEF worked with the government to spread its activities to an additional five regions, reaching more than fifty percent of Morocco's schools.

Whenever I visited Morocco during the implementation of ALEF, I became more and more convinced that commitment to improving the quality and relevance of the system of education in any country is the cornerstone of a transformational process that can propel the country forward socially and economically.

In Qatar, we were busy launching an educational program that contributed to the government's ambitious educational reform called Education for a New Era. Denise Borders and I travelled in 2004 to confer with the Supreme Educational Council in Qatar on the approach that needed to be taken. In 2005, we worked in partnership with the Supreme Education Council as a school support organization committed to achieving the vision of creating a high-quality, high-performing, and self-sustaining education system.

Working side-by-side with teachers and principals in twenty-two independent schools, we observed significant improvements in teaching, classroom management, and school administration. Our project used content specialists in math, science, and English who advised the teachers on the teaching/learning process, professional development, the new curriculum standards, classroom methodologies, and assessment of learning results. In addition, we had a school management advisor at each school to oversee daily operations, to ensure the school was well managed, and to provide coaching and support to the school administration. Denise and I paid a yearly visit to this project to monitor the progress and to discuss with the Supreme Educational Council needed adjustments in the implementation strategy.

The third large and highly visible project that was launched in 2004 was the Ambassadors Girls' Scholarship Program (AGSP) in fifteen African countries (Kenya, Uganda, Tanzania, Rwanda, Democratic Republic of Congo, Ethiopia, Burundi, Cameroon, Niger, Chad, Somalia, Sudan, Djibouti, Eritrea, and Guinea Bissau). We started AGSP in 2004 and ended it seven years later in 2011. Working closely with over thirty-six local implementing partners, our CGE provided support to vulnerable girls and boys in the form of scholarships, mentoring, community participation, and HIV/AIDS awareness activities. AGSP made a significant impact in girls' education with increased retention, passing, and graduation rates in nearly all of the countries where the program was implemented.

In addition, the AGSP team strengthened the capacity of the local implementing partners in mentor training, program administration, financial and data management, monitoring, and community participation with an emphasis on sustainability. CGE disbursed more than 188,000 scholarships; approximately 90% of the beneficiaries were girls. The mentoring materials compiled in three *Girls' Mentoring Resource Guides* were made available in English,

French, and Portuguese. The AGSP team also developed a *Tool Kit for Girls' Scholarship Programming and Related Enhancement Activities,* which served as a capacity-strengthening tool for the African organizations to create and manage sustainable, culturally appropriate scholarship programs. The resource guides and tool kits were available in hard copies and electronically to all our local partnering organizations and to any African NGO that was interested in designing and implementing girls' education programs.

As much as we appreciated receiving significant funding from USAID, my staff and I were also interested in seriously diversifying our financial support. By 2004, in addition to USAID, we also had funds from UNICEF, the Dutch government, the government of Qatar, the State Department, Coca-Cola Foundation, and the Red Cross. We decided that the pool of funders needed to be larger and even more diversified—that was part of the challenge of climbing Mount Everest. My staff and I started researching foundations and other donors who were interested in international education or gender equity, and studied their agendas. Suffice it to say, we were able to expand our pool of funders in a serious way. Between 2004 and 2010/11, we added another thirteen funders to our existing seven: the World Bank, UNFPA, UNIFEM, the government of Saudi Arabia, Cisco, Procter and Gamble, and seven foundations: Mosaic Foundation, Kenora Foundation, General Electric Foundation, Exxon Mobil Foundation, Johnson and Johnson Foundation, Alcoa Foundation, and MacArthur Foundation. It was mind stretching and sometimes challenging to work with twenty diversified funders and to understand their policies, priorities, and modalities of business. As I said earlier, those were really heady years.

My visits to the countries we were working with increased, my discussions and negotiations with funders exponentially expanded, and my learning deepened. In addition to being totally focused on work, these trips also allowed me to continue to immerse myself in different cultures, to appreciate the diversity of natural beauties, and to be moved by different human conditions. Whenever I visited countries with deserts such as Jordan, Morocco, and Qatar for example, I profoundly understood that borders were meaningless. There is nothing better than a desert to cancel the concept of divides. Deserts allowed my imagination to soar, and my mind to be extremely free. My mind never stretched as well as it did in a desert. In Mali, the Democratic Republic of Congo, (previously Zaire), Niger, Guinea, and some other African countries, my heart stretched, becoming larger and more encompassing. Poverty and hunger made me profoundly understand that we owed every human being dignity and basic human rights. I became more and more convinced that it is the responsibility of all of us to ensure the dignity of everyone in our global village. Our dignity is compromised when the dignity of a poverty-stricken child, woman, or man is compromised.

I was determined to work harder. I was determined that my staff and I could make a difference and could improve the lives of many. Climbing Mount Everest was the best decision we made.

CHAPTER THIRTY-FIVE

CONTINUING TO CLIMB

WHEN IT RAINS IT POURS, and 2004 continued to be the winning year.

I learned about a new group, the Mosaic Foundation, which was founded by the wives of the Arab ambassadors. Their objective was to improve the lives of women and children in the Arab world, and to increase awareness and understanding about Arab people and culture in the United States. From what I gathered, I thought they would be interested in improving the education of girls' in the Arab countries where girls were lagging behind. I met with the executive committee of the foundation to explain AED's capabilities and track record, and proposed working with Ministries of Education to improve the status of girls' education in their countries. The foundation invited us to submit a proposal for Yemen, Djibouti, and Egypt. We did as requested and were awarded the funds for implementation. We named the project Approaches and Methods for Advancing Learning (AMAL - an Arab word which translates to "hope" in English).

AMAL was launched in 2004 and continued through 2006. The project's main goal was to expand access to the underserved and to enhance the quality of education in Yemen, Djibouti, and Egypt. AMAL's two objectives were to: a) deliver in-service teacher training that improved teachers delivery by making the teaching-learning process interactive, gender-sensitive, and student-centered; and b) increase community participation in support of expanded access, improved quality, and greater accountability. The project designed and delivered in-service teacher training and low cost materials based on the following principles:

- An interactive teaching approach
- A gender-sensitive teaching methodology with educational materials
- A problem-solving teaching process
- A relevant and practical teaching/learning process
- A needs- and context-driven teaching/learning process

Increasing community participation and parental engagement in the education of their daughters and sons was the driving force of this project.

As if all the new projects in fifteen African countries and five Arab countries were not sufficient to fill every waking hour of my days, also in 2004 I was elected president of the AUB Alumni of North America (AANA). AANA dates back to 1925, when a group of young alumni met in Brooklyn, New York, and elected their first officers. AANA is a nonprofit organization, and by 2004 it represented more than 6,000 alumni and 370 former faculty and staff members. The members of AANA reside in every state of the United States and in Canada. A board of eleven members governs the national association, which had twenty-four chapters when I was elected. The purpose of AANA is threefold:

1. To bind together for mutual social, moral, and intellectual benefits all AUB graduates and former students, faculty, and staff in North America;
2. To enable them to help their alma mater in every way possible; and
3. To perpetuate AUB's ideals and fair name wherever the Association's members may live.

As president, I also became an ex-officio member of the AUB Board of Trustees. From 2004 to 2006, a new dimension was added to my life, I became fully re-engaged with AUB through AANA. I planned, prepared, and attended many AANA board meetings in New York, and participated in many AUB Board of Trustees meetings, also in the Big Apple. Being engaged with these boards was very rewarding; the engagement provided me with a strong connection to Lebanon.

I worked closely with AUB's Office of Development and alumni as well as with the board members of AANA to ensure that all the chapters of AANA were active. I assisted in creating new AANA chapters in the states where there were AUB alumni but not yet a chapter to organize them. Our work often included fundraising events, most of which were specifically to increase AUB's ability to offer financial assistance to students who could not afford the tuition. Working with other alumni to raise funds from successful Lebanese Americans and other Arab Americans to assist capable and promising students who wanted to study at AUB, or were already studying at AUB and wanted to continue their higher education, energized me. It felt so good to give back to AUB and to Lebanon.

After my election as president of AANA, I was featured in the AUB magazine *MainGate*. In the interview by Co-editor Lynn Mahoney, entitled *A Woman Who Sets No Limits*, I underscored the importance of gender equity in education around the world. The article recounts an incident in which the father of a girl student in Mali challenged me about the need to educate girls since "their job is to get married and have children." I agreed, adding that education would make them even better mothers. "You mean to tell me that an illiterate woman does not love her children as much as an educated one?" he asked incredulously. "Not at all," I replied, and gave him an example of two mothers, one literate and one illiterate, visiting a clinic and obtaining medicine for their sick children. I knew from experience that the illiterate mother would be intimidated and might well be at a loss about following written instructions. Mistakes could happen and the child could suffer the consequences. "It is not just about love, it is also about reading and writing." The Malian man considered for a moment and said flatly, "You are right. We should educate all our girls."

The Board of AANA and I planned a gala dinner as a national fundraiser for March 19, 2005. The theme of this national event was AUB's role in building East-West understanding; it was a smashing success. Our three major speakers, Congressman Earl Pomeroy, Congressman Tom Davis (R-VA, 1995-2008), and AUB President John Waterbury, all spoke about the unique role that AUB plays in improving mutual understanding between the East and the West, and how there had never been a stronger appreciation of the need for such improvement.

In my closing remarks for the evening, I spoke in the name of thousands of alumni:

As alumni of AUB, we value and celebrate the multifaceted nature of different cultures. We recognize that connecting cultures helps secure the future of humanity and its diversity. We celebrate different perspectives and continue to find in each the means to gain deeper understanding. As alumni of AUB, we learned a value system that made us recognize that freedom of thought and expression is a precious commodity and as natural to us as the air we breathe; that respect for the values that others prize highly is the foundation of tolerance; and that critical thinking is the lifeline to a better future. We also learned that it is critical to live these values and to share and discuss them. The value system we all lived at AUB changed us; the changes were subtle, but profound. We may not, in our youth, have noticed them or paid attention to this transformation, but today we recognize that AUB has changed us. It has widened our horizons and deepened our willingness to understand one another. AUB continues to help new generations contribute to the East-West dialogue, making each graduate charged with interpreting, translating, and conveying the richness, and complementarity of the various cultures that exist in the East and in the West. Today, more than ever before, given the events in Lebanon and the region, the role AUB plays is needed and is essential in contributing to the possible positive transformation.

During the mid-2000s, the AUB Board of Trustees conducted a major fundraising campaign to infuse AUB with a significant amount of money, possibly in an unprecedented way, and to strengthen the culture of giving among the alumni, friends, and supporters. My contribution to this campaign was to organize a meeting for President Waterbury and William Hoffman, AUB's Washington Office Director, with Congressman Pomeroy. As a result of this meeting, and due to Congressman Pomeroy's exposure to the role of AUB during the Building of East-West Understanding event, the Congressman agreed to spearhead a bill that resulted in an additional $5 million allocated to the American educational institutions in Lebanon, with the lion's share being allocated to AUB. When Congressman Pomeroy becomes convinced of the importance of an issue, he goes all-out in his support. That is what he had done for girls' education after his trip to Mali and Ghana, and that is what he did for AUB after recognizing its importance in producing open-minded leaders, thinkers, and professionals from whom the Middle East and the rest of the world would benefit.

While my active social life demanded a great deal of my time, my AED team's climb of Mount Everest was still ongoing. My travels to many of the countries where our programs were being implemented continued to increase. We faced a constant need to negotiate and readjust programming based on shifting priorities with the donors or the Ministries of Education, or both. The need to be present at the launch of new programs was equally important. For those reasons and others, my trips to Morocco, Qatar, Pakistan, Guinea, Ghana, and Yemen kept me quite involved with the programs on the ground.

In 2005, many new beginnings blossomed. Through the CGE, my team and I launched a multi-year, multi-million dollar educational program in Yemen. The Yemen Basic Education project was a flagship project to improve access to and quality of primary education for thousands of children in Yemen as well as to reduce gender inequality in the education system. The project, which operated in three of the poorest, most remote, and underserved of Yemen's twenty-two governorates—Maareb, Shabwah, and Amran—utilized a cross-cutting integration of gender-equity approaches while conducting school rehabilitation projects. Our team conducted pre-renovation structural engineering assessments and was responsible for the actual renovation and rehabilitation of seventy schools over a three-year period. Our team in the field had access to numerous Yemeni experts—architects, structural engineers, civil engineers, urban planners, teacher training specialists, education coordinators, women's literacy advisors and community participation specialists—who we ended up hiring as staff or consultants and who conducted assessments and school renovation projects.

In addition to renovations, the project contributed to the strengthening of capacity at both the ministry and the governorate level through its Educational Management Information Systems component. This was designed to collect and use information for decision-making, focusing initially on the governorates and schools in which the project was already working. Working in Yemen, even though challenging for security reasons, was very rewarding due to the tangible results that we could measure.

Most of the projects AED implemented in the early 2000s focused on primary education and, at best, on basic education. Very few were entirely focused on secondary education. My personal field experience and discussions with staff in the different countries made me understand that there was a need to focus more on secondary education. I decided that the climb to the top of Mount Everest needed to include the writing of a new book about secondary education. My hypothesis was that maximum individual and community benefits occur as a result of secondary education for girls. I knew that my time was nearly completely booked; however, I was aware that I still had some hours on weekends and late evenings, and I decided to proceed. Two members of my staff, Stephanie Psaki and Lisa Kays, assisted me. The book was completed near the end of 2005 and given to my excellent editor, Mary Maguire, to review. Once Mary completed her editing, I chose the title: *Keeping the Promise: The Five Benefits of Girls' Secondary Education.* AED printed the book in early 2006.

Keeping the Promise underlined the importance of a renewed push to ensure that girls worldwide had access to secondary as well as primary education if the investments made are to pay off. It detailed the barriers and challenges to girls' access and retention in education systems, and shed light on the reasons why there are fewer girls than boys in schools. The book also analyzed the health, economic, educational, and social benefits that accrue to the girl herself, as well as to her family and her community, when girls complete that educational cycle. *Keeping the Promise* explained how girls' secondary education is a tool for poverty alleviation. Finally, the book presented strategies for promoting girls' secondary education and how by doing so, communities can create a virtuous cycle in the fields of health, education, and economic productivity.

The book was disseminated widely among donors, Ministries of Education, policy makers, universities, practitioners, and educational NGOs. Many university professors used it either as a reference book for their courses or used chapters from the book as part of their curricula. Among the professors who used it were Dr. Fernando Ramirez at Harvard University, Dr. Ann Van Dusen at Georgetown University, and Dr. Elaine Murphy at George Washington University. Many other universities asked me to lecture about the book, including the University of Maryland College Park and the American University.

A few months after the launch of *Keeping the Promise*, I received a call from Ken Smith, the president and chief executive director of Jobs for America's Graduates (JAG), who wanted to discuss girls' education; one of my colleagues had told him about my work. During the meeting, Ken asked precise questions about how girls' education benefits the girls and their communities, and how we designed and implemented our programs. He also asked tough questions about how we measured results. As I answered, I focused on his capacity as president and CEO of a non-profit organization dedicated to preventing dropouts among young people who are most at risk.

At the end of our meeting, Ken surprised me by announcing he was also the head of a family foundation, the Kenora Foundation, and that he was interested in the possibility of funding a project that we would implement in Tanzania. That first meeting led to several others, to a wonderful story of the family of Ken and Nora Smith and their two daughters, and to how they wanted to contribute in making a difference in the lives of underprivileged girls in Tanzania.

Through AED, the Kenora Foundation funded projects in Tanzania, South Africa, and Guinea, and for the first time, my team and I designed a project not for several provinces in a country, but for several schools. We believed that involving small donors in our work was as important as involving big donors because the culture of giving and of compassion for others who are less privileged needs to be valued and celebrated. We were inspired by what Ken and Nora Smith were committed to, and we gladly agreed to be part of their effort to improve the lives of girls they had never met.

We named the Kenora Family Foundation project Improving Girls' Primary Education. We hired three local teams, trained them, and put them in charge of implementing this activity in three schools: Tounkourouma Primary School in Guinea, Gomvu Primary School in Tanzania, and Dietrich Moravian School in South Africa. The project was designed to improve retention and quality of education for students—with a special focus on girls—through scholarships, mentoring, tutoring, and teacher training. Scholarships came in the form of educational materials to all students, while providing mentoring and tutoring specifically to the girls. The first generation of the project benefited a total of 1,020 students, including 524 girls. The commitment of the Smith family was exceptional. They visited the projects in Tanzania and South Africa to meet the girls who benefitted from their generosity. While in country, they met with our team of local implementers to discuss the improvements that were taking place, and they visited the Ministry of Education in Tanzania to discuss expanding the project through partnerships with the Ministry that hopefully would lead to sustainability of the effort.

Ken and Nora Smith did not visit the sites alone; they were accompanied by their two daughters and their son-in-law. I had no doubt that the new generation was equally committed to the concept of assisting the less privileged. When their daughter Tara decided to get married, she included with the wedding invitation a request asking invitees not to send gifts; instead, she encouraged them to donate the gift amount to our project in Tanzania. The Improving Girls' Primary Education project in Tanzania received a generous infusion of funds as a result of this couple's wedding.

Ken and Nora, and their daughters Tara and Jennifer, inspired my staff and me for several years. They never stopped giving and caring. Their compassion, scholarships, support for teacher training, and support for mentoring made a radical, positive difference in the lives of over one thousand African children, lifting those youngsters from a possible dead-end route to a journey of hope and possibilities.

While I was busy launching new programs; overseeing the quality of implementation of our activities; traveling in Africa, the Middle East, and Asia; writing a new book and lecturing about it; chairing the board of AANA, and serving on the Board of Trustees of AUB, the Cedar Revolution took place in Lebanon.

The Cedar Revolution was triggered by the assassination of the Lebanese Prime Minister Rafik Hariri on February 14, 2005. On February 18, those who were opposed to Syrian meddling in Lebanon launched the Independence Peaceful Uprising to liberate the country from Syrian domination. Their actions motivated the Lebanese masses to gather in support. They held mass rallies in many regions of Lebanon, and in particular in Beirut. The protests continued and became larger, louder, and bolder, until the pro-Syrian government in Lebanon resigned on February 28, 2005.

On March 5, 2005, Syrian President Bashar Al-Assad bowed to Lebanese and international pressure and announced the Syrian army would pull out from Lebanon in two stages. He did not set a timeline for the withdrawal. Syrian troops began a partial withdrawal from Beirut and Northern Lebanon on March 8. The popular demonstrations continued and reached their peak on March 14, when the Lebanese people rallying against Syrian occupation held the largest demonstration in the country's history with over a million participants. Many wondered how it was possible to have a million individuals in the streets when in 2005 the whole population of Lebanon was estimated at four million. Some journalists maintained that Lebanese anger against perceived Syrian hegemony had been simmering for decades, and that the assassination of a popular leader was the spark that gave birth to the movement. Lebanese activist leader and newspaper columnist Samir Kasseer, for example, wrote: "democracy will be spreading in the region and the starting point is Lebanon."

By the end of March 2005, the Syrian government pulled out most of their troops and dismantled most of its intelligence stations in Beirut and Northerm Lebanon. While the Lebanese were celebrating the withdrawal, pro-Syrian militants made their presence known with bomb explosions around the country.

The primary goals of the peaceful Cedar Revolution and the activists who organized the popular upheaval were the withdrawal of the Syrian troops from Lebanon and the replacement of a government heavily influenced by Syrian interests with more independent leadership. Also, the demonstrators demanded the establishment of an international commission to investigate the assassination of Prime Minister Hariri, asked for the resignation of security officials who were under Syrian control, and insisted on the organization of free parliamentary elections that were not tinted by Syrian influence. The demonstrators chanted and raised banners demanding the end of the Syrian influence in Lebanese politics.

The Lebanese expressed themselves loudly and clearly, the Syrian heavy-handed interference in the affairs of Lebanon had to stop, and the United Nations and the international community held the Syrian regime and its proxy government responsible for any security problems against the people of Lebanon. On April 7, 2005, the United Nations Security Council ordered an international investigation into Hariri's assassination through Resolution 1595. In response to the continuous U.S.-led pressure, and in the face of popular protests, the Syrian government pledged to pull out by April 30, 2005, after thirty years of presence in Lebanon. At the start of the demonstrations, Syria had maintained a force of roughly 14,000 soldiers and a strong presence of its intelligence agents in Lebanon. Following the demonstrations, the Syrian troops completely withdrew from Lebanon. The pro-Syrian government was also disbanded, accomplishing the main goal of the revolution.

The Cedar Revolution created a new sense of hope in Lebanon; the demonstrators' popular motto was *Hurriyya, Siyada, Istiqlal* or Freedom, Sovereignty, Independence. These words became the mantra of the majority of the Lebanese people and a new political dawn was rising. Many Lebanese, possibly the majority, felt the future was promising.

Towards the end of 2005 and the beginnings of 2006, I met with my former AUB Professor Suheil Bushrui, who is presently Professor Emeritus at the University of Maryland and Director of the Kahlil Gibran Chair for Values and Peace. He wanted to discuss the necessity of ensuring that the Lebanese heritage remained known and valued in the U.S., Professor Bushrui believed academic institutions might be the vehicle through which this knowledge could be channeled. He noted that the Irish heritage is respected for many reasons, in large part because universities in the U.S. teach the most influential writers of Ireland such as James Joyce and William Butler Yeats. Why not teach the influential writers, philosophers, and poets of Lebanon such as Gibran Kahlil Gibran, Ameen Rihani, and Mikhail Naimy?

I thought his idea was sound and would indeed serve Lebanon. He felt the University of Maryland would be the right institution to start with, as they were interested in teaching and promoting the Lebanese heritage. We discussed at length the different ways we could help facilitate sharing the contributions of Lebanon with the civilizations of the world through its thinkers and writers. Professor Bushrui convinced me that we needed a task force to support the University of Maryland, and in the long run other American universities, in promoting Lebanon's heritage. He suggested that I create such a task force and chair it. I could not refuse the request of this distinguished professor, author, poet, and thinker. I gathered together about twenty prominent, successful Lebanese Americans from diversified backgrounds who committed themselves to our cause. Professor Bushrui suggested a name for our group: *Min Ajl Lubnan* or "In Honor of Lebanon."

At our first task force meeting, we formalized our mission: "To partner with universities in the United States to promote the Lebanese heritage." We agreed that *Min Ajl Lubnan* would partner with universities starting with the University of Maryland—in particular with The Center on Cultural Heritage, the Gibran Kahlil Gibran Chair, and the Center for International Development and Conflict Management—to plan and organize research studies, conferences, annual lectures, seminars, workshops, and publications about Gibran Kahlil Gibran, Ameen Rihani, and Mikhail Naimy.

Even though the launch of *Min Ajl Lubnan* coincided with an atmosphere of optimism in Lebanon that was generated by the Cedar Revolution, this sense of optimism did not last long. By July 2006, the Israel Hezbollah war started. The thirty-four-day military conflict destroyed a large part of the infrastructure of Lebanon. This conflict continued until a UN-brokered ceasefire went into effect on August 14, 2006. Lebanon again became the land on which regional powers fought. Hezbollah was heavily backed by Iran, and the 2006 war could be considered the first war between Israel and Iran.

The more these regional powers did not respect the rights of smaller countries like Lebanon that did not have the same military might, the more our task force became determined to make the West, and in particular the U.S., understand the legacy of Lebanon. This small country in the Middle East was the first democracy in the region, a land where Christians and Muslims lived in peace, and where writers and philosophers wrote about the unity of religion, the importance of peace, and the necessity of an East-West dialogue and understanding. *Min Ajl Lubnan* went to work. We partnered with the University of Maryland and organized a series of fundraisers to support international conferences about Lebanon and its global thinkers, and to facilitate translations and publications about Gibran, Rihani, and Naimy. These fundraisers themselves were celebrations of Lebanon's contributions.

During the first event, we honored two women from the Lebanese diaspora: Ivonne Baki, a Lebanese Ecuadorian who was a former Ambassador to the United States, and the former Trade and Industry Minister of Ecuador; and Maha Kaddoura, founder and president of the Kaddoura Foundation, trustee of Tufts University, member of the Board of the Fletcher School of Law and Diplomacy at Tufts University, and member of the Dean's Committee of the Kennedy School of Government at Harvard University.

While I was busy with the task force honoring these two esteemed women, I joined a group of professionals—Richard Irish, BJ Warren, Carolyn Long, Ralph Bates, and David Brunell—who had worked together at TransCentury, to honor Warren Wiggins. We strongly felt Warren deserved to be recognized for his leadership, creativity, and innovative approaches to international development. Warren's leadership style was built on creating mutual trust between him and his colleagues. He empowered those who worked with him by respecting and valuing new thinking, and was quick to give credit where credit was due. Because of his leadership, each of us who worked with him performed at our maximum level, supported by an enabling environment that facilitated excellent performance, clear communications, easy professional interactions, creativity, innovation, efficient and effective decisions, and an incredible joy of working. Warren created a multiplier effect, a performance multiplier.

He inspired us and valued publicly our capabilities, skills, results, and track records. Honoring him was a celebration of a unique leader to whom we owed an enormous debt of gratitude for our new ways of thinking and our shared commitment to those less privileged.

On February 18, 2006, around one hundred of us gathered on the roof of the Washington Hotel overseeing the White House and spent the evening toasting Warren. He never liked being in the spotlight, but for that evening, it was appropriate for us to recognize publicly how much we valued him. Many of us had tears in our eyes as we reflected on how lucky we were to have had the opportunity of working with him.

Also in 2006, I organized a major event at AED to mark International Women's Day on. Under the AED Knowledge Series, I organized a seminar on Women Leadership in the Arab World, the objective of which was to create a provocative discussion about the challenges faced by Arab women as they redefine their roles and forge pathways to participate in the leadership of their countries. The seminar took place on March 6, 2006. As an AED Senior Vice President, I moderated the seminar, which included Dr. Rima Saleh, Deputy Executive Director of UNICEF, a Palestinian; Dr. Farida Allaghi, an international human development expert from Libya; and Dr. Fatima Sbaity Kassem, the Director of the Center for Women at the United Nations Economic and Social Commission for Western Asia, a Lebanese.

When one aspect of my life becomes very demanding of my time, other aspects do not go dormant; on the contrary, they remain active, and sometimes accelerate their movement forward. Launching *Min Ajl Lubnan*, organizing fundraiser events in support of an academic agenda to aid Lebanon, participating in organizing a celebration to honor Warren Wiggins, and organizing a seminar on Arab Women

Leadership, had to happen alongside my work in international development.

In 2006, my staff and I agreed the Center for Gender Equity needed to develop a variety of tools such as an organizational capacity-building protocol and a mentoring guide for girls' education which could be adapted for many cultural contexts in order to sustain local civil society efforts and capabilities. We also agreed on the need to construct a comprehensive model of complementary activities that, when implemented together, could have a tremendous impact on girls' access to and persistence in education, as well as improved academic achievement. After a series of design meetings, we detailed the activities and intervention of the model. They included professional development for teachers, community involvement and engagement, mentoring girls and boys in life skills and transitions, and scholarships. This has come to be known as the Four Pillars Model for Girls' Education.

We also doubled our efforts to work with new partners and donors. Between 2006 and 2008, we added several foundations as donors. We worked on the Four Pillars model with the Johnson and Johnson Foundation in Tanzania and Guinea; the GE Foundation in Kenya; the Exxon Mobile foundation in Nigeria; the Alcoa Foundation in Guinea; and the Coca-Cola Foundation in Mali. We also continued to expand the Kenora Foundation projects in Tanzania and Guinea. During those years, we expanded our work in Yemen, and the World Bank funded implementation of two education research studies to assess both the incentives and the quality of girls' secondary education in Yemen: the Incentives for Girls' Secondary Education study recommended cash transfers to households conditional on girls' attendance and performance in school, promotion and funding of proposals designed at the school/

community level, as well as overall policy reforms; and the Quality of Girls' Secondary Education study proposed interventions including program diversification, policy changes, and improvements in secondary-level assessment, effectiveness of libraries, laboratories, and use of ICT (information, communication, and technology) for teaching, learning, and administration.

As if that weren't enough, we also expanded our work in Qatar. In addition to our staff working directly with Qatari schools, we added an advanced training program regarding curriculum standards to reach 600 teachers, specifically K-12 math, science, and English teachers in Qatar. Our staff designed and delivered a national training program based on a gap analysis drawn from classroom observations and school site visits. The needs assessment then informed the design of the training program. National training activities were followed by cluster training and one-on-one mentoring, coaching, and modeling sessions. The project emphasized action research and best practices, and a database of international best practices was also developed.

During this three-year span, the launch of new projects became our custom, and I traveled to most of our program countries. In Yemen, I spoke in Arabic with little girls who were going to school for the first time, and with the Ministry of Education about the importance of continuous professional teacher development and the need to increase the number of qualified women teachers. In Qatar, I continued the discussions with the leaders of the Supreme Educational Council and attended teacher-training activities. In Guinea, Aly Badara Doukoure, the chief of party, arranged that I visit the Minister of Education, who immediately asked me to expand our work to more than the provinces we were covering. I explained to the Minister that more donors would be needed to fund the expansion. Aly also arranged for a meeting with the parents; they, too, wanted us to expand our work.

In Mali, I visited remote communities and met with the parents. One father told me that "educating a girl is like bringing light to a dark room," while another questioned why the girls need education. In his mind, the boy would become the head of the household and he was the one who would need a job. To him, I explained the economic benefits of girls' education.

In Niger, in a remote area in the north, a group of parents challenged me and said the best thing they could do for their daughters was to have them married at the age of twelve or thirteen. I spent a long time explaining the health, nutrition, and educational benefits of girls' education, not just to the girl but to her family. I spoke in French and had a local translator translate my words into Tamajeq.

In Morocco, I met with USAID and ministry officials. I was delighted to hear from both that the ALEF project was becoming nationally recognized as a flagship effort and a success story. Joshua Muskin, our chief of party, related how our team succeeded in making education more relevant to the lives of the Moroccan youth in the governorates where ALEF was being implemented.

My visits to the field were always the most significant part of my work. That is where it all came together. From visiting the remote rural areas and discussing with parents, local community leaders, teachers, principals, and students the importance of education; to visiting the ministers, the directors of curriculum and teacher training at the ministries; to meeting with the donors such as the USAID missions; to discussing at length with my field staff the different aspects of the implementation of our projects—those tasks were what made my job the best job anyone can have.

My field staff and I recognized that implementation nearly always brought to the surface the need to revisit the design and to adjust several aspects of the plan along the way. When we worked in international educational development, and in particular when we worked in the field in different countries, we understood the transformative aspect of working with others and serving those who were less privileged. We understood that listening and learning was the foundation of our work, while understanding different cultures, contexts, and ways of living were the key ingredients for its success. I cannot overemphasize the importance of listening during these visits. We designed better programs when we listened. We designed useful programs when we did not come in with ready answers. We designed responsive programs and we adjusted their designs based on an acknowledgement that each community had reasons whether or not they were sending their children to school, and only after understanding those reasons could we, with their input, design useful programs or adjust the trajectory of implementation.

In 2007, I received a visit from two directors of the Salzburg Global Seminar from Austria. They invited me to participate as faculty in their upcoming seminar "Breaking the Glass Ceiling: Women in Politics and Business." The seminar was set for November, and six or seven faculty members would lead the five-day sessions for approximately forty participants. I requested time to consider the possibility, given my very busy schedule. They were clever; they asked me not to make the decision immediately, but to allow them to stay in touch over the coming weeks so they could provide further information about the Salzburg Global Seminar. After a few weeks and several discussions with the directors, I accepted. It was a decision I never regretted.

Working with the other faculty members to prepare for the seminar was a different learning experience, but most importantly, immersing myself in the Salzburg Global Seminar for five full days put me in an ideal atmosphere where intellectual stimulation had no limits, and where the luxury of dissecting new issues, ideas, strategies, and possibilities was a normal thing to do. The abstract for our seminar captured what the faculty members agreed to present:

> Unquestionably, women have made significant advances in their presence and power in both the political and business arenas. Although the numbers of women in political office and in the boardroom globally remain relatively low, there is growing evidence of marked positive impact where women have a substantial presence. Recent studies undertaken on women's leadership and power in the corporate and business arena mirror, in certain respects, studies undertaken evaluating the impact of women in the political arena: the outcomes on process, structures, and policies improve, and in business, profitability improves as well.
>
> To date, the linkages between women in the political and business arenas remain fairly limited. This session will compare women's advances in these two critical sectors and compare the information and data that exist related to the impact a significant presence of women in leadership and power positions can create. By comparing different arenas, the session will seek transferable lessons and strategies for

increasing women's presence and power, as well
as for magnifying the positive impact they have.
In addition, the session will consider prospects for
greater cooperation between and across these sectors
to overcome common barriers and support women's
ability to create significant change.

In addition to the day-long structured sessions, the stimulating,
informative, and sometimes challenging discussions continued late
into the evenings. The Salzburg Global Seminar stretched our minds,
deepened our knowledge, increased our commitment, and sent us
home with renewed energy to work harder on increasing women's
presence in leadership positions.

Also in 2007, Mary Maguire, Senior Vice President at AED
for communications, suggested that we cooperate on a companion
video to my book *Keeping the Promise*. I suggested filming in Uganda,
and Mary utilized her staff and mine to create the video. It told the
story of two underprivileged girls and how through our project,
the Ambassadors' Girls' Scholarship Program, their lives were
transformed. The video *Path to Promise: Girls Making the Grade* was
completed in 2008.

In 2008, I welcomed in my office Holly Gordon of the
Documentary Group and a director of the Tribeca Film Festival.
She came to discuss the idea of creating a global movement to raise
the awareness on the imperative of girls' education, and in particular
using the media of film to help achieve this. I was delighted and very
supportive of Holly's ideas and, needless to say, we hit it off at our first
meeting. I was incited to serve as one of the first board members of
10 x10 (Ten Times Ten), the organization that Holly created to raise
the funds for the awareness campaign and movie. Holly frequently

flew to DC from her base in California and we continued to plan and strategize about the goals of 10 x10. We met at least three or four times a year and held several conference calls. Holly's vision, energy, and commitment, convinced many experts in girls' education to join our board and to support this worthy effort. Together, we raised the funds needed to film the story of nine girls in nine countries: Afghanistan, Cambodia, Egypt, Ethiopia, Haiti, India, Nepal, Peru, and Sierra Leone. Nine women writers were selected from the countries chosen for the movie to research and write the stories of the girls. The movie Girl Rising was filmed in nine countries; it depicts the strength of human spirit and the power of education to transform lives. The nine girls featured in the movie confront tremendous challenges and overcome nearly impossible odds to pursue their dreams of going to school. In 2012, the movie Girl Rising was produced, and in early 2013 it was premiered at the Sundance Festival and later released to movie theaters. I was delighted that the Washington Premiere was at the World Bank and that CNN subsequently aired the movie. The main message was: Educating girls can break cycles of poverty in just one generation. Forbes magazine named the Girl Rising movie and movement the number one most dynamic social initiative of 2012. Having a movie about the transformative power of girls' education has been a cherished dream of mine and I was ecstatic that we were able to produce it and witness its wide impact.

In the spring of 2008, my staff and I held a retreat to assess how far we were in our climb of Mount Everest and to plan our next steps. During the session, we noted that from the CGE's launch in 2001 until 2004, the center had established solid foundations, we also noted that from 2004 on the center's growth was accelerating at a quicker pace than expected, and concluded this was largely the consequence of the intense dedication of the staff, who believed passionately that a programmatic focus on girls' and women's issues was essential to ensure equal access to life's opportunities as well as national economic growth and overall human development.

One of the Center's hallmarks was the diversity of its clients and partners. We were pleased to note that by the beginning of 2008, in addition to core activities with USAID, the Center had worked with a large number of other international donors. The staff and I recognized that our collaboration with the diverse donors, clients, and partners enabled CGE to make longer-term commitments to educational reform in at least nine countries. Long-term work in those countries enabled CGE to achieve substantial impact at the local, regional, and national levels. We also recognized that CGE had been successful in creating and strengthening civil society organizations to improve girls' education and women's empowerment in at least twenty countries.

We wondered if we would ever reach the top of the mountain, recognized there was a lot more to do, and reflected on the fact that possibly the journey of working with the underserved was by itself reaching the top of the mountain. At the end of the retreat, the staff and I felt energized, invigorated, and inspired to maximize our efforts.

On April 10, 2008, I was surprised with the Kahlil Gibran International Award during an annual dinner held by the Kahlil Gibran Chair for Values and Peace of the University of Maryland. I had no doubt that Professor Bushrui was the one who suggested the honor. When Dean Edward Montgomery presented the award, he said it was "in recognition of [my] outstanding leadership in promoting women's education throughout the world, and in appreciation for [my] services to the legacies of Kahlil Gibran and Ameen Rihani." I am not sure I deserved such an honor. I truly think there is so much work still to be done to advance girls' and women's education, and so much work to be done to inform the West about Lebanon's cultural contributions. My efforts are only a small wave in an ocean of needs. I was touched and humbled.

Two months later at the international conference of UNGEI in June 2008, during its Global Advisory Committee meeting in Kathmandu, Nepal, I was elected co-chair of UNGEI. Again, I was honored and humbled. During that meeting, we revised and updated UNGEI's vision to read "A world where all girls and boys are empowered through quality education to realize their full potential and contribute to transforming societies where gender equality becomes a reality."

On the flight from home Kathmandu to Washington, D.C., I realized how important my new role and responsibility were and kept thinking about what could be done to make UNGEI even more powerful and impactful than it was at the time. What if UNGEI were to bring about the tipping point in girls' education? Given that UNGEI relied on a broad alliance of committed partners who were major players in international development, I thought that might be possible. I reviewed all the members of UNGEI: large UN agencies such as UNICEF and UNESCO; powerful donors such as the World Bank, USAID, the Swedish International Cooperation Agency, the Norwegian Agency for Development Cooperation, the Department for International Development of the UK, and the Danish Development Assistance Program; and civil society organizations with a proven track record from Africa, Asia, the U.S. and the UK. The question became: What if these committed partners could raise the collective awareness about the centrality of girls' education and its transformative power in order to make all international development stakeholders prioritize girls' education on their global and national agendas? The possibility of bringing about that tipping point was there.

Even though the flight back took many long hours, I could not sleep on the plane; the excitement about the new global possibilities in the field of girls' education kept me awake and jotting notes. I reread the mission of UNGEI; it clearly said that the members of UNGEI were "mobilized to provide direct support to countries and facilitate an enabling educational environment where girls and boys can flourish and unleash their untapped potential." It also said, "The UNGEI partners work together on mobilizing resources for targeted project interventions, country programs, and large-scale systematic interventions designed to affect the education system as a whole." Several ideas came to mind, among them the thought that I should work more closely with the Secretariat of UNGEI, which was based at UNICEF in New York, to ensure that every member of the Global Advisory Committee—not only the major active ones— becomes as pro-active as could be. Another idea was to find ways to leverage the power of the donors in future educational conferences; a third one was to make UNGEI even more visible than it was at the time. I decided to suggest to the Secretariat that the UNGEI should have an honorary chair, an internationally visible personality who was committed to girls' education and women's empowerment. I immediately thought of Queen Rania of Jordan.

During my first meeting with the Secretariat after my election, I presented several suggestions, among them the three ideas conceived on the plane ride home. The Secretariat supported my suggestions and acted immediately on the idea of the honorary chair. Through UNICEF, they contacted Queen Rania and she agreed to the task. No doubt with Queen Rania as our honorary chair, the global visibility of UNGEI would increase. The Secretariat and I also worked in subtle ways to ensure that the other members of UNGEI's Global Advisory Committee became engaged and proactive. During our several meetings and conferences during my tenure as co-chair, the Global Advisory Committee and the Secretariat worked closely together to achieve the objectives of UNGEI which included: improving the quality and availability of girls' education, accelerating action on girls' education, and revitalizing the broad social mobilization and high-level political action needed to ensure that every girl—as well as every boy—received a quality education. At UNGEI, we also advocated for a holistic approach to education with balanced investment in education across the lifecycle, addressing early childhood education, primary and secondary education for all children—with a focus on the children of poor families, and literacy and empowerment of women.

CHAPTER THIRTY-SIX

MAXIMIZING EFFORTS ON ALL FRONTS

M Y EFFORTS EXPANDED ON ALL fronts in 2008- 2009. Co-chairing UNGEI meant working with UNGEI's Secretariat to plan several meetings for the Global Advisory Committee, and then co-chairing those meetings in New York. It also meant attending UNESCO's Education for All (EFA) meetings in Paris where the Global Monitoring Report (GMR) was presented. The GMR was developed by an independent team of education analysts and published by UNESCO. The Education for All GMR was an authoritative reference that aimed to inform, influence, and sustain genuine commitment towards education for all. One of our objectives at UNGEI was to ensure that the team working on the GMR would analyze the quantitative and qualitative information they were studying with a gender lens.

Co-chairing UNGEI also meant representing UNGEI at the EFA meetings of the High-Level Group, which brought together representatives from national governments, development agencies, UN agencies, civil society, and the private sector. Its role was to generate political momentum and to mobilize financial, technical, and political support towards the achievement of the EFA goals and the education-related Millennium Development Goals (MDGs).

Still further, co-chairing UNGEI meant participating in the annual UNGEI conference in Kathmandu, Nepal, and then working with the Secretariat on planning UNGEI's conference in Dakar, Senegal, which I also co-chaired.

On the AED front, overseeing such a large number of projects, staff, and budgets meant increasing the number of overseas trips I took every year, and increasing the numbers of hours I worked on a daily basis. I am grateful that long trips did not create serious jet lag for me, and that I did not need more than six hours of sleep a day. In one year, I made eleven overseas trips: one for a vacation, and the other ten for work.

During those years, I had my initial meeting with a Saudi educational delegation visiting Washington, D.C. They spoke eloquently about King Abdallah's vision to assist the education ministry in the kingdom in its drive to transform the K–12 education system and to accelerate its continuous quality improvement in the future. The delegation also spoke about the King's plan to ensure that the kingdom's public education sector would be a major contributor to the national knowledge economy and an enabler for the new generations of Saudis to compete in the global marketplace. I was fascinated by what I heard.

Also during that time, *Min Ajl Lubnan* reamained very active, organizing cultural events and collaborating with the University of Maryland in College Park, in particular with Professor Emeritus Suheil Bushrui, in planning and organizing international conferences, seminars, workshops, and annual lectures on Gibran and Rihani. Our objective—ensuring that the new generations of American students, as well as international students studying in universities of the greater

Washington, D.C. area were exposed to the contributions of the main Lebanese thinkers, philosophers, and writers, and recognized the richness of the Lebanese heritage—drove us onward and fueled our energies.

The year 2010 was another one filled to the brim. In January, I had a poetry reading at Georgetown University which was organized by Al Waref Institute, an Arab American organization that addressed issues of human rights, women's empowerment, the role of civil society, and other relevant issues in the Arab world. At the end of the poetry reading, Marah Bukai, the founder and chair of Al Waref, surprised me with the award of the Institute.

On the professional front, my team and I were busy responding to new questions from the Kingdom of Saudi Arabia, given that we have been selected among the three finalist organizations that bid on supporting Tatweer. Tatweer was an organization established by a royal decree from King Abdullah bin Abdulaziz to strategically plan the improvement of the K–12 educational system in the Kingdom. The possibility of working with the Saudi government on reforming the educational system was exciting and energizing.

In May 2010, I flew to Dakar to co-chair the UNGEI Conference, "Engendering Empowerment: Education and Equality (E4)." UNGEI issued a press release that stated:

> The conference aims to examine ways to transform the global partnership to support girls' education in view of reaching particularly the Millennium Development Goals (MDGs) two and three, and to reaffirm that girls' education is a development imperative. With the Millennium Development Goal target date of 2015 only five years away, the conference will put girls

front and center with the goal of strengthening and expanding partnerships for girls' education around the most pressing obstacles they face in pursuit of education. The conference will also examine issues of violence, poverty, and quality education, and their intersection with participation, climate change, and health.

The press release also mentioned the opening and closing session speakers: Kalidou Diallo, Minister for Education and National Languages in Senegal; Anthony Lake, Executive Director of UNICEF; David Wiking, UNGEI Global Advisory Committee Co-Chair and Director from the Swedish Development Cooperation; and me, as the UNGEI Global Advisory Committee Co-Chair and Senior Vice President at the Academy for Educational Development. Two hundred participants including scholars, government officials, and education experts, deliberated for two full days. At the end of the conference, the participants, the Secretariat, and the co-chairs produced the "Dakar Declaration on Accelerating Girls' Education and Gender Equality," which read as follows:

We the participants of the United Nations Girls' Education Initiative global conference "Engendering Empowerment: Education and Equality," assembled in Dakar in May 2010, call for urgent action in support of girls' rights to education, gender equality, and empowerment opportunities. The rights of girls and women are guaranteed by the Convention on the Rights of the Child, the Convention on the Elimination of all Forms of Discrimination against Women, the Convention against Discrimination in Education, and the Beijing Platform for Action. In Jomtien in 1990, we established the Education for All Framework; in Dakar in 2000, we strongly endorsed the need for targets for education, especially for girls. Since then, there has been considerable progress: about 22 million more girls enrolled in primary schools from 1999 to 2007, and gender gaps in primary school enrolments have narrowed in many countries. Despite the progress that has been made, poor quality of education, extreme poverty, structural inequality, and violence against girls continue to jeopardize the achievement of the education- and gender-related Education for All and Millennium Development Goals by 2015.

Powerless and poor girls make up the most disadvantaged group in education. Achieving equity in education will entail putting in place a rights-based empowerment framework that will target the most vulnerable and transform power hierarchies in learning spaces, communities, and policy structures in order to give poor and vulnerable girls a voice and ensure that their right to quality education is sustained.

Gender equity is at the center of transformative, quality education. Attention to the physical, social, and academic aspects of multiple learning environments is necessary to enhance opportunities, especially for adolescent girls, and to move beyond basic education. Recognition of teachers as professionals, supported by gender-responsive curricula, is also key to ensuring gender equality.

Because poverty is both structural and multidimensional and has differential impacts on girls and women, interventions for girls' education must cover multiple sectors. Education policies, strategies, plans and budgets must all be gender-responsive.

Gender-based violence remains an obstacle to the full achievement of girls' rights to education. We call for effective strategies and for enforcement of legislation and policies to ensure safe and secure learning environments for girls. Protective and innovative learning opportunities must also be created for children and young women affected by HIV/AIDS and for those in armed conflict and emergency situations. We envision a world in which a special initiative for girls' education is no longer needed—a world in which all girls and boys are empowered through quality education to realize their full potential and contribute to transforming their societies, so that gender equality becomes a reality.

While in Washington collaborating with the UNGEI Secretariat on planning the conference, and while in Dakar co-chairing the sessions and working with several committees on finalizing the Dakar Declaration, I also worked late in the evenings to finalize the list of proposed staff and consultants who will go to Saudi Arabia and work side-by-side with the Saudi Tatweer staff.

The good news came sometime in the spring of 2010. The director of Tatweer invited us to collaborate with the Saudi leadership in designing a strategic plan for the implementation of the educational reform. Before the conference in Senegal, my team and I had planned for this possibility. When the news came, I worked sixteen hours a day, flew to Dakar, and came back to continue the planning process to help ensure the success of this project in the Saudi Kingdom. An international team of seven educational planning experts (including Arab American experts) had to be fielded to Saudi Arabia in June. I decided to spend around ten days with our team in Riyadh to ensure that the launch was well done. I wanted to make sure that we shared the expectations of the Tatweer leadership, that what we were expected to deliver was clearly understood by the members of our team, and that the understanding of the working relationships with the leadership of Tatweer was also clear.

However, at the end of May, before we all embarked on this exciting trip, I had my routine yearly physical check-up. My doctor discovered a complication related to my earlier cancer operation and recommended immediate surgery. I explained the importance of the Tatweer project and that I would be traveling to Saudi Arabia in a week or so. While she insisted my health must come first, I stressed that I could not delay the fielding of my team of experts and that my presence was necessary for at least the first ten days. After several discussions with my doctor, my oncologist, the surgeon, and Zuheir, I convinced them I had to make the trip to Saudi Arabia, but that upon my return I would agree to the recommended operation.

In early June 2010, seven international education-planning experts and I traveled to Saudi Arabia. The experts would spend approximately seven months in Riyadh while I and another colleague stayed for the first ten days. I wanted to ensure the team was sensitive to the context and culture of Saudi Arabia in an in-depth way. Of course orientations about the kingdom's history, culture, and education system had taken place before we arrived, but I strongly felt that a continuation of such orientation was necessary once we were on the ground in Riyadh. My ten days with the team were unforgettable. Even though I had visited Saudi Arabia twice before as part of the planning for the project, this third visit was incredibly fascinating, in great part due to the fact that I got to know in a more profound way the leadership of the Ministry of Education and Tatweer. His Highness Prince Faysal bin Abdullah bin Mohammed Al Saud, the Minister of Education; Dr. Khaled Al-Sabti the Vice Minister; and Dr. Ali Al Hakami, the general manager for King Abdallah bin Abdulaziz's Public Education Development Project—Tatweer—represented an ideal enlightened leadership to lead the reform effort. They were pragmatic visionaries. Dr. Al-Hakami, with whom I worked closely, was a superb leader, a creative thinker, an effective planner, an efficient manager, and an analytic professional. Working with him and his team was inspiring and rewarding. After the first ten days, I knew we could do the expected work, but I also knew that I had to change the leader of my team in Riyadh. On the flight back to Washington, I was more concerned about how to find the most qualified and appropriate leader for the team than I was about my upcoming surgery.

As soon as I returned from Saudi Arabia, I entered the hospital. What was expected to be a two-hour surgery took five, as the operation was more serious than anyone expected. My recovery also took a little more time than I wanted since I was eager to go back to work. Advancing girls' education, contributing to educational reforms, designing projects that mitigated gender-based violence, and participating in forums to promote women's leadership were, in my mind, more important than my health problems.

Toward the end of July, I went back to my office. For the next few months I immersed myself in the program issues that needed attention in Saudi Arabia, Yemen, Morocco, Tanzania, Kenya, Nigeria, Guinea, Djibouti, Ethiopia, and the Democratic Republic of Congo. I also supported the staff planning for a workshop for the African NGOs from twelve African countries who were our implementation partners in the Ambassadors Girls' Scholarship Program (AGSP). In addition, my staff and I worked on proposals for Djibouti, Ethiopia, Qatar, India, and other locations.

During those months I continued regular health check-ups, and new issues surfaced. A second operation was scheduled for mid-December. I was frustrated that my body was no longer as capable as my mind. Health problems seemed to be creating obstacles on the road, but I continued to believe that our programs and projects were more important than health distractions. I kept moving ahead, working as hard as possible, putting in my long hours, planning, designing, and overseeing the implementation of our programs. I delivered on my intention to change the leader of our team in Saudi Arabia when I asked Dr. El-Houcine Haishour to lead the AED efforts for Tatweer. Changing team leaders in the middle of the course is never an easy affair; however, I consider that particular decision to be one of the best I ever made. Dr. Haishour turned out to be exactly what Tatweer needed. His vast educational experience with the World Bank and AED, his work on educational reform in many countries, his cutting-edge knowledge of the intersection of education and technology, his creative and analytic mind, his powerful capability of planning long-term, as well as his mastery of several languages including Arabic and English prepared him well to partner with Tatweer on leading a strategic planning effort for one of the most wideranging and comprehensive educational reforms in the Middle East. After all, the educational reform in Saudi Arabia had the potential of impacting the educational reforms of many Arab and Muslim countries.

Another decision I made before I entered the hospital in December was to agree to travel to Kenya in January 2011 with my staff, Michele Akpo, and her team to deliver a workshop to forty-two leaders of African NGOs on how to advance girls' education in their countries in a sustained manner. The workshop was for five full days and the plan was to deliver two simultaneous workshops—one in English and one in French—given that the participants were coming from twelve African countries, approximately half Francophone and half Anglophone.

A third important decision I made at the end of November/ beginning of December and before my operation, was that I needed to start thinking of my successor at AED. Given my health situation, I did not believe I could continue traveling the way I did or working twelve-to-fourteen hours a day on a regular basis.

December arrived, and I was busy with our project in Saudi Arabia and the important capacity-building workshop for the African NGO leaders when I heard shocking news: AED had been suspended by USAID due to financial difficulties faced by one of AED's projects in Pakistan. AED was so large at the time that a senior vice president like me was not able to know everything that was going on within the organization as a whole, and specifically not the issues that a project not under my supervision could be facing. That announcement came on December 9, and I was to enter the hospital on December 13 for the second follow-up surgery. The doctors had insisted on complete rest for the remainder of December if I wanted a full recovery.

I spent the rest of the month at home recovering and meeting with a variety of doctors for follow-up examinations. I also tried to remain up-to-date with how AED was addressing the financial difficulties. I had a quiet Christmas at home with Zuheir and the rest of the family.

My New Year's wishes were more than the usual. Silently, I prayed for the recovery of my health, and for good health for my husband and brothers. Professionally, I prayed for AED to resolve the difficulty in an appropriate way. On a global scale, I prayed for a miracle in Lebanon, or rather the coming together of the different political parties and for the agreement on policies and strategies that protected Lebanon from regional negative impacts. I am sure I joined much of the world in praying for peace in the Middle East, but I also prayed for the end of hunger in Africa; for more equitable systems of basic public education and health services in Africa, Asia, and the Middle East; and for the end of wars wherever conflict existed in the world.

January 2011 dawned. I felt energized and ready to travel to Kenya. The AGSP team led by Michele Akpo had designed a workshop based on a decade of accumulated knowledge and best practices in girls' education and scholarship programming. The session was designed for the African NGO partners who had been sharing in the implementation of this robust program, and given their interest in sustaining their work in advancing girls' education, my team and I decided to present, in addition to the capacity-building topics planned, a strategic workshop that would focus solely on how to sustain the programming and implementation of girls' education projects. The workshop was designed with the underpinning philosophy that programming for girls' education included: teacher training, curriculum relevance, community engagement, life skills, mentoring, provision of scholarships, HIV/AIDS' education, leadership engagement, public-private partnerships, and more. The sessions were entirely participatory and included debates on specific topics:

1. Analyzing the environment: stakeholder identification, stakeholder interest and involvement, and assessing needs;

2. Planning the program and engaging stakeholders: assessing needs with stakeholders, and engaging the stakeholders on a strategy that leads to results;

3. Implementing a set of activities: designing a work plan that encompasses the needed activities such as: scholarships, life skills mentoring, teacher training, role models, community engagement, HIV/AIDS' education, and other activities that enhance girls' education;

4. Sustainability: strategy for effective capacity-building, strategy for effective advocacy, types of advocacy, leveraging funds from diversified sources, and continuous capacity strengthening; and

5. Monitoring and evaluation: measuring results and impact, using the results of the monitoring and evaluation to inform the stakeholders and to continue the improvement of the implementation.

The five days in Nairobi, Kenya, delivering this capacity-building and strengthening workshop with four of my staff was so powerful. The sessions deepened my knowledge about the emerging leaders of Africa. I understood better the depth of their commitment to transforming their societies and their vision for a future where equity and equality were basic pillars. I experienced their willingness to face all kinds of challenges to level the playing field for the new generations in their countries, and to work strategically to eradicate poverty and illiteracy. I shared their beliefs in the potential and aspirations of every man and every woman as well as every boy and every girl, and their hope for a better tomorrow. These five days also reaffirmed my knowledge that in Africa, singing and dancing often become part of serious, analytic workshops; such a creative addition makes the debates easier to continue over dinners and into the evenings, and the reflection process on such matters becomes even more natural.

As I returned to Washington, D.C., towards the end of January, I read about demonstrations in Tunisia that started on December 18, 2010, in Sidi Bouzid following Mohammad Bouazizi's self-immolation in protest of ill-treatment by the police. These demonstrations had spread to Egypt, Libya, Yemen, Bahrain, and Syria. I could not help but think that the 2005 Lebanese demonstrations for freedom from foreign hegemony, for freedom of speech, and for basic rights of those who oppose the domination of regional governments, were the starting point of an Arab awakening. The Cedar Revolution demonstrated that those who are oppressed will eventually revolt. However, the huge difference was that the Cedar Revolution was peaceful and did not use force, weapons, or violence. The later demonstrations which were dubbed "Arab Spring" were both non-violent and violent, and were met with greater violence from the regimes of the countries where these events took place.

I had mixed feelings about the Arab Spring from the beginning. Violence is a non-starter for me. Change through peaceful marches and continuous non-violent demonstrations, yes. Change through civil disobedience, yes. However, I was convinced that change through violence would lead to a horrific cycle of violence. Violence breads violence; violence moves on a slippery slope and creates a cycle of destruction. I was weary of the fact that what seemed to have started as a non-violent set of protests in Egypt immediately turned into violent street altercations.

Syria was another story. From day one, the Assad regime used utmost violence against children, youth, and adults, and against any and all demonstrators who voiced dissatisfaction with his government. I was concerned for the future of the Syrians and for the spill-over effects on Lebanon. Syria's borders with Lebanon are a gateway through which refugees from Syria can flee. Lebanon's size and fragility might not be able to absorb many Syrian refugees.

At one point in early 2011, I realized I was very worried about the political upheavals and the violence in several Arab countries and in Syria in particular, but alas, I recognized that this is one of the situations where an individual like me cannot make a difference and that it would take international political will to stop the blood shed. I decided to continue focusing my attention on work—specifically the strategy that our executive team at AED had decided to undertake to merge with another not-for-profit organization with an excellent reputation that also worked in international development.

I wanted to continue strengthening AED's Center for Gender Equity and the leadership of the Center, given that my health situation was not improving. My doctors strongly recommended that I change my lifestyle, stop jet-setting from one continent to another, and end the twelve-to-fourteen hour workdays.

Yet my staff and I continued designing and winning new projects, including "Arab Youth and Employability" and "The Four Pillars Plus Approach to Girls' Education in Nigeria." The GE Foundation funded both projects. The Arab project was to design and implement a series of symposia on youth and employability in order to take the pulse of one of the most vital populations in our global community. At the first symposium, held in Qatar, we would explore the commonalities and differences among the youth of the Gulf, the Levant region, and North Africa, as well as among young men and women in Arab countries. The symposium would also look at the challenges and opportunities that Arab youth faced, and the pathways to employment and enterprises that were open to them.

The Four Pillars Plus project in Nigeria aimed at improving the quality and relevance of education for orphans and vulnerable children—especially girls—in junior and senior secondary schools. The project focused on the four-pillar approach of scholarships, teacher professional development, girls' mentoring, and community mobilization. We would, of course, enter into a dialogue with the Nigerian communities about the particular challenges facing girls and their families, and engage these communities in finding solutions to overcome those obstacles. The "Plus" aspect of the program took into account the particular culture and context of Nigerian regions where the project would be implemented, and would incorporate activities that were most appropriate for building support for girls' education, enriching local economy, and ensuring sustainability through skills training and employment. I strongly recommended that GE and my senior staff not work in the northern region of Nigeria since I was not sure that we could deal with the strong opposition that Boko Haram had declared regarding girls' education.

While my staff and I planned the launch of these two projects, I worked with the executive team at AED to finalize the merger between AED and Family Health International (FHI). In July 2011, the two organizations became one under the agreed-upon name of FHI360.

Immediately after the merger, I began searching for an appropriate date to announce my resignation so I could begin changing my lifestyle. I wanted to do three things before I retired: appoint and train my successor at the helm of the Center for Gender Equity; launch the program on Arab Youth and Employability; and secure one last large girls' education project.

As luck would have it, I was able to do all three in a short period of time. I appointed Andrea Bertone, a most capable senior director in CGE, to be my successor. Andrea had worked with me for eight years and had proven to be a superb professional and leader.

We launched the work on Arab Youth and Employability in Doha, Qatar, in November 2011 with excellent Arab analysts from different parts of the region. Robert Corcoran, the president of the GE Foundation, and I moderated the sessions of the symposium which featured many excellent speakers. Those who analyzed the status of Arab youth, and who discussed present policies and future solutions—as well as the way forward, included Dr. Tarik Yousef, the CEO of Silatech, an Arab think-tank; and Dr. Rami Khoury, from the American University of Beirut.

Finally, during the months of December 2011 and January 2012, I negotiated with Price Waterhouse to ensure that FHI360 would be a significant partner and subcontractor on a proposal they were submitting to the Department for International Development (DFID). The proposal involved twenty countries in Africa and Asia, and was in response to DFID's Girls' Education Challenge (GEC). I was delighted to be able to end my involvement with AED—now FHI360—by engaging the organization in the British-funded GEC. Its goal was to help up to a million of the world's poorest girls improve their lives through education. The initiative called on NGOs and the private sector to find better ways of getting girls into school and of ensuring they received a quality education to transform their future. GEC would support projects that could demonstrate new and effective ways to expand education opportunities to marginalized girls, and which could be robustly evaluated to widen their impact.

I announced my resignation in February 2012. My colleagues and staff organized a farewell party that took place at Academy Hall at FHI360 around the end of that month. The celebration included videotaping interviews with those who worked with me, theatrical skits about episodes of my professional life, poems and tributes, slide shows, photos, and of course, speeches. I was humbled and honored by the words spoken during that farewell event. To illustrate what happened during this moving celebration, what follows is the speech of Stephanie Funk, a USAID deputy director of one of USAID's Missions in Africa:

> First, I want to thank you for letting me say a few words in honor of May today. It's a privilege to recognize someone I respect, admire, and care for so greatly, both personally and professionally. Personally, May and I have known each other for decades, and although we met in the workplace, we have become close friends. Professionally, I have to say that of all the people I have met in all the countries I have lived, I have never met anyone who so adeptly mixes academics, philosophy, technical know-how, advocacy, and common sense like May. I have watched with awe as she has applied her unique set of skills and made a difference to women and girls around the world.
>
> While the development community's interest in women in development, gender equity, and girls'

education has waxed and waned, almost as many times as the name has changed, May's commitment has remained steadfast. Like many of you have said today, her achievements have been remarkable, but what I find equally remarkable is her human touch.

I first met May twenty-two years ago when I joined USAID's Office of Women in Development. To say that I knew nothing about Women in Development would be a vast understatement. I was young and inexperienced, and I'm pretty sure I was selected for the position to cover the Africa portfolio only because I'd lived on the continent as a Peace Corps volunteer for two years. Soon after I joined the office, I was assigned to be the CTO for the girls' education component of an Africa Bureau education contract. The WID Office funded the girls' component and May was the Chief of Party for the sub-contractor responsible for implementing it. She was an extremely accomplished professional in the field, and I was constantly perplexed by the fact that she was reporting to me rather than vice versa. I kept waiting for her to complain, but she never did. Instead, she took me under her wing and she taught me. She taught me everything I know about girls' education. She was kind, she was patient, and she was fiercely smart, always respectful, and forever wise. She made me believe that I could actually do this job and she infected me with a "righteousness" of girls' education that I have never lost.

To manage the contract, we formed a core group which consisted of the Africa Bureau, the WID Office, the S&T education office, and the prime and sub-contractor on this award. We held weekly meetings in a small, dark, windowless office in USAID/W. Early on, May ensured that the project bought into a World Bank study on the value of girls' education, and for the first time ever, the direct link between six years of girls' education and reduced fertility rates, reduced infant mortality rates, and increased life expediency was documented. Before I knew it, May and I were teaching that core group and the field about the benefits of educating girls. We were on a mission and we were armed with evidence. It wasn't easy. Some were not the most willing or quickest learners, and others were outright hostile or patronizing. But we never gave up. We advocated, and advocated, and advocated. Within a year, the contract was overstretched with requests from the field. We went from creating demand to being in demand. That small, dark, windowless office became bright and busy as we struggled to find consultants to answer all the calls. Most importantly, the number of girls attending school in Africa started to climb, and it has been increasing ever since. I have no doubt that those girls now live longer, healthier, and happier lives. Most of them have never met May Rihani and may never know the role she played in helping to better their lives. I, on the other hand, know full well the role she played in my life. And my guess is that if I asked every woman in this room who has been coached, mentored, inspired, or improved by May to raise their hand, there would hardly be a hand that wasn't raised. You simply can't know May and not learn from her.

So as one of, and on behalf of, the innumerable women that May has developed, I want to say thank you. Thank you for loving us, for believing in us, for encouraging us, and for making us better. Most of all, thank you for your human touch—that precious touch that like no other continually and uniquely breathed life into a concept called women in development. Thank you, May.

Stephanie's speech is an example of how my staff and colleagues showered me with their generosity and appreciation. I must admit that receiving a huge amount of emails and letters from staff, colleagues, and partner organizations as a result of my resignation made me reflect on if I truly deserved all those accolades. I concluded that everyone was way too generous with their remarks, and that while the occasion of my resignation made them reflect on the importance of international development, I was only the conduit of these reflections. Even though I felt that I did not deserve all that they said, the emails, letters, speeches from D.C., and from overseas, are among the most precious and valued gifts I have ever received.

I would be remiss if I did not acknowledge that I also received equally moving correspondence from family members. The following letter from Ramzi is an example:

Today you resigned from decades of work as a specialist and authority in gender equity and girls' education. You have given so much to people around you, starting with your family, to your friends and colleagues, and all the way to little girls in Africa without them knowing what you are offering. And this is the greatest gift of all.

You have done all this with love, dedication, determination, hard work (I mean *very* hard work), and made a positive difference in the lives of people from Afghanistan to Malawi. I doubt I know anyone who can claim this type of achievement both in quantity and quality. It is no surprise that a celebration of the magnitude, intensity, and potency which was held yesterday at FHI360 to honor you, your achievement, and your career has the imprint of "Life Achievement Award" written all over it. I can understand why people call you "mentor," "teacher," life-changer," and "legend." You certainly are one, and I am so proud of my sister who has reached the stars in her field.

For all of this, allow me, my dear May, to offer you a small token of appreciation and gratefulness for all your contributions and generosity, so numerous and so varied, some known and others remain unknown. I would like you to accept this gift towards a couple of vacations, piano lessons, and towards publishing your new book.

> Thank you for allowing me to make this gift from the
> heart. I only hope it brings you as much happiness as
> it does for me.

Of course, tears covered my face while reading Ramzi's letter, the way tears ran down my cheeks when I listened to the tributes of my staff and colleagues; and the way tears rolled down my cheeks when I read letters and emails of other members of my family.

I have no doubt that I do not deserve all that was said about me. Instead, I am the one who needs to thank so many for providing me with the opportunity of working in international development. Being involved in international education and serving others made my soul more encompassing, my heart more responsive, and my brain more agile. I am the one who needs to thank all those who facilitated my career; those who worked with me; those who allowed me to enter their countries, cities, villages, and rural areas; those who allowed me to visit their schools; those who had endless meetings with me; and those who spoke words of wisdom to me under a tree or in a ministry conference room.

By having the career I have had, I could not have been more privileged. I am utterly thankful.

Starting March 2012, I decided to spend my time writing books, serving on boards of organizations I believe in, and doing a few selected consultancies every year. I did not know that other things would also take place.

Charito Kruvant, the president of Creative Associates, nominated me for Creative Associates' International Women's Leadership Award, and the Temple of Understanding in New York nominated me for the Juliet Hollister Annual Award. I was surprised and humbled.

Yet while I learned of these two nominations, the conflict in Syria was spreading and becoming more violent, and I was becoming even more concerned about the loss of innocent lives as well as the negative impact the Syrian war would have on Lebanon.

CHAPTER THIRTY-SEVEN

SYRIA'S BLOODY MESS AND LEBANON'S MESSAGE

THE YEAR 2012 WAS FULL of immense contrasts. On one hand, Syria's bloody mess and deepening civil war had already left thousands of people dead and was widening the divide between the different Syrian factions. On the other hand, many voices from Lebanon continued to highlight the need for the peaceful co-existence of religions and the importance of diversity and pluralism. Professor Suheil Bushrui, for example, had published a book in English, *The Spiritual Heritage of the Human Race*. In 2012, an Arabic translation of his book was published and disseminated heavily in Lebanon. *The Spiritual Heritage of the Human Race* is a call for the utmost respect of all religions and for a deeper understanding of the common ground among different spiritual schools.

In September 2012, Pope Benedict visited Lebanon. In his speeches, he praised the country as an example of cooperation among faiths. He said, "Like me, you know that this equilibrium, which is presented everywhere as an example, is extremely delicate...

Sometimes it seems about to snap like a bow which is overstretched or submitted to pressures which are too often partisan." He added, "This is where real moderation and great wisdom are tested." Pope Benedict's visit reminded us of Pope John Paul II's when he had said Lebanon is a "message" about peaceful co-existence. In his document "A New Hope for Lebanon,'" Pope John Paul II had outlined the need for co-existence and for all Lebanese to look toward Lebanon for their future. Speaking in French, Pope Benedict told the stadium crowd, "In this holy land, Christians, Muslims, and Jews are called to work together with confidence and boldness, and to work to bring about without delay the day when the legal rights of all peoples are respected and they can live in peace and mutual understanding."

In 2012, it became clear that the Arab Spring did not transform the Arab societies into the democracies that the first waves of demonstrators were aspiring for, as if the voice of the demonstrators—and in particular the voice of the new generations—got lost and was pulled down by the heavy weight of the traditions of dictatorship and oppression. The Arab Spring stumbled and fell on its face and the Arab youth became disappointed and disillusioned.

In 2012 in Lebanon, despite extraordinary political constraints due to the gridlock between the March 14 political alliance and Hezbollah, many Lebanese writers and journalists, as well as young professionals, continued to believe in the possibility and value of democracy, diversity, pluralism, and equal basic rights. That strong belief emanated from many reasons including the fact that Lebanon was never ruled by a dictator, and that the army in Lebanon never used its guns, tanks, or airplanes to silence and oppress the people in general, or to side with a dictator against children, women, youth, and demonstrators.

Lebanese writers and journalists wrote about the importance of peaceful co-existence, sharing their voices of moderation and hope. Individuals such as Marwan Hamade, Philip Salem, Nadim Koteish, Henri Zghaib, Akl Al Awit, Melhem Khalaf, Sahar Baasiiri, Mohammad Sammaq, and Edmond Rabat highlighted the uniqueness of Lebanon as the meeting point of Christianity and Islam—the land where the dialogue between Christianity and Islam continues on a regular basis. They wrote about the need to transcend divisions based on religion and ethnicity; the need to not allow anger or hatred to make us forget that golden age when freedom reigned, where Muslims and Christians governed together, built business companies together, and together made the economic status of Lebanon rise beyond expectations. In their articles and speeches, they underlined the importance of continuing to value both the differences and the common ground, the premise that Lebanon's essence is diversity, and that no one faction should ever dominate. Their words continued to remind us that we owe it to ourselves and to the world to demonstrate that religions can peacefully co-exist, and that countries are less promising if they believe that one religion—or one ethnicity, or one race—should dominate.

At least in Lebanon, despite the political stalemate, and despite the extreme positions of Hezbollah and others, there were still voices that believed the golden age of Lebanon was evidence that democracy and freedom are part of the essence of Lebanon. These voices considered the years between 1950 and 1975 as proof that a Middle Eastern country can be democratic, can be built on a foundation that believes in diversity, and can practice freedom of beliefs, freedom of speech, and freedom of thought. These voices recognized that Lebanon cannot be divorced from its surroundings and that what was happening in Syria in particular, and in the Middle

East in general, would have a negative impact on the fragile country; however, they also believed that Lebanon can and will overcome these extreme difficulties.

Certain writers and journalists believe that Lebanon is a message; it is a position about respect for diversity and pluralism. They underlined the fact that the essence of Lebanon is based on a continuous dialogue between Christianity and Islam, and that the central idea within the concept of Lebanon is that the East and the West meet and interact in Lebanon, and a new culture is born. Many Lebanese continue to believe that even with the existence of all the extremist movements in the Middle East, and even though these movements will affect Lebanon, they will not succeed in destroying the essence of Lebanon.

If Lebanon stops being the place where minorities live together and where no one group dominates, then the whole Middle East, the Arabs and Israel, will lose that window of hope and that opportunity to prove to the world that the Middle East is not just a region where war, conflict, and violence exist. Lebanon continues to be the promise of a better future in the Middle East.

CHAPTER THIRTY-EIGHT

HUMBLED BY AWARDS

A S I MENTIONED EARLIER, AS soon as I announced my resignation from my years of globetrotting and international work and service, I was nominated for two prestigious awards.

On March 13, 2012, at the National Press Club in Washington D.C., Creative Associates launched its Center for Women's Leadership in International Development. The Center supports women around the world, helping them to realize the positive change they seek by promoting women's leadership in international development, and highlighting the contributions women leaders make to effective and sustainable development.

At this event, Creative Associates' President Charito Kruvant presented me with the first International Women's Leadership Award. In her speech, she mentioned they had selected me because of my "outstanding leadership and dedication to girls' education and women's empowerment." Greg Niblett's introduction included a highlight of my accomplishments. I was moved by what Charito and Greg said. My acceptance speech reflected on the meaning of leadership:

To have Charito Kruvant and Greg Niblett offer me the first leadership award of the Center for Women's Leadership in International Development is a true honor. I am very appreciative of this tribute.

Yesterday, I was reflecting on what leadership means and what I have learned through my years of experience in international development. What came to mind are some key dimensions of leadership. These are not the only elements of leadership, but I believe key ones.

First, a leader must have a vision, be able to articulate that vision clearly, be utterly committed to it, and be able to help others embrace it and make it their own. That capacity of ensuring alignment between one's vision and helping others make that vision their own is what makes someone a real leader.

Second, a leader must be able to motivate and mobilize others—in particular those who stand to benefit from the vision, or who can help others benefit from it. To mobilize others is an art and a science; once someone perfects that skill, she or he is close to the top of the leadership ladder.

Next, I strongly believe a leader must practice active listening. While it may not be an easy skill to master, active listening is an important condition of leadership. *Active* is the key word here. Active listening requires the ability to set aside your agenda and concerns and open yourself to listen very carefully to what is being communicated to you. Active listening is about immersing yourself in a new context, a new framework, and a new mindset, and then reconnecting the new information with a broader agenda. Once that is done, you are able to align your objectives with new concerns. No doubt a hard skill, but once mastered, leadership becomes easier to attain.

Fourthly, one cannot be a leader without empowering others. It is an act based on self-confidence, and an act that makes continuity and sustainability possible. Empowering others creates a path that reaches the goals, or creates a movement that no one can stop.

Finally, the above dimensions still need the glue to bring all the elements of leadership together. That glue is compassion. Through compassion, a leader will discover the energy to translate her vision into a plan, that plan into the plan of others, and the collective plan into action.

I thought I would share with you one example of my work where some elements that I learned about leadership were utilized.

In 1993, while at Creative Associates, I was asked to understand and analyze why girls' education in all of Afghanistan, other than Kabul, was only at 2.7%

—the lowest percentage anywhere of girls going to school at that time.

Dressed in a *chador* (but leaving my face uncovered), I met with the arch-conservative and bearded men of the Afghan rebel forces' shadow Ministry of Education during the civil war. We met in Peshawar for four days while I worked to get them to help me understand the situation concerning girls' education. Believe me, I listened very actively.

Many explanations were given that were not convincing. For example, they said, "The Soviets have declared war on us and we cannot send our daughters to school; bombs falling on schools might kill them." I asked: So you value the lives of your daughters more than the lives of your sons? They quickly backed off from this theory. They offered other explanations, but they were equally unconvincing. For four days, they seemed at a loss as to how to explain the 2.7%, and I continued to listen. Finally, one of them said, "We do not send our daughters to school because of our religion; the mullah tells us not to send them to school."

I felt this was my opportunity. Being versed in Arabic and being knowledgeable about Islam, I quoted a sentence from the Hadith, the collection of Prophet Mohammed's sayings: "Education is the responsibility of every Muslim man and every Muslim woman." I asked, who is more important, the mullah or the Prophet? To make a long story short, we discussed this at length, and as a result, they allowed me to design with them, the home schools for girls.

Yesterday, recalling this event from 1993 made me think of my whole career and the leaders with whom I worked: my father Albert Rihani; my first development teacher, Maurice Gemayel; and my first American boss and mentor, Warren Wiggins.

I thought of many world leaders who have inspired me, and remembered the voices of some of these leaders:

The Dalai Lama, who said, "Compassion is a necessity, not a luxury. Without it, humanity cannot survive."

Eleanor Roosevelt, who stated, "Where...do universal human rights begin? In small places, close to home— so close and so small that they cannot be seen on any maps of the world. Such are the places where every man, woman, and child seeks equal justice, equal opportunity, equal dignity without discrimination. "

Mahatma Gandhi taught us, "We must be the change we wish to see."

The work of true leaders withstands the test of time. True leaders like these dedicate their lives to their vision. Their hard work and the ability to endure when

it would have been far easier to lay down their efforts—
and their constant optimism that a better world can be
achieved—is a measure of their contribution.

I wish us all, each and every one, a vision that drives
us, a dedication that keeps propelling us forward, and
a constant positive outlook that makes us recognize
that we can make a difference in this word.

Thank you for honoring me with this leadership
award. I see that its true value is its recognition of
the importance of girls' education and women's
empowerment to achieve equality between genders.

On October 16, 2012, I received the Juliet Hollister Award
from the Temple of Understanding in New York. The Temple
of Understanding states that its main objective is "developing an
appreciation of religious and cultural diversity." When they nominated
me, I was humbled to be in the company of past awardees such as:
Nelson Mandela, the Dalai Lama, Archbishop Desmond Tutu, Prince
Hassan Bin Talal, Queen Noor, Ravi Shankar, Mary Robinson, and
others. I was sure that the little girl from Freike did not deserve this
honor; however, I would not be honest if I do not confess that I was
delighted to receive such an award.

At the award ceremony, my dear friend Professor Suheil Bushrui
introduced me, and his introduction brought tears to my eyes. Here
are paragraphs from his introduction:

The award we are bestowing on May Rihani bears
the noble name of Juliet Hollister. Juliet Hollister

had realized what Mahatma Gandhi many years ago proclaimed: "There will be no lasting peace on earth, unless we learn not merely to tolerate, but even to respect the other faiths as our own."

In many ways, May Rihani has followed the example set by Juliet Hollister in seeking to establish peace not only among the nations, but also among its diverse religious communities. May Rihani has understood that in order to achieve such a goal, it is imperative to restructure education, and above all, to encourage and develop the education of girls and women.

May Rihani has spent, in fact, a major part of her professional life engaged in what could aptly be described as the "silence of good things." Her dedication, her commitment, her sacrifices, her indefatigable efforts, her sharp intelligence, her noble vision, and her capacity for winning the love and respect of others distinguish her as one of the great servants of humanity, and, in particular, as a promoter of the emancipation and empowerment of girls and women throughout the world.

I came to know May Rihani in the '70s, when she was very young. I met her first in the house of her parents, Albert Fares Rihani and Loreen Schoucair, a remarkable couple who embodied the noblest qualities of human love and dignity—her distinguished father a man of literary distinction, and her saintly mother a talented author of children's literature. I may say, indeed, that she was nobly fathered and divinely mothered. For her, academic distinction alone was not sufficient—for it had been inculcated into her from childhood that she had the duty to make this world a better place. Whatever distinction she achieved, she had learned, she must dedicate to the service of others. The circumstance of her Lebanese birth had also a great influence on the shaping of her thought and character. I am reminded here of a letter addressed by L.A.G. Strong to William Butler Yeats, which I have taken the liberty to adapt to May, because it depicts so eloquently her relation to her native land, where her early years up to adulthood were shaped. In this extract I have recast L.A.G. Strong's observations about Yeats and Ireland to make them applicable to May Rihani and Lebanon.

The first thing to be borne in mind is that you are a Lebanese. No one who loses sight of this will understand you. To some characters, nationality is not important: they have no striking racial traits, and one remembers their origin with a shock of surprise. Others adopt a nationality, and so vehemently identify themselves with it that their real birthplace and parentage become misleading. You have always been a Lebanese; no other country could have produced you

May Rihani is imbued with the spirit of her native land. She seems particularly to have benefited from that rich blend of historical happening and legendary association, which is her birthplace. May has been influenced alike by the mythology of her homeland and the mysticism of the Sufi tradition. In fact, all the religions have a special place in her heart. In honoring May Rihani tonight, we are also honoring her great country, which through the ages has remained a meeting point of cultures, civilizations, and great spiritual traditions: the land of Lebanon.

Time does not permit me to describe in detail May Rihani's professional career, and I must therefore content myself with the following brief cameo. Her services in the international arena have taken her to areas which even the most hardened of men might hesitate to visit. Her main purpose in this has been to help underprivileged girls in remote and rural areas of Africa, Asia, and the Middle East. Her activities have exposed her to considerable dangers. The news, last week, of the shooting of the fourteen-year-old rights activist Malala Yousafzai serves as a reminder of the kind of risks May has run in order to champion the cause of girls' education.

For May, her profession is her vocation. She has brought to her work a poet's vision—for she is a distinguished poet in her own right. In my last anthology, just published in London, entitled *The Literary Heritage of the Arabs*, I include some of May's work as representative of the most important writing in modern Arabic literature.

It was Shelley who declared that poets are the unacknowledged legislators of the world. The vision of the poet combined with an acutely intelligent practical mind has enabled May Rihani to provide for us all an example worthy of emulation. May Rihani not only believes in the interconnectedness of all religions, but has also demonstrated it through her marriage, for she, a Christian Maronite, is wedded to a Sufi Druze, Mr. Zuheir Al-Faqih. Their union presents an image of that oneness, that unity in diversity, that blissful peace which we all pray will one day be the lot of the whole world. It is my honor and privilege to introduce to you, May Rihani.

While walking toward the podium to deliver my acceptance speech, I thought of my parents and silently thanked them for what they taught me. Following is my acceptance:

Thank you, Professor Bushrui, for your kind introduction. I am honored and humbled by this prestigious award that the Temple of Understanding has graciously bestowed upon me. I share this award with Malala Yousafzai and with the underprivileged girls who live in remote, rural, impoverished communities in Africa, Asia, and the Middle East, especially those girls and young women who braved all odds to go to school.

My life has been enriched by working to ensure that girls in more than forty countries, such as in the remote mountains of Yemen, in drought-stricken areas of Mali, in the war-torn communities of the Congo, and in the religiously conservative rural areas of Pakistan and Afghanistan, are able to go to school and learn what benefits them, their families, and society at large.

Progress has been made; however, according to UNESCO, in 2009, about sixty-seven million children remained out of school, the majority of whom are girls.

I believe that every human being, man or woman, adult or child, American, African, Asian, or Middle Eastern, white or black, Christian, Muslim, Hindu, Jew, or of any other faith, is a sacred being.

I believe that it is the duty of each one of us to do all we can to help ensure that the basic rights of each human are extended to everyone else, regardless of gender, race, creed, geographic origin, or economic status.

I believe no country can advance without the input of all its human beings: men and women.

I believe children's education—all children, girls and boys—forms the foundation of a forward-looking society.

I believe the more we work to close the gap between rich and poor, and men and women, the better our planet becomes.

I believe these principles and these basic human rights that include education help create a win-win environment: no one loses, everyone gains.

I learned many of these principles in Lebanon, the country of my birth. I learned that communities and countries could not prosper except through the unified and concerted effort of all.

Christians, Muslims, and Druze built the culture of Lebanon, a culture that is based on the notion that Lebanon is not only a country, but also an idea that unites all religions and cultures, fulfilling the principle of "unity in diversity." Also, in Lebanon, I learned the value of educating everyone, absolutely everyone, girls and boys. I learned that every child, rich or poor, girl or boy, has the right to dream great dreams, and to contribute in a great way.

As an adult, I wanted to apply what I learned in my country of origin. That is why I made the journey of my life a journey that contributes to improving the destiny of remote rural children, especially girls.

I consider myself fortunate to have worked in the field of girls' education and women's empowerment.

Speaking on behalf of those voiceless girls in rural and remote areas is an honor.

Advocating on their behalf is a privilege.

Designing educational programs that serve them is a sacred duty.

Contributing to policies that facilitate their inclusivity in the educational system is the noblest of all goals to achieve.

As Saint Francis said more than 700 years ago, "It is in *giving* that we *receive*."

Working hard to contribute to lifting the poor from their poverty through education purifies our heart.

Working on spreading a culture of equality helps us cross to a place of enlightenment.

Working on building connecting bridges between different continents by promoting education, and in particular girls' education, expands our soul.

Working to establish the foundations for equity and respect for all human beings and cultures vastly enriches our vision.

I do not think anyone should tire of building bridges of commonality, dialogue, coexistence, and tolerance, to touch the shores of the different continents of our small planet.

I believe these dialogues of tolerance and peaceful coexistence happen in a more genuine way when everyone, including the girls of poor communities, has the opportunity of attending school and learning, and therefore are able to participate in an ongoing global dialogue.

I believe the waves of extremism will recede as everyone is educated, especially the girls who are the future mothers of society, and who are the first teachers that shape our minds and hearts.

Once equity and equality become part of the value system of every culture, and once all human beings are valued as sacred, our planet will breathe better and deeper.

Someone might say this is an idealistic and optimistic dream. I say: transformative, positive, and grand actions always start with great idealistic and optimistic dreams.

CHAPTER THIRTY-NINE

SEARCHING AND REFLECTING

RECEIVING THESE TWO MUCH-APPRECIATED HONORS gave me motivation and cause to reflect on my professional journey, on how far we have come and how much we have yet to accomplish.

Our task is not finished until humanity makes a wonderfully stubborn commitment towards disrupting and eradicating poverty, and towards lifting poor families from hopelessness by facilitating the education of every girl and every boy on this planet.

Our task is not finished until humanity takes a clear, courageous, and bold position against violence. It is as clear as the sunshine that violence breeds violence, and puts those who inflict it—as well as those who suffer from it—on the slippery slope of a vicious destructive circle.

Our task is not finished until humanity wakes up to the fact that we are all equal: Americans, Africans, Europeans, Asians, Europeans, Middle Easterners, Lebanese, French, Italians, Malawians, Saudis, Senegalese, Indians, Christians, Muslims, Jews, Druze, Hindus, and Buddhists, and that only when we awaken to and internalize that fundamental fact can we begin the journey of love, goodness, service, and justice.

Our journey is not complete until humanity strives in the most genuine way towards equality and the basic human rights of women and men, majorities and minorities, dominant and less-dominant religious and linguistic groups; only then may we walk on a path that is built on respect and recognition of the value of diversity and pluralism.

Our journey is not complete until human beings open their minds and hearts to other cultures, allow their curiosity to dig deep and discover the luminous gems that each culture offers; only then we might begin to erase the unhealthy stereotypes we often use as a false lens to see others.

Our journey is not complete until we allow our hearts to embrace an all-encompassing love of humanity, until we work hard on building stronger connections with those who are like us—and particularly with those who are *not* like us, who do not belong to our country, who do not speak our language, who do not share our skin color. A fundamental genuine concern for others, especially those apparently different from us, will help us discover how vast the common ground is among the people of all cultures and contexts.

Our journey is not complete until we learn about the major religions of the world and contribute to the dialogue of these religions; only then can we shape a true understanding among the people of the world and strengthen those who believe in common values while minimizing the impact of those extremists who believe in division and violence.

Our journey is not complete until every country facilitates the education of all its children, and ensures that the vast majority of girls and boys complete secondary education. Those countries where girls are not able to or are not allowed to complete their secondary education will get stuck in the past and will not be able to advance.

Our journey is not complete until we believe that every hungry child and every illiterate girl and boy are *our* children and *our* responsibility, and that the Other is only a reflection of our Self.

Let the river of erasing borders and divides flow.

I still have a lot of work to do.

INDEX

505

R

Rabat 167, 173, 338, 340, 362, 365, 485
Rabat, Edmond 485
Racine 40, 126, 237
Rafeh, Lily 37
Rahbani Brothers 50
Ramirez, Fernando 440
Ras Beirut 35, 50, 52, 150
Research Triangle International 361
Riachi, Fadia 37, 180
Riegleman, Maryanne 140 , 152, 154, 155, 156, 158, 159
Rihani, Albert v 6, 7, 13, 14, 15, 16, 18, 19, 20, 21, 22, 24, 25, 26, 27, 28, 29, 30, 33, 35, 36, 39, 40, 41, 43, 58, 60, 61, 64, 67, 73, 74, 75, 76, 77, 79, 80, 81, 82, 83, 85, 86, 87, 88, 89, 90, 93, 97, 103, 123, 126, 127, 129, 130, 131, 132, 134, 135, 136, 138, 150, 151, 152, 177, 179, 180, 192, 230, 240, 244, 245, 246, 247, 248, 249, 250, 251, 252, 254, 255, 257, 258, 265, 266, 278, 285, 296, 297, 299, 300, 301, 302, 305, 306, 318, 326, 327, 328, 329, 330, 340, 341, 342, 343, 344, 345, 346, 353, 354, 360, 412, 491, 493,
Rihani, Ameen Albert 13, 14, 62, 83, 104, 152, 180, 246, 248, 256, 257, 266, 340, 416
Rihani Ameen Fares 20, 21, 22, 23, 26, 39, 47, 48, 68, 74, 95, 100, 118, 171, 180, 224, 226, 230, 231, 244, 328, 330, 399, 400, 401, 407, 420, 445, 446, 456
Rihani, Loreen v, ix, 14, 15, 16, 20, 24, 25, 28, 29, 30, 31, 32, 33, 35, 39, 41, 43, 57, 60, 61, 80, 81, 82, 83, 84, 85, 86, 87, 88, 89, 90, 91, 92, 93, 100, 101, 107, 109, 123, 126, 127, 128, 129, 130, 131, 132, 136, 138, 148, 150, 151, 152, 177, 192, 220, 230, 244, 245, 246, 247, 248, 249, 250, 251, 252, 254, 255, 257,
265, 266, 285, 297, 301, 302, 305, 314, 326, 327, 328, 329, 341, 342, 343, 344, 345, 346, 350, 351, 352, 353, 354, 355, 356, 357, 358, 359, 360, 412, 493
Rihani Publishing House 25, 78
Rihani Ramzi vii, 14, 47, 48, 49, 62, 83, 87, 125, 126, 127, 128, 131, 132, 138, 150, 151, 152, 172, 176, 177, 179, 180, 246, 247, 248, 249, 250, 251, 252, 253, 255, 256, 265, 266, 270, 271, 273, 274, 275, 276, 277, 278, 284, 286, 296, 297, 299, 300, 301, 302, 305, 314, 329, 330, 337, 338, 339, 340, 345, 347, 351, 352, 353, 354, 355, 356, 357, 358, 359, 360, 370, 394, 407, 416, 420, 423, 479, 481
Rihani, Roberto 112
Rihani, Sarmad 14, 49, 62, 82, 87, 113, 125, 127, 138, 150, 151, 179, 180, 246, 247, 253, 255, 256, 265, 266, 275, 330, 339, 340, 347, 351, 353, 354, 355, 356, 357, 358, 359, 394, 416
Riyadh 466, 467
Robinson, Mary 492
Rodin, Auguste 229
Rodionov, Mikhail 401
Romania 103, 104, 199, 263, 425
Rome 59, 63, 64, 65, 66, 67, 71, 74, 82, 93, 228
Roosevelt, Eleanor 491
Rothko, Mark 236
Rouhana, Charbel 282
Rugh, Andrea 381
Rumi 187
Russia 400
Rwanda 404, 430

S

Saab, Najla 32
Saba Rahhal, Mona 95
Sader, Fuad 330, 418
Said, Abdul Aziz 187, 313, 399, 413

UNESCO 2, 126, 132, 134, 135, 139, 141, 142, 182, 203, 388, 457, 460, 497

UNICEF 162, 165, 305, 306, 332, 333, 334, 335, 403, 422, 426, 431, 457, 458, 463

UNIFEM 427, 431

Union National des Femmes Tunisiennes (UNFT) 278, 279

United Arab Emirates 154, 155, 159, 199

United Kingdom 400

United Nations Decade for Women 110

United Nations Development Program (UNDP) 154, 155, 156, 159, 160, 388

United Nations Food and Agriculture Organizations (FAO) 63, 64, 65, 66, 203, 215, 265

United Nations General Assembly 110

United Nations Girls' Education Initiative (UNGEI) ii, 1, 399, 422, 457, 458, 459, 460, 461, 462, 463, 465

United Nations Population Conference 103

United States ii, 20, 48, 73, 99, 143, 155, 190, 311, 370, 382, 398, 433, 434, 446, 447

United States Agency of International Development (USAID) i, 155, 156, 158, 159, 161, 162, 165, 166, 167, 168, 199, 200, 242, 279, 291, 292, 295, 319, 320, 321, 325, 336, 338, 340, 361, 362, 363, 364, 367, 368, 370, 373, 374, 376, 379, 381, 382, 384, 385, 389, 390, 404, 406, 420, 427, 428, 431, 451, 456, 457, 469, 476, 477, 478

University of California at Davis 125

University of Maryland i, 313, 440, 445, 446, 447, 456, 461

University Women of Lebanon 90

U.S. ix, 2, 21, 24, 43, 46, 62, 69, 72, 84, 95, 99, 118, 124, 125, 127, 128, 129, 130, 131, 132, 134, 135, 136, 138, 139, 145, 146, 152, 153, 156, 160, 161, 170, 177, 179, 187, 190, 191, 192, 197, 198, 200, 201, 203, 204, 221, 234, 235, 237, 238, 251, 273, 274, 275, 277, 278, 280, 284, 285, 286, 288, 289, 307, 319, 320, 328, 342, 344, 353, 355, 360, 372, 385, 395, 398, 400, 402, 404, 405, 444, 445, 446, 457

U.S. Department of Justice 398

V

Vance, Cyrus 197

Van Doren, Mark 73

Van Dusen, Ann 440

Vatican 2, 64, 65

Vatican Museum 64

Vautier, Bulle 133, 172, 263

Vautier, Michel 133

Venice 178

Venus 59

Verlaine, Paul 134

Via Veneto 65

Victoria Station 182

Villa Borghese 65

Ville Lumière 131

Virgil 58

Virginia 234

W

Waldrop, Gideon 172, 198, 235

Wali, Sima 330

Wallace, Steven 171

Wanna, Said 235

War and Peace 23

War Arun Temple 184

Warren, BJ 125, 134, 141, 146, 147, 151, 152, 447

Washington, D.C. 56, 125, 126, 127, 128, 130, 134, 138, 146, 147, 150, 151, 171, 176, 179, 189, 190, 197, 233, 234, 240, 241, 246, 252, 253, 266, 268,